The Rise and Fall of China's Economic Miracle

For Eugene, Juno, and the post-Covid generation

The Rise and Fall of China's Economic Miracle
1950–2030

Kent G. Deng

polity

First published in 2026 by Polity Press Ltd.

Polity Press Ltd.
65 Bridge Street
Cambridge CB2 1UR, UK

Polity Press Ltd.
111 River Street
Hoboken, NJ 07030, USA

ISBN-13: 978-1-5095-7035-5
ISBN-13: 978-1-5095-7036-2 (pb)

A catalogue record for this book is available from the British Library.

Library of Congress Control Number: 2026933794

Typeset in 10.5 on 12 pt Sabon by
Cheshire Typesetting Ltd, Cuddington, Cheshire
Printed and bound by CPI Group (UK) Ltd, Croydon

For further information on Polity, visit our website:
politybooks.com

CONTENTS

Tables and Figures viii
Abbreviations xiv

Introduction **1**
1. An Overview of China's Growth Trajectories 1
2. Methodology 4
3. Structure of this Book 5

Chapter 1. China's Openness and Economic Growth before 1950: A *Longue Durée* Narrative 7
1. Laying out the Background: 'Open Era' on Whose Terms? 7
2. State Capacity: Taxes and Silver Deadweight to the Economy 11
3. Secret of Qing Growth: Better Resource Base and Allocation in Favour of Farming 16
4. Unintended Consequences of the Ming and Qing Policies 23
5. China's Economic Status Prior to the Opium War 23
6. Economic Impact of the Opium War 27
7. China's Indigenous Growth Trajectory 29
8. Final Remarks 31

Chapter 2. The Road to the PRC, Maoist Growth Traps and State Failure 32
1. Pre-Mao China as Land of 'Murphy's Law', 1850–1950 32
2. Rise of 'Militocrats' (or Stratocrats) and Maoism in the Making, 1850–1920 42
3. Mao's Career Choice and Strategy 46

4. Mao's Moral Economy and His Political Economy after 1930 50
5. Impact of Maoism on Performance of the Economy 57
6. Mao's Legacy Debated 68
7. Final Remarks 71

Chapter 3. Deng's Termination of Class Struggle and the Pursuit of Growth 72
1. Exogenous Party-State and Resistance from the Population 72
2. Deng's Personal Qualities: Key to Reforms 79
3. Top-down Reforms during the Vital Years, 1980–1984 81
4. Boom in Tertiary Education 83
5. Spontaneous Changes in Rural Institutions 86
6. Rural Industrial Enterprises and 'Urban Substitution Industrialisation' 87
7. Surge of the Urban Private Sector 93
8. End Results: Changes in Economic Performance 97
9. Evaluation of Deng's Reforms 100
10. Final Remarks 109

Chapter 4. State Capacity and 'Getting Prices Wrong' 110
1. Institutional Determinism: State Capacity and Its Changes 110
2. State Capacity Riding on Reforms 112
3. 'Getting Prices Wrong' *by* the State and *for* the State 119
4. State Capacity's Externalities and Unintended Consequences 126
5. Final Remarks 137

Chapter 5. The 'China Model': Constraints and Unsustainability 138
1. Defining the Nature of the 'China Model' 138
2. From Unproductive Cheap Labour to an 'Absolute Advantage in Trade' 142
3. State-led 'Absolute Advantage in Trade' for Market Dominance 146
4. State-led 'Import-Export Combo' 151
5. The Limits and Unsustainability of the 'China Model' 158
6. The Covid-19 Shock: A World without China 169
7. The Fallacy of the 'Global Value Chain' and What China May Look Like by 2030 171
8. Final Remarks 174

Conclusion 175

Appendix 1. Changes in China's Regional Population Densities 179
Appendix 2. Domestic Flows of Cotton Goods during Qing Times 183
Appendix 3. Technical Illustrations of Economic Mechanisms 184
Appendix 4. Qing Salary Bonuses and Their Abolition 195
Appendix 5. Crude Information from the GDP Accounting Approach 197
Appendix 6. China's Import Dependency 207
Appendix 7. Distribution of Issues in China's State Five-Year Plans 209

Notes 213
Figure Sources 263
Index 269

TABLES AND FIGURES

Tables

1.1. Landmarks of China's Openness, 1550–1700 10
1.2. Revenues Sources, the Early Ming, 1414 AD 13
1.3. Changes in Farmland in China, 1644 versus 1887 17
1.4. Shares of Farmland under New World Crops in the 1920s 22
1.5. Recorded Qing Government Annual Revenues, the 1830s 25
1.6. Marketed Goods, Total Value, the 1830s 25
1.7. Seasonality and Labour for Cotton Weaving 26
1.8. Labour and Land Productivity Indexes, 1870–1930 29
2.1. Mandatory Annual Government Granary Stockpile, 1748–1766 36
2.2. Population Decline in Taiping-affected Provinces 37
2.3. Number of Qing Officials versus General Population, 1700–1850 38
2.4. Composition of Governor-Generals of Provinces, 1644–1911 40
2.5. Ethnic Composition of Military Officers, 1644–1911 40
2.6. New Standing Armies across Provinces, *c.*1880 43
2.7. Provincial Arsenals and Mass Production of Modern Arms 44
2.8. Political Factions and Foreign Sponsors, 1912–1949 45
2.9. Mao's Purges, 1931–1976 51
2.10. Soviet Control over Mao's Party, 1920–1937 53
2.11. Shift in Military Balance of Power, 1945–1948 54

2.12. Ownership Changes in Mainland China, 1957 56
2.13. Industrial Workforce versus Total Population, 1930–1974 59
2.14. Nominal versus Real Wages in the State Sector, 1957–1978 60
2.15. Agriculture-dependent Growth Patterns, 1952–1975 61
2.16. China's Perpetual Food Deficits, 1956–1978 62
2.17. Food Rationing, 1960s–1970s 65
3.1. Collectivisation and Decline in Farming Output and Draft Animals 74
3.2. Investment Bias, 1953–1975 77
3.3. Decline in State-run Investment Returns, 1963–1978 78
3.4. Distribution of Higher Educational Qualifications, 2010 85
3.5. Maoist Investment Pattern 1953–1975 89
3.6. Monopolistic Prices of Consumer Manufactures, Prior to 1980 89
3.7. Employment Structures, TVEs versus SOEs, 1978–2000 90
3.8. SEZ Growth Engines, 1978–2008 108
4.1. Housing Price-to-Income Ratios, 1998–2017/20 116
4.2. Extent of River Water Pollution, 2001–2020 128
4.3. Exposed Cases of 'Secret Coffers', 2003–2013 133
5.1. Imports-Exports Shifting to the West, 1970–1974 154
5.2. Japan's Import Pattern, 1965–1989 156
5.3. Taiwan's Import Pattern, 1960–1980 156
5.4. Agricultural TFP Performance, 1996–2007 158
5.5. Research Outputs, China versus G7, 1980–2020 159
5.6. Cases Formally Filed against China, 1995–2024 161
5.7. Mismatch between Domestic Household Savings and Investment Sprees, 1978–2024 166
5.8. Impact of Covid on G7 Trade, 2019–2022 170
5.9. Unemployment Rates, High-end Labour Market, 2023–2024 171
A–4.1. Annual Honesty and Uprightness Bonuses, *c.*1720–1740 195
A–4.2. Donation of Honesty and Uprightness Bonuses, 1820 196
A–5.1. Sectoral GDP Shares, 1980–2020 200
A–5.2. Sectoral Labour-GDP Efficiency Indexes, 1980–2020 201
A–5.3. China's Tax Revenue-to-GDP Ratio, 1880s 202
A–5.4. Tax Revenue-to-GDP Ratios in Advanced Economies, 1760–1860 203

A–5.5. Taxes as % GDP, China vis-à-vis other Economies, 2013–2020 203
A–5.6. Economic Recovery of G7, 2023 versus 2019 206
A–7.1. Ranks and Weights of Issues on Government To Do List, 1986–1990 209
A–7.2. Ranks and Weights of Issues on Government To Do List, 1991–1995 210
A–7.3. Ranks and Weights of Issues on Government To Do List, 1996–2000 210
A–7.4. Ranks and Weights of Issues on Government To Do List, 2001–2005 210
A–7.5. Ranks and Weights of Issues on Government To Do List, 2006–2010 211
A–7.6. Ranks and Weights of Issues on Government To Do List, 2011–2015 211
A–7.7. Ranks and Weights of Issues on Government To Do List, 2016–2020 212

Figures

1.1. Sinicised European Knowledge of the Orbit of the Moon 10
1.2. China's Cumulative Silver Imports, 1640–1910 11
1.3. Silver-to-Gold Exchange Rate, China versus Other Countries 14
1.4. Trends in Farmland and Population, 1650–1890 18
1.5. Annual Silver Imports versus Annual Qing Treasury Silver Stock, 1645–1910 19
1.6. China's Cropping Systems, 1920s–1930s 21
1.7. China-wide Farm Size Distribution, 1920s 24
1.8. Silver Imports and Sampled Exchange Rates of Bronze Coins per Silver *Tael*, 1700–1900 28
1.9. Growth Performance: Benchmark versus Reality, 1830–1978 30
2.1. China-wide Rebellions in the 1850s and 1860s 34
2.2. Disasters and Disaster Relief, 1645–1910 34
2.3. Trends in Labour Inputs, 1950–2020 60
2.4. Hypothetical Growth Trajectory of the Maoist Economy until 2002 62
2.5. Birth Rate in China, 1950–1980 66
2.6. Per Capita Private Household Savings, 1978–2023 67

2.7. Opinions on Mao's Legacy 69
3.1. Growth in Higher Education, 1978–2010 84
3.2. Sectorial Fixed Capital Investment, 1980–2020 97
3.3. Per Capita Agricultural Output Volumes, Indexes, 1978–2023 98
3.4. Per Capita Industrial Output Volumes, Indexes, 1952–2023 99
3.5. Qing Benchmark versus Actual Growth, 1970–2020 101
3.6. Decline in Engel Coefficient, Rural versus Urban, 1978–2010 102
3.7. Rise in Household Consumption, Rural versus Urban, 1978–2000 103
3.8. De-ruralisation, 1978–2010 104
3.9. Growth Indexes for Foreign Trade, 1978–2023 105
3.10. Capital Investment in China by Category, 1995–2020 106
4.1. Tax Growth Indexes, 1980–2020 114
4.2. Housing Sales Prices versus Construction Costs, 2000–2023 115
4.3. Government Direct Involvement in Housing Construction, 1980–2022 116
4.4. Government Living-Cost Subsidies, 1978–2006 120
4.5. RMB–US$ Exchange Rates and Trade Balance, 1978–2023 121
4.6. China's Import–Export Balancing Act, 1978–2023 122
4.7. Foreign Currency Sources and Foreign Reserves, 1978–2023 123
4.8. Cash FDI, Trade Surpluses, and Foreign Currency Pool, 1978–2023 125
4.9. 'Getting Prices Wrong' by the State and for the State 126
4.10. Water Pollution in Seven Rivers, 2001–2020 129
4.11. China's CO_2 Emission Track Record, 1949–2023 130
4.12. General Pattern of Convicted Officials, 1980–2023 132
4.13. Breakdown of Convicted Officials, 1987–2001 135
4.14. China's Corruption Control Ranking in Asia, 1995–2024 136
5.1. China's World Standing in Physical Inputs and Outputs, 2022–2024 141
5.2. SEZs' Share of China's Industrial Workforce, 1998–2011 143
5.3. Industrial Output Values, Domestic versus Foreign Firms, 1999–2011 144

5.4. Footwear Output and Exports, 2016–2022 145
5.5. Growth Gap between GDP and Urban Wages, 1985–2023 147
5.6. Urban Wages Affected by RMB–US$ Exchange Rates, 1985–2023 148
5.7. Impact of the 996 Regime on Wages, 1985–2023 149
5.8. Industrial Strikes, 2023 and 2024 150
5.9. China's First Import-Export Combo, 1950–1965 153
5.10. China's Imports Worldwide, 2024 155
5.11. United States' Annual Trade Deficit with China, 1985–2023 160
5.12. Recurring Issues in the State-run Five-Year Plans, 1986–2020 162
5.13. Mismatch between Domestic Savings and Domestic Consumption 163
5.14. Endogenous Domestic Growth Constraints 164
5.15. Investment-driven and Supply-driven Domestic Construction, 1992–2024 165
5.16. Growth in Government Debt versus Total GDP, 1995–2023/4 167
A–1.1. Population Density, Yellow River Region, 1000–1910 179
A–1.2. Population Density, Yangzi River Region, 1000–1910 180
A–1.3. Population Density, South-east Coast, 1000–1910 180
A–1.4. Population Density, North-west Hinterland, 1000–1910 181
A–1.5. Population Density, South-west Hinterland, 1000–1910 182
A–1.6. Population Density, North-east Hinterland, 1000–1910 182
A–2.1. Cotton Trade Patterns, *c.*1750–1800 183
A–3.1. Ming Silver Trade as a Burden on the Economy 185
A–3.2. Ending Population Stagnation 186
A–3.3. Maoist Rural Growth Trap 187
A–3.4. Economic Decline under Mao's Rule 188
A–3.5. Post-Mao Production Possibility Frontier 189
A–3.6. RMB Depreciation and Rise in External Demand 190
A–3.7. Negative Externalities 191
A–3.8. Supply-Driven Model and the World Market 192
A–3.9. China's Stifled Domestic Consumer Manufactures Market 193
A–3.10. Tariffs and Their Impact on the Market 194

A–5.1. Agricultural GDP, State Expenditure and Food Imports, 1980–2010 198
A–5.2. China's GDP Leap, 1980–2020 199
A–5.3. China's Tax-to-GDP Ratio, 1950–2020 202
A–5.4. Import Dependency Seen from China's GDP, 1978–2023 204
A–5.5. CO_2 Emissions per Unit of GDP, 1978–2022 205
A–6.1. Pattern of China's Imports from the United States, 2023 207
A–6.2. Pattern of China's Imports from the European Union, 2023 208

ABBREVIATIONS

BRICS	Brazil, Russia, India, China, and South Africa
CCP	Chinese Communist Party
CPTPP	Comprehensive and Progressive Agreement for Trans-Pacific Partnership
EOI	Export-oriented Industrialisation
FDI	Foreign Direct Investment
G7	Canada, France, Germany, Italy, Japan, Britain, and United States
GATT	General Agreement on Tariffs and Trade
GVCE	Global Value Chain Economy
IOI	Import-oriented Industrialisation
OECD	Organization for Economic Cooperation and Development
PPF	Production Possibility Frontier
PRC	People's Republic of China
R&D	Research and Development
RMB	Renminbi Currency of China
SOEs	State-owned Enterprises
TPP	Trans-Pacific Partnership
TVEs	Township and Village Enterprises
USI	Urban Substitution Industrialisation
WTO	World Trade Organization

INTRODUCTION

1. An Overview of China's Growth Trajectories

Imagine an economic superpower in the pre-industrial world possessing such state capacity that the government could tax the population to the point of demographic stagnation and then spend its revenues on building the longest land-based defence system in world history, on constructing a new capital city stretching 34 km^2, and on maintaining an ocean-going armada of 200 ships. Moreover, due to this government's preference for receiving taxes in silver – a precious metal that was not plentiful domestically – large quantities of manufactured products were exported in exchange for imported silver from near and far. The silver intake of this economy was hitherto unprecedented across the world. Furthermore, although this power still possessed technological advantages by world standards at this time,[1] information exchange with the outside world was tolerated to the point that its indigenous calendar system, which was considered sacred and inviolable, was contracted to foreigners to achieve accuracy. In addition, this country had a total of 127 diplomatic and information connections beyond its borders. This mysterious power was not situated in Europe but in Asia: it was the Ming Empire (1368–1644) when China reached a pre-modern pinnacle in growth and development. When thinking in terms of 'path dependence', there should have been no reason for China not to continue along this distinctive path for the next, say, 500 years.

During the following Qing Dynasty (1644–1911), however, China's state capacity crumbled under ultra-low taxes in the name of Confucian benevolence. It was a voluntary and unforced policy change initiated by the ruling clique in 1712. Although prolonged low taxes bailed China out of its Ming population stagnation and fuelled an unprecedented population explosion, it crippled the provision of public goods, which became clear during the Little Ice Age from the 1840s to the 1880s. Nationwide unrest broke out which had little to do with the tax burden and everything to do with state failures. By 1860 Qing rule was on the brink of total collapse. This would normally trigger China's 'dynastic cycle' mechanism to give birth to a new imperial dynasty. Indeed, there should have been no reason for the dynastic cycle not to continue for the next 500 years.

But against all odds, China took a third way which was neither an extension of the Ming superpower approach nor a continuation of Qing low-tax benevolence. Military rule emerged during the Qing rebellions with a strong tendency towards feudalism – the antithesis of empire. Institutionally, the ending of the Imperial Examinations for the civil bureaucracy helped establish a militocracy run by less educated individuals who were more familiar with modern weapons than Confucian books.

This new breed of military officers delivered results in the war against rebels. But they did not stop there. In 1911, three dozen military officers (who now controlled all of China's provinces) forced the last Qing Emperor to abdicate in a bloodless revolution. This was a top-down *rebellion* that worked. What followed was a republic run by competing militocrats until Mao's army reunited the mainland in 1949. Mao's unification of China did not change the militocratic nature of the state despite a communist camouflage. But a single militocratic ruler paved the way for a dictatorship in the country. Such a dictatorship turned out to be a curse for social welfare with disastrous outcomes: the economy remained rural, the population lived at the subsistence level, education was ignored, investment was wasteful, and China became one of the poorest countries in the world. In this context, the notorious anti-life 'one child policy' was implemented as a last resort to reduce human consumption that production failed to match. Meanwhile, it was a high-maintenance society in terms of putting down resistance. Political purges became the order of the day. Even so, China could have continued with Maoist man-made ruralisation, low literacy, mass poverty and so on indefinitely, as these things served the Maoist utopia well. Indeed, similar systems persist elsewhere in the world today.

So, China's ascent in the post-Mao years (after 1976) was far from inevitable. The seed for change was planted long before Mao seized political control over China in 1949. Deng Xiaoping was a rare breed, one of a handful of leaders who had first-hand experience in both the West (in France) and the Soviet Union. Deng's personal qualities turned out to be vital for enacting change in a country under a one-party dictatorship. It takes a good dictator (Deng) to cancel out a bad dictator (Mao) in the absence of regime change. But history has not produced many good dictators. Ordinary people had no say at all.

Deng's reforms began with 'looking and moving backwards' into history, a renaissance of the good old market economy and meritocratic schooling that Ming-Qing Chinese were brought up with. Looking and moving backwards worked. The Maoist straitjacket was shaken off. This was comparable to the Renaissance in late medieval Europe, when society looked backwards to find solutions for contemporary problems. But Deng's reforms went beyond a renaissance by establishing two new goals for China: (1) higher incomes for households, and (2) greater national strength for China in defence, output, and technology (in that order). To achieve these goals, foreign inputs – capital, technology, and materials – were the *sine qua non*. So, a new era of 'import-oriented industrialisation' began, which in turn has driven China's exports in the past four decades. External luck has also helped China during this time: WTO-mediated globalisation has turbocharged the 'import-export combo' to transform China into the world's second largest economy. But an inborn problem looms large for China's 'supply-driven' growth model, which sends the value and the volume of China's exports in opposite directions: the more China exports the cheaper its exports become. Profit margins have collapsed as China's cheap exports have taken over more and more overseas markets, forcing other countries' manufacturing sectors to retreat, and thus causing unemployment to rise and disposable incomes to fall in those countries. Now, China must sell its exports more cheaply by the day to continue operating. This is self-defeating and is already happening on an industrial scale.

To sum up, although China's long and continued existence as a civilisation may be the envy of the world, China has had its fair share of contingencies and ups and downs. China's economic history is messy, and as time goes by, there is no sign that China's historical messiness is being reduced. Against this backdrop, there has been no linear and teleological inevitability to lead China towards a particular destiny that one may hope for, even though its economy currently ranks no. 2 in the world.

2. Methodology

This fact-based book navigates China's history through what actually occurred, taking a long-term perspective in order to avoid any inappropriate baseline being arbitrarily adopted whereby a wrong growth trajectory and growth story are portrayed – a common practice these days, unfortunately. Typically, 1911 or 1949 is used as the starting point, as if these years mark the beginning of Chinese history. 'Growth' has then been calculated from these baselines. But what if one pushes the observation point back a century and sets the baseline there? It then becomes obvious that China's economy suffered from long-lasting underperformance and decline.

Additionally, each chapter has its own internal historical logic and dynamics and can be read and understood independently. This is to avoid the common practice of filtering historical facts and pigeonholing human and societal experiences. To do so, one often sets 'arbitrary and subjective assumptions *ex post*' for history. But the bottom line is that history has no direction *ex ante*, it simply 'happens'.

Moreover, this book is fact-driven (or data-driven). Existing opinions are subject to the acid test of facts. A good example is the commonly circulated 'export-oriented industrialisation' growth model for post-Mao China. From historical documents and China's own statistics, exports were only half of the story and they served the primary purpose of imports. So, the actual model was instead 'import-oriented industrialisation'. Another common view is that China's Special Economic Zones in the coastal regions boosted exports. But again, from historical documents and China's own statistics, we see that exports were unable to match imports into Special Economic Zones, let alone be a growth engine for the whole of China. The real propellers driving China's thriving exports were humble rural townships and village enterprises. The list goes on.

Furthermore, the data-driven approach adopted here is multifaceted and multi-polar in nature. The handling of historical data in this book is intentionally disciplined in interpreting it as realistically as possible despite historical intricacies, rather than employing pedantic streamlining or reconstructing the data to fit a neat framework. As a result, the text sometimes gives off the appearance of lacking structure. But important historical linkages are always included and indicated. On the subject of data, I am sceptical about GDP accounting because the metric has generally proven to be untrustworthy especially in historical growth trajectory extrapolations. This is largely due to the component 'average prices' which is often inaccurate or biased. More specifically, China's modern GDP data have been notoriously problematic.[2] As late as 2004, GDP figures for China's manufacturing sector were 33 per cent unreliable; those of China's commerce, 51 per cent unreliable; and those of China's primary sector and real estate sector, 100 per cent unreliable.[3] Likewise, China's provincial GDP figures do not sum to the national GDP figure, with discrepancies between them of 10–30 per cent from the 1990s to the 2010s.[4] China's all-rounded information opaqueness makes data verification difficult. It becomes rational to regard China's official GDP numbers as guilty until proven innocent. The better alternative is physical inputs and outputs that are difficult to manipulate and falsify.

Finally, I try to avoid too much economics terminology, as it may put off the general reader. The downside is that the text may become long-winded at times.

3. Structure of this Book

First of all, despite the title of the book covering the period 1950–2030, it is essential in my view to go back to earlier times that were intimately linked to China's modern era. China's Ming-Qing past (1368–1911) – the subject of chapter 1 – provided many of the key foundations of Chinese civilisation that have carried into the present day.

Secondly, the key factor that exerted continuous and consistent pressure and influence on China's growth and development has been the dichotomy of (and interplay between) the state and the market. Considering this key factor, this book identifies a major discontinuity between Maoist foolhardy mismanagement that resulted in famine and poverty (1949–1980) and Deng Xiaoping's reforms that offered hope and progress (post-1980). Simply put, the former were anti-growth and anti-developmental in nature, made China *unprecedentedly* poor, and were thus unsustainable. The latter have steered China back to modern growth and mainstream development and have made China *unprecedentedly* rich, but they are also self-defeating and unsustainable.

Thirdly, the five chapters of this book collectively serve the purpose of explaining China's non-linear historical path of growth and development. Chapter 1 provides historical background all the way up to the rise of Mao. Chapter 2 investigates the self-imposed growth limits of Maoism. Chapter 3 describes Deng Xiaoping's innovations that successfully reversed Maoism and undid its damage. Chapter

4 explains what has made China 'great' again. Chapter 5 demonstrates why and how China's current expansion has *already* reached its upper limits.

Finally, with the knowledge of China's long and bumpy track record in mind, I conclude that (1) China's current 'import-export combo' has now led the country to a major domestic recession on a mammoth scale, and (2) China's growth and development is likely to be set back for decades, until China's own domestic household income level becomes capable of supporting China's manufacturing sector autonomously. The latter requires a range of path-breaking socio-political changes towards a democracy that empowers ordinary workers to share proportionately the fruits of economic growth. But this is easier said than done.

— 1 —

CHINA'S OPENNESS AND ECONOMIC GROWTH BEFORE 1950: *A LONGUE DURÉE* NARRATIVE

1. Laying out the Background: 'Open Era' on Whose Terms?

Conventionally, the 1839–40 Opium War and the consequent 1842 Nanking Treaty (whereby China's domestic market was forced open) have been regarded as the very beginning of China's 'Open Era' (which also implies 'modernness').[1] This is based on two principal criteria: (1) 'market openness' and (2) colonisation attempts by foreign powers. However, this Anglo-centric periodisation of China's history is deeply questionable.

Firstly, there is an issue whether China's door was truly closed until 1839. Scholars commonly cite China's official maritime bans as hard evidence, as if Ming-Qing China was just another Tokugawa Japan with a policy of *sakoku* (isolationism, literally 'locking the nation's door up'), ignoring the key facts that (1) China's masses were private land owners free from feudal control of the Tokugawa type, and (2) China's state structure and statecraft were also non-feudal. As a result, it was difficult to implement maritime bans due to a mismatch between a small number of law enforcers of the Imperial government and China's super-long coastline together with a large private economy. So, all such bans were eventually paid only lip service.[2]

Furthermore, according to classical and neo-classical economics, as long as trade exists, the market is open. Prior to the Opium War, international trade indeed existed in China. The official trade in Canton was prosperous: according to a House of Commons committee, the British East India Company made £17 million in total profit from trade with China between 1793 and 1810, before involvement in the opium trade.[3] On China's side, the amount of Canton trade duties increased from 780,000 *taels* in 1828 to 1.2 million *taels* in 1832 with an annual double digit growth of 11.4 per cent.[4] Some 3.8 million pounds of tea was exported from Canton in 1773, rising to 40.3 million pounds in 1843.[5] Meanwhile, gold and silver drained out of China in 1837–8 on the eve of the Opium War: £1.7 million-worth to India alone.[6]

Apart from the official trading port of Canton where legal trade was conducted, there was a significant smuggling trade along China's coast. In the first 30 years of the opium trade (1809–39), illegal sales of the drug in China increased ten-fold to 40,000 chests per year,[7] with an annual growth rate of 8 per cent. In this context, the Opium War was triggered by British losses in opium cargos, known as 'Opium Compensation',[8] not by the Canton system that did not control opium smuggling at all.[9] Nevertheless, it was a fact that maritime bans did not work and trade went on.

For students of Chinese history, the mid-Ming (Ming: 1368–1644), not the post-Opium War era, should be seen as the period in which China was willingly open to post-Renaissance reliable knowledge and a European-controlled silver trade. To begin with, the Ming Court had a total of 127 diplomatic connections, including to Italy in Europe.[10] The main players in this openness were the Ming *literati* and arriving western Europeans (sea traders and Jesuit missionaries).[11] The latter managed to ship a record amount of silver to China together with a range of post-Renaissance technology, including mathematics, astronomy, mechanical clocks, firearms, and fine arts. At the heart of these cross-ocean exchanges was the Manila Galleon Trade (1565–1815), which was purposely created to transport silver from Acapulco to meet Asia's demand for the metal.[12] China exported large quantities of manufactured products, typically porcelain and silk textiles (and later tea) to purchase silver.

Foreign silver took China's monetary market by storm prior to the Qing (1644–1911). Europeans were welcomed. Portuguese were permitted to settle in Macao and acted both as go-betweens to link China to Europe and as watchdogs to monitor any wrong-doings by other Europeans in the region to protect China's interests.[13] Moreover, Europeans began to provide new useful knowledge to Chinese. For example, Jesuits were responsible for (1) the creation of the very first *Atlas of the World* in 1602 in Beijing which was later adopted in Europe, (2) the translation of Euclid's *Elements* into Chinese in 1607 in Beijing, which soon became standard textbooks for the Chinese, and (3) the production of a European-style calendar by Jesuits for the Ming Empire in 1634 which, among many other things, hugely benefitted farming. Thus, Jesuits dominated the Imperial Board of

Astronomy and became an integral part of the Ming-Qing state apparatus, not to mention Portugal's permanent footing in Macao as a gateway to China from 1557.[14] The best-known Europeans in Ming China included Matteo Ricci (1522–1610) and Ferdinand Verbiest (1623–88), roughly a century apart.[15] Their collaborators on the Ming side included Xu Guangqi (1562–1633), a prime minister at the highest level that Jesuits could hope for. So, to associate the Opium War with China's openness is a clear anachronism. It finds no justification from China's own track record, although it has been promoted by the ruling Chinese Communist Party (CCP).

The 'Opium War narrative' is motivated by the alleged anti-colonial attitude of Leninism which is, however, incompatible with the behaviour of Russia (be it Tsarist Russia, Soviet Russia, or post-Soviet Russia) towards China. Over the past centuries, China has lost a vast amount of territory only to Russia.[16] To be exact, China ceded about a quarter (24.4 per cent) of Qing-ruled territory to Russia (3.1 million km^2).[17] So, real colonisation of China on an industrial scale began with the 1689 Treaty of Nerchinsk. The 1842 Nanking Treaty was more than 150 years too late, not to mention that the physical size of Hong Kong cannot compare with China's territories lost to Russia in Central Asia, Mongolia, and Siberia.

Whichever way one looks at China's history, the 1839–40 Opium War and the 1842 Nanking Treaty did not unilaterally open China from outside. Table 1.1 shows the range of outside influences from 1550 to 1700. In the table, four categories are chosen to reflect openness: silver influx, knowledge intake, the Catholic church from Europe, and colonies granted to outsiders. Ming openness began in 1557 when Macao was obtained by the Portuguese, some 280 years prior to the Treaty of Nanking when Hong Kong was obtained by the British.

The evidence of openness during the Ming period is hard to dispute. European astronomy was used as China's own. Figure 1.1 shows the orbit of the moon being explained in technical detail matching any modern science textbook fit for the twenty-first century.

China also incorporated imported silver into its monetary system. China not only tolerated the inflowing foreign silver, but also allowed its economy to become 'silverised'.[18] That said, China only began minting its own silver coins in 1888 and established a silver standard in 1909,[19] three centuries after silver began flowing into the country. It is remarkable that a sovereign country accepted foreign currency voluntarily for so long. The data displayed in figure 1.2 begin in 1644 when the Manila Galleon Trade had already taken place annually for about eight decades. By 1900, the cumulative silver absorbed by

Table 1.1. Landmarks of China's Openness, 1550–1700

Year	Imported silver	Imported knowledge	Catholic church	Colony
1557				Macao until 1999 (Portuguese)
1565	Manilla Galleon Trade until 1815 (Spanish)			
1582			Matteo Ricci (Italian)	
1602		*World Atlas* (Italian)		
1607		Euclid's *Elements* (Italian)		
1624				South-west Taiwan until 1662 (Dutch)
1626				North Taiwan until 1642 (Spanish)
1634		Gregorian calendar until today (Jesuits)		
1689				Siberia, north of the Amur River until today (Russia)*

Note: * During the reign of Peter the Great (1672–1725, r.1682–1725).
Source: Based on the author's own research.

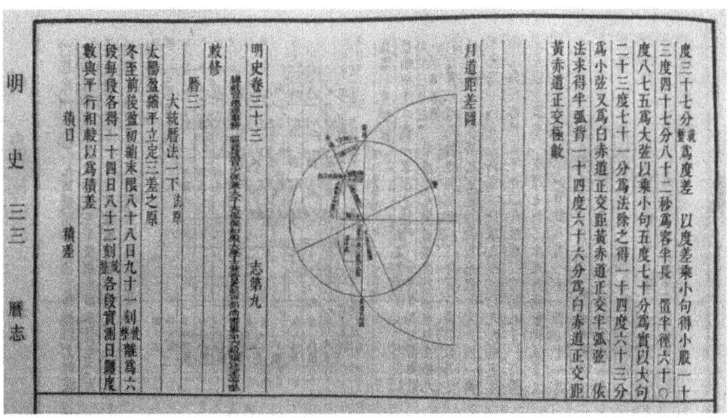

Figure 1.1. Sinicised European Knowledge of the Orbit of the Moon

Sources are available in the separate section of 'Figure Sources'.

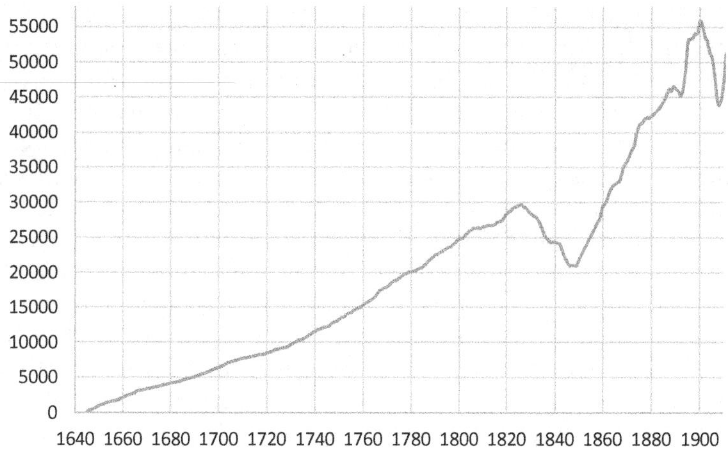

Figure 1.2. China's Cumulative Silver Imports, 1640–1910 (in tonnes)

Note: A trough from 1820 to 1860 overlapped with the opium trade.

Sources are available in the separate section of 'Figure Sources'.

China amounted to 55,000 tonnes (or metric tons) from all external sources, or 146–149 grams per capita,[20] making a silver standard possible for China's monetary system.[21]

2. State Capacity: Taxes and Silver Deadweight to the Economy

The ongoing debate on state capacity sheds new light on why the Ming period should be included in China's modern history. Simply put, the Ming state imposed heavy taxes and rolled out huge public infrastructure projects in a short space of time. Good examples are the Great Wall, the ocean-going armada, and the construction of the new Ming capital of Beijing. They set the performance trajectory of the state in China in the fourteenth century. If the Ming state-capacity trajectory had continued through the seventeenth and eighteenth centuries, there would have been no room for Maoism to take root in China later.

The incentives behind the Ming rebuilding of state capacity came from a rather unexpected source of infighting in the Ming Imperial Court. A string of intended and unintended consequences led to the Ming high tax regime. It began with the questionable emperorship of Zhu Di (1360–1424, r.1402–1424) who dethroned his nephew Zhu Yunwen (1377–?, r.1398–1402), the second emperor of the Ming, in 1402. In a bid to secure his throne, from 1398 to 1402 the young emperor Zhu Yunwen had launched pre-emptive attacks on his powerful uncles. But the war he waged did not go well, and the young monarch was instead defeated. One of those uncles, namely Zhu Di, crowned himself as the third emperor of the dynasty. In this context, Zhu Di was *not* an undisputed monarch of the Ming. This created a chain reaction towards the building of state capacity in China.

Meanwhile, Zhu Yunwen disappeared without a trace, meaning that the dethroned young emperor remained a threat. This led to a knock-on effect. Firstly, there was a decade-long manhunt organised by the new emperor Zhu Di across China and overseas. The Ming armada was built and sent out to look for the dethroned nephew.[22] This was how the Ming ocean-going activities were first designed. Second, the decision was taken to move the Ming capital city 1,000 km to the north from Nanjing to Beijing where Zhu Di's own power base, the royal fief of Yan, was located.[23] This necessitated the construction of the new capital city on the site of the obsolete Mongol Yuan headquarters. Third, by moving the capital city virtually onto the Ming northern line of defence facing the powerful Mongols and Manchus, it made sense to rebuild the Great Wall.

All three projects – the armada, the new capital city, and the new Great Wall – were the *sine qua non* for Zhu Di's emperorship. But these projects needed money. So, more taxes were raised. The Ming per capita tax burden was heavier than that of the Qing by a factor of two.[24] The Ming taxation system was almost certainly inherited from the Mongol Yuan (1279–1368) when heavy taxation was associated with stagnant population growth.[25] The Mongol household tax was twenty times higher than the previous Song level (Song: 960–1279).[26] In provinces like Fujian, the land tax was set at three *piculs* per *mu*, equivalent in many cases to the farmland's entire annual yield.[27]

Evidence for Ming heavy taxation comes first of all from the construction of the new Great Walls of China, which remains standing to this day. The old walls constructed during the Qin Dynasty (221–207 BC) became obsolete during Song-Yuan times (960–1368). The total cost of the Ming reconstruction has been estimated as equivalent to US$360 billion (in presumably the 2021 prices) and among the top five most expansive public works projects in world history.[28] The project began in 1381 and ended 187 years later in 1568, costing the economy about US$2 billion per year or US$200 per household per annum. Over time, the total burden of the wall project on the Ming population was in the region of US$36,000 per household, which almost certainly played a part in slowing down population growth.[29] The second piece of physical evidence for the Ming tax burden was the construction of the large new capital city of Beijing which was also built with a 23 km-long city wall for a city 34 km^2 in size.[30] Moreover, the Ming navy maintained an armada of 200 ships – then the largest fleet with undisputed sea power in world history – which paraded across the Indian Ocean seven times from 1405 to 1431 for allegedly diplomatic purposes, until the sheer cost of the unprecedented maritime operation emptied out the Ming coffers.[31]

In addition, there was a stealth tax burden from a change in the method of paying taxes: the Ming state demanded that taxes were paid in silver for the first time in China's history with the 1581 'One Whip Method' (*yitiao bian*).[32] Why silver was selected for tax collection by the Ming has so far remained mysterious. A sensible guess is that the Ming state was informed by Jesuits that silver was the international currency of the time, although the metal was neither readily available inside China nor had it been used for tax payments before. From available data for 1414 shown in table 1.2, silver counted for a mere one per cent of tax payments. After 1581, Ming taxpayers faced the dual burden of a high tax rate and the obligation to pay in silver. Indeed, high silver prices began to weigh on population growth.

China was poor in silver deposits. Silver therefore had to come from overseas, as it did in large quantities thanks to Ming openness. Japan was the first supplier to be called upon. Its silver exports to China lasted for 170 years (1530–1700). Spanish Manilla joined in after 1565 for another 250 years.[33] Foreign silver was not a gift and needed to be purchased with tangible commodities such as porcelain and silk textiles produced by the Chinese with an 'equal value' (to assume an idealistic 'transaction-cost-free' market).[34] In reality, however, China was likely to have overpaid due to its disadvantageous position. This was the first large-scale 'import-export combo' in China's long history.

Table 1.2. Revenues Sources, the Early Ming, 1414 AD

Type	Amount collected	Value in *taels*	% Total
Grain	30,000,000 *piculs*	15,000,000	59
Plain silk cloth	20,000,000 bolts	10,000,000	40
Silver	300,000 *taels*	300,000	1
Total		25,300,000	100
Goods to silver ratio			99:1

Source: Zhang, *Ming Dynasty*, vol. 78, 'Sihuo Zhi', in *Twenty-Five Official Histories*, vol. 10, p. 7982.

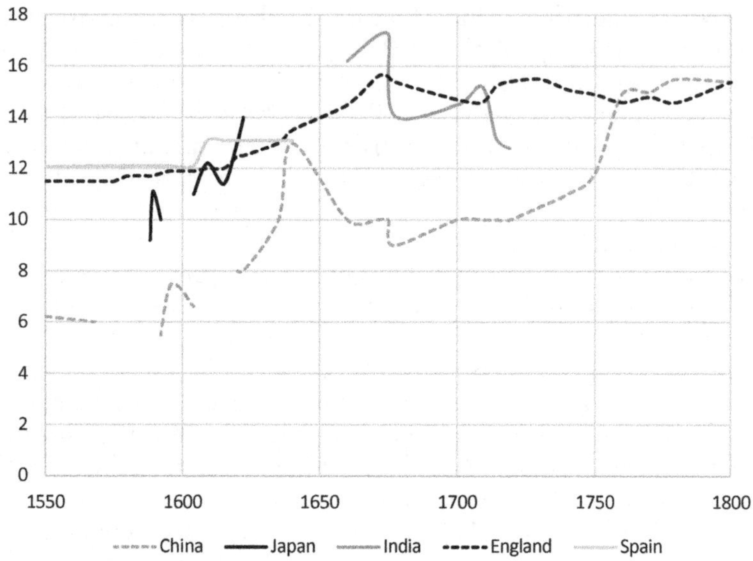

Figure 1.3. Silver-to-Gold Exchange Rate, China versus Other Countries

Note: The time framework of 1550–1800 overlaps with the Manila Galleon Trade. The price differential between China and other countries was the source of the arbitrage profit.

Sources are available in the separate section of 'Figure Sources'.

Figure 1.3 shows a pattern in which silver prices measured in gold in China were an outlier most of the time (apart from *c.*1640 and after 1770). It shows that silver dealers were able to obtain one unit of gold from China by offering the Chinese only half (during 1550–80) to two-thirds (during 1680–1720) the amount of silver that would be required in other world markets. This price differential was the engine for the one-way movement of global silver cargos to China until Chinese silver prices finally synchronised on a world par during the second half of the eighteenth century. By this time the Spanish Manilla Galleon Trade had begun its epilogue,[35] as the extra profits from silver arbitrage with China finally disappeared. As such, foreign silver was not as innocent as one may believe.[36]

A systematic study of annual silver output in New Spain suggests that production grew rapidly from 1,000 tonnes around 1550, to 3,000 tonnes in 1650, 4,500 tonnes in 1750; and finally ending at 7,000 tonnes around 1800.[37] This created a problem, as the upper bound of China's annual silver intake via Manilla was a mere 100 tonnes. In other words, Ming demand for silver imports was limited to 100 tonnes. The notion that China munched up a third of the world's dispensable silver, year in and year out, sounds like a red herring. China's demand reached 5,400 tonnes per year only in the 1830s. By then, China's farmland had more than doubled and its population had nearly quadrupled. So China was able to export more goods to buy more silver. In this context, the depth of Chinese pockets for silver imports was dictated by how much surplus China was able to export. Such a burden fell upon the fixed resource base of the Ming.[38]

Meanwhile, the Imperial Mint issued continuously large quantities of bronze coins as the Ming legal tender. Gresham's Law must have been in its element; and Ming bronze coins drove silver out of market circulation in ordinary people's daily life, as taxpayers only needed to use silver once a year. This suggests that imported silver was more likely to be a *deadweight* to the economy. Ming population growth was even weaker when silver was hoarded.

Given that the silver price in China was twice the European par, and that the Ming tax burden was twice the Qing level, the Ming tax burden payable in silver can be taken as four times the Qing level. In addition, much silver was hoarded. Something had to give. Indeed, the pace of population growth under the Ming was roughly a quarter of that of the Qing.

These internal mechanisms were not visible to the outside world. As far as Europeans were concerned, China remained open and wealthier by mercantilist standards. What the outside word did not know was the price Ming China was paying collectively in the form of population stagnation. This was because all the above-mentioned burden fell upon the fixed territory of the Ming. In other words, although the Ming period (1368–1644) was an era of openness, the economy was confined within a limited resource basis within the Great Wall. As a result, the total area of farmland did not increase much during the Ming. With various deductions on total output, including heavy taxes and the costs of silver conversion for tax payment obligations, after-tax resources were only enough to maintain the existing size of the Ming population, to the benefit of Ming state capacity. Our evidence comes from Ming regional population density estimates documented in Imperial records which show stagnant population growth (Appendix 1).[39] Some scholars have resorted to discarding the official Ming population censuses and replacing them with estimates based on backward extrapolations of the Qing population figures, when state capacity was much weaker and the tax burden much lighter.[40] Such a practice is unhelpful as it ignores the vital issue of state capacity.

3. Secret of Qing Growth: Better Resource Base and Allocation in Favour of Farming

Qing growth was different. It had an enlarged resource base that supported higher population growth while at the same time maintaining silver imports.[41] Although the Qing state may have been minimalist and lethargic,[42] it was by no means passive towards social welfare. This planted the seed for state failure.

Firstly, the Qing state made more arable land available for farming. By the end of the seventeenth century China's territory doubled through mergers with Mongolia and Manchuria in the north and north-east and Xinjiang in the far west.[43] Such expansion encompassed some of the best farming zones including the black soil region in Manchuria and the naturally irrigated land along the Great Bend of the Yellow River in South Mongolia. Efforts were also made to open the north-western hinterland (Gansu and Xinjiang) and south-western hinterland (Guizhou and Yunnan) for migrant farmers.[44] Qing reclamation schemes only left Tibet and its neighbouring Qinghai untouched. In the interior, huge areas of the Sichuan Basin and Yangtze-Han Plain were redeveloped as China's new rice exporting regions with better irrigation and more productive seeds.

The result is highlighted in table 1.3. Qing territory doubled from Ming levels (a 94.6 per cent increase in land mass) which in turn enlarged China's farmland by a third. The one-third increase in farmland may not, however, be enough to explain the doubling of China's population density in the core regions.[45] The next factor which boosted Qing agricultural output was state-led redevelopment of the vast region of the Yangzi reaches to double farming output there (205.3 per cent of the Ming level). There is no evidence that such re-development led to ecological depletion in the region before 1800.[46] So, the overall increase in agricultural output was around 235 per cent. Meanwhile, more and more households were persuaded to join farming. All these factors increased the economic base for population to take off. And it did.

China's farming labour migrated rather quickly to China's new regions.[47] Large numbers of farmers left old core regions (such as Hebei, Henan, Shandong, Shanxi, and Shaanxi) to resettle elsewhere.[48] The Qing state saw this migration as crucial for 'total employment' (as distinct from Keynesian 'full employment'). It issued policy guidance called 'filling regions of land abundance with people from regions of high population density' (*yi zhai bu kuan*). The matching policy was

Table 1.3. Changes in Farmland (km^2) in China, 1644 versus 1887

Territory	Total land	Privately farmed land*
Ming (I)	5,964,000	467,598
Qing	11,604,000	607,984
Qing addition (II)	5,640,000	140,386
II:I (%)	94.6	30.0
Redevelopment		
Sichuan Basin		560,000
Yangtze-Han Plain		400,000
Redevelopment total (III)		960,000
III:I (%)		205.3
Grand total (IV=II+III)		1,100,386
IV:I (%)		235.3

Note: The Ming territory as in 1644; the Qing territory as in 1812. Conversion of *mu* to square kilometres with a ratio of 1,500:1. * Privately farmed land was about 90–95 per cent of the Ming-Qing total farmland.
Source: Based on Liang Fangzhong, *Zhongguo Lidai Hukou Tiandi Tianfu Tongji* (*Dynastic Data for China's Households, Cultivated Land and Land Taxation*), Shanghai: Shanghai People's Press, 1980), pp. 346, 380.

'farming new land by invitation' (*quannong*), with property rights for new farms, free passage for farming migrants and tax holidays for new farming settlement.

Two large regions were purposely targeted: Manchuria and Mongolia. By 1668, Manchuria alone had absorbed 14 million immigrants from China's interior.[49] In the nineteenth century, the number of immigrants to Manchuria totalled approximately 600,000 a year. Even towards the end of the Qing, in 1907, 'farming new land by invitation' programmes continued and moved two million people a year to Heilongjiang.[50] Large-scale immigration also took place in Mongolia. In 1712, immigrants from Shandong totalled over 100,000.[51] Migrants moved to China's southern frontiers, too.[52] The third region was Sichuan. During 1743–8, a quarter of a million migrants moved there under the scheme of 'filling up Sichuan'.

Qing migration has left permanent marks on recipient regions to the present day, namely Manchuria, Mongolia, Sichuan, and Yunnan, where there are clear lineage and dialect links to migration donor regions such as Shandong, Shanxi, Hebei, Hubei, and Hunan.[53]

New lands and migrations in turn created synergies for the economy. Labour reduction in donor regions improved the 'marginal product of labour' there.[54] The labour recipient regions turned idle land into productive farms. So, overall, China gained twice regarding factors of production (from labour and land). From 1750 onwards, Manchuria supplied the Yangtze Delta with 10 million *piculs* (725,000 tonnes) of wheat, rice, and bean-cakes (as fertilisers) annually.[55] In return, the Yangtze Delta supplied Manchuria with cotton goods.[56] Meanwhile, by 1760, the Yangtze-Han Plain had doubled its food output capacity from the Ming level to 2.2 million tonnes of cereal a year,[57] not to mention large quantities of raw silk, raw cotton, and cloth.[58] The market economy expanded as a result.

Internal migration and agricultural development changed the distribution of China's demography and farmland: the share of the population in advanced farming regions in China's total dropped from 72 per cent (as of 1787) to 55 per cent (as of 1933), while the share of farmland in the same regions dropped from 74 per cent (as of 1787) to 49 per cent (as of 1933). The population and the newly cultivated land increased 17 per cent and 26 per cent, respectively.[59]

On the micro level, by the 1750s, China's average family size had increased by 20 per cent (one extra person in a family of five).[60] On the macro level, growth went continuously from strength to strength until China's population reached its peak of 398.9 million (1833), hitherto an Asian record.[61] This growth picture perfectly mapped onto China's enlarged resource base. Such changes delayed the onset

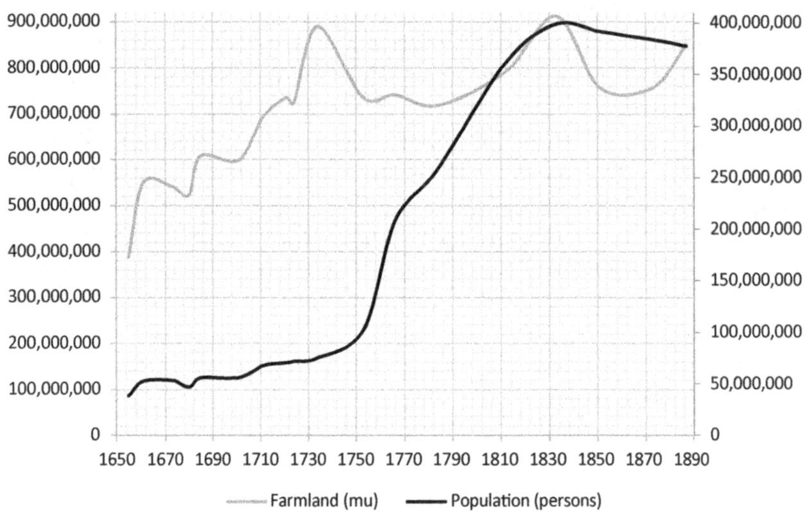

Figure 1.4. Trends in Farmland and Population, 1650–1890

Note: Left Y-axis: Farmland (*mu*). Right Y-axis: Population (persons).

Sources are available in the separate section of 'Figure Sources'.

of the Malthusian crisis which Ming China suffered. Figure 1.4 indicates general trends in farmland and population. It is obvious that an increase in farming land occurred first, taking the lead from 1650 to 1810. Population growth initially followed rather slowly (1650–1750) and then took off in the following century (1750–1850). So, intuitively, this was farmland-led population growth. This population growth model was not available during the Ming period.

Meanwhile, the Ming single-minded desire for receiving taxes in silver was over as Qing tax collection switched back to a combination of payments in both currency and grain.[62] This took the pressure off taxpayers regarding exporting China's surpluses in exchange for foreign silver. As a result, from 1650 to 1800 China's appetite for the monetary metal was sluggish (below 200 tonnes a year). The silver trade became volatile once again only after 1800 when the British East India Company entered the ring.[63]

Even so, silver piled up in government coffers, faster than silver imports. Figure 1.5 shows that from 1645 to 1820 China's annual silver intake was stable but at a low level (well under 200 tonnes per year). But the silver stock in the Qing Imperial Treasury behaved rather independently and increased from 700 tonnes in 1685 to over 2,000 tonnes in 1770.

However, there is a hypothesis that attributes China's population growth to a new food source consisting of maize and sweet potatoes

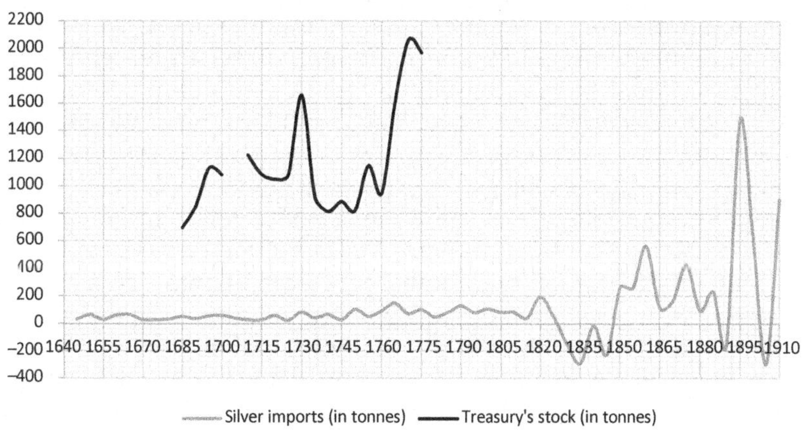

Figure 1.5. Annual Silver Imports versus Annual Qing Treasury Silver Stock, 1645–1910

Note: Data in five-year intervals, in tonnes.

Sources are available in the separate section of 'Figure Sources'.

from the New World.[64] It carries a subtle message of 'inferior food for the poor'.[65] An obvious reason was their low nutritional value. Maize yields per unit of land are about 30 per cent higher than wheat, but maize offers two-thirds of the protein for the same weight.[66] Fresh sweet potatoes yield ten times that of rice per unit of land, but contain only one-sixth of the energy of long-grain rice at the same weight.[67] In this context, if maize and sweet potatoes had replaced wheat and rice, the Qing population story becomes one of being 'larger but poorer'. From a social welfare point of view, such an increase in population size may not be worth having. In addition, if 'bad food drives out good', economics textbooks may need overhauling simply because China's population counted for about one-third of humanity at that time.

Anecdotally, an American journalist who covered China during the 1927 famine reported that in Shandong refugees lived on millet gruel, not maize or sweet potatoes.[68] Another American journalist was told by some 'proletarian soldiers' of the Communist Red Army in 1935 their food preferences: cooked rice was first; wheat-flour buns second; millet third; maize fourth; sweet potatoes fifth; and cabbages last.[69] In 1943, the same 'poor men's army' was known to live exclusively on wheat and millet.[70] A year earlier, in 1942, only when the food supply became desperately tight in Japanese-controlled Nanjing was maize forcefully introduced by the puppet government as an emergency measure.[71] There was no mention of sweet potatoes at all.

Prima facie, maize and sweet potatoes gained at best the status of an auxiliary food. Firstly, in a China-wide survey of 16,786 farms in 168 localities between 1929 and 1933, none of the regional units were said to specialise in maize or sweet potatoes, as demonstrated in figure 1.6.[72] More importantly, figure 1.6 shows that New World crops were adopted in only three regions, far from enough to feed the whole population. This simple fact discredits the notion of 'New World crops feeding China'. The implication here is that the Qing population was fed better than what the New World crops hypothesis implies.

Only seven out of twenty-two provinces adopted New World crops. Maize was adopted mainly in mountainous hinterlands in China's north-west, south-west and west regions, sweet potatoes mainly in China's south-western hinterland, the south-east and south coast (table 1.4). Inside those regions, new crops occupied on average 21 per cent (for maize) and 15 per cent (for sweet potatoes) of farmland. China-wide, the combined share of the two crops accounted for 3.6 per cent of farmland usage (table 1.4). The message is clear: with or without New World crops, China's population increased with more or less the same momentum.

Figure 1.6. China's Cropping Systems, 1920s–1930s

Note: (1) Upper circle marks where maize was cultivated: Shanxi-Shaanxi hinterland which was dominated by millet-wheat farming; (2) Lower-left circle marks where maize was also cultivated: Sichuan-Yunnan-Guizhou hinterland which was dominated by rice farming; (3) Lower-right circle marks where sweet potato was cultivated: south-east coast which was also dominated by rice farming.

Sources are available in the separate section of 'Figure Sources'.

Moreover, according to the same survey, in the south-western hinterland of Sichuan 20 per cent of sweet potato output was used as animal fodder; in Guangdong on the south coast, the share was 50 per cent.[73] Maize did not fare any better. In the core wheat region, about 35 per cent of maize was used as animal fodder; in the core rice region, it was 50 per cent.[74] So, maize and sweet potatoes indeed entered the human food chain. However, they were converted to animal protein first. Chinese consumers now obtained cheaper animal protein instead.[75]

Finally, labour inputs are a factor that has been overlooked so far. Farming maize and sweet potato was more labour-intensive per hectare than China's traditional crops. They needed 189 (sweet potatoes) and 205 (maize) working days per hectare per year, compared with

Table 1.4. Shares of Farmland under New World Crops in the 1920s

Maize	North-western hinterland (Shanxi-Shaanxi)	South-western hinterland (Yunnan-Guangxi)	Western hinterland (Sichuan)	*Average*
Nominal share* %	25.0	25.0	25.0	*25.0*
Multiple cropping index	118	152	167	*146*
Adjusted share† %	21.2	16.4	15.0	*21.0*
Sweet potatoes	South-western hinterland (Sichuan)	South-east coast (Guangdong)	East coast (Fujian)	
Nominal share* %	25.0	25.0	25.0	*25.0*
Multiple cropping index	167	176	169	*171*
Adjusted share† %	14.9	14.2	14.8	*14.6*
% of China's total farmland§				*3.6*

Note: * Mean value of Buck's range of 20–30 per cent. † Calculated with one New World crop in a multi-cropping system. § China-wide weight after taking regional variations of the introduced crops into account.
Sources: John L. Buck, *Land Utilization in China: Statistics* (London: Oxford University Press, 1937), pp. 174–5; Buck, *Atlas*, pp. 48, 50–1, 62, 82.

95 working days for wheat and 105–120 days for rice.[76] This was a 1.6- to 2.2-fold increase despite their low nutritional values. As such, adopting New World crops made little economic sense for farmers.

For all the above reasons, the New World crops did not become a main food source in Ming-Qing China; and China's population growth did not ride on an inferior food source. Rather, population growth was fuelled by improved resource allocation. So, the rationality presented in figure 1.5 stands. Nevertheless, China's door remained open prior to the Opium War. If it had not, maize and sweet potatoes would not have appeared at all until 1840.

4. Unintended Consequences of the Ming and Qing Policies

It is now clear that state policy in the Qing period was very different from that in the Ming period. As in many modern states, the Ming policies were geared towards maximising tax revenue. By contrast, the Qing policies aimed to maximise household output and incomes, which was rare in world history. The change in China's demographic patterns suggests that both policy objectives were achieved.

However, two very different unintended consequences arose from these policy differences. The Ming tax collection in silver (which had to be purchased through China's exports) and the spending of tax revenue (on the Great Wall, Beijing city and shipbuilding for the Ming armada) all encouraged monetisation of the economy. As a result, the Ming economy became highly diversified and the Ming social strata had more people making a livelihood outside farming. Such an employment structure was compatible with international trade, domestic specialisation, urbanisation, and proto-industrialisation. So, China stood a real chance, similar to Japan of the late Tokugawa era (Tokugawa: 1603–1868), of becoming a capitalist society should the Ming trend have continued for the next 500 years.

But the Qing physiocratic approach with a low tax burden encouraged universal farming. While this produced a well-fed population, such an approach discouraged international trade, domestic specialisation, urbanisation, and proto-industrialisation. Meanwhile, by persuading most Chinese to take up full-time farming, China's social structure was altered towards a mono-class society of 'peasant power'. Such peasant power eventually became the socio-political foundation of Maoism which, apart from lip-service propaganda, showed little tangible interest in international trade, domestic specialisation, urbanisation, and industrialisation.

5. China's Economic Status Prior to the Opium War

The Qing economy was strong yet overwhelmingly rural. China's unprecedented population growth took place mainly in the rural sector. Comparing with Japan's 12–15 per cent in *c.*1700, China's urbanisation rate remained low: at best 7 per cent (upper bound) for 1843,[77] or 6 per cent (lower bound) for 1893.[78]

Even so, China's rural economy was capable of supporting the market with its surplus produce.[79] Studies estimate that 20–40 per

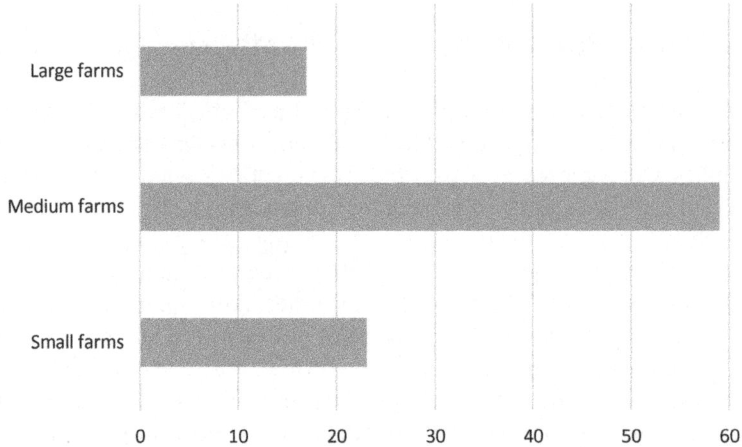

Figure 1.7. China-wide Farm Size Distribution, 1920s

Sources are available in the separate section of 'Figure Sources'.

cent of rural output was marketed,[80] thanks to a large proportion of 'well-to-do households' (large and medium farms) that formed a 76 per cent rural majority without a detectable trend of landholding polarisation even at the *passé* stage of China's traditional growth.[81] Our evidence comes from figure 1.7 where large farms accounted for less than 20 per cent of rural households. The well-to-do group of medium farms accounted for about 60 per cent of all households. Statistically, this group is where the mode and median values lie. The small farms that made up the remaining 22 per cent could be as poor as they liked but they were an outlier, not representative of the farming population statistically. Thus, Mao's rural revolution may have appealed to this 22 per cent. But it is deeply doubtful it had the support of the rural majority, as the Maoist propaganda claimed.

Quantitatively, prior to the 1839–40 Opium War, the value of China's 'marketed goods' was about eight times the government's annual revenue. This estimation is based on (1) the 47 million *taels* of tax collected in silver and rice by the Qing government (table 1.5) and (2) China's total marketed goods output worth 385 million *taels* (table 1.6).[82] One may look at it another way: marketed goods generated 8–40 per cent of Qing GDP, while Qing tax receipts were only 1–5 per cent of GDP.[83]

Two observations can be made from the data in table 1.6. Firstly, as much as 60.7 per cent of China's marketed goods were not for export. Secondly, exportable manufactures (metals, silk textiles, and porcelain)

Table 1.5. Recorded Qing Government Annual Revenues, the 1830s

	Value of various forms	Converted to silver × 10^6 *taels*
Land-poll	37,140,000 *taels*	37.1
Salt tax	6,080,000 *taels*	6.1
Maritime trade duties	1,800,000 *taels*	1.8
Stipend rice	4 million *piculs**	2.0
Total		47.0

Note: * The official conversion of stipend rice tax to silver payment was set artificially at 0.5 *tael* per *picul*; see Zhao Erxun, *Qingshi Gao* (*Drafted History of the Qing Dynasty*), vol. 122, 'Shihuo Zhi', in *Er-shi-wu Shi* (*Twenty-Five Official Histories*) (Shanghai: Shanghai Classics Press, 1986), in *Twenty-Five Official Histories*, vol. 11, p. 9286. There are estimates in circulation, too.[84]

Sources: (1) Land-poll and salt tax, see Zhou Bodi, *Zhongguo Caizheng Shi* (*A Financial History of China*) (Shanghai: Shanghai People's Press, 1981), pp. 421, 434; (2) Stipend rice tax, see Zhao, *Drafted History*, vol. 122, 'Shihuo Zhi', in *Twenty-Five Official Histories*, vol. 11, p. 9264; (3) Upper bound of Guangzhou maritime trade duties (1790–1840), see Anon., 'Tianzi Nankude Guanzhou Shisanhang' (Imperial Coffers in the South: The Thirteen Maritime Dealers in Guangzhou). https://www.gzass.gd.cn/whzc/wenhuaziyuan/wenhuagushi/131.html.

Table 1.6. Marketed Goods, Total Value, the 1830s

	Value (million *taels*)	Share of total (%)
Grain[85]	163.3	42.4
Salt	58.6	15.2
Raw silk	12.0	3.1
Sub-total		*60.7*
Tea	31.9	8.3
Metals	6.0	1.6
Porcelain	4.5	1.2
Silk textiles	14.6	3.8
Cotton cloth	94.6	24.5
Sub-total		*39.3*
Total	385.5	100.0

Source: Based on Wu Chengming, *Zhongguode Xiandaihua: Shichang Yu Shehui* (*China's Modernization: Market and Society*) (Beijing: Sanlian Books, 2001), pp. 148–9.

accounted for only 6.6 per cent of China's marketed goods,[86] since cotton textiles were mainly for domestic trade and consumption.[87] Silk exports now faced head-on competition with Japan. Thus, the Qing economy was almost certainly less export-oriented (and thus less open) than its Ming counterpart. Part of the reason was Qing China exported predominantly primary products such as tea and raw silk instead of China's traditional manufactures such as silk cloth and porcelain sets (for which Ming China is still famous). Many countries now exported tea and raw silk side by side with Qing China.

Meanwhile, China's inward-looking 'cotton economy' strengthened the dominance of agriculture in the economy, a phenomenon which has not been fully addressed. Two factors influenced cotton expansion as the main force of domestic manufacturing and trade. Firstly, as a close substitute for silk, cotton was able to keep silk from daily consumption and fetch higher market prices, especially from the export market. This was the reason why cotton was promoted by the Mongol Yuan state in order to increase silk exports. Secondly, the cotton production process was 'democratic' at the grassroots level: from sowing seeds to weaving cloth, all could be organised by rural households autonomously. It offered an income-making opportunity for idle labour in the agricultural off-season.[88]

In table 1.7, a typical household's annual working days are calculated for weaving and farming. In southern China, the labour allocation ratio was 1.8:1 in favour of weaving, while in northern China the ratio was as high as 5.5:1. The indication here is that the rise of household weaving was highly rational. China's rural 'industrious revolution' was inevitable thanks to cotton.[89] Bear in mind, China was not alone as Tokugawa Japan had a rather similar past.[90]

The Qing cotton trade was thriving. It has been estimated that between 20 and 100 million bolts (*pi*) of cotton cloth were produced per year prior to the Opium War.[91] In a simple estimation, if an upper bound of 100 million bolts is used as an annual output benchmark, it can be converted to 900 million square meters.[92] These 900 million

Table 1.7. Seasonality and Labour for Cotton Weaving, Annual Person-days

Region	Total working days minus annual holidays	Farming days	Available weaving days (husband)	Available weaving days (wife)	Available weaving days (husband + wife)	Weaving-farming ratio
Yellow River Region	311–317	95*	216–222	311–317	527–539	5.5–5.6
Yangzi Region	317–320	229†	88–91	317–320	405–411	1.8

Note: * Wheat single cropping. † Spring wheat-late rice double cropping.
Source: Buck, *Statistics*, pp. 307, 311, 314.

square meters can be divided by China's population at its peak, i.e. 398.9 million persons (1833). The result is 2.3 square meters per head per year. Given that a pair of adult-sized trousers requires 1.5–2 square metres of cloth; and a long sleeve shirt 1.6–2.1 square metres,[93] a new outfit needs 3.1–4.1 square metres of cloth. If a youngster's outfit uses half that amount, it will require 1.6–2 metres of cotton cloth per year. If a stylised family of five people in Qing China had two adults and three children, the amount of cloth needed for the family to wear new clothes every year can be estimated as 11–14 square metres, or 2.2–2.8 square metres per head, a perfect match for the 2.3 square metres of cotton cloth per head produced during the Qing. Meanwhile, there were other areas for cloth to be consumed such as shoe-making, bedding, interior decorations, as well as weddings, funerals, religious ceremonies, and communal festivals. In addition, the *nankeen* cloth was subject to export.[94] So, the said 2.3 square metres per head was barely enough. This explains why China imported large quantities of cotton yarn from India and then cotton cloth from Britain at this time,[95] meaning that the Qing cotton industry fell short of China's domestic demand. As a result, India's trade surplus with China increased three-fold from 1829 to 1837 to 6 million pounds, half of which was accounted for by cotton yarn.[96]

But together with the expansion of farming under the Qing, the industrious revolution led by cotton weaving undercut urban growth and prevented a societal division of labour. As a result, the Qing economy became far more rural than its Ming counterpart, which had a negative impact on China's growth trajectory, development possibilities, and political life in the twentieth century.

6. Economic Impact of the Opium War

By 1840, China had been open for international trade for four long centuries and a recipient of global silver for over three centuries. So, the notion that China's trading door was only opened by the 1839–40 Opium War is highly debatable, as it ignores China's history before the treaty ports. Rather, the treaty ports at best qualified as one type of opening among several. More specifically, the Opium War merely adapted China's existing openness to *British terms*. The impact may be detected from the reversal in silver flows for about a decade from 1840 to 1850 (figure 1.5). Needless to say, other foreign powers benefitted from Britain's gains in China,[97] common at the time when a sovereignty-based international order was not yet in sight.

Even so, China's demand for silver generally ran its own course. This can be inferred from silver imports and the exchange rate between bronze coins (*wen*) and silver (*taels*). From available and random observations, the Opium War had no permanent impact either on China's intake of foreign silver or on the general trend in bronze-to-silver exchange rates after 1840. Figure 1.8 contains data for silver availability (from silver imports) and exchange rates of bronze coins against silver *tael*. Silver imports to China were volatile from 1820 to 1900. But there was no sudden increase in inflation measured by bronze coins in exchange for one silver *tael*. Rather, an inflation drive occurred before 1840 when the trend of exchange rates moved upwards from 800 bronze coins per silver *tael* (1720) to about 1,400 bronze coins per silver *tael* on the eve of the Opium War (1839–40), if taking 1,600 bronze coins per silver *tael* in 1790 as an outlier. The rate rose again from 1400 to 1800 bronze coins per silver *tael* from 1840 to 1870, if taking 2,000 bronze coins per silver *tael* in 1850 as another outlier. After that, there was a downward move all the way back to the level of 1820.

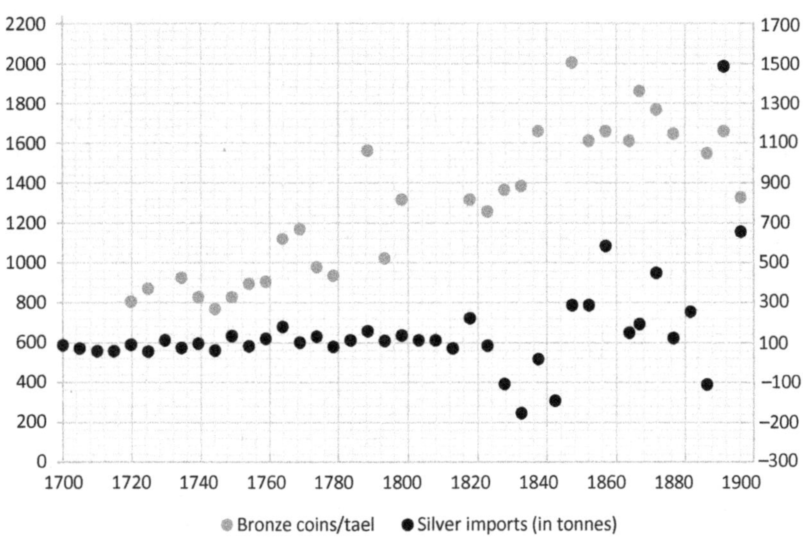

Figure 1.8. Silver Imports and Sampled Exchange Rates of Bronze Coins per Silver *Tael*, 1700–1900

Note: Left Y-axis: Bronze coins/silver tael exchange rate. Right Y-axis: Silver imports (in tonnes).

Sources are available in the separate section of 'Figure Sources'.

7. China's Indigenous Growth Trajectory

To return to the issue of China's demographic landscape, uninterrupted growth occurred between 1650 and 1830 (figure 1.4). This was also a period in which China saw a continuation in market openness since the Ming era. The best evidence was a continuous inflow of foreign silver which stacked up in the Imperial coffers (figure 1.8).

After 1850, however, China entered a different era. On the economic front, private property rights and the market economy seem to have run out of steam. During the period 1870–1930, China's labour and land productivity remained stagnant for these six decades, as shown in table 1.8, where labour and land productivity in 1870 is indexed to 100. Labour productivity was broadly flat while land productivity grew at an annual rate of just 0.13 per cent. This suggests that the economy sat along an upper limit for the farming sector, something similar to John Stuart Mill–David Ricardo's 'stationary state' or Mark Elvin's 'high-level equilibrium trap'.[98]

The last boom in China's pre-industrial economic growth came to an end around 1850. Nevertheless, the Ming-Qing growth saga provides an indigenous benchmark for later times. For this purpose, a baseline can be set in the 1830s before things went wrong for China. Indeed, on the farming front, in the century between 1830 and 1930, *per capita* output changed very little even in China's more advanced southern regions.[99]

It should be noted that China's real GDP during this period remains unknown despite several contested estimates.[100] As such, this project

Table 1.8. Labour and Land Productivity Indexes, 1870–1930

Year	Labour productivity	Land productivity
1870	100	100
1880	98	103
1890	99	103
1900	97	106
1910	99	105
1920	98	108
1930	99	108
Annal change	-0.02%	0.13%

Source: P.K.C. Liu and Kuo-shu Hwang, 'Population Change and Economic Development in Mainland China since 1400', in C.M. Hou and T.C. Yu (eds), *Modern Chinese Economic History* (Taipei: Academia Sinica, 1979), pp. 65–75.

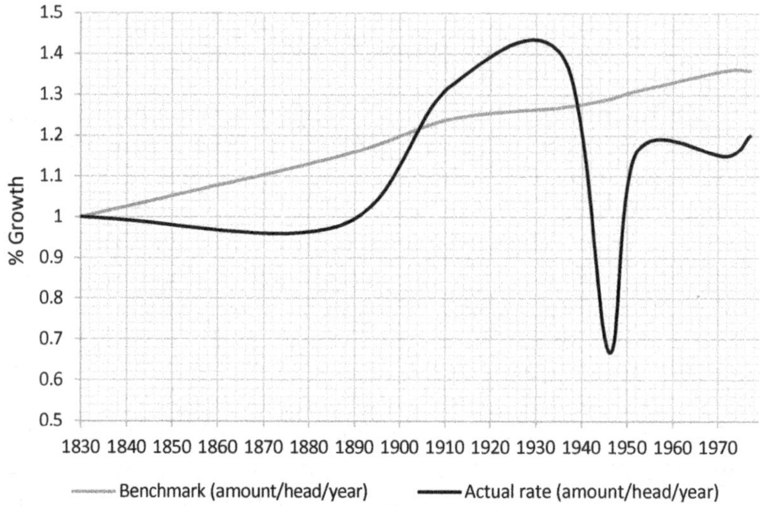

Figure 1.9. Growth Performance: Benchmark versus Reality, 1830–1978

Sources are available in the separate section of 'Figure Sources'.

uses only three growth-related percentages: (1) research indicating that China's economy grew at 0.9 per cent a year from 1750 to 1830;[101] (2) estimates showing that China's population increased 0.5 per cent a year from the 1810s to 1830s;[102] and thus (3) an annual per capita growth rate of 0.4 per cent (which does not support the notion of 'stagnation' for a traditional economy). This was much slower than even the 'Hindu rate of growth'.[103] Qing China had a weak state, so such a slow growth rate can be expected. At such a rate, however, by 1970 China's economic size would have increased 3.5-fold, and its population would have doubled. Here, one asks, was China capable of outperforming its Qing potential in the twentieth century?

Rather surprisingly, surpassing China's traditional benchmark has turned out to be a tall order. Figure 1.9 shows two growth trajectories. One is the Qing benchmark, and the other is actual growth. It reveals how poorly China's economy performed until the 1970s even by Qing standards. Across 150 years from 1830 to 1980, China underperformed most of the time, bar 35 years from 1905 to 1940. So, 76 per cent of the time China did not reach the Qing modest standards. After a soft-landing decline from 1830 to 1880, China managed to have some sort of take-off from 1880 to 1930 despite a regime change (from an empire to a republic), and a civil war between the south and the north. Thereafter, economic performance was poor thanks to the Second World War and Maoism (1949–1979). However, over the 148-year-long span (1830–1978), the only period when China's growth performance outdid its Qing benchmark was 1905 to 1940.

8. Final Remarks

So far, few historians have linked the Ming period (1368–1644) to China's modern growth. This is despite the fact that the mentality of openness and the practice of a high-capacity state were both endogenous in society at that time – a promising combination for Ming China to move towards some sort of modernity. Against all the odds, however, the Qing authorities promoted physiocracy and a small state instead, moving away from the Ming norm. As a result, China's state capacity vanished. Moreover, as the Qing story unfolded, state failures created ample opportunities for the less educated not only to meddle with but also to take over state power in China. These are the points to be dealt with in chapter 2.

— 2 —

THE ROAD TO THE PRC, MAOIST GROWTH TRAPS AND STATE FAILURE

1. Pre-Mao China as Land of 'Murphy's Law', 1850–1950

By 1800, China had changed beyond recognition from its Ming norm of 'heavy taxation with low population growth'. It would continue to do so until it claimed a quarter of the world's population and a third of world GDP.[1] A change in fortunes loomed large after 1850: anything that could go wrong began to do so internally, which had little to do with China's alleged xenophobia and the 1839–40 Opium War.

Conventional wisdom prefers a linear and teleological approach. Again, one goes back to the Opium War. The narrative runs as follows: China's international isolation was ended by British gunboat diplomacy in 1839–40.[2] As Imperial rule decayed and China's trading door was forced open,[3] a Christian-communist movement, known as the 'Heavenly Peaceful Kingdom' (*taiping tianguo*), heralded a wave of radical changes which led eventually to the '1911 Revolution'. At the same time, the '1919 New Cultural Movement' led to an ideological shift to 'modern science and Western democracy' (known as the 'May Fourth Movement'),[4] which finally and teleologically landed on the 1921–49 Communist Movement.[5]

The problem with this rhetoric is its incompatibility with China's socio-economic changes. Firstly, Christianity arrived in China with Matteo Ricci who landed on Macao in 1582 and reached Beijing in 1601. Why did it take 250-odd years for Christianity to produce the Heavenly Peaceful Kingdom? Moreover, the Heavenly Peaceful Kingdom only affected a third of eighteen Qing provinces. Can it be regarded as a national movement?

Secondly, what ended Qing rule was not a clear-cut 'revolution' but a complex process culminating in a mutiny of a few hundred army cadets in 1911, known as the 'Wuchang Mutiny'. Most tellingly, when the mutiny broke out, Sun Yat-sen, the leader of the late Qing republican movement, was not even in China.[6] So, it was either a leaderless event at its critical moment, or the munity was not part of the republican movement at all.

Finally, the '1919 New Cultural Movement', which stood for 'modern science and Western democracy', was short-lived and had little to do with the Communist Movement, which was exported to China directly from Russia, a country that was not known for either its science or its democracy at that time. Thus, although popular, the linear and teleological narrative has far too many holes in it.

Historical observations have left a conundrum: Why and how did the commonly alleged 'Open Era' of post-1840 not deliver growth any better than the sluggish Qing trajectory it inherited (figure 1.9)? The short answer is that China was dogged by 'state failures', which lasted for about a century from 1850 to 1950. During this elongated period of failure, China's private economy was negatively affected. The starting point was 1850, a decade after the Opium War, when China was swamped with internal rebellions. Figure 2.1 highlights the seriousness of the crisis. China was carved into four zones by rebels. Zone A was dominated by ethnic Han rebels divided between the Nians and Taipings; Zones B and D by Muslims; and Zone C by the ethnic Miao. The Taipings alone claimed to have a total of 600,000 troops. The Nians had another 200,000.[7] So, rebels in Zone A already outnumbered the Qing armed forces of 120,000 Eight-Bannermen (*baqi*) and 660,000 Green Standards (*lüqi*, *lüying*).[8]

As for what caused such a sudden and wide eruption of social unrest across the Qing Empire, the *force majeure* of the 1840–1880 Little Ice Age ticks many boxes. It was responsible for a colder and drier climate with more typhoon attacks on the East Asian mainland.[9] It also changed the basic conditions for farming by altering rainfall levels and the frost-free period, both vital for agricultural yields. Figure 2.2 shows how China's disasters peaked between 1850 and 1860, coinciding with the Little Ice Age. But government disaster relief efforts could not match its own level of provisions in the 1730–1790 or 1825 periods when disasters were far less severe. This was a major problem.

A causal link has been speculated by Bret Hinsch, as stated in this passage:[10]

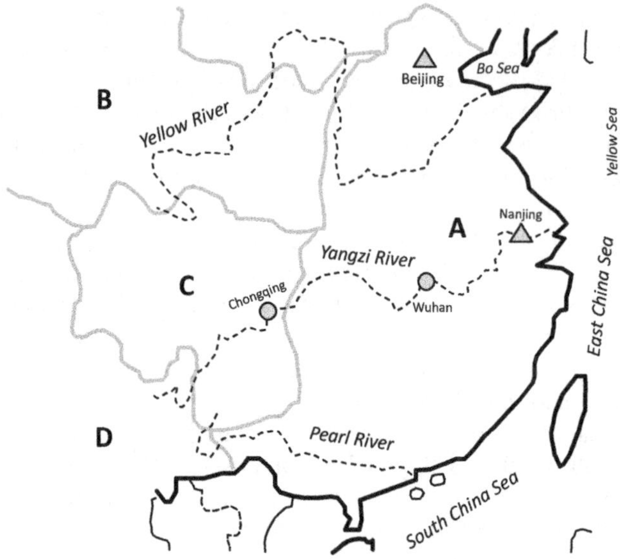

Figure 2.1. China-wide Rebellions in the 1850s and 1860s

Note: Rebels' regions: A – Nian-Taiping Zone; B – Muslim Zone$_1$; C – Miao Zone; D – Muslim Zone$_2$.

Sources are available in the separate section of 'Figure Sources'.

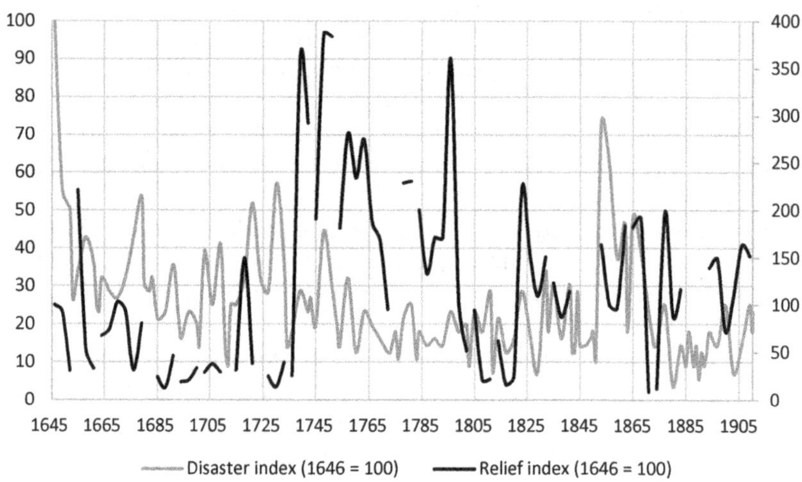

Figure 2.2. Disasters and Disaster Relief, 1645–1910

Note: Left Y-axis: Disaster index (1646 = 100).
Right Y-axis: Disaster relief index (1646 = 100), counting beneficiary counties.

Sources are available in the separate section of 'Figure Sources'.

> [In China] the climate again turned warm from 1720 to 1830, followed by a general cooling from 1840 to 1890. This final period of cold began a decade prior to the massive uprising of the Taiping Heavenly Kingdom (1850–1864). And in northern Anhui, cradle of the Nian revolt (1851–1868), natural disasters such as flood and drought struck with such regularity that local peasants lamented 'ten years saw eight years of catastrophe'. The beginnings of the rebellion coincided with three successive years of disastrous flooding.

Intuitively, the Little Ice Age seems to have correlated with the timing, the spread, and the indiscriminate nature of the rebellions. A similar situation occurred during the Northern Song period (960–1127) when an earlier Little Ice Age triggered sweeping changes in China's economy across all regions, though not rebellions.[11] Meanwhile, the 'White Lotus Rebellion' in 1796–1805 was limited to three provinces (Shaanxi, Hubei, and Sichuan) due to a localised drought in China's west hinterland. The rebellion thus never spilled over to affect the rest of the empire.[12]

Given that famine relief is a socio-political factor in determining rebellions, the role of the Qing state needs scrutiny. This was particularly relevant in imperial China due to its long tradition of a granary system (*changping cang*, literally 'ever-even or ever-equilibrium granary') which worked as a social safety net to counter-balance crop failures and food price fluctuations. Officially, this social safety net lasted until the 1900s.[13] Now, the Little Ice Age put Qing state capacity to the test.[14]

In as late as 1812, the amount of grain stock held by the system was maintained at the level of 33,508,575 *piculs* (2,429,370 tonnes), not too far off the mandatory stockpile of 36,710,000 *piculs* (2,661,475 tonnes) shown in table 2.1. A stockpile of 33.5–36.7 million *piculs* was enough to sustain 30 million adults for 100–120 days over a lean season.[15] If the charity system was included, the amount of the stockpile was about 45 million *piculs* (2.2–3.3 million tonnes) in a normal year.[16] So far so good.

Moreover, there was a network of village communal granaries (*yicang*) based on 'donated grain' (*juan gu*), which came from the local communities themselves. According to general guidance issued by Beijing, local grain donors to charity granaries were exempted from *corvée* services to incentivise grain donation.[17] In addition, according to the Qing regulations of 1725 and 1739, charity granaries were autonomous and free from government interference.[18] In 1753, Zhili Province had 1,005 communal granaries across 144 counties and prefectures (thus seven granaries per county) with a total stockpile of

Table 2.1. Mandatory Annual Government Granary Stockpile, 1748–1766

Location	Stockpile, in *Piculs* 36,710,000 (2,661,475)	Percentage of total stockpile	Percentage of total registered population*	Grain-population ratio
Northern provinces	17,200,000 (1,247,000)	46.9	42.4	1.1
Southern provinces	19,510,000 (1,414,475)	53.1	57.6	0.9

Note: Figures with brackets are in tonnes. Conversion is based on 1 Qing *picul* = 72.5 kilograms; see Liang, *Dynastic Data*, p. 545; also Kang Chao, *Man and Land in Chinese History: An Economic Analysis* (Stanford: Stanford University Press, 1986), p. 209. Grain in the granary system was unhusked for a longer shelf life. The husking/milling process normally causes a loss of 30 per cent in weight. * Qing population as in 1766; see Liang, *Dynastic Data*, p. 396.
Source: Zhao, *Drafted History*, vol. 121 'Economy', in *Twenty-Five Official Histories*, vol. 11, p. 9263.

285,300 *piculs* (20,684 tonnes).[19] So, communal granaries' capacity was small.

In addition, there was another source of food supply from the market. In a normal year, the market traded 30 million *piculs* of grain, enough to feed another 30 million adults for a season.[20] However, this was not suitable for famine relief. So, the main force of famine relief had to be state granaries.

Cereal is perishable, and its maintenance can be expensive without modern technology. So, in 1695, the official rule was to 'retain 70 per cent of the stockpile and sell 30 per cent' (*cunqi disan*) to better manage the size of the granary stockpile.[21] Still, food spoilage occurred, as reported in 1704. Officials responsible for granary spoilage had to pay for the damage or lose their job.[22] Meanwhile, in 1735 the rule for southern provinces, where a humid environment made grain storage difficult, was further relaxed.[23] Ultimately, the Qing authorities saw a reduction of the granary stockpile as a solution. In 1835, a new annual quota of 24,000,000 *piculs* (1,740,000 tonnes) was set.[24] This was roughly a third reduction from the previous level. Consequently, the number of adults that could be saved during a famine shrank to 20 million.

Against this backdrop, the 1840–80 period saw Qing state famine relief at a low ebb when it was needed most (see figure 2.2), with relief delivery falling to half of the pre-1840 level. So, the 1835 reduction of the government grain stockpile took its toll and translated into

Table 2.2. Population Decline in Taiping-affected Provinces* (Million People)

	1851 total I	1860 total† II	Survival rate (II/I)	1880 total§ III	Recovery rate (III/I)
Anhui	37.4	17.7	47.3%	19.9	53.2%
Jiangsu	44.7	28.7	64.2%	32.4	72.5%
Zhejiang	30.3	13.3	43.9%	15.0	49.5%
Hubei	22.2	15.3	68.9%	17.2	77.4%
Hunan	21.8	17.6	80.7%	19.8	90.8%
Jiangxi	24.3	11.2	46.1%	12.6	51.8%
Fujian	16.2	9.9	61.0%	11.2	69.1%
Total	196.9	113.7	57.7%	128.1	65.1%

Note: * Figures for Taiping-controlled Sichuan, Guangdong, and Guangxi are not available, but according to Cao, their total was likely to be 73.3 million; see Cao, *Demographic History*, vol. 5, p. 553. † It is known that the annual population growth rate during peace-time was 0.6 per cent in 1776–1851 just before the unrest.[25] By factoring this growth rate in, one may back-extrapolate population losses when the unrest ended before any population recovery occurred. § Figures after one-generation-long recovery.
Source: Cao, *Demographic History*, vol. 5, pp. 467, 489, 505–6, 508, 535, 540, 552–3.

China-wide social unrest. Clearly, Qing unrest cannot be attributed to a high tax burden from government rent-seeking. Rather, the unrest was caused by a lack of public goods due to the state's withdrawal from its duty, a point that will be elaborated later.

The unrest cost China dearly. To begin with, China's demographics were dramatically altered. In table 2.2, the 1851 data are the pre-unrest period benchmarks. The data for 1860 show the immediate impact of the Taiping Rebellion on population size. The data for 1880 show a modest recovery in the population one generation after the ending of the unrest. Among the seven provinces that were impacted by the Taipings, only 57.7 per cent of China's standing population survived by 1860. The loss rate was over 40 per cent. The worst affected provinces were Anhui, Zhejiang, and Jiangxi where the population was reduced by more than half in the decade to 1860. Twenty years later, China's population was still 34.9 per cent lower than the 1851 level. Not until 1919, six decades later, did China's population climb back to 432 million. The economy also underperformed (figure 1.9).

Ultimately, one wonders why the Qing state unilaterally reduced its food stock in a granary system so vital for social order. Opposing the outdated impression that there was an absolute, despotic monarchy

Table 2.3. Number of Qing Officials versus General Population, 1700–1850

Year	Population	Officials on payroll	Ideal number officials*	True Population/ Officials ratio
1700	20,411,163†	24,150	—	845.2:1
1830–50	398,942,036	26,355	472,345	15,137.2:1
Annual %	2.3	0.06		

Note: * Hypothetical, if the number of officials had grown at the same speed as the general population. † Surprisingly small as shown in the early Qing record.
Sources: Liang, *Dynastic Data*, p. 10; Yang Zhimei, *Zhongguo Gudai Guanzhi Jiangzuo* (*Bureaucracy of Premodern China*) (Beijing: Zhonghua Books, 1992), pp. 420–1.

that controlled all aspects of people's life in China,[26] the answer comes from the size of the Qing bureaucracy which fell far behind the growth of the Qing population by a factor of 38. As shown in table 2.3, in the beginning, the Qing population to bureaucrat ratio was 845:1. On the eve of social unrest in 1850, the ratio swelled to 15,137:1 due to a freeze in the number of officials working for the government. The shortage of government personnel was in the region of half a million (472,345). As a result, a shortage of manpower to facilitate public goods provision (such as maintaining granary stock and handing out relief) was inevitable.

Likewise, the small army of Qing bureaucrats was thinly spread out across the empire. A total of 2,546 key officials were in control of the centre of the empire in Beijing.[27] Another 2,650 military officers ran a standing army of 780,000 troops.[28] This left approximately 17,300 administrators to run three layers of administration with eighteen provinces (*sheng*), 190 prefectures (*fu*), 1,672 counties (*xian*), and 402 county-equivalent units.[29] They totalled 2,074 units. On average 8.3 officials ran a local government office. This constraint explains why the Qing state was incapable of penetrating at the village level let alone at household level.[30]

One may argue that there was a hidden army of 'sub-official functionaries' (*li*) whose number was elastic. However, as all these 'sub-official functionaries' were hired as officials' personal assistants, their number had to be limited by the disposable part of an official's salary. The pay scale for Qing officials was 45 *taels* per year for the county magistrate and 180 *taels* for the provincial governor without performance bonuses.[31] Meanwhile, a Qing cavalryman had an allowance of 36 *taels* a year plus stipend rice.[32] If the latter was a benchmark for a professional pay scheme, it was unlikely that a county magistrate could afford to hire a full-time 'sub-official functionary'. A provincial governor might hire a couple. Such numbers were too small to make a difference.

Of course, a bonus system (*yanglian yin*, literally 'honesty and uprightness bonuses') was implemented in 1723.[33] In theory, a bonus could be 100 times a basic salary.[34] However, so far very few documents outlining who got what can be found in Qing records.[35] Rather, a significant proportion of bonuses boomeranged back to the state coffers in the name of donations (Appendix 3). So, the small state judgement remains.

In the mid-nineteenth century, the co-occurrence of three factors – a *force majeure* shock on food production, a large population facing the threat of famine, and a small government that controlled a reduced stockpile for relief – created a perfect storm for rebellions.[36] In particular, the lack of officials on the ground made mass rebellions easy.[37] The Taipings alone systematically looted in 600 cities and towns with little resistance.[38] At the same time, the lack of officials also made the aforementioned maritime bans ineffective (as in the case of opium). In this context, China-wide social unrest during the second half of the nineteenth century was a product of state failure.

The invisible Qing state in people's daily life can be viewed as deliberate in that it adhered to Confucian moral economy.[39] The root cause of the Qing minimalist state was a unilateral commitment to 'freezing total tax revenue indefinitely' (*yongbu jiafu*) announced by Emperor Kangxi (1654–1722, r.1661–1722) in 1712, which bore the hallmark of Confucian statecraft.[40] In due course, this 1712 edict wrecked the Ming state capacity trajectory and planted the seed for Qing state failure a century or so later.

The ultimate reason for Kangxi's benevolent decision was rooted in concerns over the Manchus' legitimacy to rule China. This had haunted the Qing Court since 1644 when the Manchus agreed to act as mercenaries of the Ming state to put down a rebellion that captured Beijing in 1643. The rebels were eliminated but the Manchus failed to honour the deal, staying on in Beijing and establishing the Qing Dynasty. This was the original sin and guilt that the Manchus tried hard to redeem. So, the Manchus were *not* a clique with an undisputed claim to rule China. This created a chain reaction in China's state-capacity building.

Han Chinese were welcomed in the Qing state apparatus. Table 2.4 shows that Qing provincial governorship was chiefly made up of ethnic Han. The data in table 2.5 show that even in the military, in which Chinese had no obvious advantage, ethnic Han officers accounted for about a third.

Table 2.4. Composition of Governor-Generals of Provinces, % of Total, 1644–1911

	SZ	KX	YZ	QL	JQ	DG	XF	TZ	GX	XT
Han	92.3	59.4	77.8	51.5	69.0	69.8	88.6	71.0	81.7	40.0
Manchus	7.7	40.6	22.2	45.6	31.0	28.3	11.4	25.8	18.3	40.0

Note: SZ – Shunzhi (r.1644–61), KX – Kangxi (r.1662–1722), YZ – Yongzheng (r.1723–35), QL – Qianlong (r.1736–95), JQ – Jiaqing (r.1796–1820), DG – Daoguang (r.1821–50), XF – Xianfeng (r.1851–61), TZ – Tongzhi (r.1861–74), GX – Guangxu (r.1875–1908), XT – Xuantong (r.1909–11).
Source: Dai Yi (ed.), *Er-shi-liu Shi Dacidian, Rewujuan* (*Comprehensive Indices of the Twenty-six Histories of China, Volume on Individuals*) (Changchun: Jilin People's Press, 1993), pp. 1206–390.

Table 2.5. Ethnic Composition of Military Officers*, % of Total, 1644–1911

	Han	Manchus	Mongols	Total
1st–3rd Grades	38.5	38.5	23.0	100
7th–9th Grades	31.8	40.9	27.3	100

Note: * Based on 'Eight Banners' (*baqi*).
Sources: Zhang Deze, *Qingdai Guojia Jiguan Kaolue* (*The State Apparatus of the Qing Period*) (Beijing: Xueyuan, 2001), pp. 6, 38–43, 57, 79, 105–6, 126; Song Yuanqiang, *Qingchaode Zhuangyuan* (*Champions of the Qing Imperial Examinations*) (Changchun: Jilin Culture and History Press, 1992), pp. 477–87.

To sustain the supply of Confucian bureaucrats, the Chinese language was accorded official status. Chinese books were made available.[41] Confucianism continued as the state philosophy.[42] The Imperial Examinations to recruit bureaucrats were resumed in 1646 with a nearly seamless connection to the last Ming Examination held in 1643. No changes were made to Ming examination regulations.[43] In addition, all Manchus princes were educated from a very young age by top Confucian scholars.

Regarding economic policies, Han-specific policy was carefully adapted in the form of promoting farming. Each year, the Qing emperor performed the 'Opening of Tillage Ceremony' (*gengjili*) and held a memorial ceremony in the Temple of the First Agriculturist (*xiannong tan*).[44] The Qing authorities also sponsored more agricultural treatises than their Ming predecessor by a factor of two.[45]

When the first Qing Emperor Shunzhi (1638–61, r.1644–61) occupied the throne, he was only six years old. He died young at the age of 23. So, the Shunzhi reign was rather eventless. Then came Emperor

Kangxi (1654–1722, r.1661–1722) who ruled the empire for a record 61 years. Kangxi led a policy of reconciling relations with the Han Chinese. In 1684 he paid his respects in Nanjing at the mausoleum of Zhu Yuanzhang, the founder of the Ming Dynasty. It was reported that the emperor took the side path instead of the boulevard and ordered his entourage to dismount. He then deigned to kneel three times and kowtowed nine times (*sangui jiukou*) at the tomb, the highest etiquette that was observed by subordinates to the throne. In doing so, Kangxi symbolically recognised the Ming founder as the ultimate ruler of China.[46] Around this time, the benevolent policies of 'governing by *laissez-aller*' (*wuwei erzhi*) and 'light corvée and low taxes' (*qingyao bofu*) as idealised approaches to governance since the Western Han period (206 BC–25 AD) converted Kangxi's state craftsmanship. The result was his 1712 edict of 'freezing total tax revenue indefinitely' (*yongbu jiafu*) to win Chinese hearts. With hindsight, the whole process of Manchu redemption produced a 'ratchet effect' with no way back.

The hands of the Qing state were tied because of it. Over the next century, until 1840, the backbone of Qing tax revenue – the Land-Poll Tax – remained unchanged at the level of 30-odd million *taels* a year. Meanwhile, as the economy and population expanded, the tax burden on land declined by 50 per cent,[47] and the tax burden on people fell by 80 per cent.[48] The Qing taxation rate became so light that people 'barely noticed the tax system'.[49] In the process, Qing fiscal capacity diminished.[50] The long peace during the eighteenth century created a false sense of security. Thus, the Qing state can be thought of as a 'night-watchman state' (or a 'minarchy').

Fast forward to the 1960s, Mao's China was ruled by an army of 12 million cadres equivalent to 15 per cent of China's population, excluding Mao's army officers.[51] The civilian-to-official ratio was 5:1, over 50 times the Qing level. This ratio persisted. In 2012, China was run by over 60 million government employees, more or less the same as Mao's level.[52] So, Mao's China had no mass rebellions despite a mass famine. There was no inheritable and inevitable link between the Qing minarchy and Mao's autocracy.

Qing rule was doomed to be usurped in a process that occurred many times in China's long history and was known as the 'dynastic cycle'.[53] In such a process, a new dynasty would have replaced the Qing to maintain an empire in East Asia and to allow the cycle to continue for the next 500 years. But the cycle was broken this time by a force akin to 'feudal separatism'. And feudalism was historically the worst enemy of the empire system in China.

2. Rise of 'Militocrats' (or Stratocrats) and Maoism in the Making, 1850–1920

The Little Ice Age exposed the state failure of the late Qing.[54] The corresponding China-wide unrest woke the Qing elite up. The tables were turned when the Qing elite resolutely abandoned the self-imposed low taxation straitjacket of 1712. What followed from the 1850s through to the 1870s was the rise of proto-fiscal states with taxation self-determination at the provincial level to facilitate state re-building from the bottom up to fight the rebels.[55] This provincial approach to waging war in turn led to regionalism with a high degree of financial and military autonomy.[56] As a result, while China-wide rebellions did not end the empire, the rise of autonomous provinces did.

In the process, a new breed of provincial governors emerged. They were no longer 'litero-meritocrats' who ran civilian rule on behalf of Beijing but 'militocrats' (or stratocrats) who ran fiscal military mini-states independent from Beijing.[57] The four foundational militocrats were Zeng Guofan (1811–72), Zuo Zongtang (1812–85), Li Hongzhang (1823–1901), and Zhang Zhidong (1837–1909). The new approach gave the Qing Empire a new lease of life for another 50 years until 1911, a not trivial period of time.

Meanwhile, the role of the age-old Imperial Examinations for recruiting bureaucrats faded out fast. The system was challenged in the '1898 100-Day Reforms' and then scrapped by law in 1905. The good old days of the *literati* and civil bureaucracy were finally over. The future belonged to militocrats. Finally, in 1912, the genie of radical changes came out of the bottle when three dozen provincial militocrats joined forces with General Yuan Shikai (1859–1916) and forced Puyi (1906–67, r.1908–12), the 'Toddler Emperor', to abdicate. Consequently, the rebel General Yuan became the first President Elect of the Republic of China in the 1913 election. The leader of the Republican Movement Sun Yat-sen was no match for his stratocrat rivals and he received merely two per cent of votes compared with 62 per cent for Yuan Shikai and 20 per cent for Li Yuanhong (Vice-President Elect, who was personally involved in the 1911 Mutiny in Wuhan).[58]

The secret of the militocrats' success on the battlefield was their ability to assemble armed forces equipped with Western firearms. This ushered in the 'Westernisation Movement' (*yangwu yundong*) from 1860 to 1895, which opened the floodgates for Western ideas, technology, and institutions to penetrate China on an industrial scale.

Table 2.6 contains data for provincial armed forces by the time social order was finally re-established. Across the Qing territory, all nineteen provinces ran independent armies which accounted for a third of all troops. China was now fully militarised.

In addition, as shown in sporadic data in table 2.7, the new provincial troops were supplied by China's new arms industry in six locations, which had the capacity to produce large quantities of gunpowder, bullets, shells, and rifles, and was also capable of making cannons and building warships.

To demonstrate the superiority of new Qing armed forces over the rebels, in the period 1860–4 the fatality ratio in battle was 61:1 in favour of the Qing side.[59] Given the fact that the Taipings only had about 20,000–30,000 diehard members armed with cold steel weapons,[60] a unit of 550 men from a provincial army was capable of taking on all the Taipings put together. So, the tables were decisively turned against insurgents. By 1870, social order had been restored. In the process, China finally moved from a Confucian civilisation to

Table 2.6. New Standing Armies across Provinces, *c.*1880

Opposing rebel group	Province	New Qing troops
Taiping	Anhui	11,290
Taiping	Jiangsu	29,960
Taiping	Zhejiang	21,300
Taiping	Hubei	13,783
Taiping	Hunan	12,970
Taiping	Jiangxi	9,360
Taiping	Guizhou	9,486
Taiping	Fujian	10,540
Taiping	Guangdong	11,800
Taiping	Guangxi	16,940
Nian	Zhili	63,400
Nian	Shandong	13,950
Nian	Shanxi	4,900
Nian	Henan	9,190
Muslims	Shaanxi	14,450
Muslims	Gansu	12,500
Muslims	Xinjiang	30,277
Muslims	Yunnan	15,033
Miao	Sichuan	15,698
Total	19	326,827

Source: Zhao, *Drafted History*, vol. 132, 'Military', in *Twenty-Five Official Histories*, vol. 11, p. 9311.

Table 2.7. Provincial Arsenals and Mass Production of Modern Arms

Arsenal	Location	Start time	Annual output
Suzhou	Suzhou	1865	Bullets: 100,000 rounds
Jiangnan	Shanghai	1867	Gunpowder: 6.7 million pounds; bullets: 8.6 million rounds; shells: 1.6 million; rifles: 65,000; cannons: 742; and ships: 15
Tianjin	Tianjin	1870	Gunpowder: 6.1 million pounds; bullets:16.1 million rounds shells: 40,000; rifles: 52
Guangzhou	Guangzhou	1874	Bullets: 240,000 rounds
Sichuan	Chengdu	1877	Bullets: 3.3 million rounds; shells: 5,400; rifles: 18,681
Jinling*	Nanjing	1899	Bullets: 131,500 rounds; shells: 65,800; rifles: 18; cannons: 64
Total	6		Gunpower: 12.8 million pounds; bullets: 28.3 million rounds; shells: 1.7 million; rifles: 83,751; cannons: 806; ships: 15

Sources: Based on Xu Tailai, *Yangwu Yundong Xinlu* (*Re-examination of the Westernisation Movement*) (Changsha: Hunan People's Press, 1986), pp. 25, 28, 32, 34, 35, 36. Li Yunjun (ed.), *Wanqing Jingji Shishi Biannian* (*A Chronicle of Late Qing Economic History*) (Shanghai: Shanghai Classics Press, 2000), p. 423. For the Jiangnan Arsenal, also see Mary C. Wright, *The Last Stand of Chinese Conservatism, the T'ung-Chih Restoration, 1862–1874* (Stanford: Stanford University Press, 1957), p. 293.

a Social Darwinian one with a new doctrine of 'political power from the barrel of a gun' (*qiangganzi limian chu zhengquan*), as openly promoted by Mao and his followers later in 1927.[61]

Behind the scenes, all provincial troops needed about 20 million *taels* of silver per year to sustain themselves.[62] Money had to come from inside a province. This in turn led to an unconventional tax regime – an indirect tax called the 'one per cent transit tax' (*lijin* or *likin*). It began in 1853 by trial and error in a war zone in Jiangsu.[63] It was based on the principle of 'pay as you trade' and thus fairer than a direct tax and faced less resistance. It soon became a main revenue source in all provinces.

Last but not the least, militocrats set a precedent in liaising directly with foreign powers for weapons, loans, and technology for their war effort, a pattern which became widespread in twentieth-century China. Table 2.8 contains information for the three periods of pre-1916, 1917–40, and 1941–9. In the beginning, three foreign powers

Table 2.8. Political Factions and Foreign Sponsors, 1912–1949

Date/Group	Chinese leader	Foreign sponsors
(1) Pre-1916		
New Standard Army	Yuan Shikai	Japan
Southern Republicans	Sun Yat-sen	Japan, Britain, USA
(2) 1917–40		
Fengtian Sect	Zhang Zuolin	Japan
Zhili Sect	Feng Guozhang	Britain, USA
Anhui Sect	Duan Qirui	Japan
Hebei Sect	Feng Yuxiang	USSR
Guangdong Sect	Chen Jiongming	Britain
Guangxi Sect	Lu Rongting	Britain, USA
Guangdong Republicans	Sun Yat-sen	USSR
Nanjing Republicans	Chiang Kai-shek	Britain, USA, Germany
Wuhan Republicans	Wang Jingwei	Japan
Communists	Mao Zedong	USSR
(3) 1941–9		
Republicans	Chiang Kai-shek	Britain, USA
Communists	Mao Zedong	USSR

Sources: Liu Zhichao and Hu Yuhai, *Minguo Junfa Shilue* (*A History of Warlords during the Republic Period*) (Shenyang: Liaoning University Press, 1998), ch. 4; Larry I. Bland (ed.), *George C. Marshall's Mediation Mission to China* (Lexington: George C. Marshall Foundation, 1998); Li Jie, *Wenwu Beiyang* (*Achievements of the 'Northern Modern' Elite*) (Nanning: Guangxi Normal University Press, 2004), chs 1–5.

were directly involved in supporting two groups of militocrats. The picture became complicated in 1917–40 when ten groups of militocrats were linked to five foreign powers. Finally, two groups of militocrats were supported by three foreign powers after 1941. In the end, Japan was replaced by the USSR. Accordingly, Chinese warlords changed their patrons, good examples being Yan Xishan (1883–1960), Sheng Shicai (1892–1970), and Zhang Xueliang (1901–2001). China's alleged xenophobia was not applicable to high-level provincial politics.

In a nutshell, the fundamental weakness of Qing state capacity was exposed by the exogenous shock of the Little Ice Age in 1840–80. China-wide social unrest in the 1850s to 1860s threatened the very existence of Qing rule. Fighting the rebels militarised provinces which became independent with their own standing armies and localised taxes during the 1850s to 1870s. Collaboration between militocrats and foreign powers became necessary which led to the 'Westernisation Movement' (*yangwu yundong*) from 1860 to 1895.[64] A range of makeshift changes to rebuild the failed political system led to a republic in 1913 on China's soil. This was the whole package.

These militarised and financially independent mini-states that collaborated with foreign powers made Mao Zedong tick (1893–1976). In his own words,

> Amongst all the recent figures in history, I only admire Zeng Wenzheng [Zeng Guofan] in that he did such a perfect job to eliminate Hong Xiuquan and Yang Xiuqing [of the Taipings].[65]

Mao also openly admitted that what he learned from Zeng was 'to build a separatist regime inside China by military force' (*wuzhuang geju*);[66] and to 'encircle cities from the countryside' (*nongcun baowei chengshi*) in the war against the Taipings.

The adoption of such ideas was a conscious choice by Mao. It was neither imported Marxism, nor Leninism nor Stalinism, but indigenous 'Zengism'. Mao religiously copied Zeng Guofan's deeds.

3. Mao's Career Choice and Strategy

In essence, Zengism can be defined as 'agro-military authoritarian rule'. It left a permanent imprint on Mao's outlook. Mao's fixation with rural-based military authoritarian rule stayed with him all his life. None of these strategies can be found in the Marxist-Leninist-Stalinist doctrines. They were readily available within Mao's reach in his home province of Hunan. Zeng was indeed a fellow Hunan man whose family home was just 70 kilometres away from Mao's.

So, the principle of 'political power from the barrel of a gun' should be further elaborated as 'in the countryside'. Mao went further in 1938 in his essay 'Issues of War and Strategy' in stating: 'We can use our gun to build our party. . . . The barrel of a gun leads to everything that we ever need.'[67] Fast forward to 1966 and Mao told his party frankly that state power was a means for his personal ends:

> The essential issue of our revolution is state power. . . . Once we have the power of the state, we have everything. If we lose it, we lose everything.[68]

In 1975, a year before he died, Mao put it bluntly:

> How can we avoid struggle with 800 million people around?[69]

What a flawed motto. Mao saw 800 million potential Social Darwinian contenders for his power.

So, a democracy was out of the question for Mao. In this context, Mao seldom got himself involved in urban rebellions. He was never attracted to democracy, including the *Commune de Paris* (1870–71), something that Mao failed to comprehend all his life.

With hindsight, in the 1920s Mao could easily have become a militocrat relatively sheltered from external influence. What he needed were three '*M*s' – money, modern arms, and men – all available domestically, as Zeng Guofan had demonstrated. Bear in mind that the external influences of Marxism-Leninism and the Soviet Union are absent in Mao's career choices thus far.

This trajectory was especially attractive to Mao given that he did not receive a good enough education to make a decent living. So, Mao joined a warlord's army as a foot soldier as his first career choice when he was 18. At the age of 26, he finally landed a job – obscure but nevertheless paid – in a university library looking after a newspaper collection. This made him feel utterly unworthy.[70]

So, Mao clearly had a career problem before he became involved in the Communist Movement at the age of 27.[71] Mao's career trajectory was not unusual among China's makers and shakers at the time: Yuan Shikai (who rebelled against the last Qing emperor) received only traditional primary education (*sishu*) in Confucianism; and so did his follower Duan Qirui (1865–1936). Zhang Zuolin (1875–1928) had no school education at all. Such was the ilk to which Mao originally belonged.

About a generation later, a new crop of leaders emerged with formal education in military academies in both China and neighbouring Japan, skipping Confucian schooling entirely. This applied to Feng Yuxiang (1882–1948), Tang Jiyao (1883–1927), Yan Xishan (1883–1960), Sun Chuanfang (1885–1935), and Mao's arch-rival Jiang Jieshi (or Chiang Kai-shek, 1887–1975). Mao (1893–1976) now had a second choice to make, whether to opt for the Feng-Tang-Yan-Sun-Chiang model of enrolling in a modern military academy, preferably outside China.

Meanwhile, against the odds, China's militocrats began to get involved in a democratic experiment. Under the banner of republicanism, Asia's first democracy was born in China. From 1912 to 1928, China had, in all, eight presidents and twenty-eight premiers. Four of those presidents were in power for only a year. The longest term for a premier was seventeen months, while the shortest was just two days.[72] Most of them had a military background. So, the possibilities were written on the wall for Mao and his ilk.

In this context, contrary to the widely circulated belief, the one-off

'May Fourth Movement' in 1919 had little impact on China's future growth and development. The new republican regime in China was unable to impose its rule effectively across the whole of China. So, the experiment in democracy failed. Not until 1992 was a democracy reignited in Taiwan. Nevertheless, chaos and social experiments sent a signal to opportunists who had few other skills: to become a stratocrat was where their future lay. This was exactly what Mao decided to become.

Around this time, Russian Bolshevism landed in China (in 1921). Mao was 28. The new ideology sent an antidemocratic shockwave through the country by providing a new model for a military dictatorship. The Russian model fitted perfectly with the goal of a stratocrat. The key stratocrat hopefuls emerged as Chiang and Mao, the leaders of China's republican and communist movements. Both men were openly pro-Soviet Union at the time when their stratocratic careers took off in South China. That could not have been purely accidental.[73]

Meanwhile, China's social conditions were far from conducive to an industrial proletarian revolution, more resembling Tsarist Russia than Western Europe. According to the earliest account of communist activists, the total number of industrial waged workers in the 1920s was one million, or 0.2 per cent of China's total population of 440 million when the communist movement first started in China. If one adds another 10 million traditional urban handicraftsmen and service workers, total waged labourers were about 2.5 per cent of China's population.[74] The share of modern industry in China's GDP was well under four per cent.[75] In inland provinces like Hunan, according to Mao's own figures, modern waged workers were a trivial 0.1 per cent of the provincial population.[76]

But there was a trade-off. The absence of industrial waged workers and hence labour unions was compensated for by external aid from Moscow which made China's communist movement dependent on Russia. So, after 1921, Mao and his fellow Chinese communists depended on hand-outs from the Soviet Communist International (Comintern) to earn a living.[77] This arrangement bypassed Karl Marx. It was a marriage of convenience.

Mao himself did not detect anything inappropriate in receiving manna from the Russians. After all, he never read Marx's main works and never even mentioned Marx after 1937.[78] So, his ignorance became an advantage. After all, Mao's role model was Zeng Guofan, the Godfather of all militocrats in China,[79] and Mao's self-committed path to success was to 'encircle cities from the countryside', a 'rural path' Mao committed to for the rest of his life.

Not surprisingly, the Soviet Union and the International Communist Movement deeply doubted the authenticity of Mao's 'revolution'. The Maoist Movement was regarded as a 'petty-bourgeois peasant movement' and his party as a 'peasant organisation'.[80] Most tellingly, Zhou Enlai (1898–1976), Mao's lieutenant, confessed his plight before the Comintern officials in Moscow:

> In 1940, when I visited the Comintern, the leaders there were worried that we were not up to their standards. I told them that we had been toughened up by our long struggle in rural regions and had Comrade Mao Zedong's guidance, and that we were thus able to become proletarianised. Those Comintern comrades burst into an uproar in total disapproval.[81]

But Mao did not budge. His choice was fixed. For him, communism was merely a synonym for his stratocratic pursuit. This explains why he was particularly attracted to Trotsky's 'permanent revolution', regardless of the social classes involved. Trotskyism was introduced to China in 1927 by the Comintern agent Vissarion Vissarionovich Lominadze (commonly known as 'Luomi Nazi', 1897–1935) who supervised the Chinese Communist Party at the time and knew Mao personally.[82] Mao was indoctrinated and converted himself to Trotskyism, only re-phrasing it as an 'uninterrupted revolution' (*buduan geming*) or a 'continuous revolution' (*jixu geming*). As few communist gurus agreed with Trotskyism, Mao was undoubtedly unorthodox.

Facing doubts and criticism, Mao needed to take a cultish approach to establish his place in China's proletariat-absent society. In his own words later in 1958:

> What an uninterrupted revolution means is that our revolution is like a war. After we win a battle, we ought to set up a new target immediately. . . . They [officials and people] are thus pressurised by the new task and hence become fully occupied politically again.[83]

During the Cultural Revolution, Mao infamously proclaimed that '(If I want the result,) class struggle works perfectly [for me] every single time!' (*jieji douzheng yizhua jiuling*).[84]

4. Mao's Moral Economy and His Political Economy after 1930

In 1949, with the help of the Soviet Union, Mao triumphed over all the other militocrats. According to his own elucidation, his philosophy was to fight his personal opponents *à la* Trotsky.[85] Mao thus created a new Trotskyist norm to replace China's timeless social norms of benevolence, reciprocity, tolerance, and filial piety. Mao needed political opponents to make his philosophy work. His main target was the *crème de la crème* of society and his weapon was a never-ending purge on a scale larger than Stalin's. Mao in fact cared less about external threats after he obtained state-of-the-art weaponry, including the nuclear bomb,[86] a model which has been copied by dictators worldwide today.

According to the official account, Mao was responsible for eleven major purges with 114 million victims in total, as demonstrated in table 2.9.[87] Purges were simply the means to establish a dictatorship. So, while Mao might have begun his career as some sort of rebel, he ended it as a fully fledged despot.

Towards the end of his life, Mao became increasingly paranoid and irrational. This was exemplified by his Cultural Revolution from 1966 to 1976. In 1966, Mao asserted that a large number of 'bourgeoisie agents' had infiltrated all levels of his party, his government, and his army to impose 'bourgeoisie dictatorship' on behalf of an alleged 35 million landlords and capitalists.[88] He decided that the alleged 'capitalist elements' inside his party were 'antagonistically confronting the interests of workers, peasants and soldiers'.[89] Despite a lack of evidence, Mao's assertion led to the decade-long Cultural Revolution.

Mao's purges were underpinned by a propaganda of 'low-class emancipation' (*fanshen*, literally 'turning misfortunes') and a policy of 'worker-peasant alliance under the leadership of the party' (*dang lingdao xiade gongnong lianmeng*).[90] Both were articulated in his 1949 essay on a 'democratic dictatorship'.[91]

After 1949, Mao conveniently added a third 'good class' of 'soldiers' with overwhelmingly rural background (*bing*). All the post-1949 'Trotskyist purges' were backed by Mao's military. During the Cultural Revolution, Mao imposed China-wide martial law (*jun guan*) and planted his army representatives (*jun daibiao*) in all levels of government until 1976. Mao made sure that the barrel of his gun was visible all the time.

In this context, Mao did not worry much about people like himself –

Table 2.9. Mao's Purges, 1931–1976

Time	Name	Target	Victims
1930–1	'AB League' Purge	Own officers	±100,000
1941–5	Yan-an Rectification	Party intellectuals	±40,000
1950–3	Suppression of Anti-revolutionaries	Republican sympathisers	±12 million
1951–2	Three-Anti and Five-Anti Movement	Political dissidents and black-market operations	±1.2 million
1954	Gao-Rao Clique Purge	Party rivals	–
1955	Hu Feng Clique Purge	Party intellectuals	2,100
1957	1957-Rectification	Party rivals	–
1957	Anti-Rightist Movement	Intellectuals	±500,000
1959	Lushan Purge	Army rivals	–
1964–5	Four Cleansings	Grassroots disloyalists	–
1966–76	Cultural Revolution	Technocrats and intellectuals	±100 million
Total	11		±114 million

Sources: (1) 'AB League' Purge, see Li Rui, *Li Rui Tan Mao Zedong* (*Li Rui's Memoir on Mao Zedong*) (Hong Kong: Time International Publishing Co., 2005), p. 2; Peter Vladimirov, *The Vladimirov Diaries, Yenan, China: 1942–1945* (New York: Doubleday, 1975), pp. 167–78; Li Weiming, 'Huifu Lishi Benlai Mianmude Jiannan Licheng' (Difficulties in Restoring Truth in History), *Yanhuang Chunqiu* (*History of Chinese*), 11 (2008): 57. (2) Yan-an Rectification, see Li, *Li Rui's Memoir*, p. 39; Vladimirov, *Diaries*, pp. 513, 514. (3) 1950–3 Anti-revolutionaries, see Bai Xi, *Kaiguo Da Zhenfan* (*Sweeping Suppression of Anti-revolutionaries in the Early Days of the People's Republic*) (Beijing: Chinese Communist Party History Press, 2006). (4) Three-and-Five Antis, see Wu Jue and Ye Junjian, *Sanfan Wufan Yundong Jishi* (*Documentary of the Three-Anti and Five-Anti Campaign*) (Beijing: East Press, 2014); (5) Gao-Rao Clique, see Li Yunhui, *Chong Kao Gao Gang Rao Shushi Fandang Shijian* (*Re-Examining the Gao-Rao Clique*) (Hong Kong: Chinese University of Hong Kong Press, 2017). (6) Hu Feng Rao Clique, see Li Hui, *Hu Feng Jituan Yuan-a Shimo* (*A History of the Fabrication of the 'Hu Feng Clique'*) (Wuhan: Hubei People's Press, 2003); Sheng Guofan, *Wo Suo Qinlide Hu Feng An, Faguan Wang Wenzheng Koushu* (*My Personal Experience of the Hu Feng Clique, Memoir of Judge Wang Wenzheng*) (Beijing: Chinese Communist Party History Press, 2007). (7) 1957 Rectification, see Deng Xiaoping, *Report on the Rectification Campaign* (Beijing: People's Press, 1957). (8) 1957 Anti-Rightist, see Cong Jin, *Quzhe Fazhande Suiyue* (*Period of Tortuous Development*) (Zhengzhou: Henan People's Press, 1989), p. 61; see also Li, *Li Rui's Memoir*, p. 132. (9) Lushan Purge, see Li Rui, *Lushan Huiyi Shilu* (*Records of the Lu Shan Conference*) (Beijing: Spring-Autumn Press, 1989). (10) Four Cleansings, see Lin Xiaobo and Guo Hongde, *Wegede Yuyan: Siqing Yundong Shimo* (*Rehearsal of the Cultural Revolution: A History of the Four Clearances Campaign*) (Beijing: People's Press, 2013). (11) Cultural Revolution, see Song Yongyi, *Mao Zedong He Wenhua Dageming* (*Mao Zedong and His Cultural Revolution*) (Taipei: Jinglian Press, 2021).

less educated with no obvious skills or qualifications. Rather, he needed support from them. What Mao did to his supporters was to grant blue-collar workers, poor peasants (*pinnong*, *xiazhongnong*), and army soldiers the privilege of political immunity from his Trotskyist purges on the one hand, and the reward of farmland or full employment on the other. After 1949, food rationing for all at subsistence level was also added. This alliance did most of the dirty work of making and maintaining Mao's dictatorship while Mao was alive.

However, among industrial workers, peasants, and soldiers, Mao saw peasants as his ultimate base to rule China. Any decline in peasant numbers was viewed as a reduction in his power base. Indeed, Mao deliberately kept China's urbanisation rate low for just such a reason.[92] This approach undoubtedly came from the late Qing militocrats in general and from Zeng Guofan in particular. China's urbanisation rate suffered.[93]

However, after the abrupt ending of Mao's 'class struggle' under Deng Xiaoping's leadership, Mao's moral economy of Trotskyism was in tatters. Mao's fight against the modern tide of urbanisation failed, too.

Regarding Mao's political economy, it was modelled after the Soviet Union with three ingredients: (1) a one-party state, (2) overwhelming state ownership of capital, technology, and land, and (3) state control of economic outcomes via state-run allocation of factors of production and consumption at all levels. All these ingredients were compatible with a stratocracy.

The story began in the 1920s when external financial and military aid from the Soviets played a vital role in keeping both nationalist and communist movements alive in South China. The Soviets' double dipping between nationalists and communists aimed to create a pro-Russian China to counter other powers, especially Japan. In this context, Mao and his fellow Chinese communists acted on behalf of Moscow. Table 2.10 contains details of the control possessed by the Comintern over Mao's party, demonstrating how it dictated policy from the very beginning. It is no exaggeration to state that Mao's party had no independence from Moscow before the death of Stalin in 1953.

From the Soviets, Mao and his fellow Chinese communists secured two *M*s: money and modern weapons. That was half the battle won for a budding stratocrat. The task that remained was to recruit men to join him. Mao himself recognised this by declaring that 'under the leadership of the Communist Party, we can create any miracle as long as we have men'.[94] The urban sector where the Bolsheviks were based was out of his comfort zone, so Mao kept himself away from it.

Table 2.10. Soviet Control over Mao's Party, 1920–1937

Date	Comintern agent	Comintern-imposed policy
1920–1	Voitinsky and Sneevliet	Formation of a communist party
1921–3	Sneevliet	Urban uprisings
1922–3	Sneevliet	First amalgamation with the Republican Party
1925	Borodin*	'Red bases' in China's north-western frontier near USSR
1926	Borodin and Roy†	Appeasement with warlords
1927	Lominadze and Neumann§	Armed mass uprisings in cities
1928	Bukharin, Mif and Stalin	Building 'communism in one province' and 'Bolshevisation' of the party
1931	Mif	Replacing Qu Qiubai with Wang Ming as the party chief
1937	Stalin	Second amalgamation with the Republican Party¶

Note: * Borodin: he double dipped as the top adviser to the Citizens' Party (*guomin dang*, often translated as the 'Nationalist Party') at the same time. † Roy: an Indian-born Comintern agent, real name Manabendra Nath Roy (known as 'Luo Yi' or 'Lu Yi', 1887–1954). § Vissarion Vissarionovich Lominadze (also known as 'Luomi Nazi', 1897–1935). Neumann: German-born Heinz Neumann (also known as 'Niu Man', his dates remain unknown). This was not followed through due to the 1927 Communist-Republican Split. Eventually the communists survived precisely because of their red base located on the Shaanxi-Gansu-Ningxia Border (*Shan Gan Ning Bianqu*) in Northwest China from 1935 to 1945. ¶ This was one month after the Xi-an Incident when Chiang was taken hostage by the two mutinous generals Zhang Xueliang (1901–2001) and Yang Hucheng (1893–1949) to force Chiang to accept an anti-Japanese united front.
Sources: Li Ying (ed.), *Cong Yida Dao Shiliu Da* (*Memoirs of Participants of the First to Sixteenth Congress of the Chinese Communist Party*) (Beijing: Central Documents Press, 2003), vol. 1, pp. 58, 73–4, 124–9, 132–3, 165, 257–8, 268, 274–5, 308, 317, 325, 362, 376–7, 383, 394; Otto Braun, *A Comintern Agent in China, 1932–39* (London: C. Hurst, 1982); Jung Chang and Jon Halliday, *Mao: The Unknown Story* (London: Vintage Books, 2005), p. 197; Li, *Li Rui's Memoir*, p. 101; Li Weimin, 'Gongchan Guoji Yu Zhongguo Kangri Minzu Tongyi Zhanxian' (Comintern and the Making of China's National United Front against Japanese Invasion), *Yanhuang Chunqiu* (*History of Chinese*), 3 (2006): 22–6.

As far as Mao was concerned, the missing *M* (men) could come from the peasantry with whom he identified throughout his adult life. In 1927, Mao led the 'Autumn Harvest Uprising' (*qiushou qiyi*) across three provinces (Hubei, Hunan, and Jiangxi) and created an agro-military 'red base' around Mount Jinggang in Jiangxi. It was the first territorial communist state inside China, encompassing 42,000 square kilometres and five million people (in 1934).[95] This was equivalent to 0.4 per cent of China's total land and 1.1 per cent of China's total population. After that, the rural sect of communists survived a near-death experience in the Long March and started all over again in the rural Shaanxi Plateau in North China in 1936. The *raison d'être* of such a repetitive pursuit had no Eurocentric inspiration. Rather, it all came from Zengism.

In comparison, the state of Mao's rival Chiang Kai-shek was urban and assisted by the West after 1930. Chiang controlled three-quarters of China's territory, three-quarters of China's towns and cities (1,545 in all), and two-thirds of China's population (*c.*339 million).[96] Chiang's forces were also able to deliver punches, as demonstrated by the Siping Offensive in South Manchuria in 1946.[97] The manoeuvre pushed Mao's troops all the way out to Harbin in the northern corner of Manchuria, facing certain annihilation.

But both Stalin and the American mediator George C. Marshall interfered. Chiang's troops spared Harbin. A big mistake. Barely two years later, the 'Harbin communists' swept not only across Manchuria but also all the way to China's southernmost tip of Hainan Island.[98] In the process, Chiang lost 1.5 million troops.[99]

Meanwhile, Western powers – the United States, Britain, and France – turned down Chiang's call for help to stop the escalation of Mao's military advancement *à la* the North-South Korea Model. Mao, on the other hand, had the full support of Stalin to take over the rest of the mainland. A dramatic shift in the military balance of power occurred between 1945 and 1948. As shown in table 2.11, in 1945 when the Second World War ended in East Asia with Japan's unconditional surrender, Chiang possessed the military superiority by a factor of 10–12. Three years later, in 1948, Chiang and Mao were even.

By the time Chiang retreated to Taiwan in December 1949, his party membership had shrunk 99.3 per cent; and his territory, 99.6 per cent

Table 2.11. Shift in Military Balance of Power, 1945–1948

Type	1945	1945	R-C ratio	1948	1948	R-C Ratio
	Republicans	**Communists**		**Republicans**	**Communists**	
Troops	3,700,000	320,000	12:1	2,180,000	2,600,000	0.8:1
Rifles	1,600,000	160,000	10:1	980,000	970,000	1:1
Cannons	6,000	600	10:1	2,100	2,280	0.9:1

Note: R-C: Republicans vs Communists.
Source: Based on Fuk-Fai Liu, *A Military History of Modern China, 1924–1949.* (Princeton: Princeton University Press, 1956), p. 254.

from the 1946 level.[100] Now, it was the communists – twice losers in 1927 and 1934 in wars against the republicans (nationalists) – that emerged triumphant. Mao's victory in 1949 was not as inevitable as one may think. The communist victory in 1948–49, however, reinforced Mao's path dependence on Stalin for two of the '*Ms*' – money and modern arms. Mao now fully orbited Stalin (and the Soviet Union) and enacted a 'Sovietisation Movement' in Mainland China to return Stalin's favour. Mao's gratitude also led to his decision to defend Soviet military interests in the Korean War (1950–53).[101]

From the viewpoint of Stalin (and the Soviet Union), the dream of creating a pro-Soviet China came to fruition. Mao's unorthodox agro-military communism was finally accepted by the international communist movement after the importation of '156 Projects' from the Soviet Union from 1950 to 1959 plus the installation of a central planning mechanism to rebuild China's administration and economy,[102] mainly for military purposes. An insightful report was written by the CIA's 'China Watch' in 1966:

> The core of Communist China's program for rapid industrialization was the Soviet commitment to assist China in the building of 291 industrial plants by 1967. The Soviet equipment for these plants was valued at $3.3 billion. . . . With Soviet and Eastern European support, Communist China expanded production of heavy industry from 1952 to 1959 at an annual average rate of about 25 per cent; without this aid the rate would have been far lower. This flow of equipment and technical assistance had a vital effect on the quality of China's industrialization, enabling China to produce such prestige items as jet aircraft, submarines, large electric generating equipment, metal-cutting machine tools, tractors, trucks, and electronic equipment, . . . (and) the supply of experimental reactors and other nuclear related technology, designed to eventually provide a base which could support native Chinese production of Soviet-designed weapons.
>
> . . .
>
> At the height of Sino Soviet Commercial relations in 1959, Communist China rivalled East Germany as the Soviet Union's principal trading partner. China supplied one-fifth of the Soviet Union's total imports, two-thirds of her food imports and three-quarters of her textile imports. Soviet willingness to accept Chinese agricultural raw materials and large amounts of industrial consumer goods, especially textiles, permitted China to pay for the large-scale imports of machinery and equipment needed for industrialization.[103]

Comparable reports were written much later in China with similar conclusions.[104]

Sovietisation, however, potentially jeopardised Mao's jealously guarded rural power base in the long run. In the short run, Mao swallowed the bitter pill for the sake of the patron-client relationship with the Soviet Union.

From a political economy perspective, China was on track to become a 'second Soviet Union'. Firstly, to facilitate China's import-oriented industrialisation, up to 20,000 Soviet advisors were sent to China.[105]

Secondly, the 'Sovietisation Movement' created the largest state in Mainland China hitherto with 932,000 cadres (officials-officers).[106] In 1950 China's population-to-official ratio rose to a record level of 592 to 1,[107] an increase from the late Qing level by a factor of 25. The number of cadres grew to 12 million during the 1960s out of a total population of 723 million (1965), excluding army officers.[108] Now the population-to-official ratio settled at 60 to 1.[109] Such a state was fully capable of penetrating all levels of society for the first time in China's history. Such a new and powerful state made Mao's 'uninterrupted revolution' easy.

Thirdly, there was a sweeping nationalisation (collectivisation) of capital and natural resources including farmland. All such changes were completed by 1957 thanks to Mao's all-mighty one-party state. China's sophisticated system of private ownership was outlawed and uprooted. A rural utopia was born. Data in table 2.12 show that land-based properties were 100 per cent 'de-privatised'. Manufactures and services were 99.6 and 92.0 per cent 'de-privatised', respectively. So, by 1957 China's timeless private economy had been arbitrarily ended.

Fourthly, China's functional market was effectively banned (unlike the symbolic maritime bans during the Ming) and replaced with centralised economic planning in the form of 'Five-Year Plans' to square resource allocation between inputs and outputs.

With all these changes in China's political economy, new growth should have followed *à la* the Soviet Union where the state powered

Table 2.12. Ownership Changes in Mainland China, 1957

Sector	State ownership
Farmland	100.0%
Transport	100.0%
Industry	99.6%
Services	92.0%

Source: Luo Pinghan, 'Jianlun 1957 Nian Nongcun Liangtiao Daolude Dabianlun' (The 1957 Debate on the Two Developmental Paths in Rural China), *Shixue Yuekan* (*History Review Monthly*), 11 (2002): 42.

industrialisation through the combination of city-bound migration and modern schooling. From 1926 to 1959, the Soviet urbanisation rate rose from 13.3 per cent to 38.2 per cent with an average annual growth rate of 2.8 per cent.[110] By 1960, the rate passed the 50 per cent threshold,[111] giving Russia a modern economic structure. Moreover, city-bound migration claimed about half of the increase in urban population,[112] meaning that the rural sector was marginalised. Furthermore, the Soviet case shows a positive and close correlation between urbanisation and industrialisation.[113] Finally, modern schooling acted as a necessary condition for city-bound migration for urbanisation. In 1926, the Soviet national literacy rate was 57 per cent. It increased to 75 per cent in 1937 and to 99 per cent in 1959 with an annual growth rate of 1.47 per cent.[114]

With such a combination of changes, the Soviet economy achieved an average annual GDP growth rate of between 3.3 and 3.9 per cent from 1928 to 1985.[115] The Soviet population increased 195 per cent with an average annual growth rate of 1.07 per cent.[116] Thus, the per capita GDP growth rate was around 2.2–2.8 per cent annually. This establishes a crude version of the Soviet input–output standard.

But the Soviet trio did not go down well with Mao. Good education for technocrats and urbanisation through city-bound migration presented a threat to Mao's psyche. In particular, the Soviet perspective made Mao increasingly urban-phobic and education-phobic, seen from his policy propensity after 1949. Inevitably, Mao departed from the Soviet model, switching back to his rural stratocratic mode where his comfort zone lay. The communist overlord Stalin's timely death in 1953 did Mao a favour.

5. Impact of Maoism on Performance of the Economy

By 1957, Mao had decided to abandon the Soviet urbanisation-*cum*-industrialisation model and build agro-communism in China instead. Mao's new system had several distinctive features. First of all, farming became China's national priority through the slogan 'grain production as the national primacy' (*yi liang wei gang*).[117] As a result, not only was most of the labour force locked into farming, but over 80 per cent of farmland was devoted to grain.[118] With this policy, the ceiling for industrial growth was set.

Secondly, ruralisation was encouraged at the expense of urbanisation. Mao saw his collective communes as the means to promote the 'all-round development of farming, forestry, animal husbandry, by-production and fisheries' (*nong lin mu fu yu*).[119] He even planned to break up large cities into small towns of 20,000 to 30,000 people each and ultimately to replace these towns with communes.[120] The best example was the 'Great Leap Forward' (1958–60), a mass campaign that drafted 90 million able-bodied rural labourers from the newly established 26,500 centrally controlled 'people's communes'. Given that in 1958, when the Leap began, China had a total rural workforce of 155 million, the draft rate for the Leap was 58 per cent.[121] But household-wise, the draft rate was as high as 81 per cent.[122] The aim of the Leap was to push China's iron and steel output from 5.35 million tonnes in 1957 to 10.7 million tonnes in 1959, and then to 18 million tonnes in 1960, all achieved with bare hands.[123] To meet Mao's target, traditional furnaces were built to produce what were called 'traditional iron' and 'traditional steel' (*tutie, tugang*).[124] In the process, one million backyard furnaces were hastily built, some of which were converted from brick kilns and lime kilns.[125] The Qing elite's 'Westernisation Movement' was totally forgotten.

Consequently, according to China's official statistics, in 1959 China's labour input in farming decreased by 35 per cent;[126] and 10 per cent of farmland (173.9 million *mu*) lay idle.[127] Earlier in 1958, crops were left in the fields to rot due to the shortage of labour.[128] The resulting food shortages caused 30–40 million deaths (with one victim per 2.4–3.2 rural families) in what was the largest peace-time and good-weather famine in world history.[129] China's double-digit death rate continued until 1966.[130] Mao's programme of rural industrialisation went disastrously wrong.

Thirdly, external conditions for China changed dramatically in the wake of the Korean War. Mainland China was embargoed by the West. Mao genuinely welcomed it, as the embargo gave him the rare opportunity to prove how great he could be in the way of 'self-reliance' (*zili gengsheng*). In 1956, Mao announced the 'General Growth Guidelines' (*zongluxian*) for his party and state which involved 'better, faster, and more growth with fewer inputs' (*duo kuai hao sheng*) in an official braggadocio which led to the disastrous Great Leap Forward in 1958.[131]

Fourthly, and invisibly, China's urban workforce remained stagnant despite its weak starting point in 1930.[132] The headcount data in table 2.13 show that after the Great Leap Froward not only was there an employment ceiling for industrial growth (less that 7 per cent of the total population) but also that the growth of China's industrial workforce (1.7 per cent a year) consistently fell behind

Table 2.13. Industrial Workforce versus Total Population (Million People), 1930–1974

Year	Industrial workforce (A)	Total population (B)	A/B %
1930	11.0	440.0	2.5
1959	45.5	672.1	6.8
1974	59.1	908.6	6.5
1959–74 annual %	1.7	2.0	–0.3

Sources: Data for 1930, see John K. Fairbank (ed.), *The Cambridge History of China, Republican China 1912–1949, Part I* (Cambridge: Cambridge University Press, 1983), vol. 12, p. 36; Li, *Memoirs of Participants*, vol. 1, pp. 26–7. Data for the post-1949 industrial workforce is based on National Bureau of Statistics, *Zhongguo Laodong Tongji Nianjian, 1998* (*China's Labour Statistical Year Book, 1998*) (Beijing: China's Statistics Press, 1998), p. 81. Data for China's population figures are based on National Bureau of Statistics, *Statistical Year Book, 1986*, p. 91.

China's population growth (2 per cent a year). Each year extra manpower joined the rural sector (0.3% per year). Mao's economic model thus resembled François Quesnay's *Tableau Économique* (1758) for a closed pre-industrial economy.[133] In doing so, Mao's trajectory towards making China a second Soviet Union failed to materialise on the economic front.

Figure 2.3 captures the dynamics of China's labour employment structure, which is more reliable than the GDP data, simply because it is harder to falsify headcounts. Clearly, until 1976, the Maoist economy was rural. A turning point finally occurred in 1995 at which point the share of labour inputs in the primary sector (mainly farming) dropped below half of the workforce for the first time in China's history. Any claim that China was industrialised before 1995 is dubious.[134]

Meanwhile, the Mao-Quesnay approach led to a tight resource constraint for the growth of the industrial sector. This is evident from the data in table 2.14. Workers' nominal wages in the privileged state sector were frozen for two decades. In that time, real wages halved. The annual decline in real wages was 2.1 per cent from 1957 to 1965. It sped up to 4.3 per cent during the Cultural Revolution. A halving of China's industrial labour productivity was likely to have been the root cause of this real wage collapse.

China's urbanisation process also stagnated. Data in table 2.15 reveal the reasons. To begin with, China's total workforce grew faster than the general population by 0.6 per cent per year. But the extra working population (2.7 per cent per year) did not go to cities to facilitate industrialisation. Each year 1.3 per cent extra working people joined the farming sector. The reason was that China's food

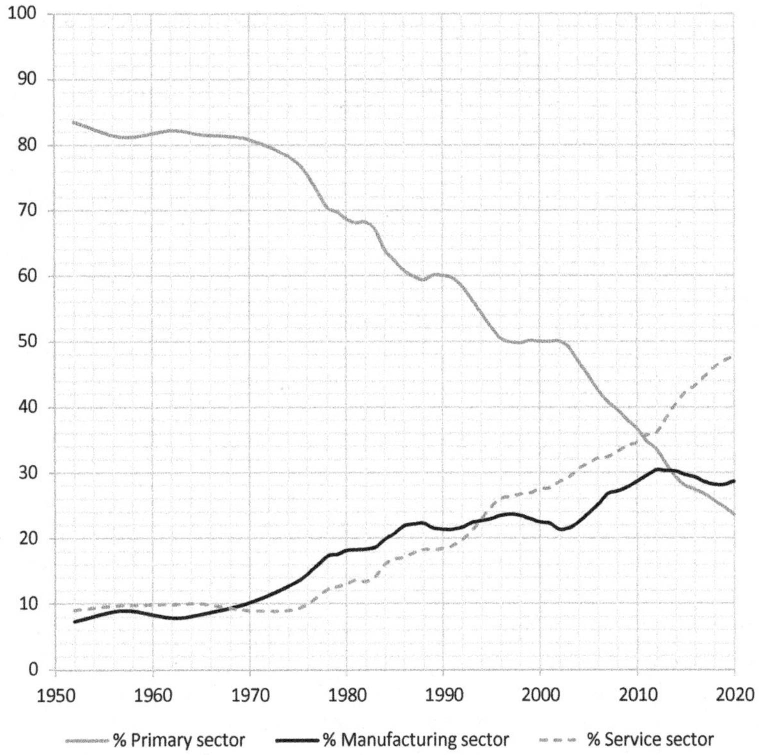

Figure 2.3. Trends in Labour Inputs, % All Workers, 1950–2020

Note: Data are based on workers' headcounts.

Sources are available in the separate section of 'Figure Sources'.

Table 2.14. Nominal versus Real Wages in the State Sector, 1957–1978

Year	Nominal wage/year	Index	Real wage (1957 prices)*	Index	Annual change
1957	637	100	637	100	—
1965	652	102	539	85	-2.1%
1978	644	101	310	49	-4.3%

Note: * Conversion is based on the average inflation rate of 2.01% per year for the period from 1950 to 1978, based on Li Jingwen, 'Zhongguo Jingji Tizhi Zhuanxing Guochengzhongde Hongguan Tiaokong' (Macro Control over the Process of Switching China's Economic System), *Xinhua Wenzhai* (*Xinhua Compilation*), 4 (1997): 49–51.
Source: Based on V.D. Lippit, *The Economic Development of China* (Armonk, NY: M.E. Sharpe, 1987), p. 150.

Table 2.15. Agriculture-dependent Growth Patterns, 1952–1975

Category	1952	1975	% Annual change
1. People			
Total population	574.8*	924.2*	2.1
Total workforce	207.3*	381.7*	2.7
Urbanisation rate	12.5%	17.3%	1.4
2. Food			
Grain outputs	164†	285†	2.2
Grain/head (national)	260§	304§	0.6
	(1,795 kcl/day)	(2,099 kcl/day)[135]	

Note: * In million persons. † Unhusked grain in million tonnes. § In kg. Figures in brackets, kilocalories/head/day after husking/milling process which reduces the weight by about 30 per cent. Husked white dry rice contains 3,600 kilocalories per kilogram, used here as a proxy.

Sources: (1) Total population figures and urbanisation rates: Anon., 'China Population since 1952', *Demographia*, https://demographia.com/db-chinapop.htm. (2) Employment data: National Bureau of Statistics, *Labour Statistical Year Book, 2004*, p. 7. (3) Grain outputs: Wei Li and Dennis Tao Yang, 'The Great Leap Forward: Anatomy of a Central Planning Disaster', *Journal of Political Economy*, 113/4 (2005): 846; cf. Justin Y. Lin, 'Rural Reforms and Agricultural Growth in China', *American Economic Review*, 82/1 (1992): 35. (4) Grain per head: Li and Yang, 'Great Leap Forward', pp. 846, 855.

output (with an increase of 2.2 per cent per year) barely kept up with population growth (at a rate of 2.1 per cent per year). This resulted in the thin margin of 0.1 per cent net growth in food, or 0.6 per cent in per capita terms.

Finally, Mao's economy faced Malthusian limits, a view which is supported by data in table 2.16. Food shortages were chronic in North China during Mao's rule to the point where at times surpluses from the south were unable to compensate for northern food deficits (as in 1961–5, 1971–5). In the end, even South China ran out of food in 1976–8.

Figure 2.4 displays what China's economy would have looked like had it continued on its Maoist growth trajectory up to 2002. By this time, China's population would have tripled and its workforce nearly quadrupled. But the urbanisation rate would only have doubled. Per capita food consumption would have remained at the subsistence level. Thus, Mao's economy would have fallen well short of the Soviet 50 per cent urbanisation rate as a benchmark for industrialisation. Rather, China would have sunken deep into a 'ruralisation' trap. Mao's Sovietisation of China's economy would have failed.

Mao's 'ruralisation trap' explains why China's urban sector was unable to create more jobs and absorb city-bound migrants. Rather,

Table 2.16. China's Perpetual Food Deficits (Million Tonnes), 1956–1978

Period	North China	South China	Domestic total	Food imports†	Agricultural imports§
1956–60	-4.7*	—	—	1.8 (100)	297.0 (100)
1961–5	-20.1	—	-13.4	28.9 (1650)	229.9 (77)
1966–70	-8.0	—	—	—	616.0 (207)
1971–5	-11.6	—	-2.1	—	3565.0 (1200)
1976–8	-11.1	-0.2	-11.3		

Note: * Negative value means food imports. † Food imports in million tonnes from Australia, Canada, Argentina, and Western Europe. Numbers in brackets show indexed growth. § Imports (mainly food) in US$ million from Australia, Canada, Argentina, and Western Europe. Numbers in brackets show indexed growth. Clearly, the Soviet Union helped China little.

Sources: Internal food situation is based on Contemporary Agricultural History Study Group, Rural Economy Institute, Ministry of Agriculture (ed.), *Dangdai Zhongguo Nongye Biange Yu Fazhan Yanjiu* (*A Study of Agricultural Reforms and Development in Contemporary China*) (Beijing: China's Agriculture Press, 1998), p. 251. External food imports in volumes are based on Anon., 'International Trade of Communist China, 1950–65', CIA, 21 October, 1966, Approved for Release 2001/04/30: CIA-RDP79 T01049A003300110001-2, p. 54, https://www.cia.gov/readingroom/docs/CIA-RDP79 T01049A003300110001-2.pdf?utm_source=chatgpt.com; external food import values are based on S.H. Chou, 'China's Foreign Trade', *Current History*, 71/419 (1976): 70.

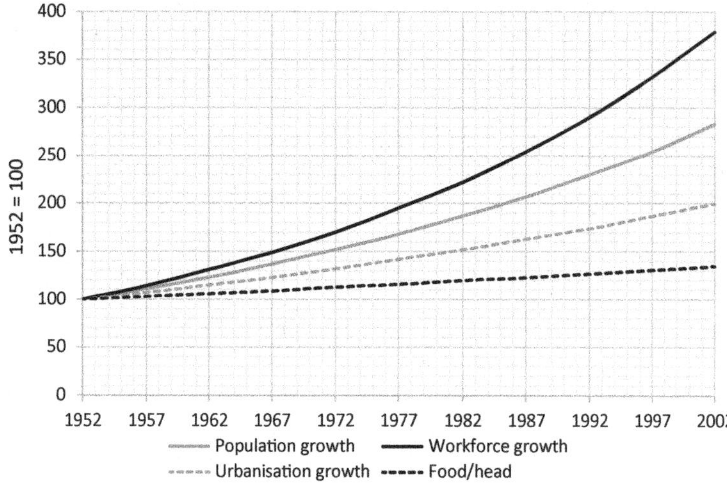

Figure 2.4. Hypothetical Growth Trajectory of the Maoist Economy until 2002

Note: Annal growth rates: (1) Workforce = 2.7%; (2) population = 2.1%; urban residents = 1.4%; food/head = 0.6%.

Sources are available in the separate section of 'Figure Sources'.

between 1967 and 1977, Mao's government sent a total of 16 million urban youngsters to the countryside in the name of 're-education' despite the fact that a cheaper alternative was to send these people to urban factories in their home cities so that they could learn from the industrial proletariat there.[136] So, fundamentally, Mao's economic planning did not take social mobility, urbanisation, and industrialisation into account which cost China economic efficiency and growth potential.

This inability to create urban employment continued after Mao died. In 1977, 15 million urban young people were jobless.[137] Two years later, this figure rose to 20 million, overburdening the urban labour market (40 million) by another third.[138] In 1980, the number of unemployed urban young reached 30 million. This translated into a 50 per cent youth unemployment rate in an urban labour market made up of 60 million people.[139]

More absurdly, the employed urban workforce was partly idle due to 'over-hiring'. As Mao's legacy, in the 1990s about 30 per cent of China's employed urban workforce was identified as *de facto* redundant.[140] So, it was common for several workers to share a workload meant for one person.[141] If so, China's 'affective industrial workforce' in 1980 was about 40 million, largely unchanged from the time when Mao's rule began. The resulting lack of technological inputs provided by the urban sector kept China's rural productivity stagnant.[142]

Finally, and worst of all, Mao's state pushed hard to re-locate heavy and military industries from coastal regions to the mountainous and rural interior (*sanxian*, literarily 'withdrawal to the third line of defence') during the 1960s and 1970s. The strategy disintegrated urban factory compounds and spread out production lines miles apart in the most difficult rural terrain.[143] There is no data on what happened to these factories. What we do know is that in 1971 less than a third of all new state investment projects were completed and less than eight per cent of production targets were met.[144] It is likely that many of the re-located factories went idle and rusty.

According to the Nobel Laureate Amartya K. Sen (1933–), people's entitlement is an issue of human rights, social security, and state responsibility.[145] Without such entitlement, Sen observed, 'the poor died from hunger in front of well-stocked food shops protected by the state'.[146] Once people's legal entitlement is protected, hunger and starvation can be eliminated.[147] Not surprisingly, Sen pointed his finger at China's failure in comparison with India's success. The poor and the hungry in Mao's China were on their own.[148] The causal link between the peasantry's lack of legal entitlement and the Great Leap Famine has been characterised as the 'powerless-starving' dynamic.[149]

As for why and how China's production possibility frontier (PPF) failed to budge, the answer lies in Mao's deliberate policy to limit the size of the urban sector, avoiding the urban Soviet path of industrialisation and modernity. But this was not the end of the story. Evidence shows that during the Great Leap campaign recorded iron and steel 'output' was to a large extent recycled metal. A scam in other words. It was witnessed in 1958 by Wang Hong, an official of the State Planning Committee:

> I was in Nanjing to inspect the Iron and Steel Drive. I visited the University of Nanjing and Nanjing Industrial College where students melted down their iron bed frames and university iron fences into piles of slag with no value. The universities had to buy new beds for students. What a double waste.[150]

In 1959, 7.2 million tonnes of slag rolled out of backyard furnaces. This represented over two-thirds (67.3 per cent) of the 1959 production target (i.e. 10.7 million tonnes). While this mountain of useless slag fed into China's total GDP that year, it did nothing for the economy. Rather, Mao's Great Leap Bubble lost the Chinese Reminbi (RMB) 30 billion in value,[151] equivalent to 20 per cent of China's GDP in 1959.[152] An industrial recession soon followed. All backyard furnaces were shut down. China's iron and steel output dropped back to 6.7 million tonnes in 1962, a decline of over 60 per cent from 1961; and China's coal output dropped back to 220 million tonnes, a decline of 45 per cent from 1961.[153] Meanwhile, in 1962 China's industrial workforce was cut back by 8.5 million (a 17 per cent annual drop) and China's urban population declined by 20 million (a 15 per cent annual fall).[154] Mao's rural iron and steel growth model had significantly failed China's system of resource allocation.[155]

So far, the assumption has been that the rural sector was still functional under Mao's rule, thanks to its official status as the most important sector in the economy. In reality, however, Maoism removed most economic incentives from the peasantry. Mao's first targets were market incentives associated with *homo economicus* (Adam Smith). Mao's abolition of private ownership over land and farming capital removed individuals' desire to invest and raise their efficiency within the rural sector. As a result, farmers became lazy and resource allocation sub-optimal. For Mao's economic planners, the way out was food rationing. Data in table 2.17 provide a comprehensive picture of food availability at the subsistence or famine diet level not only in the urban sector but also in rural China where the food came from.[156]

Table 2.17. Food Rationing, 1960s–1970s

Age and occupational groups	Raw cereal kg/year	Net weight* kg/year	Kilocalories† per day
North, rural	**Actual amount**	**Actual amount**	**Actual amount**
2–5	62	43	400
6–10	144	100	929
11–15	185	129	1,198
15+	225	158	1,467
North, Beijing		**Actual amount**	**Actual amount**
0–3		52	513
10+		180	1,775
Clerks		180	1,775
Manual workers		270	2,663[157]
South, rural	**Official guidelines**	**Official guidelines**	**Official guidelines**
2–5	60	42	414
6–10	90	63	620
11–15	190	133	1,310
15+	240	168	1,660
South, Shanghai		**Actual amount**	**Actual amount**
0–3		42	414
10+		150	1,480
Clerks		168	1,660
Manual workers		240	2,367

Note: * The husking/milling process reduces cereal by about 30 per cent in weight.
† One kilogram of wholemeal wheat flour contains energy of about 3,390 kilocalories and one kilogram of dry rice 3,600 kilocalories; see Anon., 'Whole Wheat Flour', https://www.fatsecret.com/calories-nutrition/generic/flour-whole-wheat?portionid=52100&portionamount=100.000&frc=True; Anon., 'Calories in Rice', https://www.nutracheck.co.uk/calories/calories_in_pasta_noodles__rice/calories_in_rice#url. All energy calculations are based on 1 kg = 3,600 kilocalories.
Sources: Rural north: Zheng Weidong, 'Jitihua Shidaide Fenpei Zhidu Yu Renko Shengyu' (Distribution System and Baby Births during the Collective Era), *Kaifang Shidai* (*Age of Openness*), 5 (2010): 107; Rural south: Elisabeth Croll, *The Family Rice Bowl, Food and the Domestic Economy in China* (Geneva: UNRISD, 1983), p. 80. Data for Beijing and Shanghai: Croll, *Family Rice Bowl*, pp. 118, 211; also Liu and Yeh, *Economy of the Chinese Mainland*, pp. 48–50.

Recent research has revealed the negative impact calorie rationing has on adult heights across gender and age groups. In China heights remained stagnant from 1956 to 1978 and began increasing only after 1980.[158] Not surprisingly, the People's Liberation Army (PLA) had difficulty in recruiting soldiers. In rural Guangdong, 99 per cent of army hopefuls were under-weight in the 1970s.[159]

Calorie rationing went hand in hand with Mao's policy of rural egalitarianism which tied a family's income to its size.[160] This involved '70 per cent of family income coming from food rationing according to family size and 30 per cent from family wages'.[161] This encouraged a higher birth rate to maximise household food rationing. In other words, food rationing encouraged population growth to eat up surplus grain. This was a variation of the 'tragedy of the commons' when individuals scoop the maximum from a communal pot.

Figure 2.5 shows that a high birth rate (> 4 births per 1,000 women) persisted during Mao's rule. The main force of China's national fertility rate was the rural sector which accounted for about 80 per cent of China's total under Mao's rule.[162] Mao was clearly in favour of maintaining the rural component of China's population because his power depended on it. The downside is that more births diluted per capita GDP to the point that China remained near the bottom of the international league table during Mao's rule.[163] In comparison, China's birth rates nosedived after the 1982 Birth Control Law, which has boosted China's per capita GDP figures ever since.

Meanwhile, state control over personal incomes was also imposed on the rural population. In real terms, only 30 per cent of all output

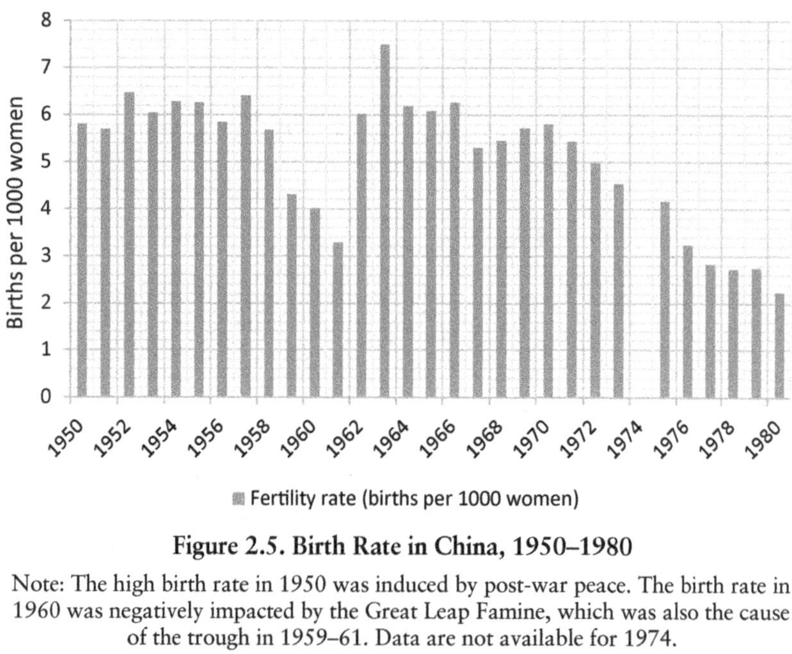

Figure 2.5. Birth Rate in China, 1950–1980

Note: The high birth rate in 1950 was induced by post-war peace. The birth rate in 1960 was negatively impacted by the Great Leap Famine, which was also the cause of the trough in 1959–61. Data are not available for 1974.

Sources are available in the separate section of 'Figure Sources'.

was distributed among villagers including official functionaries, schoolteachers, 'barefoot doctors', and accountants, as well as ordinary labourers according to an internal work-point system (*gongfen*). The lion's share, 70 per cent, was routinely extracted for internal capital accumulation (*gongjijin*) and for public goods provision (*gongyijin*).[164] It was common for individuals to come out empty-handed after all the deductions, even in a year of a bumper harvest.[165] This was known as 'no income increase after output increase' (*zengchan bu zengshou*). Indicative of this situation, in a 1978 survey of 803 million collective farmers, 97 per cent had a cash income between RMB 0.1 and 0.2 (US$0.06–0.13, the period exchange rate) per day,[166] enough for a pack of no-frill cigarettes, a candle, or a visit to a public bath.[167] In another account, rural bank deposits were a mere RMB 6.9 per head.[168] So, rural China remained extremely poor.[169] Given that the rural population constituted the vast majority of China's population (over 70 per cent until 1995), this savings level was where China's mode sat (be it unimodal or multimodal). Mao's China was thus extremely poor.

Ironically, ordinary people had to wait until Mao died to become better off. After 1978, private household savings per capita increased 711-fold with an annual rate of 15.7 per cent, as shown in figure 2.6.

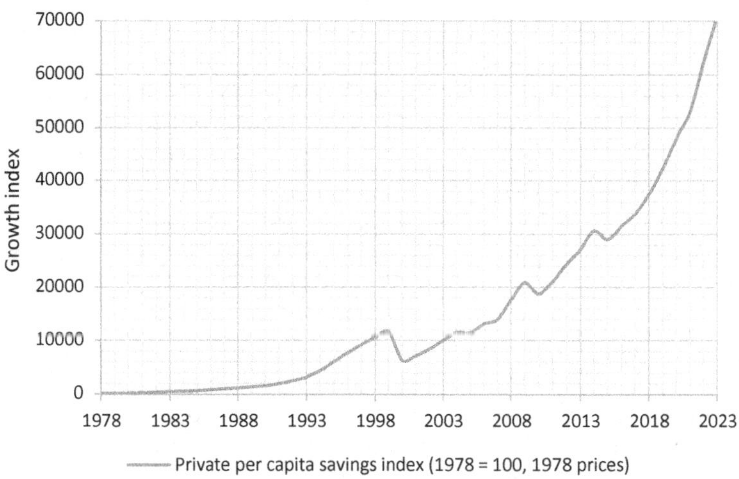

Figure 2.6. Per Capita Private Household Savings, 1978–2023

Note: Barely any private savings existed due to Mao's policy of artificial subsistence wages for all. Constant price conversion is based on National Bureau of Statistics, *Statistical Year Book, 2023*, ch. 3.

Sources are available in the separate section of 'Figure Sources'.

This was a *bona fide* sign of the economy coming out of the Maoist absolute-poverty trap, although too much saving could weaken the growth of China's domestic consumer market. But that is a different issue.

Finally, as city-bound migration was no longer available,[170] the mechanism associated with social mobility was removed; and so was the desire to have better education across all walks of life and among the rural population in particular. By the time Mao died, a third of adults in China remained illiterate.[171] Government provision of rural education was minimal. A government survey in the 1980s revealed that a great many rural schools were mere 'dark classrooms, earth tables and dirty kids' where teachers 'barely made both ends meet'.[172] Poor education took its toll. During the 1970s, a third of all farm tractors were permanently out of service, while another third suffered technical defects, leaving only a third that worked properly.[173]

To sum up, Mao's policies led to social immobility, low incentives, low efficiency, low economic growth but high birth rates. The rural sector suffered the most.

6. Mao's Legacy Debated

Even though his crimes against his own people and his failures in economic growth and development are something of a closed matter, Mao's legacy has been hotly debated and opinions remain divided. A general taxonomy can be established across three distinctive opinion groups shown in figure 2.7 where Mao's performance is assessed according to two stylised indicators: the state and the economy.

In economic history, though, any verdict depends on historical evidence, not on opinions. As far as data are concerned, the most commonly used indicator is GDP, especially total GDP,[174] although what really matters is per capita GDP. So far, we know that China's low per capita GDP growth was closely associated with a low urbanisation rate and low employment opportunities in urban factories. It is now time to see what China's total GDP looked like under Mao's rule.

Here are the basic facts provided by the People's Republic of China (PRC). First, in terms of capital formation and investment, it was documented that under Mao: (1) the amount of state investment was worth a quarter of China's annual GDP each year; and (2) the state capital assets to GDP ratio (hence new capital investment's GDP yield level) was about 1:1 after 1957.[175] Second, after each round of capital re-investment worth a quarter of China's GDP (25%), China's total

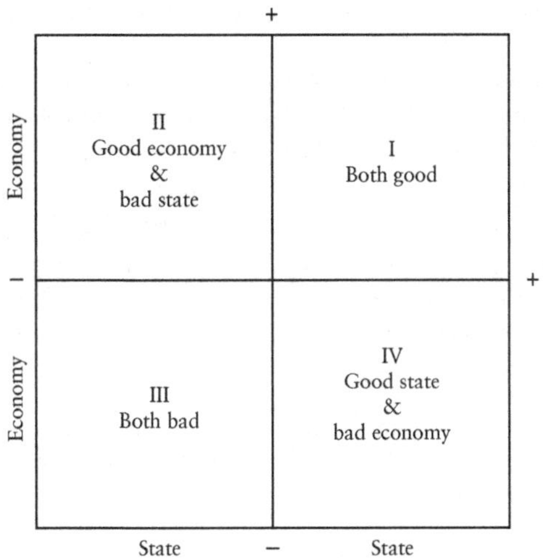

Figure 2.7. Opinions on Mao's Legacy

Authors belonging to Quadrant I: William Hinton, *Fanshen: A Documentary of Revolution in a Chinese Village* (New York: Monthly Review Press, 1966), and his *The Great Reversal: The Privatization of China, 1978–1989* (New York: Monthly Review Press, 1990); Maurice Meisner, *Mao's China and After: A History of the People's Republic* (New York: Free Press, 1986); Mark Selden, *The Political Economy of Chinese Socialism* (London: M.E. Sharpe, 1988); John Gittings, *The Changing Face of China: From Mao to Market* (Oxford: Oxford University Press, 2005); Giovanni Arrighi, *Adam Smith in Beijing: Lineages of the Twenty-First Century* (London: Verso, 2007); Dongping Han, *The Unknown Cultural Revolution: Life and Change in a Chinese Village* (New York: Monthly Review Press, 2008); Yasheng Huang, *Capitalism with Chinese Characteristics: Entrepreneurship and the State* (Cambridge: Cambridge University Press, 2008); Martin Jacques, *When China Rules the World: The End of the Western World and the Birth of a New Global Order* (London: Penguin Books, 2009). Their commonality: Mao's regime put China on a new track of social change and industrialisation.

Authors belonging to Quadrant II: Alexander Eckstein, *China's Economic Revolution* (Cambridge: Cambridge University Press, 1977); Dwight Perkins, *China: Asia's Next Economic Giant?* (Cambridge: Cambridge University Press, 1986); Barry Naughton, *The Chinese Economy: Transitions and Growth* (Cambridge, MA: MIT Press, 2007); Justin Y. Lin, *Demystifying the Chinese Economy* (Cambridge: Cambridge University Press, 2011). Their commonality: Growth in total GDP was generated despite the Great Leap Famine and Cultural Revolution.

Authors belonging to Quadrant III: Thomas Rawski, *Economic Growth in Prewar China* (Berkeley: University of California Press, 1989); Susan Shirk, *The Political Logic of Economic Reform in China* (Berkeley: University of California Press, 1993); Loren Brandt and Thomas Rawski, *China's Great Economic Transformation* (Cambridge: Cambridge University Press, 2008); Roderick MacFarquhar, *The Origins of the Cultural Revolution* (New York: Columbia University Press, 1999); Jasper Becker, *Hungry Ghosts: Mao's Secret Famine* (London: John Murray, 1996); Minxin Pei, *China's Trapped Transition: The Limits of Developmental Autocracy* (Cambridge, MA: Harvard University Press, 2006); Roderick MacFarquhar and Michael Schoenhals, *Mao's Last Revolution* (Cambridge, MA: Harvard University Press, 2008); Frank Dikötter, *Mao's Great Famine: The History of China's Most Devastating Catastrophe, 1958–1962* (London: Bloomsbury, 2010), and his *The Tragedy of Liberation, A History of the Chinese Revolution 1945–1957* (London: Bloomsbury, 2015); Ezra Vogel, *Deng Xiaoping and the Transformation of China* (Cambridge, MA: Harvard University Press, 2011); Nicholas Lardy, *Markets over Mao: The Rise of Private Business in China* (Washington, DC: Peterson Institute for International Economics, 2014). Their commonality: Maoism cost China more than China gained.

Authors belonging to Quadrant IV: No one fits in with this category. This untaken option remains the only common ground across all parties.

Sources are available in the separate section of 'Figure Sources'.

GDP would increase by a quarter, *ceteris paribus*. Theoretically, in line with the Solow–Swan model of self-propelling growth,[176] after 20 years (1957–77) China's GDP would expand 86-fold. Given that China's total GDP was RMB 1,071.4 billion in 1957 and RMB 3,250 billion in 1977,[177] real growth was a mere three-fold over the twenty-year period. If so, a quarter of GDP re-invested per year yielded 5.7 per cent extra GDP, meaning that 77 per cent China's GDP that was re-invested ended with nothing under Mao's autarky. The truth finally came out in the 1980s:

> A high rate of accumulation and large-scale capital construction alone cannot bring about sustained fast growth and good economic results. . . . [Excessive capital formation] is neither feasible nor well planned.[178]

The worst capital investment performance was in heavy industry which was marred by 'false reporting on costs and profits', and 'reckless spending once money was allotted by the state'.[179] This suboptimal investment outcome was exacerbated by China's international isolation and the absence of domestic competition. Most tellingly, China's state-run capital investment remained highly inefficient even during the post-Mao economic take-off.[180]

Moreover, there was no evidence that Mao's state favoured home-grown modern science and technology.[181] Mao's government spending on research (including that of military technology) was below five per cent of its total annual expenditure. As a result, over half of scientists and technicians received training only up to high school level or lower.[182]

The result is predictable. China's industrial sector produced mountains of capital goods, most of which simply became deadweight to the economy. This was commonly known as 'producing for inventories' (*wei cangku shengchan*).[183] For example, in 1971, China's total steel inventory amounted to 8.8 million tonnes, or 52 per cent of China's domestic output and imports combined.[184] In the 1990s, accumulated inventories still equalled 50 per cent of China's total GDP.[185] So, Maoist industrial GDP must have been over-valued by about half, to say the least. Meanwhile, piles of heavy industrial products did nothing to benefit people's material life.[186] It was documented that under Mao,

> all the material resources including land and other tangible assets and non-material resources such as power, prestige and related education and information were monopolised by the state. . . . Ordinary citizens possess little more than basic furniture, clothing, bedding, and cooking utensils.[187]

In this context, hiring more industrial workers and building more cities became untenable. In turn, China's economy remained rural and farming-dominated.

Economy-wide, the Maoist economy was unsustainable. Recent research suggests that from 1952 to 1978, China's capital productivity reduced 3.1 per cent a year; and China's total factor productivity, 1.4 per cent a year.[188] China's urbanisation rate also declined from 1960 to 1978.[189] So, like the agricultural sector, China's industrial sector could not have performed any worse.

Against this backdrop, China's growth downturn began in 1946 and continued until the 1970s. As such, Mao's legacy has to land on Quadrant III of figure 2.7.

7. Final Remarks

There was a causal link between Qing failure in public goods provision administered by Imperial-degree-holding civilian officials and the rise of less educated military strongmen. This outcome encompassed the 1850 rebels (e.g., the Taipings), the provincial warlords (e.g., Yuan Shikai) and finally Mao and his rural followers. Fundamentally, late Qing China was punished by civil wars and foreign invasions for its conscious abandonment of the Ming fiscal state which had been capable of running the largest and most expensive public-work projects in Asian history: the Great Wall, the Ming armada, and the Ming capital city of Beijing.

— 3 —

DENG'S TERMINATION OF CLASS STRUGGLE AND THE PURSUIT OF GROWTH

1. Exogenous Party-State and Resistance from the Population

What produced party dissidents and kept them motivated was Mao's persistent failure in handling agriculture and peasants rather than his inability to industrialise China. After all, all dynastic rulers in China's long history were judged by how they dealt with agriculture and peasants. Mao was no exception.

To begin with, one should go back to 1940 when Zhou Enlai tried to persuade Moscow that the Chinese Communist Party had discovered a shortcut to joining their European comrades by artificially making China's rural society 'proletarianised'.[1] Indeed, Mao's adoption of Trotskyism served the same end, as his track record shows.

Needless to say, this top-down proletarianisation violated head-on Karl Marx's doctrine of 'historical materialism' in which proletarians (or waged labourers) were a logical product of modern market-based industrial capitalism. Any attempt to artificially manufacture such a class without the necessary condition of modern market-based capitalism is anti-Marxist and flawed.

Mao's muddling with Karl Marx aroused intellectual resistance in society.[2] Inside the CCP, Liu Shaoqi (1898–1969) clearly held a different view. He opposed the ideal of de-privatising the peasantry. He also emphasised the absence of a sizeable industrial waged worker class in society.[3] Liu's policy recommendation on the eve of the communist takeover of Mainland China was a democratic coalition between the communist state, ordinary peasants, and the national bourgeoisie to foster 'class competition' but not a class war.[4] His view on the peasantry was largely in line with Alexander Chayanov's theory on peasantry being self-exploitative and thus harmless to the state.[5] But Mao's penchant was to build a dictatorship through Trotskyist endless revolutions (i.e., purges) backed by Stalin's Gulag model from the Soviet Union.[6] This was a problem for the ruling clique of the People's Republic.

Meanwhile, with Mao's 'General Guidelines of Land Law' (*tudifa dagang*) issued in October 1947, tillers were entitled to hold equal amounts of land as a reward for supporting the communist regime. Clause 11 states that

> The state recognises tillers' rights in operating land, trading land and in certain cases leasing land [for rent].[7]

Hand in hand with the initial land redistribution, there was in 1949–50 an 'expansion of the middle peasants' from 66 per cent to 85 per cent of all farming households (*zhongnong hua*).[8] At this time, there was no sign of any resistance against Mao's rule. The situation soon changed.

The outcry against 'man-made proletarians' came mainly from the grassroots in society. By April 1956, one million or so farming cooperatives (*hezuoshe*) were set up for Mao's utopia to accommodate a total of 106.7 million rural households (90 per cent of all).[9] In the process, a total of 100 million hectares (1.5 billion *mu*, as in 1949) and RMB 200–300 million in capital assets were taken from their lawful owners without compensation.[10]

Evidence shows that a vast majority of peasants did not join cooperatives voluntarily. Resistance was common. In Guangdong, only 30 per cent of households joined of their own volition; in Yunnan, only 20 per cent.[11] In Xianshu County (Zhejiang), 81 per cent of households stayed away from cooperatives.[12] Those who welcomed cooperatives were the poorest, as they had something to gain.[13] Soon, a spontaneous counter-campaign emerged across 1956 and 1957. In Guangdong, 130,000 farming households quit cooperatives one year after collectivisation.[14] In another account, 127,000 farming households chose to quit.[15] In Xiangzhong County (Hunan), 30 per cent of cooperatives ceased to exist after the autumn harvest in 1956. In 1958, in a village in Zunhua County (Hebei) only three of the poorest peasants (*pinnong*) decided to stick together in favour of Mao's programme.[16] Economic Maoism was clearly unpopular.

Mao's collectivisation targeted and harmed the rural majority, something that has been overlooked so far.[17] Amongst those who stayed, 20 per cent lost their incomes in 1956.[18] Income decline was recorded as being over 50 per cent in Hunan Province.[19] Physically leaving Mao's China seems to have been a choice in frontier regions. One investigator reported that:[20]

> In the beginning, peasants were unclear about the implications of collectivisation. But after hills, forestry, land, water buffalos and even personal belongings were collectivised, peasants were alarmed and began to resist furiously. They first worked slowly; then they cut down trees which deforested large areas. They also rushed to kill water buffalos and pigs. After that they escaped to Burma with 20,000 to 30,000 villagers at one go. Some villages were completely evacuated.

In 1958, 100,000 villagers in Menglian and Ruili Counties (Yunnan Province) voted with their feet and escaped to Burma.[21] In Guangdong, rural exodus in the hundreds of thousands to Hong Kong (*tao gang*) continued until the 1970s.[22]

This raises the question that occurs to many citizens living in communist countries: if communism is so wonderful why have so few Westerners escaped from their countries to join a communist economy? Most tellingly, two decades after Mao's forceful proletarianisation, when quitting collective farming was officially allowed by Deng's state, the withdrawal rate was close to 100 per cent among all farmers.

Back in the 1950s, after the '1957 Anti-Rightist Movement', quitting was no longer permitted. Angry peasants in the hinterland began to destroy assets. Two million working animals were slaughtered hurriedly in 1956 to avoid confiscation.[23] By 1959, 7.5 million rural households stopped raising pigs to boycott collectivisation.[24] Meanwhile, output of major agricultural products universally declined at a time when China's natural conditions – rainfall and temperature for farming – were very favourable.[25] Data in table 3.1 show that farming output of both food crops and cash crops declined across the board. But cash crops (oil seeds, sugarcane, beet, and tobacco)

Table 3.1. Collectivisation and Decline in Farming Output and Draft Animals

	Wheat kg/*mu*	Soya kg/*mu*	Oil seed kg/*mu*	Sugarcane kg/*mu*	Beet kg/*mu*	Tobacco kg/*mu*	Draft animals (ten thousands)
1955	57.5	53.0	47.0	2,647	926.5	79.0	8,775
1957	57.0	52.5	40.5	2,599	628.0	48.0	8,323
Change	–0.5	–0.5	–6.5	–48	–298.5	–31.0	-452

Source: Contemporary Agricultural History Study Group, *Agricultural Reforms and Development*, p. 88.

declined much further in yields per unit of land. This makes sense as the rural market was outlawed by Mao's state which made cash crops useless. Moreover, the number of draft animals, which represented farming capital, also decreased.

It was in this context that Mao promoted 'free meals for all' from rural communal canteens (*da shitang*) to lure peasants back into the communist system. At the 1958 Party Conference in the Beidaihe Sea Resort, Mao defined his new offering as 'free meals in communal canteens qualifies communism'.[26] Party officials were assessed by the percentage of peasants on free meals in their districts.[27] Mao also created an illusion that his state was prepared to back the free-meal utopia indefinitely. Given the Marxian principle of 'from each according to his ability, to each according to his need', Mao's 'free meals for all' removed incentives to work and opened the door for free riding and abuse. This was just another case of Mao's ignorance towards the Marxian doctrine.

The twisted logic of free meals captured the public imagination. Peasants flocked to communal canteens in large numbers. The spread of people's communes went hand in hand with free meals. By the end of 1959, there were allegedly 3.9 million communal canteens across China serving 400 million diners free of charge.[28] Now, Mao outwitted the peasantry by providing them with their own produce, but presented it as Maoist manna. No penny from Mao's state coffers was ever paid to finance such free meals. The harsh reality was that the alleged free meals all came from the output and reserves of villages. Within a year, by April 1959, food reserves in rural China had run dangerously low on an unprecedented scale: fifteen provinces were reportedly suffering from food deficits and 25.2 million villagers were going hungry.[29] A government minister recalled that

> People came to dine in a public canteen. The food they got was thin rice porridge and vegetable soups. Everyone was hungry and short of energy even for walking. In the field, they all lay down and did absolutely nothing. . . . Weeds grew taller than crops. . . . The market which could have provided a way to make a living was closed down. Rural people were not permitted to enter cities to beg for food. Their only choice was to die of starvation inside their villages.[30]

Meanwhile, food shortages became a nationwide problem. It was documented that

> Due to widespread food shortages, people suffered malnutrition. Oedema cases were reported in a great many places.[31]

Then, from 1960 to 1962, 30–40 million communal diners (and also 'Great Leapers') paid the ultimate price. They died as a result of the free meal scam in conjunction with the iron and steel scam of backyard furnaces. Regions that were hit the hardest by the famine, such as Henan, Anhui, and Sichuan, were where 'free meals' had the highest participation rates.

The Great Leap Famine forced Mao's state to abandon free-meal communism, relaxing control over peasant backyard food production, known as 'family plots' (*ziliu di*) to top up the meagre food rationing. This policy, announced in 1961 as a compromise to the losses suffered by the peasantry, created a dual farming system inside rural communes. These family plots took up about 5 per cent of the farmland inside a commune, but produced about 80 per cent of vegetables and 50 per cent of grain to sustain the rural population.[32] In another account, family plots yielded at least 50 per cent of the annual family income of the peasantry.[33] According to a survey in Inner Mongolia, the yield level of family plots was 10 times their collective counterparts.[34] Thus, 10 per cent of China's farmland could produce all the grain needed to feed China's rural population if it were converted into family plots. This also means that over 90 per cent of land under collective farming hopelessly under-performed.

With the dual approach, confidence in collective farming collapsed. For example, it was reported that:

> Changes in agricultural output clearly reveal that People's Communes performed worse than rural co-operatives; . . . co-operatives performed worse than mutual aid groups; and mutual aid groups performed worse than private farmers.[35]

It was officially admitted that, under Mao:

> for more than 20 years, there was virtually no progress in labour productivity in collective farming. The enormous waste of labour power presents agriculture a serious problem.[36]

The output gap between family plots and commune land embarrassed officials. In some cases officials swapped collective plots with family plots. They went as far as allocating plots of saline-alkali soil to peasant families to even out the disadvantages of collective farming. To their amusement, peasants were not deterred and soon converted the barren land into high yield plots while the re-collectivised former family plots simply went barren after the swap.[37]

Inside the commune system, a principle–agent problem loomed large. It was a yearly struggle in terms of how much produce was to be reported to the state. It was common for villages to have three different accounts: One for individual families, one for the village accountant, and one for the commune's officials.[38] Under-reporting was widespread, described as:

> When sun-dried grain entered the village granary for registration, we discounted its weight by 20 per cent as 'moisture content'. We also counted 100 *jin* as 80 *jin* for the pool of village food rationing. During the harvest season, our production brigade offered free lunches with one *jin* [500 grams, one-day ration] per head a day outside the mandatory food rationing. When officials came to inspect fields, we always showed them the worst plots. At the end, we only reported 800 *jin* per *mu* although we actually produced 1,200 *jin*.[39]

Even Mao himself was aware of this problem:

> Nowadays, rural production teams commonly under-report their output and retain their output illegally. They even dig deep cellars to hide grain. These cellars are protected by village security guards.[40]

It has been estimated that a total of 120 billion *jin* (60 million tonnes) was retained 'illegally' across China between 1958 and 1976.[41] Food hoarding was the reason for Mao to launch his 'Four Cleansings Campaign' (*siqing*) in 1964–5 to force the peasantry to give up this practice.[42] In doing so, not only did Mao's agrarian economic base become shaky but also his 'worker–peasant alliance' irreversibly broke down. The result? China became a net food importer from 1956 to 1978 (see table 2.16).

China's industrial sector did not fare any better. Resistance took the form of negligence. Irrational plans went ahead, as state-owned enterprise (SOE) managers did not really care. But the bad planning simply kept going. Data in table 3.2 demonstrate how Mao's state gambled with heavy industry by channelling investment into it at the expense of light industry. The implication here is that such biased

Table 3.2. Investment Bias, % Total Investment Value, 1953–1975

	Heavy industry (I)	Light industry (II)	I/II
1953–7	36.2	6.4	5.7
1958–62	54.0	6.4	8.4
1963–5	45.9	3.9	11.8
1966–70	51.1	4.4	11.6
1971–5	49.6	5.8	8.6
Average	47.4	5.8	8.2

Source: National Bureau of Statistics, *Statistical Year Book, 1992*, pp. 149, 158.

investment in heavy industry almost certainly led to low efficiency, high waste, and diminishing returns.

Moreover, the establishment of heavy industry was poorly executed,[43] showing not only asymmetric information as party officials were typically technically illiterate,[44] but also passive resistance from the professional-managerial class mistrustful of Mao's policies. This became known as 'party laymen guiding non-party experts' (*waihang lingdao neihang*).[45] Factory managers had no incentives to improve efficiency. Their replacement by ordinary and thus incompetent workers during the Cultural Revolution produced a similar effect. So, the system kept generating waste.[46] This was clear in the sharp decline in investment returns. Available data in table 3.3 show that in the beginning, state investment returned 57 per cent. This figure halved to 26 per cent when the Cultural Revolution began. It halved again to 15 per cent towards the end of the Cultural Revolution. The drop from peak to trough was 74 per cent. In this context, the writing off of state assets was a regular event.[47]

Inside the ruling party, resistance from the 'urban sect' kept a link to the outside world via diplomacy. A key figure was Huan Xiang (1909–89), one of a handful of agents operating in Western Europe. He sent reports back to China with a great deal of honesty and integrity, which potentially landed him in political trouble (as a form of resistance to Maoism) on how the welfare state of Western Europe benefitted ordinary citizens with a living standard much higher than in Mao's China.[48] This contradicted Mao's assertion that the capitalist world would fall into decay and give way to communism.

Then, in the heydays of the Cultural Revolution, party officials of the highest level began to doubt Mao's leadership. In September 1971, Marshal Lin Biao (1907–71) sensationally defected to the Soviet Union, though unsuccessfully.[49] Lin had been loyal to Mao since 1927. He performed military wonders after the 1946 Siping-Harbin

Table 3.3. Decline in State-run Investment Returns, 1963–1978

Period	Investment returns % annual	1963–5 = 100
1963–5	57	100
1966–70	26	46
1971–5	15	26

Sources: Yu Guangyuan (ed.), *China's Socialist Modernization* (Beijing: Foreign Language Press, 1984), p. 458; Zhang Hua and Su Caiqing (eds), *Huishou Wenge, Zhongguo Shinian Wenge Fenxi Yu Fansi* (*Recollection of the Decade of Cultural Revolution, Analyses and Soul-Researching*) (Beijing: Chinese Communist Party History Press, 2000), p. 396.

fiasco, and was thus highly respected within the CCP inner circle. Lin was hand-picked by Mao as his successor, which was even written into the 1970 Constitution of the Party. Lin's failed defection – the ultimate form of resistance to Mao's rule – fundamentally undermined Mao's reputation and personal image.[50] After 1971, Mao lost his grip on the barrel of his gun.[51]

Resistance also took the form of 'underground listening to enemy radio stations' (*touting ditai*),[52] which was a common practice among intellectuals. 'Enemy stations' included the BBC, Voice of America, Radio France Internationale, Voice of Free China (Taiwan), and even Radio Moscow (post-1960).[53] Interestingly, underground listening was unintendedly facilitated by government-run, mass-produced portable radios as a way to bypass China's high illiteracy rate under Mao's rule.[54] Collective listening to party propaganda radio was compulsory at the village level.[55] Large numbers of radios were sent to villages as government gifts.[56] Short-wave radios were easy to obtain even during the Cultural Revolution as a means for the government's voice to travel across China's landmass. The fact that 16 million urban young people were re-settled in the countryside allowed the younger generation to easily tune in to 'enemy' radio stations, as only large cities had jam stations to block foreign broadcasting signals. Ironically, ruralisation of the urban young thus boosted audience numbers of enemy radio stations.

2. Deng's Personal Qualities: Key to Reforms

The Soviet party-state maximises the personal influence of its leaders and more often than not creates personality cults, as in the cases of Lenin, Stalin, Mao, Ho Chi Minh, Kim Il Sung, and Kim Jong-Il. Despite its natural propensity for absolutism, the Soviet party-state may be used as an effective tool to implement economic reforms quickly and on a large scale. In this regard, the personal qualities of the paramount leader make a crucial difference, as in the cases of Mikhail Gorbachev (1931–2022, r.1985–91) of the Soviet Union and Deng Xiaoping (1904–97, r.1978–89) of Mainland China.

Unlike Mao, Deng was an open-minded and adventurous youngster. He signed up for a work-study programme and travelled all the way from China's western hinterland of Sichuan to France. At that time, the French economy had been industrialised with modern textiles, metallurgy, mining, railways, electricity, chemicals, and automobiles (in that order). So, Deng parachuted himself from an Oriental rural outpost to a heartland of European democracy, modernity, and capitalism. He was only sixteen.

Deng spent six years in France and gained work experience in a steel plant and a car factory.[57] He probably considered making modern cars in China at that time. Undoubtedly, his experience in France made Deng both urbanised and Westernised, something that was entirely missing in Mao's life. Deng joined the communist movement at the age of twenty, and in 1926 moved to a party institute in Moscow (called 'Sun Yat-sen University', 1925–30) designed to nurse Chinese collaborators (commonly known as the 'Moscovians').[58] Now, Deng not only understood capitalism but also authentic Bolshevism, another thing that was completely absent in Mao's life.

Deng returned to China in 1927 and joined General Feng Yuxiang (1882–1948) – a stratocrat with a pro-Russian background.[59] Deng was then involved in an urban workers' movement in Shanghai and Wuhan in 1928–9, which represented the mainstream of the Chinese communist movement, under instructions from Moscow. The urban operation (known as 'white-base communism') separated leaders like Deng from Mao's rural 'red-base communism'. Party insiders often viewed the white-base and red-base groups as two separate entities inside the CCP.

During the 1947–9 Civil War, Deng acted as Political Commissar of the Second Field Army of the communists. Even within the military, there was no evidence that Deng was interested in a career as a military commander.

Fast forward to 1950 and Deng became a leading civilian official (Vice-Premier) in charge of China's finance and thus became, in many respects, a technocrat. From 1955 to 1966, he became General Secretary of the party until the outbreak of the Cultural Revolution which aimed to topple Deng and his fellow 'Moscovian' Liu Shaoqi (1898–1969).[60] Both men were accused by Mao of being 'capitalist roaders inside the party' (*dangnei zouzipai*), although nobody knew whom these 'roaders' worked for other than the party itself and got paid by the party. Astonishingly, Deng survived (1966–74, 1975–7). But his Moscovian comrade Liu did not.

Mao may have been right. There was a force inside his party contemplating a different economic model. In 1964, Zhou Enlai (1898–1976), China's Premier, announced at the Third National People's Congress a comprehensive developmental goal of 'four modernisations' (*sige xiandaihua*) across agriculture, industry, the military, and science and technology. A decade later in 1975, the same goal was announced again by Deng Xiaoping at the Fourth

National People's Congress. How did Mao respond? He wrecked these modernisation plans by cleansing his party with two of his purges: the 'Four Cleansings' (1964–5) and the 'Anti-Right-Wing Overturning Verdicts' (*fan youqing fan-an*) in 1975–6 concurrent with the Cultural Revolution (1966–76). Mao could not tolerate anything modern.

Finally, in 1978, the same goal was announced for a third time by Hua Guofeng (1921–2008), China's new Premier at the time, at the Fifth National People's Congress. Third time lucky. It worked this time because Mao was dead and Mao's die-hard supporters – the Gang of Four – were arrested in 1976 and convicted in 1980.

Deng's leadership reforms took China by storm across three dimensions: (1) a new ideology, (2) new internal stability and unity, and (3) external peace.[61] Each goal shared the same aim: to dismantle Maoism.

3. Top-down Reforms during the Vital Years, 1980–1984

Economic Maoism had entered a cul-de-sac with the Great Leap Famine. Even so, Mao forged ahead to impoverish the economy further. When Mao died, China was among the poorest countries in the world. Deng put a stop to this. In Deng's own words,

> Poverty is not what communism means. . . . Although we claim that we are undertaking communism, we are not really qualified. Only in the mid-21st century when we reach the mid-developed level, can we say that China practises communism.[62]

> If we do not reform and open up, do not develop the economy, do not improve people's material life, we are all dead.[63]

This principle was elaborated later at the 2003 Resolution of the Third Plenary of the Sixteenth Communist Party Central Committee as follows:

> We must uphold the principle of people as the foundation, establish a comprehensive, harmonious, and sustainable outlook for our future, and hasten all-round economic, social and humanistic development.[64]

But the first task was to abandon Mao's ideology. The party sponsored a path-breaking debate in May 1978 on 'what qualified as truth' and concluded that 'practice was the only criterion for testing truth'. This was a return to Frances Bacon's empiricism, which disqualified Mao's notion of 'class struggle' in a classless society and the mantra of 'uninterrupted struggles' for the sake of it.[65] This debate achieved 'ideological emancipation' both inside the party and in society. A new rule of 'no political purges any more' (*bugao zhengzhi yundong*) was written into the new party constitution in 1978. De-Maoification had begun.

The next step, taken in great haste, was to redress all the unjust and false convictions of Mao's victims since 1949. Almost all victims of Mao's purges were exonerated and reinstated.[66] The beneficiaries included over 10 million 'communist enemies' and 3 million 'political dissidents'.[67] If their family members are included, the number is likely at least 60 million. This move released China's stifled elite human capital which Mao so despised.

The termination of Mao's fake class struggle was also extended to foreign policy. China began to make peace with the West and stopped supporting Maoist guerillas in Southeast Asia. In Deng's own phrase, 'to fulfill reforms and opening up, we need political stability and unity at home (*anding tuanjie*) and a peaceful international environment (*guoji heping*)'.[68]

Meanwhile, unlike Mao's numerous empty promises, the goals of the reforms were explained quantitatively as a 'moderately comfortable life' (*xiao kang*) with a price tag of US$1,000 per head so that everyone was able to understand it. Deng recalled in 1984:[69]

> Our 1978 original aim was as follows: In the first step, we doubled our GDP in the 1980s from the 1980 GDP baseline. China's per capita GDP was merely US$250. To double it meant US$500. Our second step was to double it again to reach US$1,000 per head. In realising this goal, we would become a 'moderately comfortable society'. . . . More importantly, our third step was to quadruple our per capita GDP in the 2030s to the 2050s to reach the level of US$4,000 per head to allow China to reach a moderately developed level.

Deng's programme echoed Japan's ten-year income-doubling plan in 1960 under Prime Minister Hayato Ikeda (1899–1965) and Taiwan's ten-year income-doubling plan in 1973 under Premier Chiang Ching-kuo (1910–88). Implicitly, China began for the first time to adopt the growth model of capitalist Asia.

What followed was a five-pronged approach from 1977 to 1982 to unleash the economic power of the market:[70]

(1) Restoration of law and order and termination of 'class struggle' (1977).
(2) Resumption of higher education and meritocracy for modern growth (1977).

(3) Establishment of 'special economic zones' (1979), resumption of foreign trade and foreign investment (1980) with a new doctrine of 'two systems in one country' (1980).
(4) Abolition of Mao's provincial barriers to form a single domestic market (1980); resumption of formal taxes (1981); and implementation of operational duties for managers of state enterprises (1981).
(5) Deregulation of Mao's control over consumer goods (1982).

As outlined by the State Council Communiqué of 10 October 1985, economic Maoism was discontinued and Mao's man-made economic hardship was turned around between 1980 and 1984:

> By 1980, our agriculture had been in a very difficult state. Large quantities of agricultural staples such as grain and cotton needed to be imported. But since 1981, our agriculture has grown at a high speed of 10 per cent per year on average. . . . Our food is now self-sufficient and our cotton is in surplus. . . .
>
> By 1980, our energy output had stalled. The situation has changed in the recent 2–3 years. Our crude oil and coal output have grown at more than 8 per cent a year. Our electricity has also increased as a result. . . .
>
> By 1980, our light industry had severely fallen behind people's needs. Consumer manufactures were scarce. Since then, our light industry has increased on average over 10 per cent a year with more output varieties. We now have a consumer market boom unprecedented since 1949. . . .
>
> By 1980, our government revenues had continuously declined with huge budget deficits. Since 1982 our government revenues have stopped declining and begun to break even. . . .
>
> By 1980, we had large numbers of unemployed people in the urban sector which we inherited from the past. In the past five years, 30 million new jobs have been created; our aggregate urban wages have increased 50 per cent in real terms, . . . and peasant net income has increased 80 per cent. Improvement in people's living standards has been unprecedented since 1949.[71]

No further explanation is needed.

4. Boom in Tertiary Education

Deng's measures also radically overhauled tertiary education in China. In October 1977 university entry examinations were resumed after a decade-long suspension. University graduates were permitted to take government jobs which had been preserved for Mao loyalists since 1949. Talented rural students were on a fast track of social mobility to obtain urban residential status and to apply for city jobs.

It reminded society of China's long Confucian tradition of schooling and Imperial Examinations for social mobility. In figure 3.1, higher education started from zero because all universities were forced to close down by Mao after 1966. Over three decades from 1978 to 2010, university enrolments went through the roof. The number of undergraduates increased 26-fold (10.7 per cent a year); the number of postgraduates, 140-fold (16.7 per cent a year); and the number of students studying aboard, 331-fold (19.9 per cent a year). These

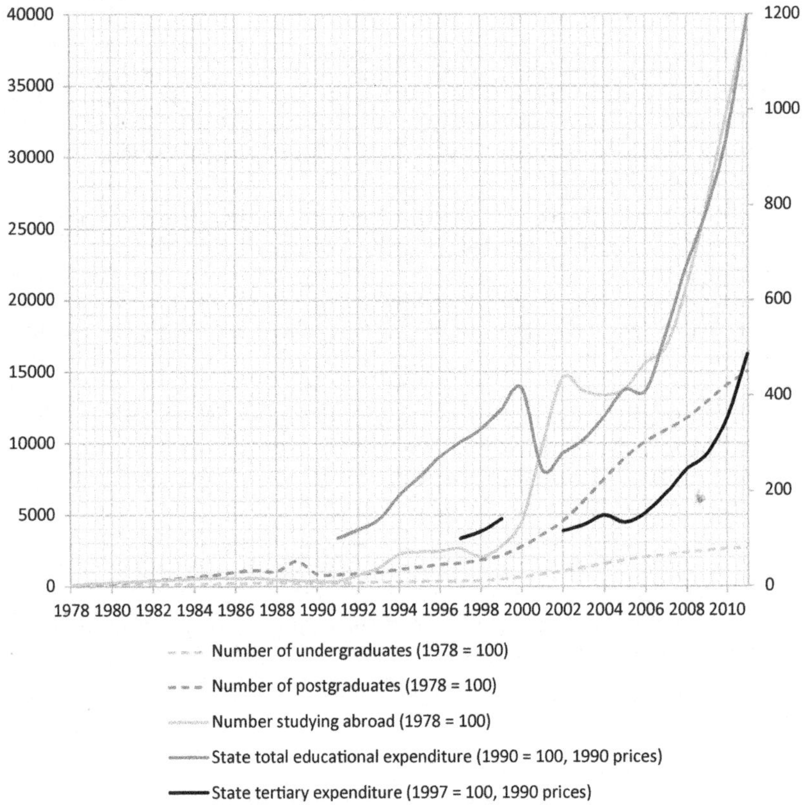

Figure 3.1. Growth in Higher Education, 1978–2010

Note: Left Y-axis: Student growth index (1978 = 100). Right Y-axis: State educational expenditure index (1990 = 100, 1997 = 100). Most students studying aboard were privately financed. Only about 10 per cent were sponsored by the government although the exact number is unavailable.[72] The constant price is based on National Bureau of Statistics, *Statistical Year Book, 2023*, ch. 3.

Sources are available in the separate section of 'Figure Sources'.

remarkable rates were achieved with minimal financial assistance from the state. There had been no such precedent in world history.

In comparison, state investment in education was delayed for at least a decade: educational expenditure increased 9.4-fold, or 12.5 per cent a year (data beginning in 1991), and the amount earmarked for university education increased 3.5-fold, or 10.1 per cent a year (data beginning in 1997).[73] Also, according to the available data for 1990–2010, state higher educational expenditure was on average 19.2 per cent of its total educational expenditure. Thus, the state's priority was primary and secondary schooling.[74]

In this context, China's growth in higher education was mainly 'demand-driven' from students and their families. Such demand was self-motivated and self-incentivised. What the post-Mao state offered was sensible deregulation rather than direct financial injections. Even so, the state made rational judgements for a change.

As a result, China's human capital was modernising fast. The data in table 3.4 show that by 2010, China had a newly emerged white-collar class that dominated education, finance, administration, health, and information technology (IT). In the process, loyal guards

Table 3.4. Distribution of Higher Educational Qualifications, % of Employees, 2010

Sector	Undergraduate degrees (I)	Postgraduate degrees (II)	I+II
1. White-collar sector			
Education*	66.5	4.7	71.2
Finance	59.7	2.9	62.6
Administration*	56.5	1.9	58.4
Health*	53.2	2.3	55.5
IT	51.6	3.4	55.0
2. Blue-collar sector			
Mining†	12.8	0.3	13.1
Manufacturing†	9.5	0.3	9.8
Catering	6.2	0.1	6.3
Construction†	5.9	0.1	6.0
Farming†	0.6	0.01	0.61

Note: Foreign languages were compulsory in university curricula since the late 1980s. Thus, most university graduates were open to Western information. * State-run sectors. † The previous 'revolutionary classes' that were privileged to man Mao's party and government until 1978.[76]

Source: National Bureau of Statistics, *Zhongguo Laodong Nianjian, 2011* (*Labour Year Book of China, 2011*) (Beijing: Labour Press, 2011), Section 1–33.

of Maoism who had often not received formal schooling were systematically replaced.[75]

5. Spontaneous Changes in Rural Institutions

The debate on how to establish truth, the reinstatement of purge victims, and the decriminalisation of 'free marketers' had a knock-on effect on people's perspectives. Spontaneous changes without the party's *ex ante* permission took place first among the poorest people – the peasantry – with whom the workings of private landownership were still in their living memory. So, their choice was simply to revert to how things were in the past.

In 1978, behind the back of party officials, eighteen farmers in Fengyang Village in Anhui Province decided to break the law and divided commune land into plots for *de facto* private farming. Although illegal, going back to private farming offered farmers a chance to break an economic dead end. Fengyang was so poor that begging had become farmers' winter occupation.[77] Official endorsement was not guaranteed in the beginning, as it was so diametrically opposed to Maoism. It finally arrived in 1982 as part of a 'truth finding exercise'.

The new system was called 'family output tenure' (*jiating zerenzhi*, literally 'household output responsible land tenure'). It was formally endorsed by a contract between the party-state officials and individual farming households. New land tenures were legally binding and tradable. This bore a close resemblance to the market conditions the peasantry used to be familiar with.[78] In the process, the party-state became a *de jure* landlord; and farmers, its tenants. Within five years, rural 'people's communes', the very core of Mao's rural utopia, had collapsed nation-wide like a house of cards. By 1985, communes had vanished completely.[79] Good riddance to Mao.

With the demise of the rural communes, producers' incentives and the power of the market were both unleashed. In North China, immediately after the new landholding tenancy system began, labour productivity increased 50 per cent; and land yield, 300 per cent.[80] For instance, in the early 1980s, in Funan County (Anhui), a family was able to produce the same amount of crop surplus as the whole village achieved previously; and the total cash income from farming in a single year surpassed the 20-year aggregate under Mao's rule.[81] In rural Zhejiang, private earnings became the main source of people's incomes.[82] Realistically, however, much of such 'growth' was by definition 'recovery' back to where China had been in the 1920s and 1930s.

A reliable measure of China's recovery in agriculture was the change in total factor productivity (TFP) which turned from perpetually negative during the period 1958–78 under Mao to positive in 1980 for the first time.[83]

In value terms, over the three decades from 1980 to 2010, China's agricultural GDP increased 9.2-fold (averaging 7.7 per cent a year); agricultural GDP per rural capita, 10.8-fold (8.3 per cent a year). These rates were all unheard of during Mao's time. Admittedly, help was available. Government expenditure on agriculture grew 12.6-fold (8.8 per cent a year) and food imports (in value) increased 7.7-fold (7 per cent a year).

The historical lesson here is that moving backwards to a traditional model worked. Mao's rural communism had been a waste of time.

6. Rural Industrial Enterprises and 'Urban Substitution Industrialisation'

The real challenge to the post-Mao reformers came from the state-owned industrial sector which had turned both parasitic in nature and zombie-like in operation despite its privileged position politically and financially.

The sheer scale and scope of Maoist inefficiency and waste, the best kept secret of Mao's reign, finally came to light in the 1980s when all the state-run firms were given fitness tests through exposure to the market. It turned out that about a third of state-owned enterprises (SOEs) lost money chronically; another third barely broke even; leaving only a third managing to stay in the black.[84]

Against all the odds, the situation deteriorated further throughout the 1990s despite the rest of China's economy becoming more efficient. In a survey of 50,000 state-owned firms conducted in 1992, 15 per cent still retained the value of their registered capital, 62 per cent had lost part of their capital value, and 23 per cent possessed only negative equity.[85] In the end, one-third of the entire state workforce was laid off as a last resort (*xiagang*).[86] But by 2000, after several rescue attempts, the state sector stubbornly remained the least efficient sector in the economy. It possessed half of China's fixed capital but produced less than a third of China's industrial GDP, which was 60 per cent lower than the non-state sector.[87]

The same problem still haunted the Chinese economy after the year 2000 in three ways. First, state-owned assets routinely lost large proportions of their face value when they were subjected to market scrutiny.[88]

Second, the state sector continued its energy-wasting practices. In 2006, to produce US$1 of GDP, China used three times more energy than the global average and four times more than the United States.[89] This inefficiency was largely compensated for by China's cheap labour (at one-tenth the cost in Europe and the United States).[90] But this was another matter. Third, there were non-performing loans and bad debts hanging over the industrial sector. In 1991, the national aggregate debt to capital asset ratio in all SOEs was 0.6. It quickly increased to 0.8 within a decade by 1997.[91] A third of all SOEs had a debt-to-capital asset ratio of 0.9 that year.[92] It was documented in 1998 that

> The current average debt to capital asset ratio in China's state-owned enterprises is 0.83. The source of debts is almost exclusively state-owned banks. Most such debts have no prospect of being repaid in future.[93]

It has been estimated that total bad debts in 2002 were equivalent to 40 per cent of China's GDP.[94] Nation-wide, the loan repayment rate by SOEs was just 3.3 per cent.[95] So, the prospect of any sizeable repayment of these debts was slim. If so, 40 per cent of GDP was almost certainly a write-off.

So, Mao's industrial sector was crippled from the start with no known cure. Unlike the rural sector, the industrial sector was the emperor's new clothes for Maoism, routinely showered with easy money and protected by monopoly, a practice that came from the Soviet tutelage of the 1950s. It created vested interests. While the stakeholders of this sector might not have agreed with Maoism, they nevertheless resisted Deng's reforms. This was a different beast altogether compared with agriculture.

Changes, if any, had to come from the outside in the fashion of 'reverse-forcing reforms' (*daobishi gaige*). Eventually, two forces came together in these reverse-forcing reforms: the newly privatised rural economy, which represented a 'push factor' from inside China, and private companies, Chinese or foreign, which represented a 'pull factor' from inside and outside the country.

Regarding the push factor, the mechanism was 'encircling cities from the countryside'. No less. It all began with a rise in demand for consumer manufactures after the rapid increase in rural household income. Rural households now had disposable incomes for goods that were price and income elastic, typically non-food products,[96] which were unaffordable under Mao's rule.

However, apart from the said inefficiency of the industrial sector, there was a structural problem. The lion's share of state investment was devoted to heavy industry. Investment in light industry for consumer manufactures was artificially depressed. Table 3.5 highlights the Maoist investment pattern.

Meanwhile, under Mao's rule, the availability of consumer manufactures was tightly restricted by state rationing with 'consumer-manufacture coupons' (*gongye quan*). On the one hand, such coupons covered a wide range of products from cloth, light bulbs, soap, matches, to wristwatches, radios and bicycles. By 1962 over 50 categories of non-food wage goods had been on the hit list. On the other hand, there was discrimination against the rural consumption. For example, in 1961 cloth rationing was set at 3 m^2 per head per year for city residents but 1.5 m^2 for each rural soul.[97]

In addition, consumer-manufactures were all sold at inflated monopolistic prices to discourage growth in light industry. The following items were on the 'must have' list for urban working-class families: bicycles, watches, and sewing machines. Thanks to the monopolistic prices, they took months or even years to save up for. For acute poverty-stricken farmers, they were far out of reach. Table 3.6 shows

Table 3.5. Maoist Investment Pattern, % Total Value, 1953–1975

Period	Heavy industry (I)	Light industry (II)	I/II
1953–7	36.2	6.4	5.7
1958–62	54.0	6.4	8.4
1963–5	45.9	3.9	11.8
1966–70	51.1	4.4	11.6
1971–5	49.6	5.8	8.6
Average	47.4	5.4	9.2

Source: National Bureau of Statistics, *Statistical Year Book, 1992*, pp. 149, 158.

Table 3.6. Monopolistic Prices of Consumer Manufactures, Prior to 1980

Type	Retail prices (RMB)	= Post-apprenticeship wage (months)
'Butterfly' sewing machine	187	6.0
'Phoenix' bicycle	156	5.0
'Shanghai' wristwatch	120	4.0
Total	463	15.0
Savings needed after food*	—	37.5

Note: * Based on China's urban Engel coefficient of 60 per cent; National Bureau of Statistics, *Statistical Year Book, 2012*, ch. 10.

Source: Ling Zhijun, *Lishi Buzai Paihuai* (*History, No More Hesitation*) (Beijing: People's Press, 1997), p. 99.

that a sewing machine cost six months' pay without taking the cost of food into account, a bicycle five months' pay, and a wristwatch four months' pay. Realistically, these three humble items cost an ordinary urban worker three years' worth of savings.

Now, years of scarcity and high prices of consumer manufactures created strong incentives for the rural sector to take matters into their own hands and undertake the task of manufacturing in villages and towns and hence ushered in a unique episode of 'urban substitution industrialisation' (USI) in China.

The confidence of the rural sector was deeply rooted in its past when large quantities of silk and cotton were manufactured in rural China and exported overseas. Deng Xiaoping's new guideline to 'increase real GDP and consumer goods',[98] which was accompanied by government deregulation of wage-goods rationing and price controls in the early 1980s, could not have come at a better time.

With the Maoist institutional barrier demolished, China entered an era of village industrial enterprises – or township and village enterprises (TVEs) – spontaneously rising to meet new consumer demand from within the rural sector itself.[99] Labour employment data as a proxy for production commitment in table 3.7 demonstrate the overwhelming preference of TVEs for manufacturing over more traditional rural production undertakings (building construction,

Table 3.7. Employment Structures, TVEs versus SOEs, % All Workers, 1978–2000

Sector	Manufacturing	Construction	Mining	Farming
1. TVEs				
1978	79.5*	12.2	4.4	3.9
1985	76.5*	16.8	4.2	2.4
1990	78.2*	15.7	4.2	1.9
1995	72.9*	22.0	4.0	1.2
2000	62.6*	31.5	4.2	1.7
TVE average	*74.0**	*19.6*	*4.2*	*2.2*
2. SOEs				
1978	57.5†	10.5	13.8	18.2
1985	60.1†	11.0	14.3	14.7
1990	62.2†	9.9	14.4	13.5
1995	61.6†	11.2	15.4	11.7
2000	52.2†	13.7	16.5	17.5
SOE average	*58.7†*	*11.3*	*14.9*	*15.1*

Note: * Mainly in light industry. † Mainly in heavy industry.
Source: National Bureau of Statistics, *Statistical Year Book, 2003*, ch. 5.

mining, and farming) by a 74 to 26 split on average. Such a manufacturing bias was largely dictated by a prolonged 'industrial goods famine' in the rural sector. Thus, rural communities had to produce manufactures for themselves. In comparison, SOEs had a 58.7 to 41.3 split on average. It means that TVEs were even more specialised in manufacturing than SOEs.

It is worth knowing that new rural industrial enterprises were the first market-oriented businesses on Chinese soil since the 1950s, despite a lack of property rights protection.[100] Usually, they operated highly autonomously under a shareholding arrangement between villagers (often local clans) and external business partners to lower risks as well as technical barriers to entry.[101] It was all about market pragmatism.

The result was USI on a massive scale in post-Mao China.[102] It all began in rural Jiangsu Province. Regarding factor input, within a decade from 1978 to 1988, non-farming investment grew 15-fold (31.1 per cent annually); the number of rural industrial workers more than doubled (7 per cent per year); and non-farming labour productivity increased 9-fold (24.6 per cent per year).[103] In terms of output, rural manufacturing accounted for 68 per cent of Jiangsu's total GDP, not to mention another 15 per cent of provincial GDP also coming from rural services.[104] With 83 per cent of GDP coming from the 'rural but non-farming' economy (an oxymoron), Jiangsu heralded a new development path which did not exist in economics textbooks, nor did it come from any *ex ante* economic planning.

China-wide, from 1980 to 2000, the total number of TVEs multiplied 14-fold (a 14.4 per cent increase per year) to 21.1 million. The number of workers these firms hired more than trebled (growing 6.2 per cent per year) to 128.2 million, twice the size of Mao's industrial workforce of 59 million in 1974. During the same period (1980–2000), total revenues of TVEs grew 18-fold (29.7 per cent per year in current prices) to RMB 1,078.3 billion; and their net profit increased nearly six-fold (22.2 per cent per year in current prices) to RMB 648.2 billion.[105]

In this context, working in rural factories became a new employment trend. Workers stayed rural but quit farming.[106] By 1984, about 100 million rural workers had been exclusively engaged in local manufacturing and services. Given that in 1985 China's total rural working population was 332.4 million,[107] and a third of the rural workforce no longer farmed at all, the number of manufacturing and services workers reached 125 million versus a total rural working population of 353.6 million in 1990.[108] This growth peaked around the year 2000 at 128 million out of a total of 355.8 million rural workers, translating into a non-farming share of 36 per cent.[109] Deng Xiaoping was impressed, saying that 'growth in township and village enterprises takes place in the manufacturing industry . . . and [they] provide fifty per cent of rural labour with employment opportunities. Peasants no longer move to cities. Rather, they have built a large number of rural towns.'[110]

In addition, from 1985 onwards, the output of TVEs spilled over China's borders into overseas markets, known as 'opening domestic and international markets simultaneously'.[111] In doing so, USI was now fused together with 'export-oriented industrialisation' (EOI), or a rural 'USI-EOI combo' at a time when China's urban sector had not yet woken up. More growth was to be generated by this symbolic USI-EOI mix. In the beginning, in 1985, the total value of TVE export sales was RMB 4.9 billion. It increased 10-fold to RMB 48.5 billion in 1990; and 10-fold again to RMB 539.5 billion in 1995 until it reached RMB 887 billion in 2000, which was now 180 times their 1985 level (on average 41.4 per cent a year for 15 years).[112] In another account, in the period 1988–99, China's exports grew at 13 per cent per annum. This figure was overshadowed by TVEs whose exports grew at an annual rate of 28 per cent on their own.[113] Alas.

In a nutshell, by 1998 TVEs were responsible for 20 per cent of government tax revenues, 28 per cent of China's total GDP,[114] and 35 per cent of China's exports (in value).[115] In 2000, at their peak, TVEs were responsible for 47 per cent of China's total industrial output and 48 per cent of China's total exports.[116] So, the rural 'USI-EOI combo' really worked.

The wonders of TVEs persuaded Professor Fei Xiaotong (1910–2005), the LSE-trained Chinese sociologist, to declare USI as an alternative developmental model for industrialisation and modernisation in a large economy to differentiate China from all known models.[117] In 1985, he explained how capital accumulation and industrial growth took place the Chinese way:[118]

> Industrial growth needs primitive accumulation of capital. . . . [To build up their industrial capital] Chinese farmers like those in Changle County [in Fujian] have worked without pay for two long years. It worked.
>
> Nowadays [1985], the rural sectoral industrial output value in Jiangsu matches the total industrial output value of the entire province back in the 1970s. This year it has even surpassed that of Shanghai![119]

7. Surge of the Urban Private Sector

But what followed was not a TVE-centred economic system, as one might hope for. Instead, TVEs began to stagnate around the year 2000 and declined thereafter.[120] A new development came from the *bona fide* private sector with well-defined property rights. China's growth now moved back to the economics textbook.

It all began during the 1990s when TVEs attracted all the media attention. During that decade, the number of sole traders increased 12.8 per cent per year; the number of workers hired by outright private firms, 28.1 per cent per year; and the number of workers hired by foreign firms (categorised as 'private' in China), 31.7 per cent per year.[121] Some provinces became fully privatised. For example, in 2000, the private sector in Zhejiang controlled 80 per cent of all assets and provided over 90 per cent of jobs, sales, and profits.[122] The private economy made Zhejiang the second wealthiest province in China (only three per cent lower than Guangdong).[123]

One obvious factor was differences in business leadership between formally private firms and TVEs. The former were typically urban, educated, and well-connected. They often had a 'desirable' social background even by Maoist standards. In other words, these people were elites, a strata of society that TVEs could not access. Politically, according to a 1999 survey, the vast majority (over 80 per cent) of China's newly emerged private entrepreneurs had a family status of either 'workers' (*gong*) or 'peasants' (*nong*) back in 1949 when Mao took over the mainland. Descendants of the previous landlords and bourgeoisie were negligible among the new business elite. As such, these old 'undesirable classes' had been effectively 'liquidated' *à la* the Marxian model.[124] So, the post-1980 entrepreneurs came as a brand-new capitalist class.

This new social class expanded rapidly. In 2000, it had four million members.[125] Just three years later, in 2003, this figure had doubled to eight million.[126] In another account, China's millionaires grew at the speed of one million per year after China joined the World Trade Organization (WTO) in 2001.[127]

But unlike TVEs, this urban private sector was closely connected to the party-state. To begin with, Communist Party membership became one's political capital to boost a capitalist business. The rule of the thumb was that individuals became capitalists more easily if they were party members.[128] According to the 2003 official statistics, 70 per cent of capitalists in China were party members prior to their business successes.[129] In another account, of six million private firm-owners, four million were former government officials.[130]

Given that there had been no 'old money' or 'family silver' left after the 1950s, the capital of new capitalists had to come from the current economy.[131] The main source of the initial capital (conventionally called 'primitive capital accumulation') came from the state sector, often via state-to-private price arbitrage.[132] Unfortunately, information on this practice is scarce. That said, it has been estimated that the total sum of state-to-private price arbitrage benefitting individuals was RMB 400 billion in 1988, equivalent to 20 per cent of China's GDP.[133] Such a capital source was a huge advantage that TVEs were never able to access.

Not surprisingly, from 2001 onwards, ruling party membership became more inclusive: capitalists were allowed to stay on (as existing members) or join in (as new members). A state-run China-wide survey reads:[134]

> [Our survey indicates that] the number of Communist Party members has visibly increased among the class of private entrepreneurs. . . . This is the result of large numbers of party officials and state-owned enterprise managers joining in the private sector since 1992. This in a way reflects an improved political status of the private sector.
>
> On the other hand, the number of Communist Party members has noticeably declined among industrial workers. . . . This shows the deteriorating political status of the working class and its alienation from the party.

Similarly, from the 1980s to the 1990s, the proportion of workers and farmers in the National People's Congress (the 'Congress' in China) declined by 60 per cent and 62 per cent, respectively.[135] Thus, the CCP and PRC were no longer what they had claimed to be prior to 1980. Also, the principle of *cui bono* applies here: who benefits most?

Now under the crossfire of TVEs and private and politically well-connected firms, the state sector retreated. By 2000, non-state workers accounted for a massive 92.5 per cent of all employed workers (354 million out of 383 million), leaving the state sector with a tiny share of 7.5 per cent (29 million).[136]

Astonishingly, when the state sector laid off 48.1 million of its workers (70 per cent of Mao's industrial workforce), it was the private sector that came to the rescue by creating a total of 182.1 million vacancies, offsetting state job losses by 134.0 million new jobs.[137] This overcompensation of job losses kept China's unemployment rate extraordinarily low: 2.7 per cent from 1980 to 2000 during the post-Mao take-off.[138] This was truly remarkable compared with the appalling unemployment rates suffered by former Soviet Bloc countries during their reforms.

In the process, for the first time in China's history a majority of industrial workers were qualified as 'waged labourers' (or proletarians) according to the orthodox definition of Karl Marx.[139] Looking back, for 50 years (*c.*1927–77) Mao and his party could not make China's rural population 'proletarianised' despite 'class wars', purges, and famine deaths. The market did so peacefully in 20 years (from 1980 to 2000).[140] Ironically, by offering seemingly unlimited new jobs, the capitalist economy also saved the failing communist system in China.

The party seemed grateful and officially upgraded the status of the non-state-owned economy from 'a supplement to the national economy' to 'an important component of the national economy'.[141] On the theoretical front, Party General Secretary Jiang Zemin (1926–2022) announced twice, in 1997 and 2002, that business people were citizens with full rights and that their capital was entitled to yield profits.[142] This marked a Faustian U-turn from the Marxian labour theory of value to economic liberalism.

New capitalists were soon encouraged to join the party as 'red-hat capitalists' without worrying about their obvious political mismatch with Marxist fundamentals.[143] By 2001, 100,000 capitalists had joined the party.[144] By 2003, over 9,000 of them had entered parliaments at various levels, called People's Congresses (*renda*); and another 32,000 served as policy consultants in the party-run Political Consultative Conferences (*zhengxie*).[145]

But why and how did Mao's urban industrial sector fail to respond to the market's call for consumer manufactures? The answer lies in both the technical and institutional nature of that sector. Mao's moribund urban industrial sector was dominated by heavy industry with huge sunk capital and often outdated technology which was either unsuited to be converted to produce consumer products or unable to produce any goods efficiently for the market. Mao's urban industrial sector was left alone as an 'industrial island' (or more appropriately an 'industrial desert island').[146] So, during the 1980s, the rural sector took the matter into its own hands and produced consumer manufactures inside the rural sector to meet the new market demand from new rural incomes,[147] hence the episode of TVEs and USI.

As USI put pressure on SOEs with large quantities of competitive products, in terms of price and quality, large numbers of SOEs were simply closed down. Some turned coat, joining village and township firms to survive. Cities once again lost to the countryside, this time in economic warfare. Even Deng Xiaoping agreed and told his party that 'our reforms began in the countryside. . . . With our rural experience with reforms, we now have turned our attention to urban economic reforms.'[148]

To be fair, some attempts were made to save the frail SOEs. The first step was a 'managers' responsibility system' from 1978 to 1993, copied from the rural reforms. It did not work well. Rather, it caused double crises of hyperinflation and high urban unemployment. What followed from 1993 to 2003 was a decade-long policy of surgical reforms, known as 'keeping conglomerates with the state and letting small and medium enterprises go' (*zhuada fangxiao*). The scheme kept only 512 SOEs intact and privatised over 10,000 SOEs, which together equated to RMB 6 billion in assets and 400,000 workers.[149] This boosted the strength of the rising urban private sector by a considerable margin which slowed down the expansion of TVEs in relative terms at least.

Meanwhile, the state's share in the economy dwindled. The central government budget-cum-investment – once the prime force of fixed capital investment in the economy – shrank from 28.2 per cent per year (in 1980) to a mere 3.1 per cent per year (in 1995), a decline of 15.9 per cent per annum.[150]

The twists and turns are highlighted in figure 3.2, where fixed capital investment is used as a proxy for the strength of each sector in the economy. Firstly, China was not short of capital, as its main source of capital investment (about 90 per cent) was domestic. External (foreign) investment was insignificant. So, China's alleged openness is now questionable as far as capital investment is concerned. Secondly, there was a zero-sum relationship between state and non-state investment. After 2000, most capital investment came from the 'non-state sector', fully compatible with the decline of economic Maoism.

There is a caveat. Since 2010, there has been a new type of investment called 'shareholding capital investment controlled by the state' (*guoyou konggu*) of which a substantial percentage (often 50 per cent) of the capital stock came from non-state sources. With this device, the state could ride on the non-state sector for large amounts of capital. In 2011, when this new practice first came to light, state-controlled investment through shareholding was RMB 30 trillion, 3.7 times the official state investment of RMB 8.2 trillion in the same year.[151] In 2017, state-controlled investment became RMB 63.2 trillion while official investment was RMB 13.9 trillion, a ratio of 4.5 to 1.[152] This was, however, the last time such data were published. Instead, only growth rates of state-controlled shareholdings are available.

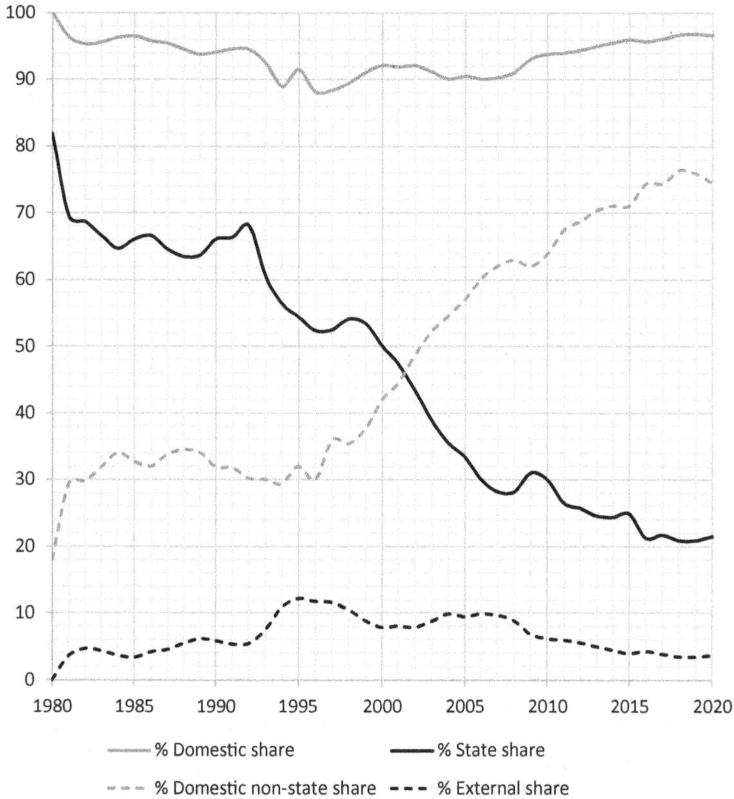

Figure 3.2. Sectorial Fixed Capital Investment, % Total Value, 1980–2020

Note: Data are in percentage shares, current prices. The years 1993 to 2003 were dominated by the policy of 'keeping conglomerates with the state and letting small and medium enterprises go' (*zhuada fangxiao*).

Sources are available in the separate section of 'Figure Sources'.

8. End Results: Changes in Economic Performance

The first aspect to look at should be people's livelihoods as these are what Deng's reforms hinged on. In addition, there is China's traditional wisdom that 'food is people's heaven' (*min yi shi wei tian*). So, agriculture is the first to be examined. More specifically, output volumes, which determine people's food intake, are preferred to values. They are also hard to falsify.

In figure 3.3, growth in per capita output volumes is divided into two groups: basic staples (grain, cotton, and vegetable oil) and

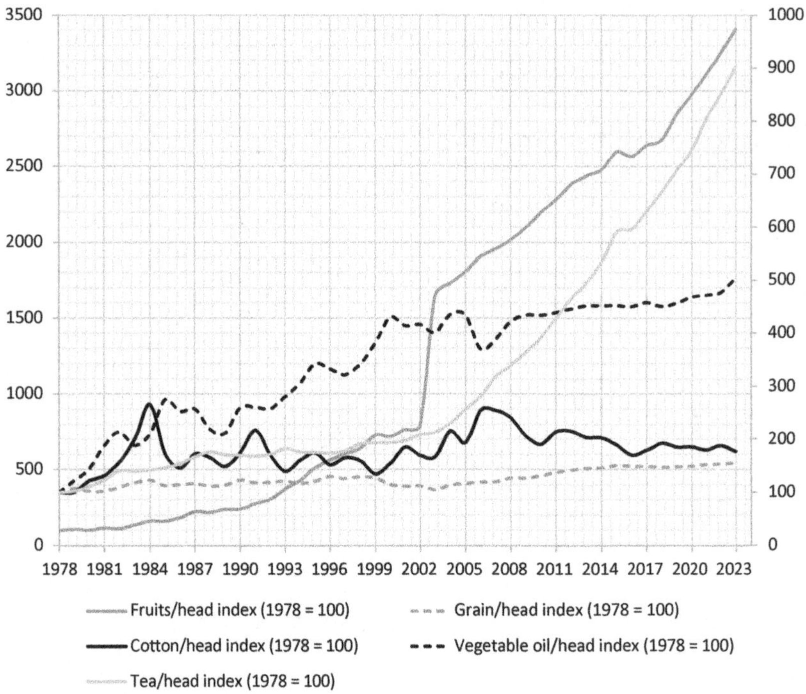

Figure 3.3. Per Capita Agricultural Output Volumes, Indexes, 1978–2023

Note: Left Y-axis: Fruits/head growth as an outlier. Right Y-axis: All the non-fruit growth. Growth in key agricultural goods was lethargic until the end of Mao's rule. Tea and fruits are typical 'price and income elastic' commodities. Their growth indicates a rise in disposable incomes in society. For crude figures of GDP as the second-order evidence, see Appendix 5, figure A–5.1.

Sources are available in the separate section of 'Figure Sources'.

luxuries (tea and fruit). Grain and raw cotton grew at merely 1 per cent and 1.4 per cent per year, respectively. Vegetable oil did a bit better at 3.7 per cent per year. Fast growth was achieved for tea (5 per cent per year) and fruit (8.2 per cent per year). Being 'price and income elastic' commodities, more tea and fruit outputs reflect higher disposable incomes and higher living standards in society.

Regarding the driving forces behind the good performance in output volumes, the role of capital investment loomed large, while the contribution of labour declined. Available data show that among the four production factors of capital, materials (such as fertilisers), land, and labour, capital contributed 13 per cent to output, materials 3.3 per cent, and land 1.7 per cent. However, labour's contribution was negative (–2.4 per cent).[153] It means that extra labour input would reduce output. Thus, China had finally departed from its traditional 'labour-intensive farming' model and embarked on a 'capital-intensive' voyage.

Now, moving onto industry. In terms of per capita output volumes, six key industrial products all had genuine 'great leaps forward' after 1980. Taking 1952 as the base year, figure 3.4 shows that take-off occurred after 1980. In per capita terms, by 2023, paper production rose 163-fold (at 7.3 per cent a year) due to a surge in education expenditure. Output of chemical fertilisers, vital for agricultural yields, increased 582-fold (at 9.3 per cent a year). Oil production grew 201-fold, or 7.8 per cent a year, to fuel modernisation (although growth was flat after 1980 due to China's limited proven oil reserves). Pig iron, steel, and cement output grew 180-fold (7.5 per cent a year), 304-fold

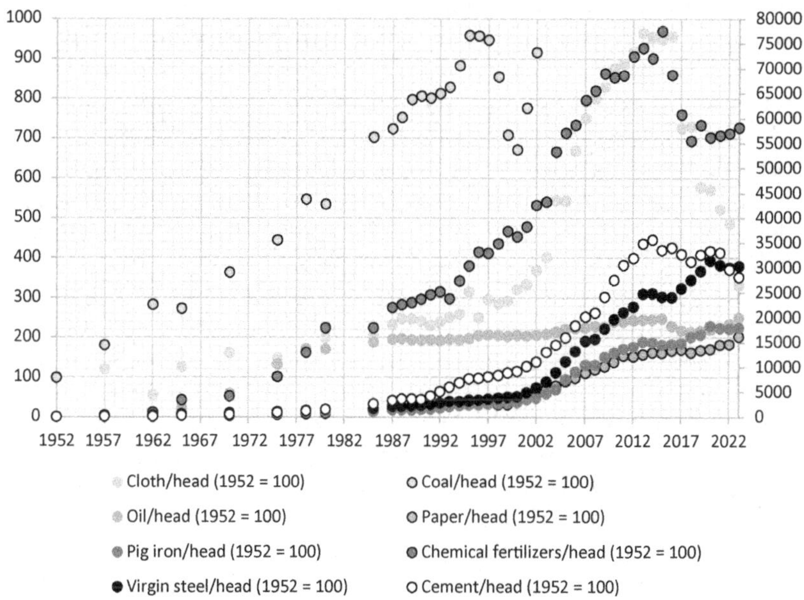

Figure 3.4. Per Capita Industrial Output Volumes, Indexes, 1952–2023

Note: Left Y-axis: Slower index growth in coal and cloth per head. Right Y-axis: Faster index growth achieved by the remaining types. Growth of key industrial goods was lethargic until the end of Mao's rule. Per capita growth in coal (energy) and cloth (daily consumption) output has remained lethargic after Mao. Growth in oil production flattened out after 1980. This can only be revealed by output volumes without the noise of prices (inevitable with the GDP approach).

Sources are available in the separate section of 'Figure Sources'.

(8.4 per cent a year), and 282-fold (8.3 per cent a year), respectively, to support a construction boom. But growth in coal production (27-fold, or 4.8 per cent a year despite China's vast coal deposits) and cloth production (33-fold, or 5 per cent a year) was weaker.[154]

Last but not the least, the rural population declined at a rate of 1.7 per cent per year, from 82.1 per cent of China's total in 1978 to below 50 per cent in 2011 for the first time in China's history.[155] So, China's demographic structure finally became 'modern' for the first time, too.

9. Evaluation of Deng's Reforms

Undoubtedly, China changed enormously after Deng Xiaoping took over the party leadership and made the best use of the party-state. Even so, Deng's deeds should be subject to the very same evaluation of 'practice as the sole testing criterion for truth or fallacy', which successfully stripped Mao of his self-declared ownership of 'truth'.[156]

To conceptualise the essence of the post-Mao changes, Deng's reforms created (1) high-quality human capital via higher education, (2) high-performance agriculture via household landholding, and (3) a high-saving society via improved household incomes. Jointly these changes rejuvenated China's national economy. China finally departed from Mao's growth cul-de-sac, which kept Mao's China below the growth track record of the Qing.

But the journey of reforms was far more complicated than self-propelled tertiary education and private farming. USI with TVEs was an unexpected growth path. It required some 'social engineering' to put seemingly unrelated factors together and make them work in unison. That was a miracle. Then came the bombshell of 'red capitalists' with the seal of approval from the largest communist party in the world. Even more bizarre.

Figure 3.5 shows that with Deng's reforms, not only did China finally outperform its Qing benchmark, which had cast a shadow over the economy for 150 long years from 1830 to 1980, but it also redeemed growth dysfunctions under Maoism by achieving a GDP per capita of US$1,000 from the meagre pre-reform level of a mere US$190 per head. With it, for the first time since 1949, China departed from being a product-scarce economy and became a product-rich economy again. In that regard, Deng was the greatest economic developer in China since the 1830s.

On the household front, for the first time since 1950 ordinary Chinese had disposable income for consumer goods without state

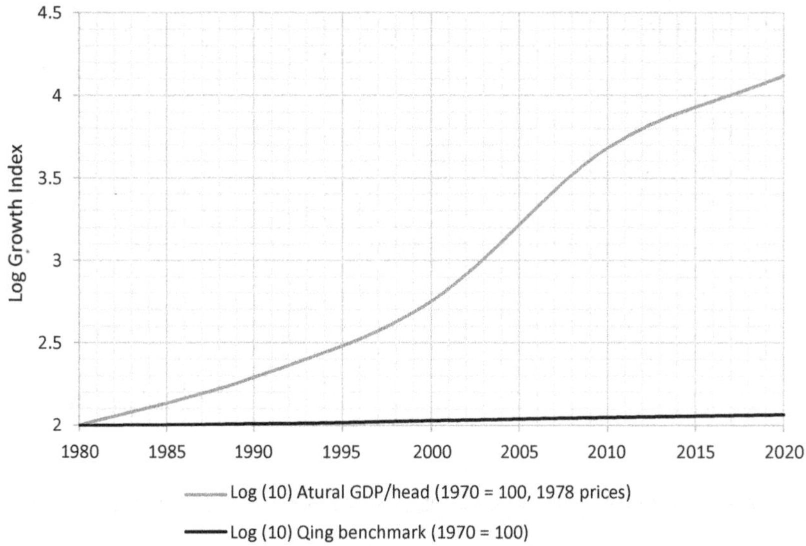

Figure 3.5. Qing Benchmark versus Actual Growth, 1970–2020

Note: (1) Due to the huge gap in magnitude, logarithmical numbers are used ($\log_{10}$) here. Y-axis begins with Log_{10} (2) = 100. (2) Crude GDP numbers are used on this occasion as no other aggregate growth information is available. (3) For the Qing Benchmark, see figure 1.9. (4) The constant price is based on National Bureau of Statistics, *Statistical Year Book, 2023*, ch. 3.

Sources are available in the separate section of 'Figure Sources'.

rationing. Figure 3.6 shows a 60 per cent decline in households' Engel coefficient (the food bill as a percentage of household income) for both the rural and urban sectors. A decline is desirable because the lower the food bill, the higher the disposable income, given that food consumption is more or less fixed due to its price and income inelasticity.[157] More interestingly, in terms of speed, the rural Engel coefficient declined faster than its urban counterpart by 0.2 per cent a year, something that had never happened before.

Meanwhile, on the other side of the same coin, China's household consumption level (including food) increased four-fold in both the rural and urban sectors. Again, rural growth moved ahead that of China's once privileged cities until the late 1990s (figure 3.7).

In addition, household savings became possible for the first time after 1949. Mao's sumptuary regime of maximum austerity left ordinary people with little savings as 'incomes of individuals and families were pushed to the subsistence level and citizens lost much of their capacity as the main force to perform saving. . . . The Maoist state

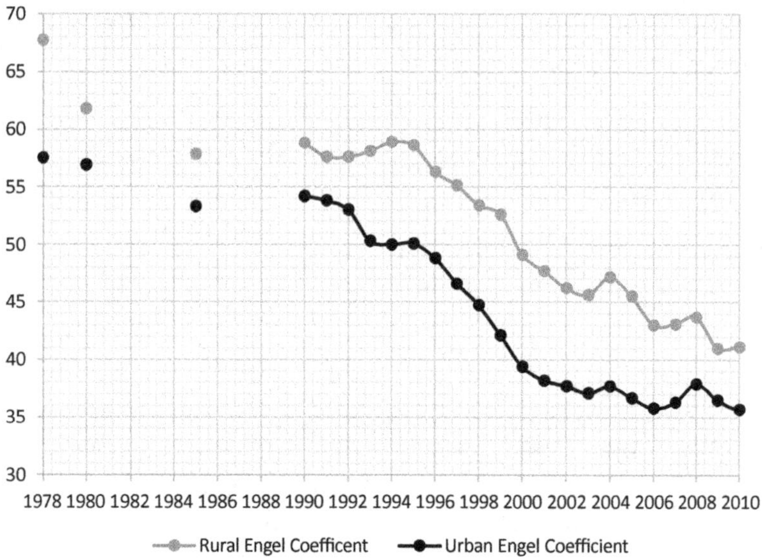

Figure 3.6. Decline in Engel Coefficient, Rural versus Urban, 1978–2010

Note: China's urban Engel coefficient in 1930 across 17 cities was 56.3,[158] better than its Maoist counterpart in 1978. Little progress was made from 1949 to 1978.

Sources are available in the separate section of 'Figure Sources'.

became the sole saver and sole capital accumulator'.[159] The notion that Maoism 'made the state rich but people poor' (*guofu minqiong*) is well supported by data.[160] This dire situation was reversed after Deng's reforms, seen from the dramatic shift in the centre of gravity in bank deposits (% shares):[161]

	State deposits	**Household deposits**
1979	76.5	23.5
1995	30.0	70.0

In absolute terms, per capita private savings increased 53-fold from 1980 to 2010 with an annual growth rate of 14.1 per cent (see figure 2.6), faster than China's GDP growth during the same period. This facilitated a 'domestic capital investment model' for growth to be sustained.

Demographically, China became a different country, too. This comes as a bonus, as Deng Xiaoping did not expect rapid urbanisation as part of his reforms. Large-scale city-bound migration took place in the 1990s despite the notorious internal migration controls. In 1995, 80 million people were regarded as part of a 'floating population'

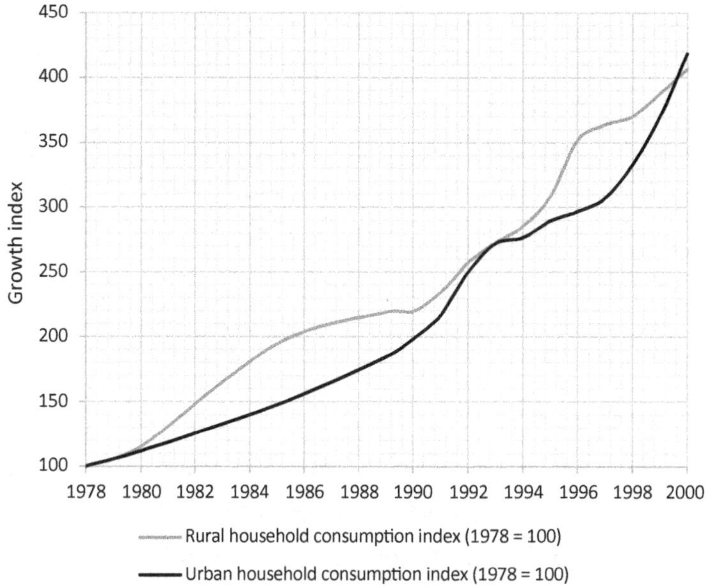

Figure 3.7. Rise in Household Consumption, Rural versus Urban, 1978–2000

Note: The constant price is based on National Bureau of Statistics, *Statistical Year Book, 2023*, ch. 3.

Sources are available in the separate section of 'Figure Sources'.

(*liudong renkou*), a synonym for 'city-bound rural emigrants'.[162] According to the 2000 national census, 88 million rural people had successfully settled in cities.[163] The real figure was likely many times larger due to the general ambivalence of the party-state towards the urban masses.[164] In this context, the best measure is in fact 'de-ruralisation' to show progress made since the Maoist past (when over 80 per cent of the total population was rural). Figure 3.8 shows that the share of the population that was rural was slashed from 82 per cent in 1978 to 50 per cent in 2010. The decline was 61 per cent with a de-ruralisation rate of 1.5 per cent per year.

There was both a 'pull factor' and a 'push factor' that made rural people willing to leave their home villages: (1) better employment opportunities and choices, (2) higher incomes, (3) better public goods provision such as law and order, education, and health care, and (4) compatibility of workers from TVEs for urban factories. To get rich and become urban (and thus 'modern') became a real possibility for ordinary rural folk.

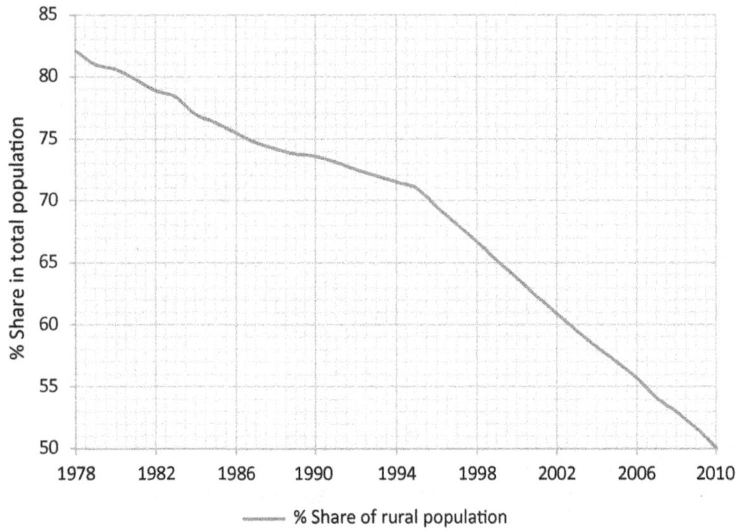

Figure 3.8. De-ruralisation, 1978–2010

Sources are available in the separate section of 'Figure Sources'.

So, China was transformed economically.[165] During the 2000s, in terms of material life, ordinary Chinese had never had it so good.

Even so, one cannot attribute all the virtuous changes to a state-led growth model (which is related to but not identical with Deng's reforms), simply because state input was often too small, as in the case of USI which was clearly market-led with little state interference. Similarly, unprecedented high enrolments in tertiary education took place without state preferential budgetary treatment. Here, the behaviour of Deng's reformist state was in line with the Qing 'night-watchman state' that tolerated ordinary people's choices, initiatives, and actions.

As far as 'opening China up' is concerned (which was central to Deng's reforms), inbound FDI, which presumably embodied advanced technology, did not really explode. China's foreign trade, which embodied less advanced technology, did. We leave this paradox here for the time being. The massive growth has stunned the world in the past 45 years. Data in figure 3.9 show that from 1978 to 2023 China's total foreign trade values increased 260-fold; total export values, 225-fold, and import values, 152-fold. The corresponding annual growth rates were 13.2 per cent for total foreign trade, 12.8 per cent for exports, and 11.8 per cent for imports.[166]

Additionally, as China rebuilt its product-rich economy, foreign

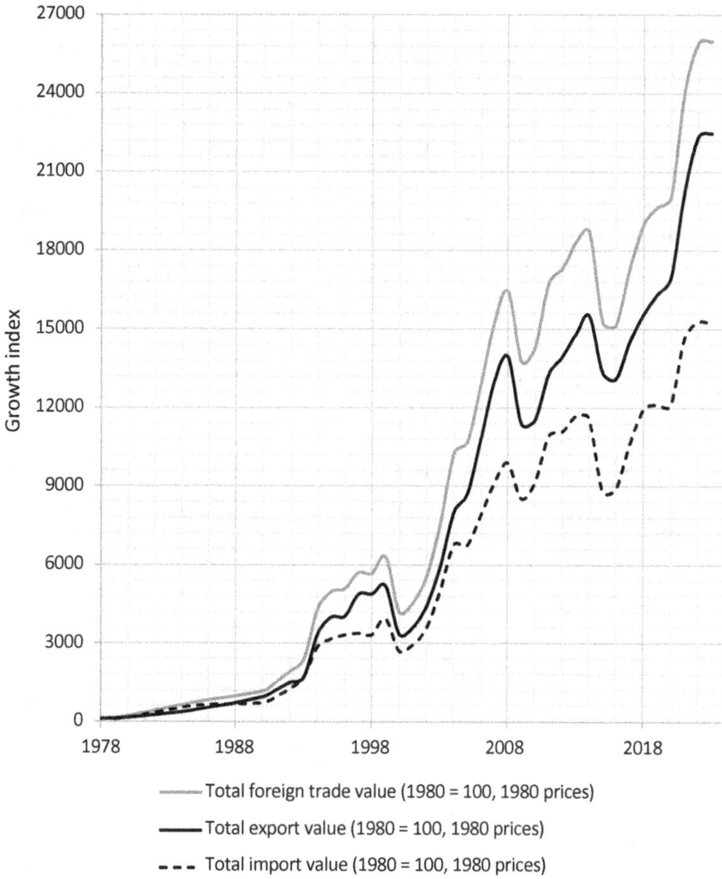

Figure 3.9. Growth Indexes for Foreign Trade, 1978–2023

Note: Not much was going on before 1978 due to Mao's autarky. The constant price in RMB is based on National Bureau of Statistics, *Statistical Year Book, 2023*, ch. 3.

Sources are available in the separate section of 'Figure Sources'.

trade regained its position in the economy. Meanwhile, exports were switched back from primary products – a norm of Mao's time – to manufactures which had made China famous during the Ming-Qing period.

Two decades after the reforms first started, China's foreign trade values reached US$474.3 billion in 2000, equivalent to 44 per cent of China's total GDP.[167] Fifty-three per cent of China's exports went to the United States, the European Union, and Japan that year.[168] In another account, from 1978 to 2000, the total value of China's foreign trade increased 110-fold (from RMB 35.5 billion to RMB 3,927.3 billion in current prices). Fast growth made China a fierce competitor at the top level: in terms of foreign trade values (imports and exports), China surpassed Japan in 2004, Germany in 2009, and the United States in 2013, climbing to the very top of the world league table.

China finally came out of its Maoist agrarian trap and became a 'Workshop of the World'. In 2000, 90 per cent of China's exports were manufactures.[169] In this context, China joining the World Trade Organization (WTO) in 2001 was logical.[170] 'Made in China' seemed unstoppable.

Data in figure 3.10 indicate that (1) FDI as a whole accounted for a tiny and declining share (6.5 per cent on average) in China's total capital investment portfolio,[171] and (2) by and large ethnically non-Chinese investors led the field of in-bound FDI with a share of

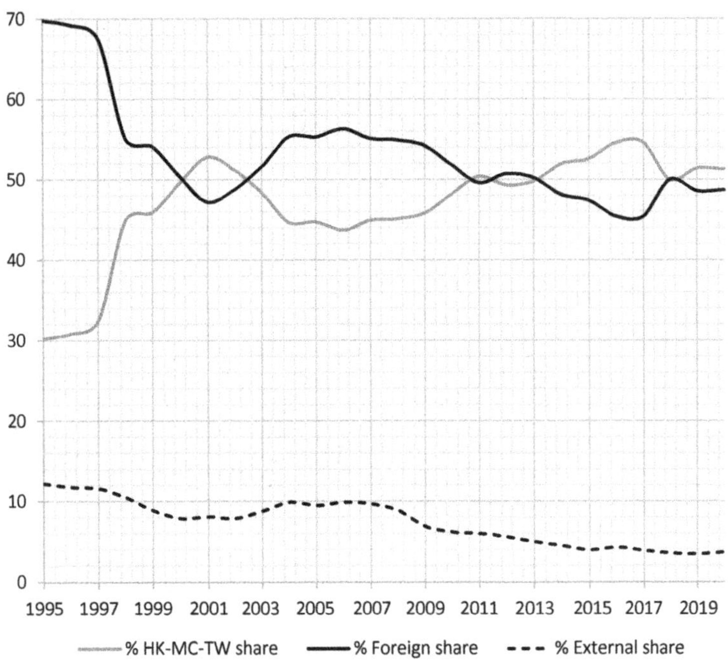

Figure 3.10. Capital Investment in China by Category, 1995–2020 (%)

Note: HK, Hong Kong; MC, Macao; TW, Taiwan.
Foreign share: Ethnically non-Chinese investors. External share: Investors outside PRC judiciary.

Sources are available in the separate section of 'Figure Sources'.

50–70 per cent of the total from 1980 to 2020, while ethnic Chinese took the lead only twice, in 2001 and 2015–19. This challenges the commonly held notion that FDI in general, and FDI from ethnic Chinese in particular, formed an important head source of China's new growth.

Moreover, the importance of special economic zones (SEZs) appears to be illusory. Prior to the 2008 Global Financial Crisis, exports from SEZs fell consistently behind either their FDI intake (as an input) or their GDP (as an output) in twelve observations out of a total of fourteen. According to the data in table 3.8, starting from 1978, annual GDP growth took the lead in Shenzhen. The role of FDI was prominent in Shantou and Hainan in annual terms. There was no persistent growth leadership of exports across all SEZs, as exports took the lead only twice, once in Zhuhai and once in Xiamen. Naturally, one expects a time lag between FDI growth and export growth, or between GDP growth and export growth. This problem can be resolved by annual growth rates that iron out time lags.

In this regard, SEZs, the flagship of China's opening up, actually practised 'import-oriented industrialisation' (IOI) which caused concerns at the highest level of the CCP and the PRC in 1985 and 1987.[172] On 1 August 1985, Deng told his party that

> We have only just begun to turn our SEZs from being import-oriented to export-oriented. SEZs produce too few exportable products. As long as Shenzhen does not break this dead clock, it does not fulfil its mission.[173]

Again, on 12 June 1987, Deng complained that

> It has taken Shenzhen seven to eight years to turn its import-orientation to export-orientation. . . . Now, the rule seems that if over 50 per cent of Shenzhen's output is exported, it breaks even with its foreign currency balance of payments.[174]

It becomes clear that the importance of SEZs should not be overplayed. Much of the credit of China's EOI goes to domestic dynamics, in particular, to China's rural-based USI until the year 2000. Statistically, SEZs played a minor part either due to SEZs' inability to turn imported technology into profitable sales overseas or owing to SEZs' real mission for upgrading China's outdated domestic technology. If so, as a national growth strategy for post-Mao China, the 'SEZ-EOI combo' was not as effective as it is often claimed to be due to a lack of supporting evidence.

Table 3.8. SEZ Growth Engines, 1978–2008

City/Year	FDI index*	GDP index†	Export index*	Annual rate comparison
Shenzhen				
1978	100	100	—	—
1990	7,117 (42.7% per year)	8,585 (44.9% per year)	100§	*GDP > FDI*
2000	35,794 (30.6% per year)	109,350 (37.4% per year)	425 (15.5% per year)	*GDP > FDI > Export*
2008	71,708 (24.5% per year)	280,600 (30.3% per year)	2,010 (16.2% per year)	*GDP > FDI > Export*
Zhuhai				
1978	—	100§	—	—
1990	100	1,971 (28.2% per year)	100	—
2000	1,180 (28.0% per year)	15,781 (25.9% per year)	720 (21.8% per year)	*FDI > GDP > Export*
2008	1,648 (16.8% per year)	33,333 (21.4% per year)	3,940 (22.6% per year)	*Export > GDP > FDI*
Xiamen				
1978	—	100	100	—
1990	100§	1,190 (22.9% per year)	975 (20.9% per year)	*GDP > Export*
2000	1,425 (30.4% per year)	10,456 (23.5% per year)	7,375 (21.6% per year)	*FDI > GDP > Export*
2008	2,701 (20.1% per year)	23,217 (19.9% per year)	33,750 (21.4% per year)	*Export > FDI > GDP*
Shantou				
1978	100	100	100	—
1990	6,093 (40.8% per year)	671 (17.2% per year)	336 (10.6% per year)	*FDI > GDP > Export*
2000	10,286 (23.4% per year)	4,167 (18.5% per year)	1,040 (11.2% per year)	*FDI > GDP > Export*
2008	10,658 (16.8% per year)	6,676 (15.0% per year)	1,320 (9.0% per year)	*FDI > GDP > Export*
Hainan				
1978	100	100	—	—
1990	100,600 (77.9% per year)	353 (11.1% per year)	100§	*FDI > GDP*
2000	430,800 (46.3% per year)	1816 (14.1% per year)	170 (5.4% per year)	*FDI > GDP > Export*
2008	1,120,000 (36.5% per year)	3,665 (12.8% per year)	383 (7.7% per year)	*FDI > GDP > Export*
Summary of 14 sets				'FDI-led' × 8 'GDP-led' × 4 'Export-led' × 2

Note: * In US$, current prices. † In Renminbi, current prices. § The base year is different from the other two categories' base years due to a lack of data. But, as the performances are all judged by an annual average, a different base year will make little difference.

Sources: Hainan Bureau of Statistics, *Hainan Tongji Nianjian, 2008* (*Hainan Statistical Year Book, 2008*) (Beijing: China's Statistics Press, 2008); Shantou Bureau of Statistics, *Shantou Tongji Nianjian, 2008* (*Shantou Statistical Year Book, 2008*) (Beijing: China's Statistics Press, 2008); Shenzhen Bureau of Statistics, *Shenzhen Tongji Nianjian, 2008* (*Shenzhen Statistical Year Book, 2008*) (Beijing: China's Statistics Press, 2008); Xiamen Bureau of Statistics, *Hainan Tongji Nianjian, 2008* (*Xiamen Statistical Year Book, 2008*) (Beijing: China's Statistics Press, 2008); Zhuhai Bureau of Statistics, *Zhuhai Tongji Nianjian, 2007* (*Zhuhai Statistical Year Book, 2008*) (Beijing: China's Statistics Press, 2008).

10. Final Remarks

Looking back to China's rich and long history for inspiration and incentives seems to have been the key to the rapport between Deng's reformist state and the general public. These incentives were deeply embedded in the Chinese traditions, which Mao had aimed to destroy all his life,[175] something that made Ming-Qing China globally attractive as a vibrant and open market (the continuous inflow of foreign silver being a reward).

So, Deng's reforms cleverly hitched a ride on China's traditional incentives. By the year 2000, 85 per cent of China's output was dictated by market forces. The marketisation process took place with minimum fuss and resistance.[176] In this regard, in place of Deng's famous metaphor of 'groping for rocks to cross the river' (*mozhe shitou guohe*), the reality was more like 'being guided by China's good old historical path dependence'.[177]

In comparison, Mao's smattering and dogmatic emulation of Trotskyism (uninterrupted and permanent revolutions) and Lenin-Stalinism (dictatorship) was the root cause of his inevitable failure. Fundamentally, *à la* Marxian historical materialism, Russia that nurtured Trotskyism and Lenin-Stalinism alike was a land where private education for social mobility or private farming for good living standards had been absent until 1861, at which time China had had an entrenched landholding peasantry for over two millennia. In terms of trade, Russia has never been a major exporter of finished industrial products.

— 4 —

STATE CAPACITY AND 'GETTING PRICES WRONG'

1. Institutional Determinism: State Capacity and Its Changes

The state and state capacity are commonly considered crucial to economic growth and development.[1] Unlike in developed countries where states are more accountable, developing countries often find their states manned by privileged officials and dogged by problems with tax collection, public goods provision, and so forth, hence the issue of 'state incapacity'.[2] State incapacity in turn leads to 'state failure', and vice versa.[3] What is intriguing is that two types of states failed in China in the nineteenth and twentieth centuries. First was the Qing *minarchy*. Second was Mao's version of Stalin's despotism.

In most cases of state failure, democracy is absent. Citizens are unable to stop bad policies. Consequently, an economy may be trapped in a developmental cul-de-sac because of an inferior state. This was indeed the case in Mao's China from 1949 to 1976 where systemic state failures occurred, as explained in chapter 2.

The logical choice after 1976 seemed to be democracy. With reforms and opening-up, among the Chinese elite, talking about democracy was no longer a taboo. Some began to discuss a new mantra of 'Western knowledge as the foundation and Chinese knowledge for utility' (*xixue weiti, zhongxue weiyong*),[4] as the antitheses of the nineteenth-century adage of 'Chinese knowledge as the foundation and Western knowledge for utility', a philosophy has already made Taiwan both modern and democratic. Whether it was Chinese knowledge as the foundation (the Qing approach) or Western knowledge as the foundation (Taiwan's approach), Maoism was obsolete. Wan

Li (1916–2015), Deputy Premier of China, asked a soul-searching question:

> Why do so many good things in the world all belong to the bourgeoisie? . . . Why can't we [communists] have freedom and democracy as well?[5]

Zhao Ziyang (1919–2005), Premier of China and General Secretary of the Communist Party, went a step further and stated in 1989 that

> Democracy has become the mainstream in the world. . . . If we do not adopt it, someone else will take the initiative from us [CCP]. I believe that a democracy [in China] is only a matter of time. Instead of being forced to take that route, we are better off to do it voluntarily.[6]

A major setback occurred with the crackdown on the Tiananmen Movement in the capital Beijing and other cities in 1989. In the following decade, however, pro-democracy was tolerated, as long as the party remainded part of the game. Books and journals on democracy were tolerated. Grassroots elections, enterprise internal elections, and the Communist Party internal elections were openly discussed.[7] In 2005, Yu Keping, a party think-tank, published *Incremental Democracy and Good Governance* (*Zengliang Minzhu Yu Shanzhi*), which tackled federalism, republicanism, social harmony, and socio-economic sustainability. A year later, his book with the title *Democracy Is Desirable* (*Minzhu Shige Haodongxi*) became a bestseller.[8] The trend continued. In 2007, Premier Weng Jiabao (1942–) openly declared that

> Democracy, rule of law, liberty, human rights, equality, and fraternity are not capitalism-specific. They are the fruits of civilisation in the long history of the whole world and hence the common values of the whole human race.[9]

And,

> We have in hand two major reforms. One is economic to promote marketisation; and the other is political to nurture a democracy.[10]

If this was not enough, for the first time credit was openly given to the West:

> As an important fruit of political civilisation, democracy belongs to the entire human kind. But we have to admit that objectively Western capitalist countries have contributed to this civilisation more [than other countries].[11]

This new approach was followed gingerly by the Third Plenary of the Seventeenth Communist Party Central Committee which announced in early 2008 that China's current Maoism-charged political system was not in accord with China's newly resumed market economy, people's rights, and social justice.[12] Later that year, in an internal debate in the party, Zhang Chunxian (1953–), Party Secretary of Hunan Province, announced that

> Our first two rounds of ideological emancipation paid attention to giving material entitlement back to our people. Our current round of ideological emancipation should pay more attention to returning the political power to our people together with their material entitlement.[13]

A social experiment in village elections for self-governance was permitted and widespread, appearing to resume the short-lived 1919 'May Fourth' agenda.[14] Preparations were also made to run internal elections for party posts.[15]

Mao's loyal personnel had to go. A path-breaking policy was put in place by Deng to end the life tenure of the party chairmanship (1982) and life tenure of all party and government officials (1984). These measures opened the door for a meritocratic technocracy to run China. A technocracy was something that Mao failed to comprehend all this life.

Jiang Zemin (r.1989–2002) went a step further to advocate for the 'Three Represents' (*sange daibiao*) in 2002, in the wake of China's WTO membership and after Deng's initial growth target of US$1,000 was reached.[16] Jiang's new doctrine redirected the party towards building 'advanced forces of production' (more output), 'advanced culture' (more art), and 'fundamental interests of the majority' (more income). It removed the fangs of Maoism and diluted Deng's conservative 'Four Cardinal Principles'.[17] In that regard, economic reforms made the ruling part malleable.

2. State Capacity Riding on Reforms

A short-hand indicator of state capacity is taxation, hence the term 'fiscal and managerial state capacity'.[18] Towards the end of the Qing period (1644–1911), the state controlled about five per cent of the empire's total GDP,[19] and thus probably fell behind advanced countries at that time by a factor of six on average.[20]

Fast forward to the People's Republic and the altered state capacity in terms of tax-collecting efficiency appears to have hugely 'improved' under Mao's rule with a double-digit share of GDP (a tax-to-GDP ratio of 28.4 per cent on average), in line with the West (G7 and

OECD). After 1980 with Deng's reforms, however, China's tax-to-GDP ratio declined by about half.[21] After 1980, it dropped to 16.9 per cent. In terms of the growth rate, from 1980 to 2020 the share of taxes as percentage of GDP fell 0.011 per cent per year. At first glance, Deng's reforms seem to have reduced the fiscal capacity of the state. But, China's post-Mao fiscal capacity moved in line with the Asia-Pacific norm and Confucius-influenced Taiwan.[22] In between the Qing and reforms, the excessive tax burden alone did not translate into a higher level of state capacity during Mao's time.

But the devil is in the details. Reforms did create unprecedented tax opportunities on a scale and scope China had never seen previously. So, China's chief sources of tax revenue climbed at double-digit rates annually. Data in figure 4.1 show that the fastest increase (370-fold from 1985 to 2020) occurred in consumption tax in conjunction with VAT (36-fold from 1994 to 2020) paid by the general public. This was followed by taxes on imports (67-fold from 1980 to 2020) and taxes on businesses (50-fold from 1985 to 2020). Worryingly, China's domestic consumer demand was restrained by the rise in consumption tax and VAT. In particular, the burden of the consumption tax weighed heavier than all other taxes by a considerable margin. Thus, the increase in the per capita tax burden clearly contradicted what may be suggested by China's tax-to-GDP ratio. A sensible explanation is that under Mao's rule, direct and indirect taxes on personal incomes or on market exchanges did not apply. All the calculation of 'taxes' was hidden by *ex ante* planned allocations of output: the state stipulated 'output surplus targets' and distributed them among urban SOEs. Thus, strictly speaking, 'beforehand deduction' under Mao's rule was just as bad as *ex post* deduction after production was completed.

There was also a tax regime hidden in the housing sector. In the 1950s, private landownership was abolished and banks were nationalised. So, when leaseholds for the residential property market were re-established in 1998,[23] the state was both the *de jure* sole landlord and the sole mortgage dealer in the economy. Ordinary consumers were subjected to artificially high prices for residential properties. On average, building costs accounted for 42 per cent of final sale prices while land contributed the remaining 58 per cent.

Over time the share of construction costs in final sales prices decreased thanks to the productivity of the construction industry. Data in figure 4.2 suggest that sales prices (growing about three-fold) grew around 50 per cent faster than construction costs (growing two-fold). But the benefit of low construction costs was not passed

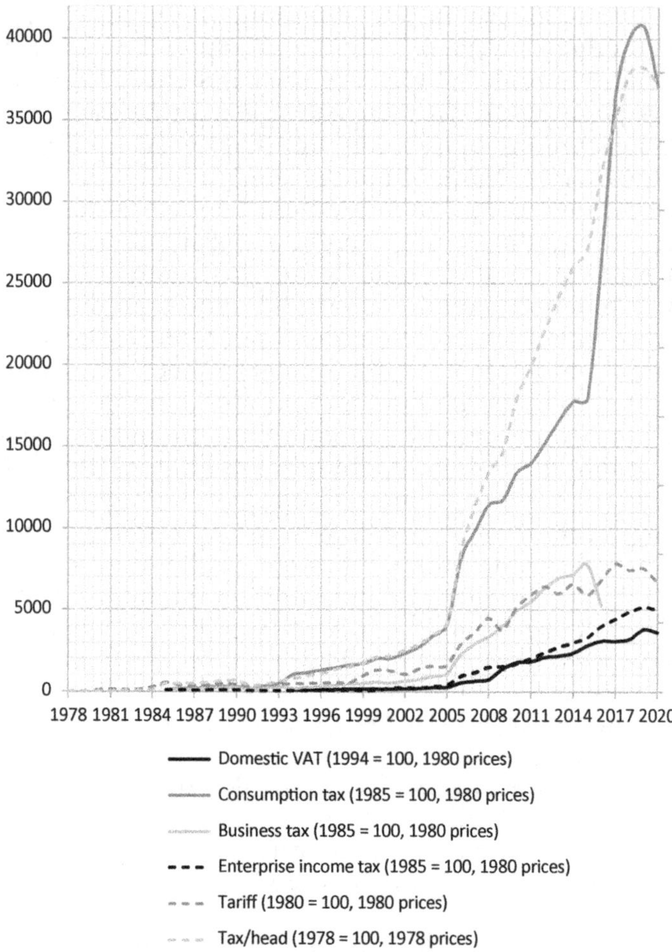

Figure 4.1. Tax Growth Indexes, 1980–2020

Note: Left Y-axis: Growth index for tax revenues. Right Y-axis: Tax/head index (1978 = 100, 1978 prices). The 1978 constant price is based on National Bureau of Statistics, *Statistical Year Book, 2023*, ch. 3. Data exclude the tax hidden in housing prices.

Sources are available in the separate section of 'Figure Sources'.

on to consumers. As such, this was not a free market but a monopoly. The gap between construction costs and final sales prices functioned as a hidden tax (although strictly speaking a 'monopolistic rent'). Monopolistic high sales prices now require 'six purses' just to cover the downpayment for a leasehold property.[24]

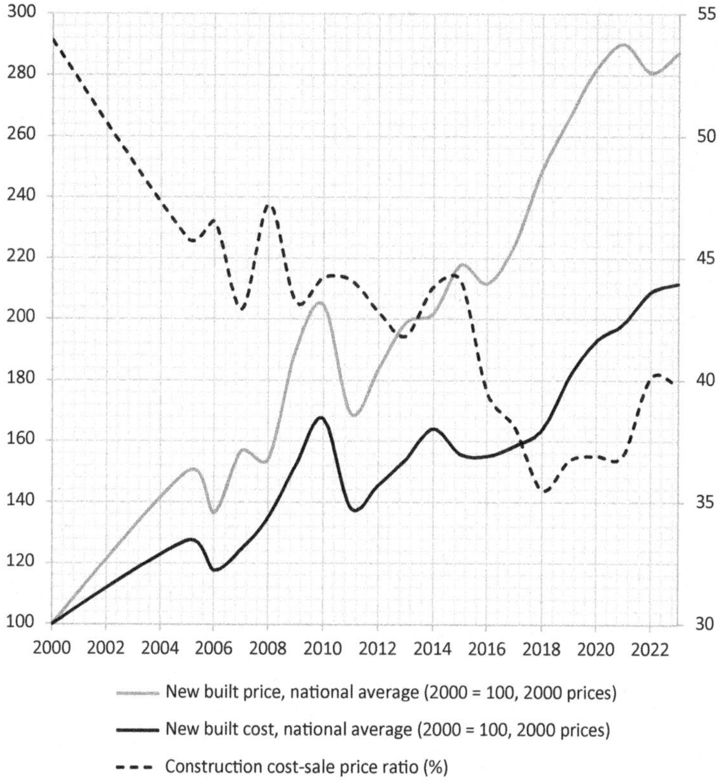

Figure 4.2. Housing Sales Prices versus Construction Costs, 2000–2023

Note: Left Y-axis: Building sales prices and building construction costs (2000 = 100, 2000 prices). Right Y-axis: Costs as % of sale prices (2000 = 100, 2000 prices).

Sources are available in the separate section of 'Figure Sources'.

China's high residential property prices become obvious when they are compared with the OECD average. Data in table 4.1 indicate that during the comparable period of 1998 to 2017/2020, housing price to income ratios increased 0.7% per year in OECD countries but 16.1% per year in China. Regarding housing affordability by the general public, on average China's housing price to income ratio became twenty-three times that of the OECD average. As a result, super high housing costs in China reduce the disposable income for consumer manufactures.

On the other side of the same coin, the state was directly involved in housing construction projects. Data in figure 4.3 show that land purchased by developers from the state remained flat, meaning that each unit of land remained expensive in what is commonly referred

Table 4.1. Housing Price-to-Income Ratios, 1998–2017/20

Period	OECD	China
1998–2017 (1998 = 100)		1,700 (16.1% per year)
1998–2020 (1998 = 100)	116 (0.7% per year)	
Growth index	0.7% per year = 100	2,300

Sources: OECD, 'OECD Affordable Housing Database', https://www.oecd.org/els/family/HM1-2-Housing-prices.pdf; see also OECD, 'Home Price-to-Income Changes since 2015', https://www.visualcapitalist.com/home-affordability-trends-in-oecd-countries-since-2015/. Fathom Consulting, 'China's house-price-to-income ratio exceeds 17', https://lipperalpha.refinitiv.com/2020/06/chart-of-the-week-chinas-house-price-to-income-ratio-exceeds-17/.

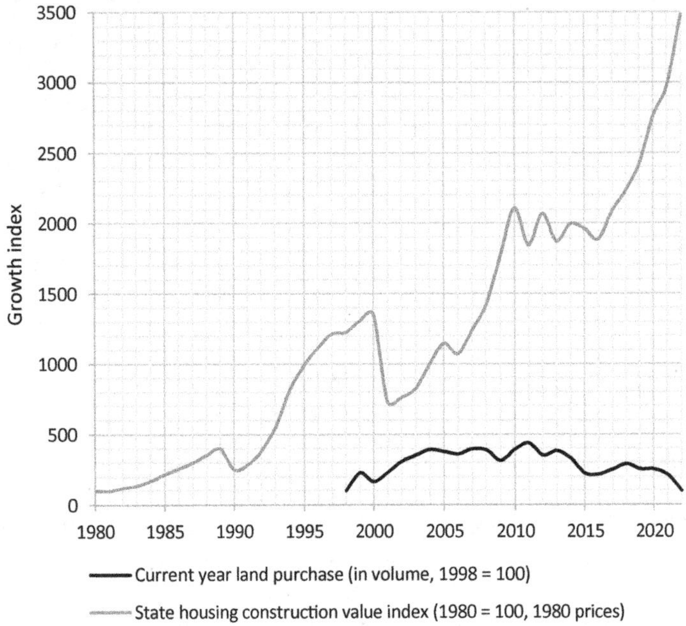

Figure 4.3. Government Direct Involvement in Housing Construction, 1980–2022

Note: The constant price is based on National Bureau of Statistics, *Statistical Year Book, 2023*, ch. 3.

Sources are available in the separate section of 'Figure Sources'.

to as 'land hoarding'. On top of leasing land to private developers, the state was directly involved in housing construction which grew 35-fold (or 8.8 per cent a year) from 1980 to 2020. Here, state double dipping in land-lease auctions and housing construction projects demonstrate maximised rent-seeking behaviour.

At the recipient end, a great many residential property buyers have become 'mortgage-debt slaves' (*fangnu*) who pay a third or more of their monthly income on servicing their mortgages, often for 30 years from the day they sign the deal.[25] The burden is so high that mortgage defaults have become common over the last decade.[26]

It is worth looking back at China's past. A China-wide survey shows that in the 1930s most tillers possessed private landholding rights (freehold or leasehold).[27] This was confirmed by China's 1954 Constitution which reads 'Clause 8: This state protects peasant ownership of land and other means of production'.[28] By April 1956, however, a total of 106.7 million peasant households (90 per cent of the total) were 'persuaded' to join one million or so agricultural cooperatives (*hezuoshe*).[29] A total of 100 million hectares (1.5 billion *mu*, as in 1949) and 200–300 million *yuan* in capital assets were confiscated from their lawful owners without compensation. After 1956, China's traditional private ownership model was no longer recognised by Mao's state. Land deeds had no bearing on land uses and yielded no dividends for previous landowners in rural cooperatives (although draft animals and farming equipment still did).[30] Trading 'collectivised land' between rural cooperatives (or 'people's communes' later) was strictly forbidden. It is worth reviewing that before 1949, state-owned land accounted for less than 2 per cent of China's total farmland.[31]

The abolition of private landownership by Mao aimed to make land available for all citizens free of charge (at least that was the image Mao tried to create); and this was written in Clause 6 of China's 1982 Constitution which stated: 'the foundation of the communist economic system of the People's Republic of China is communist ownership of the means of production, via either all-people-ownership or collective ownership.'[32] If this is not clear enough, Clause 7 of the constitution read: 'the state-owned economy is all-people-ownership communism.'[33] Period. Therefore, the notion that land in China should be free for all citizens remains.[34]

In addition, a total of US$7.9 billion (1955 prices) worth of urban business assets (or 285.5 billion *yuan* at 1995 prices) was collected by Mao's state.[35] A compensation scheme was designed to benefit 700,000 'national bourgeoisie' who collectively owned assets of US$700 million at 1955 prices (or 25.4 billion *yuan* at 1995 prices).[36] The pay-out rate was set at 5 per cent a year of the said asset value (*ding xi*);[37] and from 1956 to 1966 the total pay-out was RMB 125 million (US$34.4 million, 1955 prices) across 10 years.[38] In the end, this US$344.4 million paid to the national bourgeoisie was about half of the original US$700 million owned by the class. This US$344.4 million counted for just 4.4 per cent of the US$7.9 billion worth of the total urban capital, subject to Mao's nationalisation. If so, urban assets should be free for all citizens, too.

Stealthily, in 1982, the state reinterpreted 'all-people-ownership' (*quanmin suoyou*) of 1.4 billion citizens as 'state ownership' (*guojia suoyou*) with a single owner, according to Clause 10 of the 1982 Constitution of the PRC. It has thus opened the gate for auctioning out land plots for residential apartment blocks as a source of government revenue. If all urban land runs out, the state also has the power to buy rural farmland at a cheap price and resell it to the highest bidder in a rural–urban price arbitrage, all in the name of deregulation and marketisation.

The practice is formally termed 'revenue-making from land re-sales' (*tudi caizheng*). Land price arbitrage is officially identified as a form of taxation and the government does not even try to hide it. It has been revealed that the gap between the state purchasing price from a village and the state's re-selling price of the same land to a property developer was 40 times the original purchasing price (as of 2012).[39] This new gold mine for the post-Mao state has become *the* main source of local government revenues.[40] The real problem, however, is that selling once privately owned land (as of 1955) back to the descendants of the previously lawful owners raises doubts about the legitimacy of the tax.

The land price is only one of three components that make up the final price of a residential property. The other two are bank mortgage loans and building costs.[41] Most commercial banks in China are state-owned. The state rakes in mortgage interest as its cash cow, too. But the post-Mao state did not stop there. It acted as the ultimate rent-seeker by actively engaging with housing construction businesses in a 'catch-all' fashion, as seen in the state's direct involvement in house building (figure 4.3).

Not surprisingly, adding all the bits and pieces together, China's tax burden in per-capita terms took off. The overall increase from 1978 to 2020 was 177-fold (or 13.1 per cent a year) over four decades. There was an acceleration after 2005 to 15.4 per cent per annum from a previous 11.2 per cent per year. This demonstrates the general propensity of the state rent-seeking during the reform era (see again figure 4.1, right Y-axis).

3. 'Getting Prices Wrong' *by* the State and *for* the State

The concept of the state interfering with the market came from classical mercantilism in sixteenth- to eighteenth-century Europe, exemplified by the general principle of obtaining trade surpluses in gold, or by the English Navigation Acts from 1651 and the 1815 British Corn Laws. A modern reincarnation is Keynesianism. The Asian version of mercantilism has gained the catchy name of 'getting prices wrong',[42] although the original principle of manipulating economic conditions came undoubtedly from Gerschenkron.[43] But unlike mercantilism, 'getting prices wrong' is judged in a positive light due to its perceived ability to generate fast growth and development for a national economy, thanks to Gerschenkron and the Asian economic tigers.

In fact, 'getting prices wrong' was practised in Mao's state systematically in the form of 'rural–urban scissors-pricing differentiation' (*jiandao cha*). It took three steps. First, distorted terms of trade between farming and manufacturing were created through the state's monopsonic procurement system (*tonggou*). Second, the state arbitraged between a low price for farming products and a high price for manufactures via monopolistic resales (*tongxiao*). Third, the state raked in the price differences as tax revenue (although it was an 'economic rent' by definition). The practice combined monopsony, monopoly, and rent all in one. The consequence was a recession in agriculture and slow growth in industry (chapter 3).

Against all the odds, the practice of 'getting prices wrong' with food continued by default in the 1980s and 1990s, after Mao was gone. Deregulation of urban food price controls finally began only after China's WTO membership in 2001. The road map for state control over urban food prices from 1979 to 2006 is shown below:

The state controlled food prices by default to keep urban living costs artificially low.[44]

⇓

A low living cost kept the urban wage level competitive and allowed urban households to save.

⇓

State-owned banks took advantage of new household savings for capital formation; the urban consumption market also generated growth

⇓

Urban food prices were gradually deregulated.[45]

The available evidence comes from government living cost subsidies. Data in figure 4.4 show that food subsidies in-kind increased 800-fold (27 per cent a year) and price subsidies in money increased 600-fold (25.7 per cent a year). Both are measured by current prices. More realistically, in per capita and constant prices terms, government subsidies peaked in 2000 with a 38-fold increase (17.9 per cent a year) before declining. Even with the decline, subsidies remained substantial.

Undoubtedly, cheap food has been translated into cheap labour costs. In 2005, Chinese labour cost only one-tenth of that in Europe and the United States.[46] Even so, when one puts China's food subsidies and high house prices together, the two opposing forces cancel each other out, especially given that living cost subsidies stopped after 2006 while housing prices have been on the rise since 2000.

Then, there is the thorny issue of foreign exchange manipulation which is at the heart of 'getting prices wrong' by the state. A major unilateral change took place from 1980 to 1995 when exports from China measured in RMB became 5.5 times cheaper. With a long-term average rate of RMB 6.28 for US$1 (1980–2024), China's low-price advantage has remained until the present day. This manipulation has

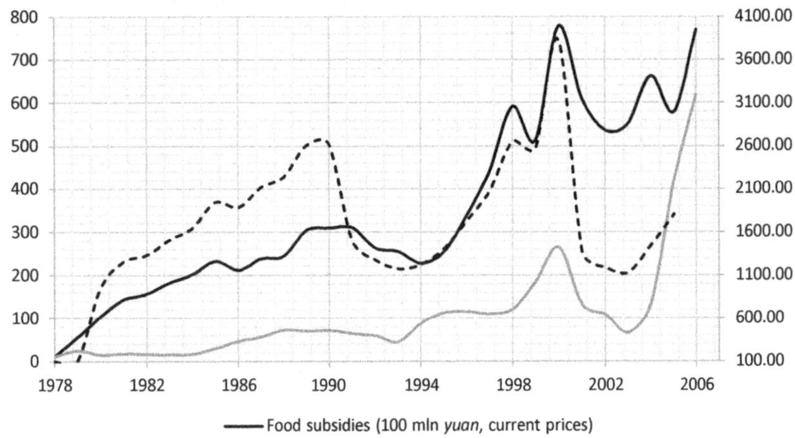

Figure 4.4. Government Living-Cost Subsidies, 1978–2006

Note: Left Y-axis: Subsidies in current prices. Right Y-axis: Subsidies/head index (1978 = 100, 1978 prices). The 1978 constant prices are based on National Bureau of Statistics, *Statistical Year Book, 2023*, ch. 3.

Sources are available in the separate section of 'Figure Sources'.

undoubtedly boosted China's goods exports on the one hand and foreign investment into China on the other, *ceteris paribus*.[47]

It marked a unilateral change in the conditions of China's international trade. Data in figure 4.5 demonstrate why and how China's trade balance entered surplus territory only after the renminbi became three times cheaper against the US dollar in 1990, and why and how China stayed in surplus territory after the renminbi became four to five times cheaper against the US dollar after 1993.

Meanwhile, let us consider the thin line between trade deficits and trade surpluses, as shown in figure 4.6. China's trade balance has toed carefully along the 50–50 line between imports and export since 1978. One cannot help wondering whether China's trade surplus is not artificially engineered.

Related to currency exchange rate manipulation was the state's handling of foreign currencies, an area in which 'getting prices wrong' has been particularly sophisticated. The conventional wisdom views a country's foreign reserves as the result of its foreign trade surpluses. True in an open economy. But one cannot take it for granted for China. Data in figure 4.7 show that from 1978 to 2015 China's cumulative foreign trade surpluses fell constantly below the growth in

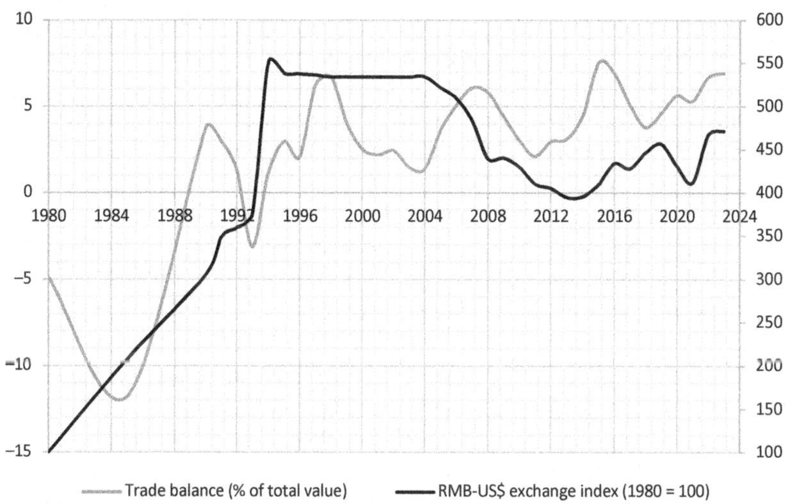

Figure 4.5. RMB–US$ Exchange Rates and Trade Balance, 1978–2023

Note: Left Y-axis: China's foreign trade balance. Below zero means a foreign trade deficit. Above zero means a foreign trade surplus. Right Y-axis: RMB–US$ exchange index (1980 = 100).

Sources are available in the separate section of 'Figure Sources'.

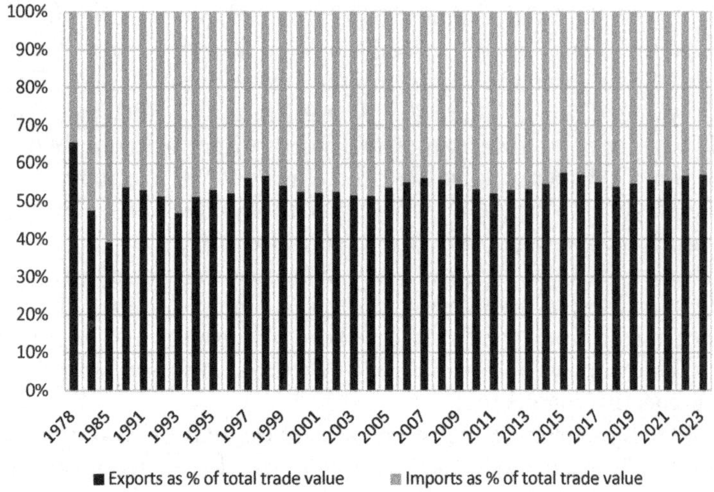

Figure 4.6. China's Import–Export Balancing Act, 1978–2023

Sources are available in the separate section of 'Figure Sources'.

China's foreign reserves. Only after 2015 did China's trade surpluses became large enough to support China's foreign reserves. Therefore, China must have had other means to bridge the obvious gap between its cumulative foreign trade surpluses and foreign reserves. A possible source was FDI.

Prior to 2012, this 'other means' turned out to include the cash component of inward foreign direct investment (a 'non-trade foreign currency source' to be precise) which was automatically counted into China's foreign reserves thanks to China's mercantilist control of foreign currencies. The policy is stated as 'compulsory conversion of foreign currencies to RMB' (*qiangzhi jiehui*),[48] regardless of whether foreign currencies came to China, left China, or remained in China.

In addition, according to the 1996 Foreign Currency Management Regulations of the PRC, the state was the sole custodian of all foreign currencies going into and out of China. First of all, inside China, any form of market circulation and transaction with foreign currencies is forbidden and the foreign currency market is governed solely by the State Council (Clauses 7 and 37). Secondly, Chinese firms operating overseas must remit their incomes in foreign currencies back to China and convert them to RMB in government-appointed banks (Clauses 9 and 10). Thirdly, Chinese citizens who possess foreign assets in currency payment certificates, foreign currency securities, and so on

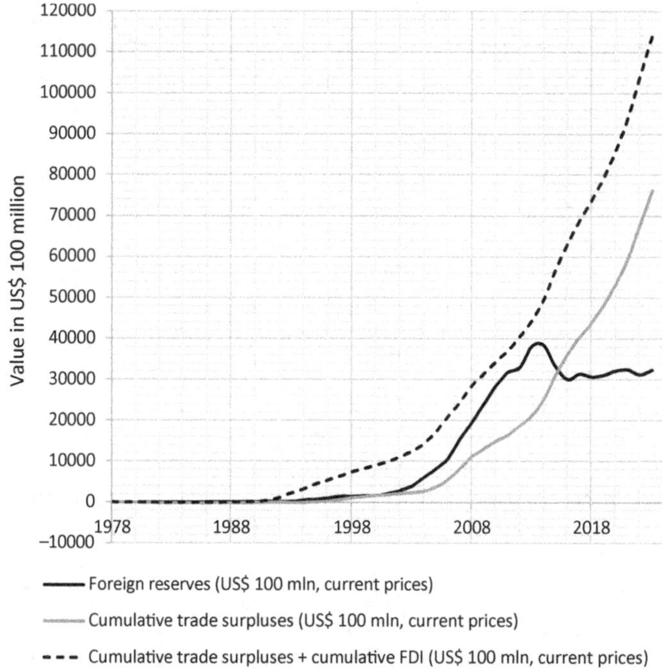

Figure 4.7. Foreign Currency Sources and Foreign Reserves, 1978–2023

Note: The distance between China's 'foreign currency ceiling' (marked by 'Cumulative Trade Surpluses plus Cumulative FDI') and 'Foreign Reserves' is foreign capital goods shipped to China for inbound FDI operations, although data for the division between FDI cash and FDI capital goods are unavailable. Cumulative magnitudes are used due to China's mercantilist propensity of foreign currency hoarding.

Sources are available in the separate section of 'Figure Sources'.

are not permitted to move their foreign assets abroad (Clause 16). Fourthly, foreign nationals can convert legitimate income in RMB to foreign currencies and remit overseas only when permitted to do so by the government's Foreign Currency Control Agency. Foreign partners in joint venture companies that complete their projects in China can convert their after-tax RMB incomes to foreign currencies in government-appointed banks; but Chinese partners in such joint ventures must sell all their foreign currencies to government-appointed banks (Clause 26).[49] Finally, all currency conversions must be conducted in government-appointed banks (Clause 17).

More specifically, the following 'normal market activities' are regarded as violation of law in China (Clauses 39, 40, 44, and 47):

(1) Keeping deposits in foreign currencies outside China (sic); (2) selling foreign currencies in China outside government-appointed banks; (3) taking or sending foreign currencies and foreign currency securities out of China without permission; (4) making any form of non-authorised conversion of foreign currencies to RMB, and vice versa; (5) making non-authorised foreign loans, or issuing non-authorised foreign bonds; (6) opening and transferring non-authorised business accounts with foreign currencies.[50]

Most rules remained unchanged in the '2008 Foreign Currency Management Regulations of the PRC'. Some relaxation has taken place regarding whether privately owned foreign currencies are allowed to remain outside China: Clause 9 reads that the overseas incomes of 'domestic individuals' denominated in foreign currencies may be sent to China or deposited overseas. The conditions and terms for sending foreign currencies back to China or keeping foreign currencies abroad are subject to the decision of the Foreign Currency Control Agency of the State Council in accordance with China's balance of payments and China's needs for foreign currencies.[51]

This is how it works. Foreign-currency owners are asked to surrender their foreign currencies to the Chinese state. In compensation, these owners receive an amount of RMB equal to the value of their foreign currencies that are now in the hands of the state, known as 'currency swapping'.[52] In doing so, the ownership of the said foreign currencies is transferred to the Chinese state who becomes the new legal owner of the foreign currencies. The state's newly obtained foreign currencies can now formally be counted towards China's foreign reserves. Here, by definition, the component of swapped foreign currencies has little to do with China's exports or its domestic market. Rather, it is a shortcut that bypasses the entire chain of investment-production-marketing-sales, and so on. So, it is *the* preferred method to obtain foreign currencies by the state.

There is, however, a catch. The RMB used to compensate foreign currencies comes almost exclusively from China's new base money supply (M_0) from China's central bank (the People's Bank of China) to ensure China maintains its existing economic balances. So, the currency swapping business creates built-in inflation pressure on RMB, hence the fast upswing in China's monetary supply beginning in 1979.[53] If, however, the central bank borrows money (say in the form of bonds) from domestic investors equal to the value of inbound FDI to pay foreign investors, this increases China's internal debt which in turn changes the money market equilibrium, as less money is available for mortgage lending. So, it is a banking problem either way.

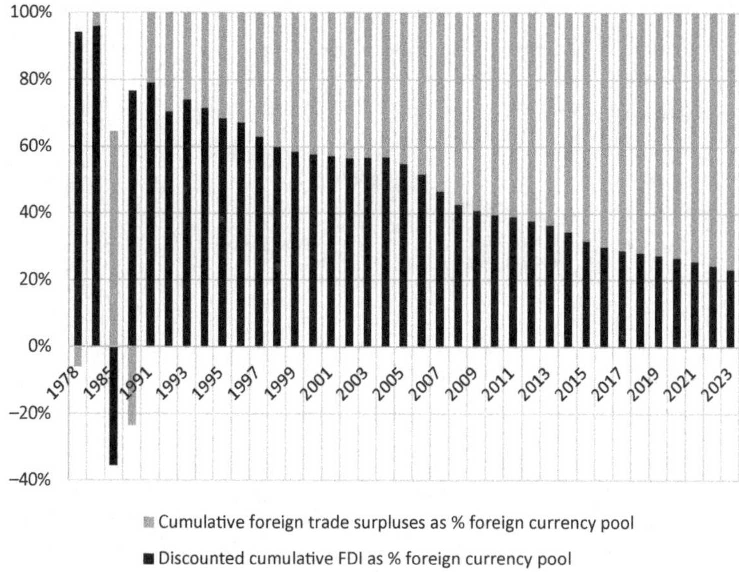

Figure 4.8. Cash FDI, Trade Surpluses, and Foreign Currency Pool, 1978–2023

Note: 'Foreign currency pool': cash FDI + foreign trade surpluses. Here, a symbolic 30 per cent share applies to inbound FDI to estimate the size of the 'FDI cash component'. The remaining 70 per cent is FDI capital goods which cannot enter China's foreign currency pool.

Sources are available in the separate section of 'Figure Sources'.

The alleged pattern of China's foreign trade leading to foreign reserves is only half true. To demonstrate the missing component 'currency swapping' of inbound FDI for foreign reserves, the data in figure 4.8 display the trends of the two components of China's foreign currency pool. In the beginning, the trade surplus component was lower than 20 per cent of China's foreign currency pool. It increased to make up half of the pool in 2007, and then 70 per cent of the pool in 2017. If this trajectory continues, China may have 100 per cent of its foreign currency pool coming from its trade surplus after 2040. In this period, the long-term average for the trade surplus component of the pool was 54 per cent. The remaining 46 per cent came from the 'cash FDI' component.

The state had two policy options: (1) reforms to allow foreign currencies to be traded and circulated freely inside China; (2) no reforms which would result in inflationary pressure from inbound FDI. The party-state opted for no reforms. As a result, from 1980 to 2015,

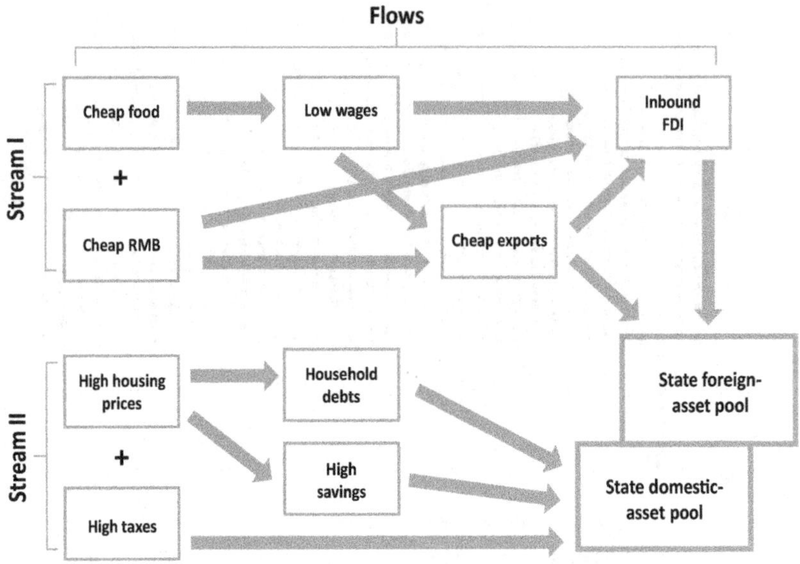

Figure 4.9. 'Getting Prices Wrong' by the State and for the State

Note: There are two streams in this framework. The upper stream aims to yield foreign assets in the form of foreign currency reserves; and the lower stream, domestic assets come from government domestic revenues. The initial push comes from the state.

China's officially published price index increased by a factor of 6.3 with an annual average rate of 5.4 per cent.[54]

In summary, figure 4.9 illustrates how 'getting prices wrong' guided two streams of wealth towards China's domestic asset pool and its foreign asset pool, both of which were firmly controlled by the state. So, from the standpoint of the party-state, 'getting prices wrong' was justifiably right .

4. State Capacity's Externalities and Unintended Consequences

There can be little doubt that China's state capacity has been rebuilt beyond recognition and that the policy of 'getting prices wrong' has been widespread. Against this backdrop, China's new growth in the post-Mao era seems to have been tailor-made. The state certainly claims so, as seen in its 'China Dream' propaganda in which the individual incentives, initiatives, and efforts so vital for a market economy are largely ignored.[55]

So, for argument's sake, teleologically growth in the said 'domestic-capital pool' and 'foreign-currency pool' may well be the goals of the post-Mao state. For the general public in society, 'positive externalities' do much of the rest,[56] be they the renaissance of China's higher education, emergence of USI, GDP take-off, mass consumption, or urbanisation, as demonstrated in chapter 3.

On the other hand, some 'unintended consequences' (or 'negative externalities') loom large, which have increased social costs and reduced social benefits.[57] The best examples are pollution and official corruption, both of which China is known for.

Firstly, industrial pollution emerged quite early on in the reform era. According to conventional wisdom, environmental damage is associated with a 'tragedy of the commons', which concerns abuses of communal resources. The tragedy can be avoided by better defining ownership and the law.[58] If all key economic resources are already nationalised and controlled by the state, then why and how has environmental damage been so severe by international standards? The answer lies in the internal divisions and frictions inside China's huge state apparatus, known as 'regionally decentralised authoritarianism' with a built-in 'centrifugal force' radiating out of Beijing's orbit.[59] Thus, common resources that do not have fixed physical boundaries such as air and river water are indeed subject to a 'tragedy of the commons'.

By 1995, environmental damage had cost China a total of US$75 billion,[60] more than China's total intake of FDI at the time.[61] After 2000, environmental damage in China achieved global significance and duly caught the attention of international communities across the sciences and humanities.[62] In terms of water pollution, of China's aggregate river length of 19,750 kilometres, 64 per cent (12,556.3 kilometres) has been polluted. This judgement comes from the information in table 4.2 where each river is measured by its degree of pollution (river length × pollution level of that river).

Among the seven main rivers, there has been a 'race to the bottom' in terms of losing good water to pollution. Data in figure 4.10 demonstrate the trends. By 2020, the share of good water across the seven rivers dropped below 20 per cent. With good water shares under 10 per cent in 2020, the Yangzi and Pearl rivers could hardly get any worse. The sharpest annual drops in good water happened in North China from 2001 to 2020: 5.3 per cent a year in the Songhua River, 7.0 per cent a year in the Huai River, 8.4 per cent a year in the Hai River, and 11.4 per cent a year for both the Liao and Yellow rivers. So far, no reversal in these trends has been detected.

Table 4.2. Extent of River Water Pollution, 2001–2020

River	% Being polluted (I)	River length (km) (II)	Length polluted I × II
Pearl	86.0	2,400	2064.0
Yangzi	82.8	6,300	5216.4
Yellow	55.2	5,400	2980.8
Songhua	45.3	1,900	860.7
Huai	41.6	1,100	457.6
Liao	39.9	1,350	538.7
Hai	33.7	1,300	438.1
Total		19,750	12,556.3
National level Σ (I × II) / Σ II			64%

Source: Qin Yang, Jingsheng Chen, Yuyi Liu, Yangguang Li, Haigang Zhang, Jing Zhang, Xiao Sun, Mingyang Lu, Rongqian Ma, and Yanlin Wu, 'Analysis of Changes in Water Quality and Treatment Effectiveness of Seven Major River Basins in China from 2001 to 2020', *Frontiers in Environmental Science*, 12 (2024).

Similarly, figure 4.11 depicts China's air pollution levels by using CO_2 emissions as a proxy for all greenhouse gases.[63] Total pollution increased 110-fold from 1949 to 2023, of which pollution from coal – the 'dirtiest' energy source – grew 85-fold as the main cause. This pattern qualifies China for a 'coal-based industrial take-off'. In per capita terms, CO_2 emissions from coal increased 68-fold (5.9 per cent per annum) from 1949 to 2023. In addition, China's energy efficiency fell short. Regarding China's low energy efficiency, see note 90 in chapter 3.

In all fairness, CO_2 emissions per unit of output now seem to be in decline, meaning that technology has played a role in improving energy efficiency.[64] It may also be a result of a push towards renewable alternatives. Better regulations may have played a role, too. Relative decreases in pollution can also be observed for SO_2 and acid rain.[65] However, this may be cold comfort as pollutant aggregates continue to rise in absolute terms by the day.

Both water and air pollution may have been unintended when China's reforms began. However, pollution can be an absolute advantage in international trade competition. In this regard, China has been known for its 'three lows' (*san di*) approach: (1) low wages, (2) low human rights, and (3) low environmental protection, as conditions working in favour of China in attracting environmental unfriendly and unwanted investment projects from the West to China. The government only needs to turn a blind eye to them.

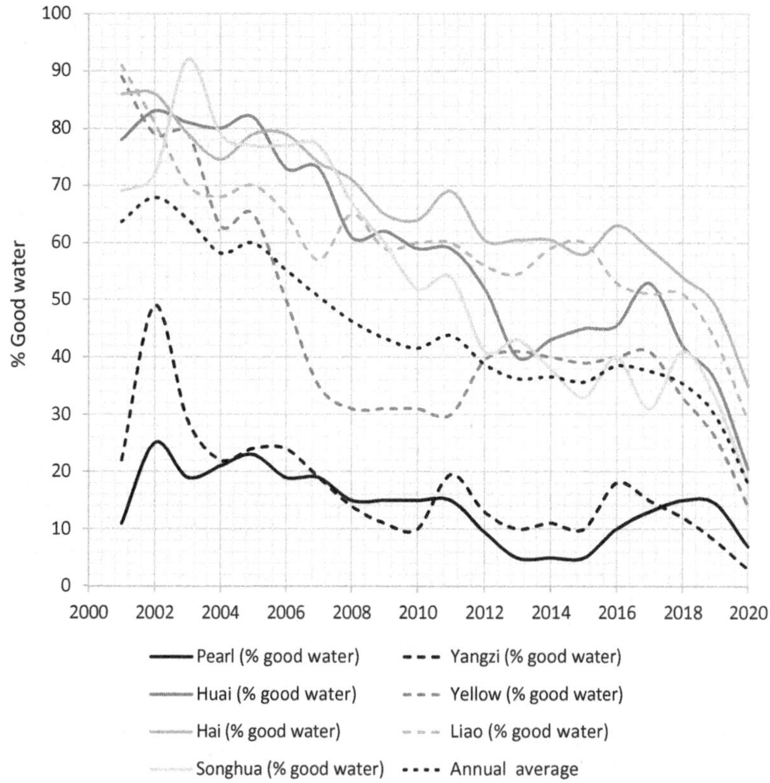

Figure 4.10. Water Pollution in Seven Rivers, 2001–2020

Note: Quality levels of 'Grades IV and V' are considered 'good water'.

Sources are available in the separate section of 'Figure Sources'.

Such projects have incurred social losses in the way of negative externalities.[66]

Unintendedly perhaps, official corruption has exploded since Deng's reforms began.[67] The market economy under the party-state has created the perfect ingredients for 'Acton's Law' of 'absolute power corrupting absolutely' to reach its full potential. The principal–agent problem common in China has only exacerbated the impact of Acton's Law.[68] As far as one can tell, 80 per cent of corruption cases have been related to China's SOEs.[69] In other words, Acton's Law and the principal–agent problem have found their ideal home in SOEs.

Official corruption has become the main concern among party leaders, top political scientists, and the general public alike since the 1990s.[70] A recent report by the Director of National Intelligence of

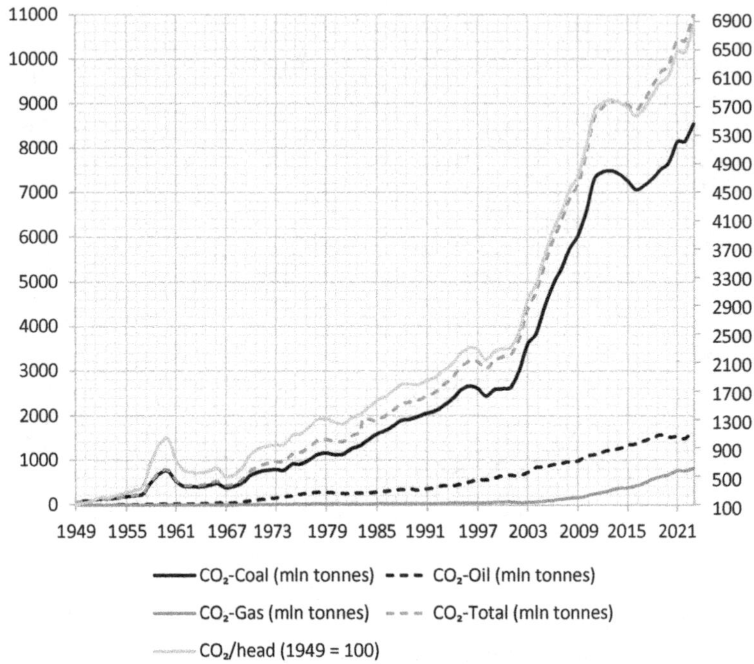

Figure 4.11. China's CO_2 Emission Track Record, 1949–2023

Note: Left Y-axis: CO_2 emission levels. Right Y-axis: CO_2 per capita index (1949 = 100). Regarding China's fuel consumption-cum-CO_2 emissions, not much was happening during Mao's era (1949–76) because China was overwhelmingly rural.

Sources are available in the separate section of 'Figure Sources'.

the United States in March 2025 with the title 'Wealth and Corrupt Activities of the Leadership of the Chinese Communist Party' opens with the stern statement that 'corruption is an endemic feature of and challenge for China'. The report cites a total of 4.7 million officials found guilty from 2012 to 2022 under Xi Jinping's leadership; and attributes China's problem to 'centralized power, eschew[ing] independent checks of accountability – especially at the provincial level'.[71]

Measures have been taken to curb corruption. The first campaign against official and business corruption began in 1978 and lasted until 2000, although the party-state decision was made public only in 1982.[72] One study indicates that in the 1990s total annual corruption revenue amounted to RMB 650–800 billion (US$78–96 billion, using the 1995 exchange rate) with the following breakdown: RMB 400 billion (US$49 billion) in illegally collected fees and dues; RMB 200–300 billion (US$24–36 billion) extracted from state-private sector arbitrage; and RMB 50–100 billion (US$6–12 billion) embezzled from SOEs.[73] There was also annual money laundering worth RMB 200 billion (US$24 billion).[74]

It has been estimated that during this period, 13–17 per cent of GDP per year was subject to official corruption.[75] It has also been estimated that during the campaign from 1978 to 2000, a total of RMB 15,037 billion (US$1,810 billion) was embezzled, equivalent to China's GDP of 1998 and 1999 put together.[76]

The most visible and mundane official corruption took the form of sumptuous banquets to benefit state officials, which cannot be detected easily from account books or officials' private bank accounts. Scattered data are as follows: RMB 37 billion in 1989, 40 billion in 1990, 80 billion in 1992, and 100 billion in 1994.[77]

The aforementioned two huge 'honey pots' – the state domestic-asset pool and the state foreign-asset pool (shown in figure 4.9) – also attracted corruption. Common forms of official corruption are either state-owned firms declaring business losses or state-run banks raking in loan kickbacks. So, managers of SOEs and state-run banks – gate-keepers of state assets on behalf of the state – are disproportionately involved in corruption cases.

Official corruption needed a platform to operate, commonly in the form of 'non-performing loans' or 'bad debts' that have dogged China's banking system since the 1980s. In 1991, as discussed in chapter 3, China's national aggregate debt to capital asset ratio in all state-owned enterprises was 0.6. It quickly worsened to 0.75 in 1995 and then 0.8 in 1997.[78]

In the 2000s, bad debts were still stubbornly high. In 2002 they were equivalent to about 40 per cent of China's total GDP.[79] In 2005, they increased to RMB 7,540 billion (or US$911 billion) and accounted for 38 per cent of China's GDP and 75 per cent of the total bad debts in the world for that matter.[80] In 2016, China's aggregate bad debts had doubled from their 2005 level and reached RMB 1.5 trillion (US$225.6 billion). Bad debts doubled again to RMB 3 trillion (US$447.8 billion) in 2022.[81] The problem continues until today. Given that most banking officials have a university education, often with degrees in accounting and finance, one wonders whether the scale and scope of bad debts are the result of human error or the deliberate acts of criminals. The latter seems to be the answer.

Data in figure 4.12 show a steady rise in the number of convicted

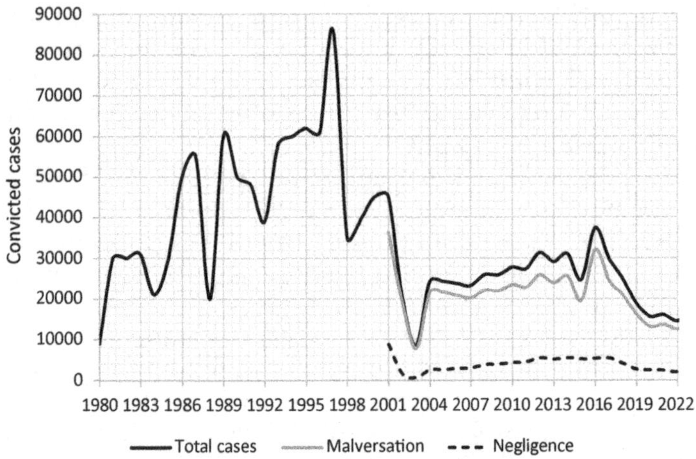

Figure 4.12. General Pattern of Convicted Officials, 1980–2023

Note: The lowest level occurred in 2002–3. The result of the new campaign after 2012 has been a mixed bag.

Sources are available in the separate section of 'Figure Sources'.

officials from 1980 to 1997, which was followed by a sharp decrease between 1997 and 2003 under the leadership of Jiang Zemin when convicted cases dropped back to the 1980 level. Even so, the annual average number of cases was 33,766 from 1980 to 2023. Moreover, data for the post-2000 period show that the ratio between malversation and negligence was 15.5 to 1.[82] The ratio became 5.6 to 1 thereafter. In other words, guilty officials were capable of doing their jobs. Given that negligence was not a major problem, these officials were particularly good at illegal profiteering.

Now, back to bad debts, which are intimately correlated to official corruption. According to a 2021 report, 26 state-owned bank managers were guilty of 'inside jobs' between bribees (i.e. state bank managers) and illicit bank loans obtained by bribers.[83] A 2025 report reveals that it was low costs and high returns for bribers that created incentives for bank loan corruption.[84] In two known cases, the illicit loan-to-bribe ratios were as high as 57:1 and 149:1.[85] The point here is that bribes ultimately came from illicit bank loans, costing bribers nothing.

In this context, bad debts are not the result of bad luck in running real businesses but a bad banking system run by crooks. Official corruption in turn has made risk in China's banking system exceedingly high.[86] Eventually, the burden of bad debts is passed onto ordinary savers and mortgage borrowers. So it is just another form of negative externality.

Outside the banking system there has been the phenomenon of 'secret coffers' or 'concealed coffers' (*xiao jinku*, literarily 'little treasuries') hidden inside institutes of the state sector,[87] be they universities, newspapers, or television stations. Sources of these coffers are dodgy (e.g., revenues from illicit fees and rents, or cuts of public funds, or outright bribes).[88] The practice is nicknamed 'financial extracorporeal circulation' (*tiwai xunhuan*) to avoid detection.[89] Sums in table 4.3 with a total of RMB 41.6 billion are almost certainly the tip of the iceberg.

Table 4.3. Exposed Cases of 'Secret Coffers', 2003–2013

Period	Event	No. of coffers discovered	No. of officials found guilty	RMB million
1995	National	—	—	4,000
1996	National	—	470	4,700
1999	Health Ministry	—	—	200
2009–11	National	60,722	10,429	31,586
2003–7	Yunnan*	6,844	2,905	159
2009–12	Ningxia*	687	—	244
2010	Yunnan*	103	—	32.4
2011–13	Guizhou*	20	—	760
Aggregate		68,376	13,804	41,681.4

Note: * Hinterland provinces.

Sources: Huang Weiting, *Zhongguode Yinxing Jingji* (*China's Invisible Economy*) (Beijing: China's Commerce Press, 1996), p. 265; Chen Bo, *Zhongguo Fan Fubai Ershi Nian* (*Twenty Years of Fighting against Corruption in China*) (Beijing: People's Press, 2000), p. 168; Yang Yu, *Shehui Zhuanxingqi Fan Fubai Yanjiu* (*Combating Corruption in a Social Transition Period*) (Tianjin: Tianjin People's Press, 2001), p. 47; Anon., 'Yunnansheng Jiaqiang Zhifa Lianzheng Chachu Xiao Jinku 159 Yi Yuan' (Yunnan Province Intensified Law and Unveiled Secret Coffers Worth RMB 159 Million), *Zhong Xin* (*China News*), 28 September 2008, https://www.shsmu.edu.cn/jw/info/1017/1927.htm; Anon., 'Yunnan Zicha Zijiu Xiao Jinku 103 Ge She Jin-e 3,239.92 Wan' (Yunnan's Self-Checks Discovered 103 Secret Coffers Worth 32.39 Million), *Yunnan Daily*, 26 October 2010, https://www.qingdaonews.com/content/2010-10/26/content_8540122.htm; Anon., 'Caizheng Bu: Sannian Chachu Xiao Jinku 316 Yi Yuan' (Ministry of Finance: Prosecuted Secret Coffers Worth RMB 31.6 Billion in Three Years', *Caixin* (*Financial News*), 7 February 2012, https://china.caixin.com/2012-02-07/100353931.html; Anon., 'Ningxia Sinian Chachu Xiao Jinku 2.44 Yi' (Four-Year Investigations in Ningxia Found RMB 244 Million in Secret Coffers), *Caixin* (*Financial News*), 11 April 2012, https://china.caixin.com/2012-04-11/100378566.html; Anon., 'Guizhou 20 Ge Xian Weigui Weiji Shiyong Fupin Zijin 7.6 Yi Yuan' (20 Counties in Guizhou Stealing Poverty Aids Worth RMB 760 Million), 5 January 2015, https://china.caixin.com/m/2015-01-05/100770892.html.

The ownership of secret coffers is deliberately undefined. But as party bosses ensure the safety of secret coffers away from ordinary employees and party watchdogs, these coffers are usually at party bosses' disposal and spending is commonly directed towards entertainment, subsidies, and downright embezzlement.[90]

By and large, party officials are disproportionately involved in corruption. From 1978 to 1998, 2.4 million Communist Party members were found guilty of corruption of various types. There were patterns in these cases. First, they were often based in SOEs. By 1998, over 70 per cent of cases were related to officials in charge of SOEs, involving over 400,000 officials who were found guilty and sentenced. Second, corruption became increasingly organised with coordinated corruption schemes counting for a third of all cases.[91] In 2000, an Amoy-based network of smugglers was exposed involving several hundred local officials. In 2001, a Shenyang ring of embezzlers had sixteen local party bosses and one hundred lesser officials. In 2002, a Tangshan-based network of embezzlers involved forty local party bosses.[92] Third, an increasing number of corrupt officials escaped overseas to avoid justice. By 2004, a total of 4,000 officials managed to take refuge overseas with an aggregate US$50 billion in illicit money.[93] Finally, the system has also been rotten from the top, as seen from high-profile banking defalcation cases each involving billions in RMB.[94] In January 2025 alone, twelve high-ranking officials in the banking sector were deposed.[95] But data in figure 4.13 reveal that over 90 per cent of guilty officials were ranked lower than the county governor level.[96] This can be explained by the existence of a principal–agent problem in a multi-layered system: the larger the political distance from Beijing, the greater the opportunities and incentives to steal from the state.

In this context, a super-wealthy class emerged in Mainland China for the first time after 1978. By 1990, 2,932 children of high-ranking officials were among 3,220 business tycoons, each worth over RMB 100 million (US$12 million, based on the 1995 exchange rate).[97] Given that there had been no 'old money' left after Mao's most-thorough nationalisation and collectivisation, the riches of these individuals had to come from the current economic system.[98] It was in this context that the 1989 Pro-Democracy Movement emerged across China petitioning to hold party officials accountable.

The numbers speak for themselves. From 1978 to 2000 corruption cases increased 22 per cent a year, much faster than China's GDP growth. By 1999, China was ranked among the 20 most corrupt countries in the world.[99] More draconian anti-corruption campaign

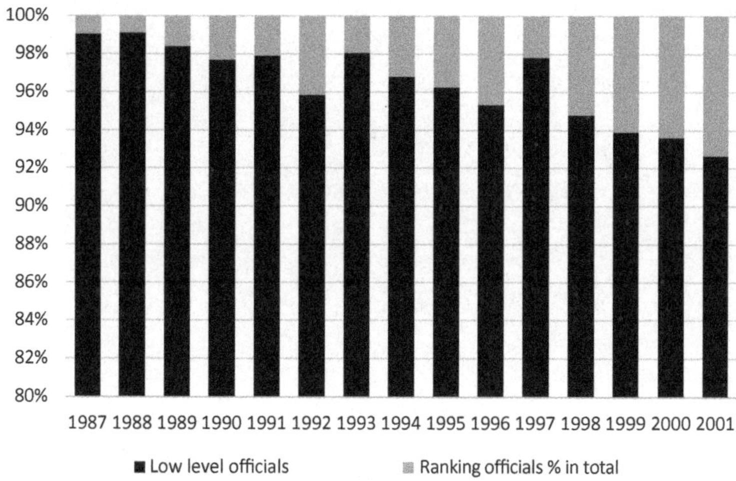

Figure 4.13. Breakdown of Convicted Officials, 1987–2001

Note: Y-axis: Percentage share of all convicted officials. Low level officials are below the county governor level; ranking officials are at the county governor level and above.

Sources are available in the separate section of 'Figure Sources'.

began in 2012 when anti-corruption became the party's priority. Similar to the earlier episode, the new anti-corruption campaign has been marred by opaqueness.

Even so, according to Xuezhi Guo's research, from 1992 to 2009, China brought disciplinary sanctions against two million officials (118,000 per year), while the Central Commission for Discipline Inspection of the CCP cites 50 per cent more per annum: 881,000 officials from 2003 to 2008 (or 176,200 per year).[100] As far as one can tell, there were two more expansions. From 2012 to 2017, the number of guilty party members reached 1.4 million (or 280,000 per year),[101] a 137 per cent increase from the 118,000 per year benchmark. Then, from 2017 to 2022, the total number rose to 4.7 million (470,000 per year),[102] a 400 per cent increase from the benchmark.

Now, the grand total of guilty party officials from 1992 to 2022 was just shy of 7 million. Given that in 2022 there were 96 million CCP members in total,[103] the 7 million convicts counted for 7.3 per cent of the party. Astonishingly, this is over 60 times higher than the criminal share (0.12 per cent) in China's general population.[104] One wonders whether this has been self-selected: to join the party in order

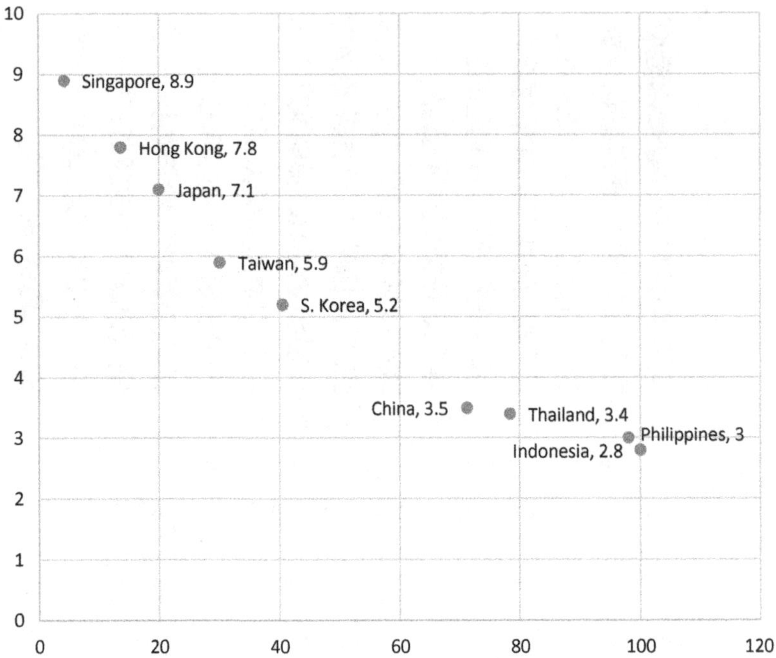

Figure 4.14. China's Corruption Control Ranking in Asia, 1995–2024

Note: Number next to each country is an average non-corruption score from 1995 to 2024. 1995 was the first year of the world rankings. X-axis: 'World Corruption Control Ranking' in ordinal numerals. China's rank was the 70th in the world. Y-axis: 'Corruption Control Score' in cardinal order (10 being the highest). China was scored 3.5.

Sources are available in the separate section of 'Figure Sources'.

to break the law. It begs the age-old question '*quis custodiet ipsos custodes*' – who watches the watchman?[105]

Comparatively, in 2012 when an ambitious anti-corruption campaign was launched by Party General Secretary Xi Jinping, China's world ranking for corruption control effectiveness was 80th with a non-corruption index of 4.0. Twelve years later, in 2024, despite the high-profile campaign, China's ranking was 76th with a non-corruption index of 4.3.[106] The improvement was but marginal: China's world standing moved up four places and its non-corruption index rose by 7.5 per cent. As indicated by figure 4.14, Asia-wide, China has remained stubbornly within the lower echelons in the anti-corruption league table, behind the Asian Tigers and Japan.

Ultimately, negative externalities – environmental damage and official corruption – have thrived on a lack of checks and balances in the Chinese system. This has been described as the 'Six No-s' (*liu wu*):[107]

1. No independent and transparent auditor to monitor the economy.
2. No independent regulator for the monetary and capital markets.
3. No central agent to control taxes and levies.
4. No institution to monitor local government expenditures.
5. No independent voice of shareholders to veto CEO decisions.
6. No independent press to guard public interests.

They are, however, all symptoms of the state lagging behind rapid socio-economic advancement. It will take the *rule of law*, which is based on ordinary citizens' rights to make the government accountable, to tackle the six No-s, something honest intellectuals in China are acutely aware of.[108]

5. Final Remarks

In China, from the Ming-Qing all the way to the present day, state capacity has been a double-edged sword rather than a panacea. The small traditional state combined with property rights for a majority of the population sustained a vibrant private economy that produced food and exported manufactures on the one hand, and imported silver and opium on the other. Such a state had a limited impact on prices, let alone enough to get them 'wrong'. This was one end of the spectrum.

At the other end of the spectrum, one sees an almighty and omnipresent state that alters prices with ease. It shows boundless appetite for revenues and assets, both domestic and foreign. But so far it has been rather toothless in pollution control and has not overturned China's low non-corruption ranking in the world, despite the fact that millions of corrupt officials have been identified and punished.

Confucius's 'Doctrine of the Mean' (*zhongyong zhidao*) may be a way forward for China's statecraft if one is 'Sino-centric'. Or, China could go with the mainstream of democracy across the world, if one is globally minded. But neither was on Deng Xiaoping's agenda.

— 5 —

THE 'CHINA MODEL': CONSTRAINTS AND UNSUSTAINABILITY

1. Defining the Nature of the 'China Model'

There can be little doubt that China has been on track for its 'four modernisations' and a 'modestly comfortable life' for ordinary people. China did not hold back after reaching US$1000 GDP per head. Rather, it has gone all the way to turn its economy into the second largest in the world, behind only the United States.

China's continuous growth from 1978 until today seems to justify the value-loaded notion of the 'Beijing Consensus' and 'China Model' to differentiate the PRC from the mainstream 'Washington Consensus' and the G7 Model. Despite variations between authors, the essence of the Beijing Consensus and/or China Model can be boiled down to a doctrine of 'state-led capitalism' which promotes and protects profit-making with rather obvious advantages, be it cheap labour, cheap land, or cheap environment.[1] Now, the Beijing Consensus and China Model have been able to show their muscles with China's global 'Belt and Road' ambitions.[2]

The economic question here is not so much why China has done what it has done, as one can list various reasons ranging from pure cost–benefit calculation to global geopolitics, or even the alleged 'Confucian ideology' (via Confucius institutes world-wide). Rather, the question is how has China done it? The commonly agreed answer seems to be comparative advantages that China, or any country in a position similar to China today, possesses, at least according to Nobel prize winning economists.[3]

Admittedly, China has comparative advantages somewhere in its economy. But such advantages are disproportionately concentrated in cutting-edge sectors such as new AI and modern weaponry, which have not yet been the centre of gravity of China's economy. That centre has so far been closer to traditional products such as foods, metals (black and nonferrous), cement, coal, and so on (figures 3.3 and 3.7). For comparison, China's AI sector only generates RMB 700 billion (or US$96 billion) (2024) versus the country's total GDP of RMB 126,058 billion (2023 figure), a negligible 0.56 per cent of GDP.[4] Thus, it is too early to draw reliable conclusions.

So, one needs to interrogate the actual nature of advantages China has possessed since 1978. According to the orthodox theory of David Ricardo, who established a theory of the economic benefits gained from trade, each autarkic country faces a matrix of opportunity costs in its national production bundle. Some national opportunity costs can be saved by producing only a limited number of products and doing so well (i.e., specialisation in production).[5] A consequence is that such a country will inevitably produce more than it can consume thanks to its newly gained efficiency, thus creating surpluses.

But Ricardo's world has multiple countries. If all countries agree upon their mutual choices of specialisation in production and then exchange their surplus domestic output with each other, the total welfare of the trading countries increases. Ricardo made it clear that in his international network no country should produce the same products as it will violate the principle of saving opportunity costs. Thus, in Ricardo's model, Portugal began with producing both wine and cloth cheaper than England. So from the perspective of accounting costs, England should stop producing either and import both. But Ricardo disagreed with an accounting cost approach. In his own words:[6]

> England exported cloth in exchange for wine, because, by so doing her industry was rendered more productive to her; she had more cloth and wine than if she had manufactured both for herself; and Portugal imported cloth and exported wine, because the industry of Portugal could be more beneficially employed for both countries in producing wine.

Thus, the rule of the game is that two trading countries should not save the same opportunity costs from the same product. Rather, via a bilateral agreement two trading countries negotiate *ex ante* who produces the product that its trading partner should give up. This is mutually agreed specialisation of commodity production for barter trade.

The Ricardian doctrine can thus be interpreted as an 'international division of labour'.[7] Here, 'division' between bartering countries is the essence of the game which means that no international competition for the same product should be permitted, which is the *sine qua non* for Ricardo's model to function. Because of this, the Ricardian doctrine is Pareto optimal at the same time.[8]

Unfortunately, misunderstandings occur. The most common mistake is to replace Ricardo's idea of international collaboration with Smith's notion of international competitiveness for profit (instead of savings). In doing so, only a lucky few countries win unilaterally.[9] If one likes this idea, chances are one looks at 'absolute advantages in trade', which are based on accounting costs and accounting-cost savings which originate from Adam Smith who clearly saw a market-fitness selection mechanism via the 'natural' (or absolute) advantages of each economy, with only the cheapest producer remaining triumphant:

> If a foreign country can supply us with a commodity cheaper than we ourselves can make it, better buy it off them with some part of the produce of our own industry, employed in a way in which we have some advantage.
>
> . . .
>
> The natural advantages which one country has over another in producing particular commodities are sometimes so great, that it is acknowledged by all the world to be in vain to struggle with them.
>
> . . .
>
> As long as the one country has those advantages, and the other wants them, it will always be more advantageous for the latter, rather to buy off the former than to make.[10]

Simply put, in a Smithian world a country's economic power is determined by what it can produce with the lowest *accounting cost.* Any mutual opportunity for cost-saving is out of the question. China does indeed tick all the Smithian boxes here: China produces a wide range of products *absolutely cheaper* than any of its rivals in the world market. For the rest of the world, as Adam Smith would agree, to buy products made in China becomes not only rational but also the only option.

This judgement is based on the wide range of products that China now dominates production of in world markets. Single-handedly China is able to take on its leading rivals put together in the world league table. Data in figure 5.1 compare China with the next nine leading economies in the world in eleven categories. Although China's population accounts for 44.3 per cent of the share of the top ten most populous countries,[11] it produces over 60 per cent of silicon, cement, rare earths, and steel among the top ten producers of these products. China exports over 60 per cent of the toys and solar panels of the

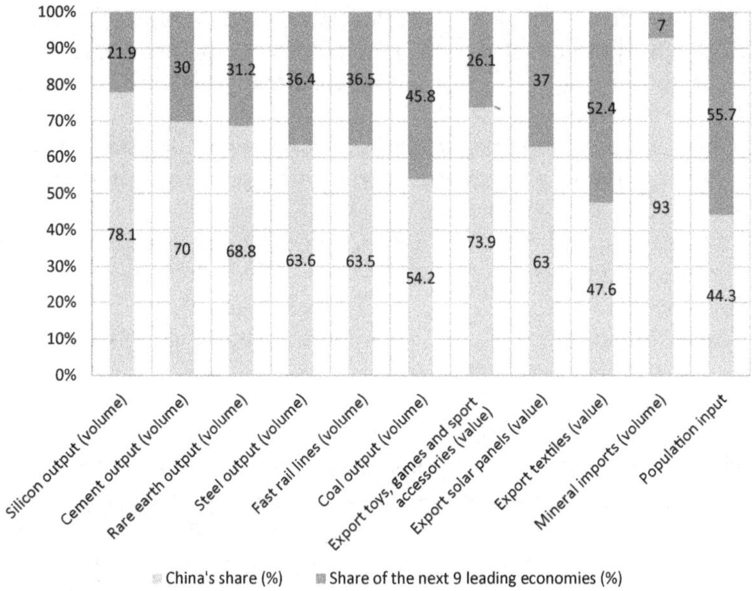

Figure 5.1. China's World Standing in Physical Inputs and Outputs, 2022–2024

Note: Numeral labels indicate percentages of the next nine leading countries combined.

Sources are available in the separate section of 'Figure Sources'.

top ten exporters of these products. To continue operating, China commands a 93 per cent share of the top ten mineral importers in the world. Here, GDP accounting can be skipped to avoid inevitable duplication.

If China's population share (44.3 per cent) in the top ten economies serves as par for China's domestic market potential (given that everybody needs consumption to live anywhere in the world), in an ideal world, China's imported inputs, outputs, and exports should all be close to the 44.3 per cent par. However, figure 5.1 shows that China deviates from this par, often by large margins. So, large quantities of China's outputs are not meant for its own domestic consumption, as follows:

Mineral imports	48.7 percentage points above the par
Silicon output	33.8 percentage points above the par
Cement output	25.7 percentage points above the par
Rare earths output	24.5 percentage points above the par

Steel output	19.3 percentage points above the par
High-speed rail construction	19.2 percentage points above the par
Coal output	9.9 percentage points above the par

As China's inputs and outputs go beyond its own domestic consumption needs, China has to export all the surpluses above the par:

Toys, games, and sports equipment exports	29.6 percentage points above the par
Solar panel exports	18.7 percentage points above the par
Textiles exports	3.3 percentage points above the par

Meanwhile, China's 44.3 per cent population share can also serve as a 'proxy par' for China's total labour inputs because the share of workers in a country's total population is relatively stable. Now, any output and exports above the 44.3 per cent proxy par is conceptually a result of higher capital inputs.[12] So, China's 'above par' position reflects the economy becoming increasingly 'capital intensive'.

Moreover, by Ricardian standards, China has not been in the internationally agreed upon opportunity cost saving game at all but has become an all-rounder that can produce many things at the lowest accounting cost, in line with Smithian standards.

2. From Unproductive Cheap Labour to an 'Absolute Advantage in Trade'

China began in 1976 with very little to offer the world in the way of either lower opportunity costs or lower accounting costs. China's low-cost labour was created during Mao's self-reliance era, when extreme low wages were combined with famine-level food rationing (tables 2.12, 2.13, and 2.15). But unlike the Ming-Qing period, international trade was replaced by Mao's autarky. So, its low-cost labour at best lay dormant. Mao and his lieutenants, who were responsible for creating China's cheap labour, tried once to employ such labour to produce cheap manufactures (iron and steel) without a market, but only succeeded in causing a mass famine instead (figure 2.6). To turn Mao's unproductive low-cost labour into an absolute advantage in trade, autarky needed to go first. It did under Deng Xiaoping (chapter 3).

What followed was a steep learning curve. China's low-cost labour needed to be employed productively in market-oriented production;

at the end of each production cycle output needed to be sold for the production cycle to continue; only then was low-cost labour tested by the market. The first taker of the cheap labour was China's domestic market; the international market emerged in a delayed fashion.

Evidently, China's coastal SEZs offered a window for export-oriented industrialisation (EOI) to marry China's cheap indigenous labour with external capital and technology. From the accounting cost point of view, there seemed no reason for this model not to work. However, from available data, the role of SEZs was limited (figure 3.2 and table 3.8). It is known that SEZs did not invest enough or export enough to constitute a critical mass in China's experiment. Now, it is also evident that SEZs failed to hire enough of China's cheap labour during the golden decade of China's WTO membership. On average, SEZs only employed 1.5 per cent of all industrial waged workers in the country (1998–2011). Data in figure 5.2 reveal that (1) the vast majority of companies that cashed in China's low-cost labour were in fact located outside SEZs; and (2) there was unremarkable 1 per cent increase in SEZs' share of China's national waged workers (from about 1 per cent to 2 per cent of China's total) over the decade after China joined the WTO.

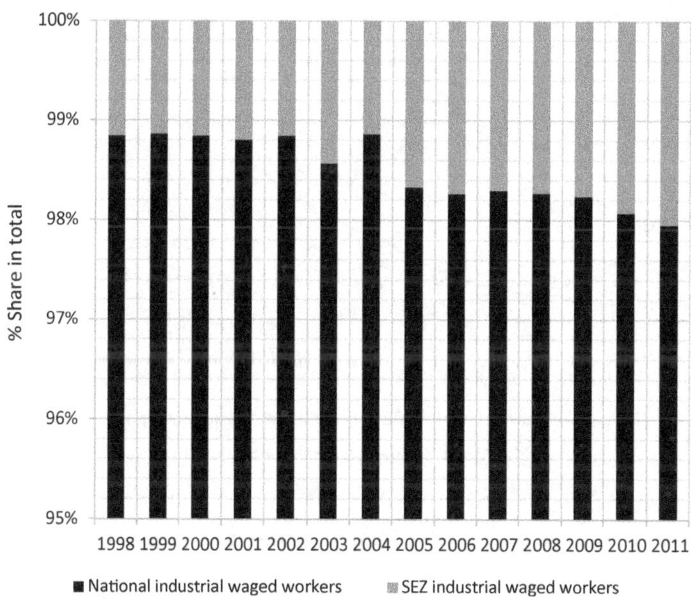

Figure 5.2. SEZs' Share of China's Industrial Workforce, 1998–2011

Sources are available in the separate section of 'Figure Sources'.

China-wide, it was again domestic industry that generated the lion's share of industrial output. Data in figure 5.3 show that China's domestic firms dominated industrial output values by a factor of 2.2 to 5.5 over foreign firms. The trough in 2004 suggests that domestic firms faced serious competition from foreign firms. If the trend had continued, then by 2008 foreign firms would have had the upper hand in China's industrial output values. But after 2004, domestic firms fought back and regained their position. This episode suggests that domestic firms narrowed the technology gap with foreign firms, as is obvious from the two linear growth lines of best fit.

As the main employers of China's low-cost labour were indigenous firms, China's 'absolute advantage in trade' did not really need FDI to cash in. Rather, the main players were TVEs; and the growth path was USI and EOI combined. Why? According to Fei Xiaotong's observation, in some cases rural labour was completely free for years.[13] In other words, labour in twentieth-century rural China may have been

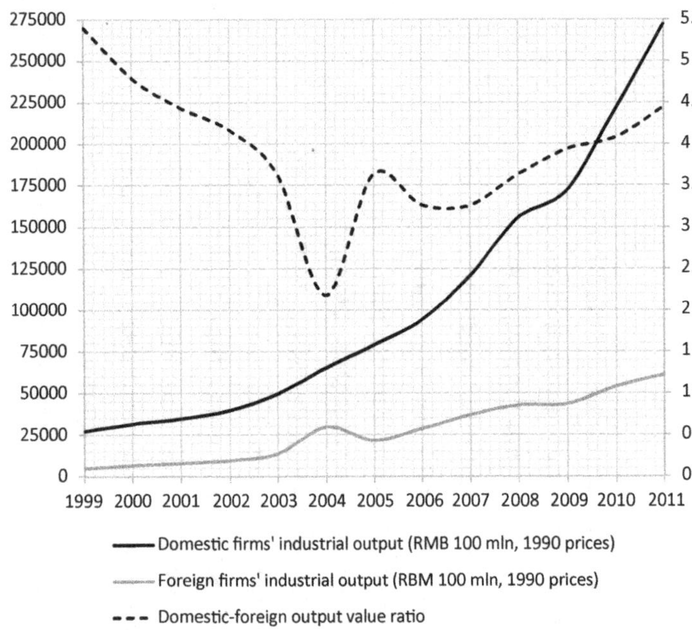

Figure 5.3. Industrial Output Values, Domestic versus Foreign Firms, 1999–2011

Note: Left Y-axis: Output value in RMB 100 million. Right Y-axis: Domestic firms' output to foreign firms' output ratio.

Sources are available in the separate section of 'Figure Sources'.

cheaper than any other known workforce anywhere in the world.[14] This zero-cost labour was not available for FDI. But it was common in the aforementioned Chayanovian model of self-exploitation, in which rural family labour was indeed free of charge.

It is also known that as early as 1985, at the time when SEZs – China's 'standing army of the economy' – practised 'import-oriented industrialisation' (IOI),[15] TVEs – China's rural guerrillas – initiated EOI and claimed a large share of China's total exports until 2000. As such, TVEs present a workable model that thrived on China's low-cost labour, a recognised growth model for East Asia.[16] If TVEs also traded, as they did, they represent the textbook example of a Smithian 'absolute advantage in trade'.

To demonstrate how China's low-cost labour was cashed in, China's footwear industry, dominated by private and often rural-based companies,[17] serves as a good example. It produces an average of 12.8 billion pairs of shoes annually and has successfully exported 9 billion pairs a year in recent decades. Figure 5.4 shows that persistently about 70 per cent of China's footwear output has been exported. Given that the current world population is about 8 billion (2022), China exports more than a pair of shoes, year-in and year-out, to every living soul on the planet. This pattern also applies to textiles, toys, games, sports accessories and, to a large extent, solar panels (figure 5.1).

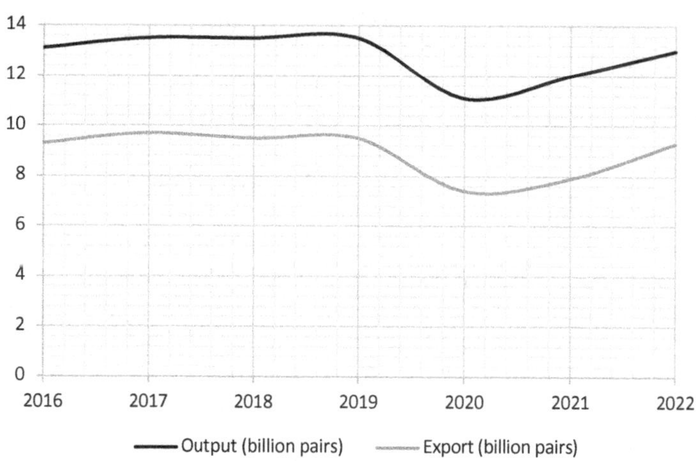

Figure 5.4. Footwear Output and Exports, 2016–2022

Note: Y-axis: Output of shoes (in billion pairs).

Sources are available in the separate section of 'Figure Sources'.

3. State-led 'Absolute Advantage in Trade' for Market Dominance

After 1978, low-cost labour became China's bankable 'endowment'. A door for foreign trade and FDI was also open. Intuitively, one correlates the two and builds a growth model. This turns out to be no more than a myth.

The problem was that China's trade balance was not guaranteed to go in China's favour when reforms began. Rather, China toes a fine line of surpluses (figure 4.6). Intuitively, with the market expansion that post-Mao China has achieved, one would expect wages in China to rise either due to labour market competition or due to living cost increases, or both. In other words, China's cheap labour should become more expansive on a *pro rata* basis with China's GDP take-off, which may explain China's thin line of trade surpluses.

The reality is very different. Urban wages fell exponentially behind GDP; although China's total GDP and urban wages both increased substantially, they, however, operated at completely different altitudes. Data in figure 5.5 are run on two scales that are over 10-fold apart. China's total GDP and GDP per head increased 138-fold (13.8 per cent per year) and 109-fold (13.1 per cent per year), respectively; and China's average wages only did so 11-fold (6.5 per cent per year) in the manufacturing industry and 13-fold (6.9 per cent per year) in the construction industry, respectively. So, urban wages have fallen desperately behind China's GDP.

Part of the explanation comes from the aforementioned government control over prices of urban food which kept urban living costs artificially low for about three decades after Mao (figure 4.4). If so, low growth in urban wages was artificially engineered by the state policy of 'getting prices wrong' (chapter 4).

Moreover, given that China's manufacturing products are in general exportable, China's RMB exchange rates with currencies of recipient countries of China's goods can be factored in for international cost accounting. If one takes the RMB–US$ exchange rate into account (as shown in figure 4.5), wages in China's manufacturing industry have fallen not only behind China's GDP but also China's domestic construction industry by 60 per cent as demonstrated in figure 5.6. Now, re-calculated growth in manufacturing wages is 5-fold for the same period, or 4.6 per cent annually, 10 per cent a year behind China's GDP.

This divergence exists because most of the output of the construction

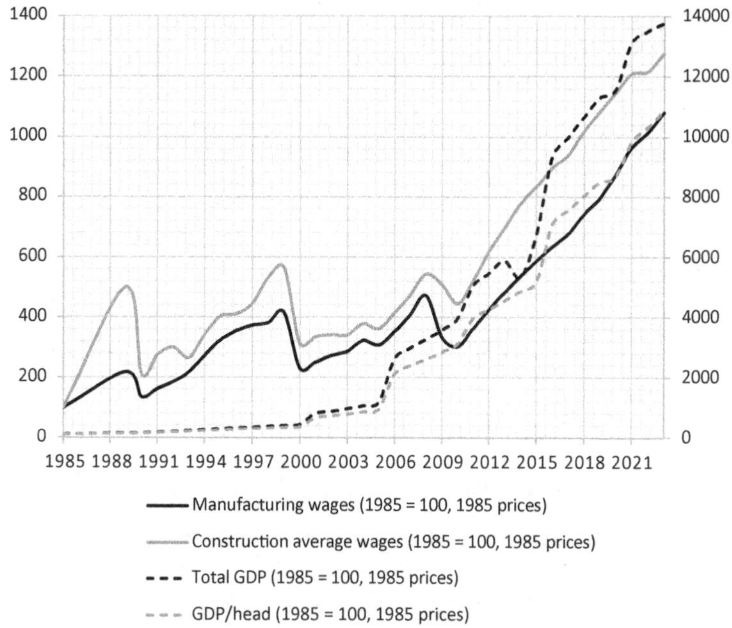

Figure 5.5. Growth Gap between GDP and Urban Wages, 1985–2023

Note: Left Y-axis: Average wage growth index (urban private sector). Right Y-axis: GDP growth index. The constant price is based on National Bureau of Statistics, *Statistical Year Book, 2023*, ch. 3.

Sources are available in the separate section of 'Figure Sources'.

industry (be it rail tracks, supermarkets, or apartment blocks) stays in China. So, the RMB–US$ exchange rate makes no difference to the sector. But changes in the RMB–US$ exchange rate make exportable manufactures cheaper by lowering China's real wages in the exporting sector. Simple.

Moreover, there is an issue regarding 'wage suppression' due to a lack of workers' rights in China.[18] More often than not, government officials side with factory bosses for the sake of 'social harmony' and local GDP performance, both being vital for bureaucrats' careers and promotions. Protecting workers' wage contracts thus rarely goes beyond lip service for officials. Wage arrears by employers (*qian xin*) and demands for unpaid wages by workers (*tao xin*) are common and often make trending lists in Chinese social media.[19] In a rare one-off report on thirty cases by the Ministry of Human Resources and Social Security, a total of RMB 36.3 million worth of wages went unpaid in 2021–2.[20] In 2024, another 1,866 cases were exposed with a total of

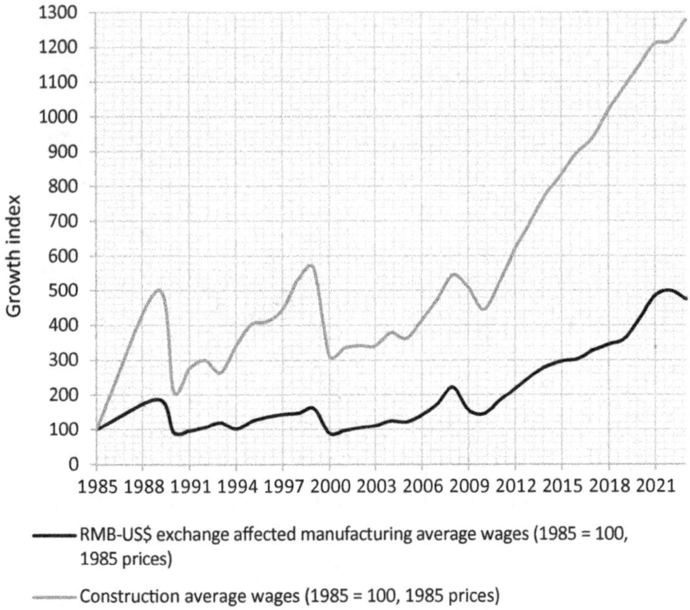

Figure 5.6. Urban Wages Affected by RMB–US$ Exchange Rates, 1985–2023

Note: The construction industry serves as a benchmark.

Sources are available in the separate section of 'Figure Sources'.

RMB 244 million in wage arrears.[21] These are likely to be the tip of the iceberg, as China's Supreme Court cited 69,000 cases with a total RMB 1.7 billion in wage arrears for 2024 alone.[22]

On top of wage arrears, since 2016 waged workers have been asked to follow a '996 Regime' common in the manufacturing industry, shorthand for a work schedule starting at 9 a.m., finishing at 9 p.m. and lasting 6 days a week (or 72 working hours per week), with no extra pay or leave,[23] despite Clause 36 of China's 1994 Labour Law, where it is written in black-and-white:[24]

> The State implements the following work-hour regime: daily working hours of all workers must not exceed eight hours; and on average weekly working hours of all workers must not exceed forty-four hours.

The law has been ignored. According to anti-996 campaigners, real wages under the 996 Regime are about 43 per cent of what workers should be paid.[25] This is within the range of 47–86 per cent of wage losses in China during the 2000s.[26] So, the 996 Regime generates a big saving for its practitioners. Others are very likely to follow suit or they will lose out to their competitors. Now, one can factor in the 996 Regime officially out of the closet in 2016. Data in figure 5.7 reveal that the suppression of wages in the construction sector reduced wage growth to 4.8 per cent a year while in manufacturing wages simply stagnated at 1.9 per cent a year. Now, the gap between China's GDP and workers' wages enlarges to 20-fold for the construction industry and 50-fold for manufacturing.

Both wage arrears and the 996 Regime can be attributed to the aforementioned low human rights which the state does little to improve on.[27] The draconian ban on any independent trade unions in Mainland China has been religiously enforced. Officially permitted trade unions are *de facto* branches of the ruling party. So, according to Clause Four of the 2021 Trade Union Law, 'all trade unions must persist in the Communist Party's leadership, socialism, a people's dictatorship, Marxism, Leninism, and Mao's thought' and so on.[28]

Even so, within the urban sector, there is a noticeable wage gap between construction workers and manufacturing workers (figures 5.5, 5.6, and 5.7), despite the fact that construction workers need less education and so should cost less to hire. So, intuitively, it should be the other way round. A sensible explanation is that workers in the

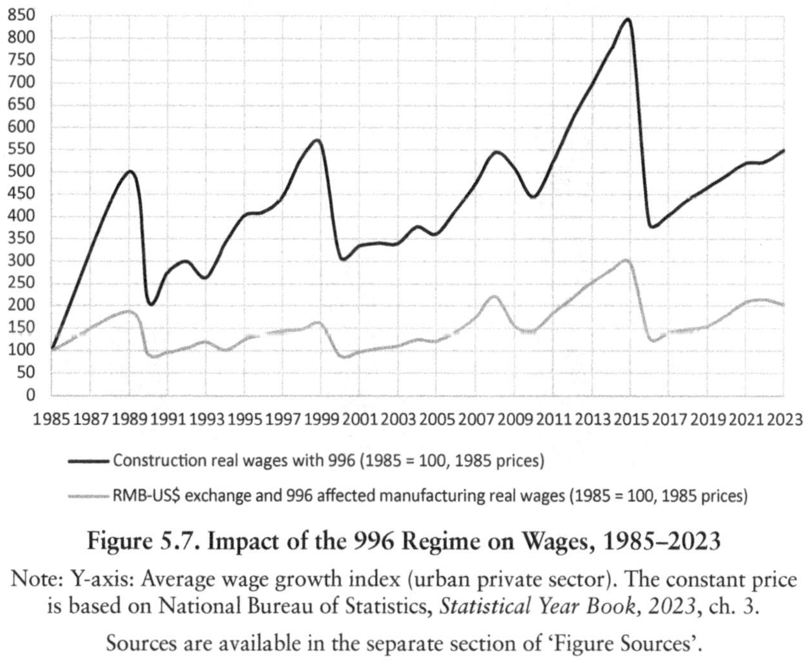

Figure 5.7. Impact of the 996 Regime on Wages, 1985–2023

Note: Y-axis: Average wage growth index (urban private sector). The constant price is based on National Bureau of Statistics, *Statistical Year Book, 2023*, ch. 3.

Sources are available in the separate section of 'Figure Sources'.

construction industry are often on seasonal short-term contracts and are thus mobile between the rural and urban sectors. These workers have home villages to fall back on. In addition, they often do not have a mortgage to pay in cities and thus losing a job is less consequential. Such an option does not exist for a large proportion of factory workers. More importantly, in the male-dominated construction industry, workers are more likely to resort to physical force against their bosses. Indeed, as data in figure 5.8 show, construction workers account for 1.6–2.2 times more strikes than their manufacturing comrades. Undoubtedly, strikes create bargaining power, and bargaining power leads to higher wages.

The whole business of keeping manufacturing wages artificially low in the past five decades cannot be justified by economic efficiency (known as Pareto optimality), and thus it is not sustainable. But why has it happened? Should it be beneficial for China to nurture a well-paid (10–50 times more to match China's GDP growth rate) working class and foster a growing domestic consumer market (10–50 times larger)? The answer cannot be found in welfare economics. Rather, one can attribute China's low wage choice to state policies which have little to do with a free market.

The accounting cost of labour aside, one wonders whether the CCP's 'socialism/communism with Chinese characteristics' is in fact

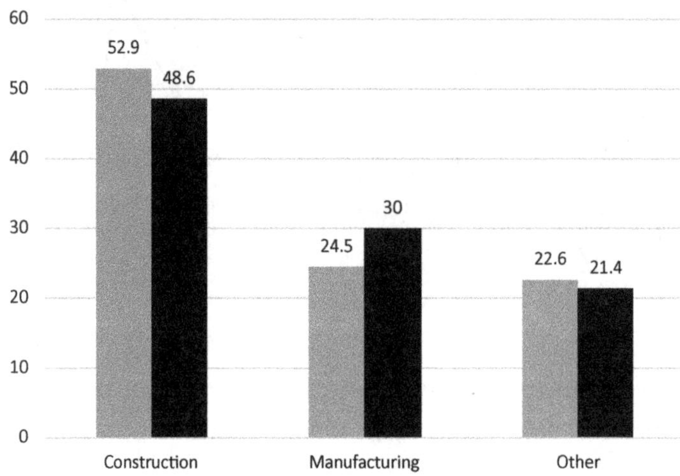

Figure 5.8. Industrial Strikes, 2023 and 2024

Note: Y-axis: % Share of all strikes in China. Left-side bars: 2023 data. Right-side bars: 2024 data.

Sources are available in the separate section of 'Figure Sources'.

'capitalism with Chinese characteristics', as ordinary workers are subject to ruthless exploitation within the law in favour of capital most of the time.

4. State-led 'Import-Export Combo'

Much of the discussion of China's economic model in the post-Mao years has been geared towards China's export performance and success.[29] On the surface, China's absolute advantage in trade with low-cost labour benefits China's exports. Even so, one must question why China has to produce and export that much. After all, Deng's income promotion scheme was humane (and even benevolent) compared with Mao's harsh policies that caused mass famine and widespread poverty. After all, Deng's programme of a 'moderately comfortable life' (*xiao kang*) with US$1,000 per head was very effective as the 'silver bullet' to re-establish the CCP's legitimacy to rule China.

With hindsight, the target of US$1,000 per head served the PRC merely in the short term. As US$1,000 per head was in sight and ordinary people's livelihoods were no longer in dire crisis, China's international power-building project regained priority on the CCP-PRC agenda. A leopard never changes its spots. For such a goal, foreign trade was viewed as a cash cow. The shift occurred in the mid-1980s. Firstly, it was China's military. Deng announced in 1984:

> To quadruple our GDP is important and will get China's annual GDP to one trillion American dollars and put China at the forefront of the world. . . . In terms of national strength, China will be a big power [in the world]. By then, if we use only one per cent of GDP for our national defence, the budget will be 10 billion American dollars which will make weapons upgrade very easy.[30]

Secondly, in 1988 Deng envisaged China's global technological standing:

> China must occupy a seat at the high table of the high-tech sector in the world.[31]

Thirdly, in terms of the end game, Deng openly declared in 1985 that economic growth in China should be categorically different from that in the West, with China's communism non-negotiable:

> Each and every policy of reform we have made so far is for both the growth of current socialism and the realisation of communism in the future.[32]

He elaborated it further in 1990 by taking industrial output as a gauge of China's communist strength:

> Our steel output needs to be 100 million to 120 million tonnes to meet what we desire, which becomes our development strategy. . . . In the next 30 to 50 years, if China's comprehensive national strength reaches the forefront of the world, the superiority of our communism will be verified.[33]

Demonstrating communist superiority over the capitalist world in terms of physical output has consistently been the ultimate goal of communist stakeholders such as Lenin, Stalin, and Mao whose materialist fixations were almost certainly inherited from the Russian Tsar Peter the Great (1672–1725, r.1682–1725).[34]

Again in 1990, Deng explained to his party:

> Whether or not China is able to resist international hegemonism and international power politics, and whether or not China keeps its communist system, all depends on the fast speed of China's economic growth.[35]

In 1992, Deng issued this instruction for Guangdong Province:

> [Communist] Guangdong needs to step up and catch up with the [capitalist] four Asian Tigers in twenty years' time.[36]

It is now obvious that GDP growth was a mere means which served a geopolitical end for the CCP. So, ordinary people's living standards made way for China's national strength.

Meanwhile, after the disastrous failure of Mao's model of self-reliance, China needed to find an alternative, hence the 'opening up' for trade. But this time, China did not aim to obtain foreign silver or opium as had happened during the Ming-Qing period (1368–1911). Rather, China required foreign industrial machines and/or their patents to upgrade China's national strength.

This returns us to the import-export combo as the key dynamic during China's opening up in the post-Mao era. Historically, the precedent for this approach was the Qing 'Westernisation Movement' from 1860 to 1895 (chapter 2). To be fair, this was also the approach with Mao's 'Sino-Soviet partnership' in the 1950s and 1960s before the relationship between the two communist countries went sour. On China's part, it was import-oriented industrialisation. Data in figure 5.9 show Mao's short-lived 'import-export combo' driven by capital-goods imports from the Soviet Union which petered off in 1965.

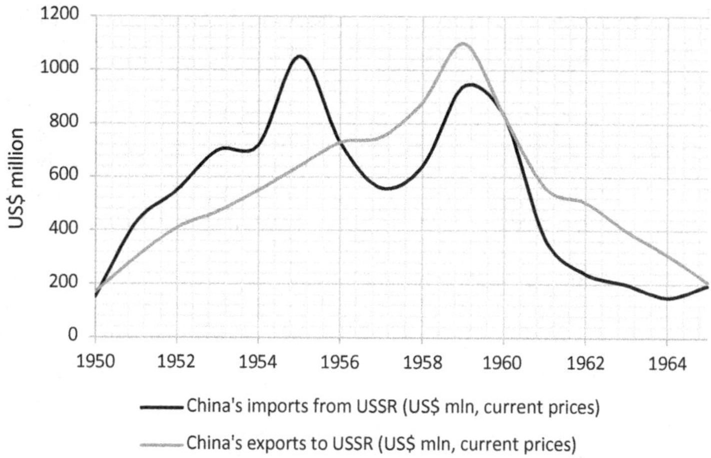

Figure 5.9. China's First Import-Export Combo, 1950–1965

Note: China's imports from the Soviet Union are traditionally called 'aid' as if they were free gifts. The harsh reality was that China had to pay every penny for such aid. By our standard, this was a straightforward textbook bilateral trade relationship.

Sources are available in the separate section of 'Figure Sources'.

After 1965, China's trade with the Soviet Union dropped to the floor. China found a new partner in the West. Data in table 5.1 show this Western dominance in trade with Mao's China in the 1970s.

However, given the fact that Mao's China was subject to the strict technological sanctions imposed by the 'Coordinating Committee for Multilateral Export Controls' (CoCom) established in 1949 in Paris, Western exports to China were overwhelmingly consumer goods mainly in the form of food (see table 2.16). Even so, the PRC's commercial connections were forged with the West. It was a matter of time before the CoCom sanctions were relaxed, as they were in the mid-1980s before ending in 1994, perfect for Deng Xiaoping's resumption of the import-export combo after China's two-decade long technological isolation from 1965 to 1985.

So, to a great extent, China had been there, done that. The formula is now repackaged and rephrased as the 'advantage of a late economic developer' (*houfa youshi*),[37] and 'overtaking the West by taking a short cut (*wandao chaoche*).[38] The following passage spells out the essence of China's chosen import dependency to obtain missing ingredients from the international market for China's four modernisations:

Table 5.1. Imports-Exports Shifting to the West, % Shares, 1970–1974

Year	Imports from USSR	From the West	Total
1970	4.0 (67)	96.0 (1602)	100 (1669)
1971	4.2 (80)	95.8 (1805)	100 (1885)
1972	5.0 (121)	95.0 (2300)	100 (2421)
1973	3.0 (136)	97.0 (4420)	100 (4556)
1974	2.1 (143)	97.9 (6535)	100 (6678)
Average	3.7	96.3	
	Exports to USSR	**To the West**	**Total**
1970	3.6 (57)	96.4 (1528)	100 (1585)
1971	3.9 (75)	96.1 (1830)	100 (1905)
1972	5.4 (134)	94.6 (2345)	100 (2479)
1973	3.3 (136)	96.7 (3960)	100 (4096)
1974	2.6 (139)	97.4 (5170)	100 (5309)
Average	3.8	96.2	

Note: (1) Values in US$ million in current prices are shown in parentheses. The Soviet share in China's imports and exports was consistently under 5 per cent. (2) Thanks to the technological sanctions imposed by the 'Coordinating Committee for Multilateral Export Controls' (CoCom), China was unable to obtain advanced technology from the West despite more trade in Mao's time.

Source: S.H. Chou, 'China's Foreign Trade', *Current History*, 71/419 (1976): 70–1.

> So long as less advanced economies can grow faster in technological changes than advanced countries through importing technology from the latter, not only will less advanced economies avoid falling into a perpetual trap of low-tech outputs, but they will also converge with [catch up with] advanced countries thanks to the higher pace of growth achieved by less advanced economies.[39]

Deng first raised the very same issue in 1978, twenty-seven years earlier:

> For our four modernisations, we need to learn how to obtain plenty of international help. Our starting point has to be the importation of internationally advanced technology and equipment.[40]

It is important to understand why China swallowed its pride and went for a self-confessed policy of state-led import dependency. As mentioned, an early attempt was made during the Sino-Soviet honeymoon in the 1950s. After the Soviet Union closed its door to China in the mid-1960s, China turned to the West when Mao was still in charge.

But Deng was more ambitious and aimed to catch up with the West more quickly as the Soviet Union was no longer a role model for China.

Meanwhile, the open market system of the post-war West could not and would not prevent China's shopping spree from being materialised. China's import dependency soon took shape.[41] Such import dependency is obvious in technology-embodied goods and materials coming to China.[42] Data in figure 5.10 reveal that technical devices and high-tech products account for 67 per cent of China's imports.

Post-war Japan also rose as an international trade giant. But the main difference between post-war Japan and Deng's China was that the former relied less and less on advanced economies for technology as time went by. Rather, Japan's main emphasis was on economic recovery from the Second World War rather than catching up with other industrial powers. To achieve it, Japan imported mainly industrial materials and food. Industrial equipment was far less important. Data in table 5.2 show that on average raw materials accounted for 79.1 per cent of Japan's imports and industrial technology-embodied equipment only 11.9 per cent which was about half of Japan's food imports in value.

Data for Taiwan in table 5.3 show a similar pattern: raw materials and consumer goods accounted for 71.2 per cent on average. Industrial equipment amounted only to 12.7 per cent. There is a lack of reliable historical data showing a breakdown of South Korea's imports.[43]

In the beginning, the West seems to have welcomed China as a new customer. After all, China's large population served as a potential market. Orders from China increased business profits and employment

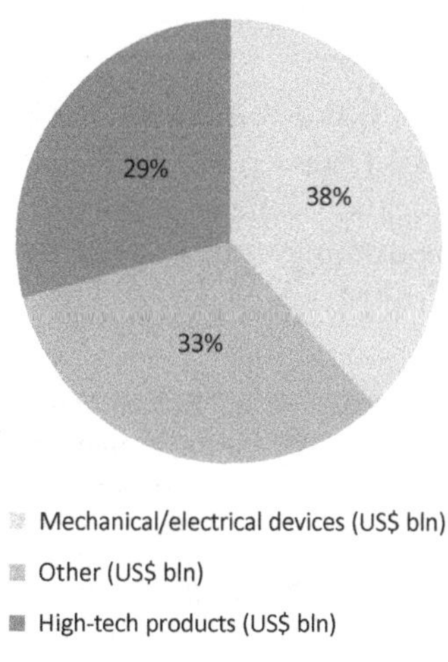

Figure 5.10. China's Imports Worldwide (US$ Billion), 2024

Sources are available in the separate section of 'Figure Sources'.

Table 5.2. Japan's Import Pattern, % Value, 1965–1989

	1965–9	1970–4	1975–9	1980–4	1985–9	Average
Raw materials	63.3	59.7	55.9	58.1	49.5	57.3
Of which oil	*16.1*	*21.4*	*36.5*	*40.5*	*20.6*	*27.0*
Food	22.7	21.5	25.0	20.8	19.2	21.8
Sub-total	86.0	81.2	80.9	78.9	68.7	79.1
Equipment	10.8	12.4	10.5	12.0	13.8	11.9
Other	3.2	6.4	8.6	9.1	17.5	9.0
Total	100	100	100	100	100	100

Source: IMF, 'Changing Structure of Japanese Trade Flows', January 1990 (Washington, DC: IMF, 1990), Table 7, https://www.elibrary.imf.org/view/journals/001/1990/107/article-A001-en.xml.

Table 5.3. Taiwan's Import Pattern, % Value, 1960–1980

	1960	1965	1970	1975	1980	Average
Raw materials	64.0	65.5	62.8	62.6	70.8	65.1
Of which oil	*6.4*	*2.3*	*3.1*	*10.5*	*20.8*	*8.0*
Consumer goods	8.1	5.1	4.9	6.8	5.8	6.1
Sub-total	72.1	70.6	67.7	69.4	76.6	71.2
Equipment	15.5	12.4	13.3	12.1	10.4	12.7
Other	12.4	17.0	19.0	18.5	13.0	16.0
Total	100	100	100	100	100	100

Source: Schive Chi, 'Trade Patterns and Trends of Taiwan', in Colin I. Bradford, Jr. and William H. Branson (eds) *Trade and Structural Change in Pacific Asia* (Chicago: University of Chicago Press, 1987), p. 311.

in the G7 economies. This was a 'win-win' for both sides at that time. China's leadership wished to keep this 'win-win' narrative: Deng told his Western audience that China's import dependency would not become a threat to the existing world order. At a 1985 meeting with former British Prime Minister Sir Edward Heath (1916–2005), Deng told his guest:

> China's current foreign trade is 50 billion American dollars. . . . To assume that it quadruples to 200 billion American dollars by the end of this century, it should not be excessive for developed countries, but will be quite enough for us.[44]

In the same year and in the same vein, Deng reassured Japanese business leaders:

> Some developed countries now worry about more products from China reducing their own exports. . . . But with their advanced technology

> and high-end products, developed countries should have nothing to be afraid of with China![45]

So, when WTO membership dropped rather naturally on China's lap in 2001, China's import dependency game was internationally granted.

But during the first decade of reforms, imports appeared to come about more easily than exports. As a result, import affordability proved to be a serious problem for China's treasury. In 1985, Premier Zhao Ziyang (1919–2005) told his party and government that the main problem was that China was importing more than it could afford:[46]

> As a developing country, it is inevitable that our shortage in foreign currencies stays with us for a long time. . . . Our opening up cannot be imports only; rather we should keep up exports in exchange for our imports. . . . We need to earn more foreign currencies to achieve a balance of payments [which we do not have at the moment].

In this context, as discussed earlier, SEZs, the brainchild of Deng's reforms, failed to export enough to fulfil what they were designed to do (table 3.8). So much so, Deng Xiaoping himself intervened in 1985–7.[47]

Despite China's self-confessed import dependency and the early mismatch between imports and exports, much of the discussion of the China Model has been geared towards China's export success along the lines of EOI.[48] It is time to set things straight: China's self-confessed state-led import dependency strategy to purchase technology-intensive foreign imports is designed to avoid risky and costly R&D in order to catch up quickly with the West. It is a simple game. Export in order to import and import in order to catch up with the West. So, exporting was merely a means to an end.

Thus, the export orientation of the Chinese economy certainly exists but it is subordinated to the purpose of buying technology-intensive foreign imports in order to catch up with the West.[49] So, as long as China had not yet reached superpower status, China had to nurture a continuous 'imports – exports – imports' cycle. China did it, but only just (figure 4.6). To highlight China's plight, Bo Xilai, China's Trade Minister, told his audience in Paris in 2005 after China ordered five A380 passenger jets: 'China has to sell 800 million shirts to buy a single A380 passenger jet!'[50] That deal for five A380s was worth 4 billion shirts made in China. China had to find ways to sell that many shirts overseas.

Against this backdrop, the state-led import dependency *ex ante* has to be the ultimate *raison d'être* for wages in China to be capped.

Technology-intensive foreign imports are relatively expansive. So labour in China as a domestic input factor has to be made cheap enough to produce sellable exports to purchase those foreign imports. The same can also be said for the motivation behind China's unilateral changes in the RMB–US$ exchange rate (figure 4.5).

5. The Limits and Unsustainability of the 'China Model'

Bearing in mind that the China Model is designed to catch up with the West, so the results are of paramount importance. The vital factor here is whether China is capable of inventing and innovating enough to make the economy technologically dynamic. Despite incomplete data, some general trends are detectable. In terms of manufactures, China has become a dominant force in the world, at least in sheer output volumes (figure 5.1). In that sector, China seems to have performed well since the 1980s.

China's agricultural productivity demonstrates a mixed bag. Data in table 5.4 show that new technology contributed 5.1 percentage points annually to China's total agricultural output growth from 1996 to 2000. That momentum, however, declined to 3.2 percentage points per year from 2000 to 2005. Then it ran out of steam and entered negative territory as a 3.7 percentage point drag on output growth after 2005. As such, after 2005 the drive to catch up with the West stopped for the sector.

Table 5.4. Agricultural TFP Performance, 1996–2007

Period	% Annual TFP gain	Cumulative gain index (1996 = 100)
1996–2000	5.1	122*
2000–5	3.2	143†
2005–7	-3.7	36§

Note: TFP: Total factor productivity, a parameter which is calculated using the simple formula 'Total factor productivity = Total output ÷ Total inputs'. Ideally, TFP > 0, meaning that an extra gain is made in the total outputs with the known total inputs. That extra gain is attributed to the role of technology that makes total inputs more efficient. * Cumulative TFP growth achieved by 2000. † Cumulative TFP growth achieved by 2005. § Cumulative TFP growth achieved by 2007.
Source: Sun Lingwang, Francis Tuan, Fred Gale, Agapi Somwarn, and James Hansen, 'Recent Trends in China's Agricultural Productivity Growth at Province Level, 1985–2007', Paper for National Bureau of Economic Research, 2011, https://users.nber.org/~confer/2011/SI2011/PRCR/Wang_Tuan_Gale_Somwaru_Hansen.pdf.

In comparison, scientific research in China seems to be catching up with the West rather quickly.[51] Data in table 5.5 show that in 1980, the G7 countries claimed a 60 per cent share of total world research output. China's contribution was negligible. Three decades later, in 2011, China's share had increased to 14 per cent of the world total and the G7's share had dropped to 53 per cent. In 2020, China's share had increased to a quarter of the world total while the G7's share had slid to 42 per cent. Overall, a 'zero-sum' game.

But counterintuitively, science and education have not been top priorities in China's five-year plans over the past three decades (Appendix 5). Earmarked state expenditure for research only doubled from 0.8 to 1.7 per cent of GDP from 1999 to 2008 (increasing 8 per cent annually).[52] Thus, if 'inventions and innovations' have *not* been generously financed inside China, the unprecedented number of privately funded young Chinese studying overseas may hold the key here (figure 3.1). Or one could look to alleged technological espionage. This line of investigation into China's 'invention-innovation black box' should be kept open, in the hope that more data become available in the future.

Assuming that China is on its way to fulfil Deng's mission of heading towards superpower status in the world, there is a catch. China's 'import-export combo' can thrive only in 'income and price elastic' markets overseas, be it for toys, clothes, white goods, or consumer electronics. To operate in such a market, as incomes of foreign consumers are out of China's control, the only factor that China can control is price-cutting to lure buyers to purchase goods made in China.[53] Now, the aforementioned domestic wage suppression begins to make perfect sense. But China's absolute advantage in trade may

Table 5.5. Research Output, % World Total, China versus G7, 1980–2020

	G7	China
1980	60* (100)	<1* (100)
2000	–	10† (1000)
2011	53§ (88)	14§ (1400)
2020	42* (70)	25* (2500)

Sources: * (1) Jonathan Adams and Martin Szomszor, 'A Converging Global Research System', *Quantitative Science Studies*, 3/3 (2022): 716–17; † (2) Sylvia S. Serger, Cong Cao, Caroline S. Wagner, Xabier Goenaga, and Koen Jonkers, 'What Do China's Scientific Ambitions Mean for Science and the World', *Issues in Science and Technology*, 5 April 2021, https://issues.org/what-do-chinas-scientific-ambitions-mean-for-science-and-the-world/; § (3) Hui-Zhen Fu and Yuh-Shan Ho, 'Independent Research of China in Science Citation Index Expanded during 1980–2011', *Journal of Informetrics*, 7/1 (2013): 213.

not persist in the long run. And the international market may not be open to China forever.

This is because China's cheap exports may be tolerated by the average consumer in the West whose total utility welfare increases in the short run by having more consumer manufactures at lower prices. The best example is China's exports to the large and open economy of the United States. Data in figure 5.11 indicate that American trade deficits with China began in 1985 at the level of a mere US$6 million that year. It had swelled 70,000 times (current prices) by 2018 until a peak was reached. From 1986 to 2018, the American trade deficit with China grew at the astonishing rate of 40.2 per cent per year for three long decades. The year 2001 was the moment when the acceleration began, coinciding with China's WTO membership.

In the long run, however, price drops create business casualties. Western companies that are unable to compete with China's absolute advantage in low wages decline or go bust and Western workers lose their jobs, a process known as 'deindustrialisation' or 'economic hollowing out'.[54] When this happens on an industrial scale, the Western consumer market slows down as its demand curve shifts to the left, and some cheap imports can no longer be sold. In other words, the market can no longer clear itself. This in turn forces China to bulldoze as many overseas markets as possible to finance its import dependency programme.

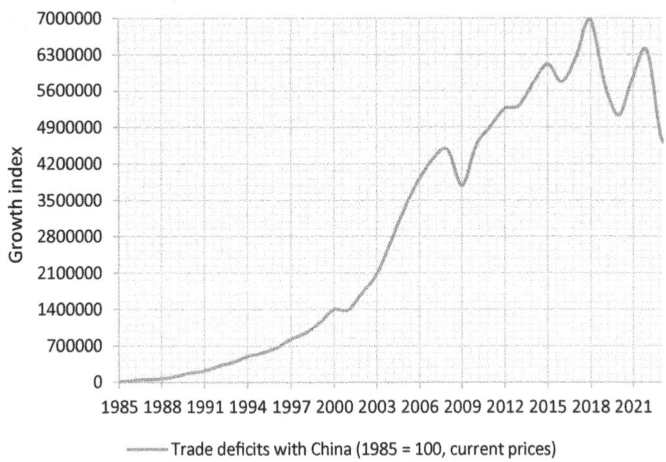

Figure 5.11. United States' Annual Trade Deficit* with China, 1985–2023

Note: * The value of goods in US$, current prices.

Sources are available in the separate section of 'Figure Sources'.

According to a study conducted in the 2000s, in the United States each new job that was supported by American exports to China was correlated with 7.1 job losses due to China's cheap exports to America. From 2001 to 2007, Sino–US bilateral trade was associated with the loss of 2.3 million American manufacturing jobs. But those were still the early days of China's cheap consumer manufactures preying on the American home market.[55]

Not surprisingly, since the 1990s, China's inroad into modernity has been littered with complaints about its foul play. China has consequently become the main target of accusations and investigations in international anti-dumping and anti-subsidy cases, with complaints made by two dozen countries. The limited data in table 5.6 reveal that annual cases levied against China's international business wrongdoings nearly doubled from 1995 to 2024. China's global share of trade disputes increased from 24 per cent in 1995 to 34 per cent in 2019. The main problem was dumping, which outnumbered government subsidy cases by a factor of 8.7 (2,479 cases versus 285 cases). This is highly consistent with China's supply-driven model underpinning its recent growth and development.

In addition, China's growth strategy has made the stifling of the domestic market a pre-condition for maximum imports. Not only is the size of China's domestic market very limited but it also tends to be insensitive to price changes.[56]

The inelastic demand in China's domestic consumer market has been deeply rooted in a combination of low wages, high costs of

Table 5.6. Cases Formally Filed against China, 1995–2024

Period	Anti-dumping	Anti-subsidies	Annual	% World total
1995–2008	1,327	—	102	24
1995–2019	—	97		34
2009–2023	945	188	81	—
2024	198*	—	198	—
Total	2,479	285		

Note: * Combined with anti-subsidies.

Sources: 'The Manufacturing Trade Remedies Alliance Report (TWC 0002)', 2019, https://committees.parliament.uk/writtenevidence/104880/html/; Simon Lester and Huan Zhu, 'The Use of Trade Remedies against China: Data since WTO Entry Shows Frequent, Steady Usage', *China Trade Monitor*, 31 July 2024, https://www.chinatrademonitor.com/the-use-of-trade-remedies-against-china-data-since-wto-entry-shows-frequent-steady-usage/; Ryan McMorrow and Wenjie Ding, 'China's Export Boom Sparks Record Number of Trade Challenges', *Financial Times*, 31 March 2025, https://www.ft.com/content/c4bce44e-9c66-4d74-bebd-0f35f0ea007f.

tertiary education and high housing prices (chapter 4), as well as a lack of social welfare, especially in the form of unemployment benefits, universal medical care, and universal old-age pensions. Data in figure 5.12 confirm that education and social welfare have not been priorities in state economic planning since reforms began.

So, ordinary households discipline themselves to save up to make ends meet in both the short run and long run. Since 1978, per-capita private household savings have increased 711-fold with an annual increase of 15.7 per cent (figure 2.6). Usually, these savings are not used to purchase consumer manufactures but for buying apartments, paying for children's education, covering family medical care, and providing old-age pensions. China's domestic demand capacity for consumer manufactures is thus far weaker than in the G7 countries. But that suits China's import dependency and export orientation (or 'import-export combo') fine, as more consumer manufactures can go overseas. The knock-on effect is that high savings by Chinese households accumulate in state-owned banks that are willing to invest in big projects only. Such projects are often of the capital-intensive type

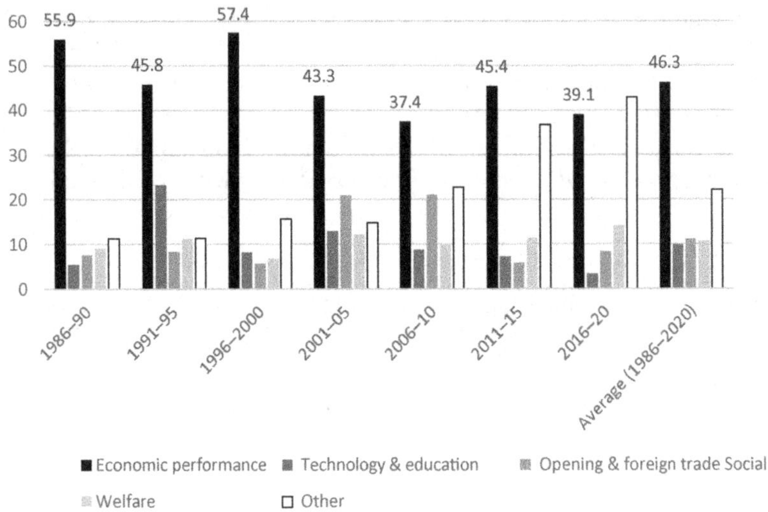

Figure 5.12. Recurring Issues in the State-run Five-Year Plans, 1986–2020

Note: Each cohort represents a five-year state planning period. Seven in total. Categories are the repertoire issues across all five-year plans. Numeral labels: percentages in the total word counts in the published state planning documents. Each plan shows a considerable degree of path dependence on the previous plans. Others: *ad hoc* issues or tasks for the designated planning periods.

Sources are available in the separate section of 'Figure Sources'.

and do not need many workers. Thus, household savings are on the rise, but jobs are not.

This mechanism is highlighted in figure 5.13 which shows how state planning feeds through the economy. It begins with domestic savings, which are channelled through the state-run priority loop to facilitate state-run imports. This then leads to exports in exchange for imports. Exports in turn incentivise domestic investment which then leads to domestic jobs and income. At this point, the economy faces two choices: either more domestic savings or more domestic consumption. Saving is favoured by households. The priority loop thus begins all over again. The subordinate loop is based on domestic consumption. But China's domestic consumption is detached from the 'import-export-combo', and cannot possibly support China's swelling output capacity. So, if for any reason foreign trade is interrupted, China faces an immediate crisis of overproduction. FDI makes the crisis even worse.

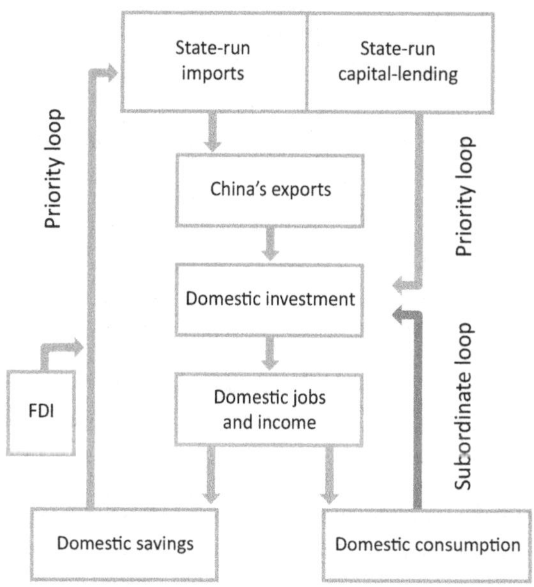

Figure 5.13. Mismatch between Domestic Savings and Domestic Consumption

Note: This is a top-heavy model. China's export market along the priority loop is powered by domestic savings and, to a lesser extent, FDI. The priority loop is also responsible for capital lending for investment projects in favour of exports. China's domestic market is limited by domestic consumption after savings.

To illustrate the model further, figure 5.14 probes China's micro-level mechanisms from the household level up. It all begins with 'household budgeting' in which household savings are given priority. Household savings then go to either banks or the stock market for returns. Given that growth in domestic consumer manufactures clashes with the households' propensity to save, it becomes a 'weak growth sector' in China. So, banks and public companies tend not to invest in that sector. The only other option is to invest in 'strong growth' sectors such as infrastructure and heavy industry. But infrastructure and heavy industry are capital-intensive, meaning that the same amount of capital investment creates fewer new jobs compared with farming or consumer manufacturing. In addition, jobs in expert

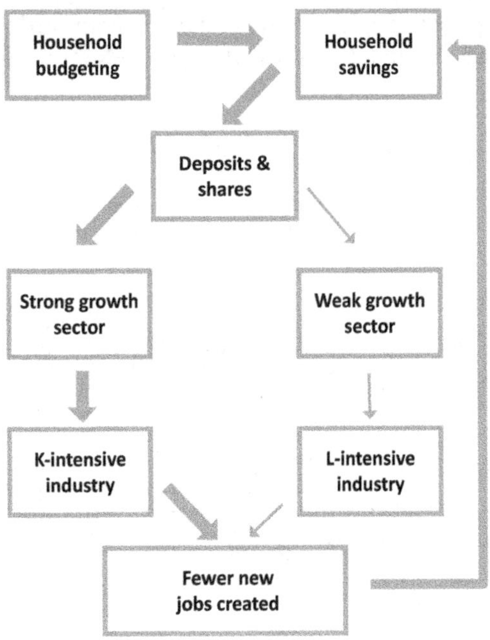

Figure 5.14. Endogenous Domestic Growth Constraints

Note: K-intensive: 'Capital-intensive'. L-intensive: 'Labour-intensive'. Thick arrows: strong incentives. Thin arrows: weak incentives. Angled arrow: re-enforced incentives. 'Household budgeting' is determined by low wages, high housing prices, and a lack of social welfare. These in turn make household savings imperative. The need for household savings weakens demand for consumer manufactures. So, banks and public companies opt for infrastructure and heavy industrial projects to invest in. But such investment will not help employment nor wage incomes due to the capital-intensive nature of these projects. So, households have to save even harder in the future.

manufacturing are low paid. As a result, households are forced to save even more. This is the self-defeating, unintended path that China is now travelling down. This constitutes China's Growth Limit Number One.

Data in figure 5.15 show (1) cumulative growth of 720-fold in infrastructure construction from 1992 to 2023 measured by completed floor area and (2) 29-fold growth in heavy industry from 2011 to 2024, here proxied by the total length of high-speed rail tracks. China has been trying consciously to invest and build its way out of the weak demand for consumer manufactures in its domestic market. But over-supply is inevitable because houses and fast rails cannot be exported after they are finished. According to a 2022 national survey, China has a total of 600 million permanent buildings, on average 2.3 persons per building.[57] A housing market recession is now spreading fast in urban China.

In addition, there is a catch. All railway lines are automatically owned by the state, all residential buildings are on a 70-year lease, all commercial buildings are on a 30-year lease, and the land beneath these buildings belongs to the state. So, all the construction projects are like putting money and assets into the government's own pocket, hence the zeal, which is disconnected from China's domestic purchasing power.

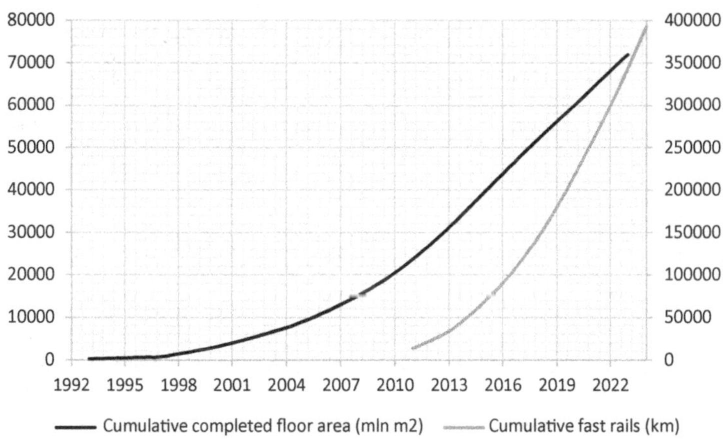

Figure 5.15. Investment-driven and Supply-driven Domestic Construction, 1992–2024

Note: Left Y-axis: Cumulative completed floor area for housing in million m^2.
Right Y-axis: Cumulative fast rail tracks in km.

Sources are available in the separate section of 'Figure Sources'.

From a balance sheet point of view, supply-driven construction growth is well in advance of the domestic investment ability of China's private sector, using household savings as a proxy.[58] In other words, even if all the cumulative savings had been released, they would still have been unable to support China's construction boom. Foreign investment could help, but dividends and interest need to be paid. Data in table 5.7 indicate that from 1978 to 2023 China's domestic household savings amounted to a maximum of RMB 11,601.4 billion, not even enough to support China's high-speed rail investment from 2010 to 2024 (costing RMB 49,979.7 billion), let alone China's housing construction boom from 1992 to 2023 (costing RMB 750,619.8 billion). So, we have a problem.

The pattern is now clear. China's domestic savings and domestic demand cannot support China's production capacity. This problem

Table 5.7. Mismatch between Domestic Household Savings and Investment Sprees, 1978–2024

	Cumulative household savings, 1978–2023	Cumulative completed floor area, 1992–2023	Cumulative high-speed rail, 2010–2024
Physically constructed		71,987.4 million m^2	392,614 km
Cost per unit		Cost per m^2: RMB 10,427.1 (2018)*	Cost per km: US$19 million (2017)
Total value	RMB 11,601.4 billion	RMB 750,619.8 billion†	US$7,459.6 billion or RMB 49,979.7 billion
Index (Savings = 100)	100	6,470	431

Note: * This is the upper bound when China's housing prices were highest on the eve of the Covid-19 pandemic. But the gap is so big that a drop of 90 per cent in housing prices after 2018 still overwhelms domestic savings 6.5:1. † To assume that all the housing construction costs are financed by foreign investment, with a 1.5–1.8 per cent annual dividend in the American S&P 500 market or 3.5–4.5 per cent annual dividend in the UK FTSE 100 market,[59] the annual dividend or interest payout will be in the region of RMB 11,260–33,778 billion. Thus China's household savings were barely enough to finance the interest payment for foreign investments.
Sources: (1) Private savings, the same as in figure 2.6. (2) Housing and fast rail construction, the same as in figure 5.14. (3) Construction cost in the final sale price, the same as in figure 4.2. (4) Fast rail construction cost, based on Martha Lawrence, Richard Bullock, and Ziming Liu, *China's High-Speed Rail Development* (Washington, DC: World Bank, 2019), p. 3. (5) RMB–US$ in 2017: 6.7, https://www.poundsterlinglive.com/history/USD-CNY-2017.

cannot be corrected on China's part because China's import dependency requires minimal consumer manufactures for China's home market and maximum consumer manufactures going overseas. So, the ongoing debate on 'turning inward to the domestic market' (*nei xunhuan*) and 'double dipping in the export market and domestic market' (*shuang xunhuan*) remains a moot point.[60] This is China's Growth Limit Number Two.

This gap between limited household savings and ever-increasing investment projects has been bridged by domestic debt, which has been in the media headlines in recent years.[61] In particular, government debt has quadrupled from 21 per cent to 88 per cent of China's total GDP at an annual rate of 5 per cent, faster than China's GDP. Figure 5.16 shows that China's total GDP expanded 50-fold (1980 constant prices) at a rate of 15 per cent per annum. But government debt swelled 200-fold at a rate of 20 per cent a year over three decades, all happening in peace-time.[62] The sustainability of such a practice is highly questionable.

Meanwhile, geopolitically speaking, now that China has harvested all the low hanging fruit, such as clothes, shoes, and white goods, the West has become less tolerant towards China marching all the way into the G7 Club. The first warning shot was fired in 2018 by the US Trump Administration after Huawei took the West off guard by its ability to provide the global telecommunication market with

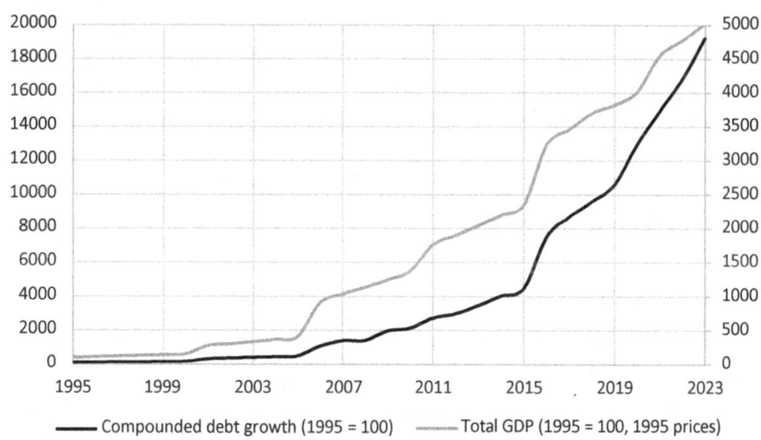

Figure 5.16. Growth in Government Debt versus Total GDP, 1995–2023/4

Note: Left Y-axis: Compounded Government Debts Growth Index.
Right Y-axis: Total GDP Growth Index.

Sources are available in the separate section of 'Figure Sources'.

cutting-edge 5G technology. It served as a wake-up call. The United States and its allies were alarmed after sleepwalking for decades into China's state-led supply-driven universe.[63]

As a beneficiary of globalisation, free trade, and the WTO, China sees nothing wrong with its publicly announced Smithian absolute advantage in trade and its bet on modernity and superpower status. So, there seems no difference between, say, Huawei's 3G and Huawei's 5G, as long as Huawei's tech sells outside China. After all, there has been a 'flying geese model' with which manufactures of different levels pass on from a leader to followers peacefully in an East Asian relay.[64] So, China openly announced in 2015 its hitherto most ostentatious package known as 'Made in China 2025', aiming to become a new world leader in ten technological fields.[65] This plan was accompanied by plans for a new China-centred world order called 'the East rising and the West declining' (*dongsheng xijiang*) and a new confrontational style of 'wolf-warrior diplomacy' (*zhanlang waijiao*),[66] both effectively removing any misunderstanding of China's true ambition.

For the G7, however, the flying geese model is permitted on condition that the G7 remain as the leaders as the model suggests, because the livelihood of the leading goose depends on it. China clearly challenges this world order.[67] Since 2015, trade quarrels and rifts between the G7 and China have not only increased but also become highly politicised with a heavy dose of national sovereignty and security.[68] It is obvious to the G7 that China's unilateral pursuit of an 'absolute advantage in trade' is a zero-sum game and produces losers.

Meanwhile, since the 2010s, two doors have been closing on China. The door for goods heading to China (vital for China's four modernisations) and the door for goods heading out of China (vital for paying for China's imports). This is likely to end China's uninterrupted 'import-export combo' loop. The 2018 Trade War and the 2025 Tariff War between the United States and China have become part of a new normal for the world. This is China's Growth Limit Number Three.

Last but not the least, the resource constraint looms large for the China Model. One wonders how long the world's natural resources can support China's growth that craves all known resources on this planet. As demonstrated in figure 5.1, China imports 93 per cent of minerals among the top ten importers but produces only 54 (coal as a proxy) to 78 (silicon as a proxy) per cent of output among the top ten producers. It hints at China's resource inefficiency, not to mention the high degree of industrial pollution inside China (figures 4.14 and 4.15). This is China's Growth Limit Number Four.

6. The Covid-19 Shock: A World without China

Despite the ongoing trade rifts and frictions (table 5.6), the fact that China has climbed out from Maoist autarky to become the undisputed main importer (figures 5.9–5.12) and main exporter in the world has created an obvious path dependence for China for the rest of the twenty-first century. The question seems not whether China will become the largest economy in the world, but when.

China's ability was tested by the financial meltdown in 2008, when the G7 economies collectively suffered from a banking crisis. China, however, survived largely unscathed with uninterrupted growth (figures 3.3, 3.4, 3.6 and 3.10). So much so, China gained the reputation of being the ballast of globalisation during a major crisis.[69] It seems that the world may have to put up with China for good or bad, thanks to China's sheer weight in the global economy. In this context, the 'Belt and Road Initiative', which began five years later in 2013, expanded China's influence in a truly global manner across time zones and war zones.[70] National boundaries seem no longer relevant to China.

The West was alarmed. To counter-balance China's advancement, the 'Comprehensive and Progressive Agreement for a Trans-Pacific Partnership' (CPTPP), nicknamed the 'mini-WTO', was formed in 2018. It has twelve member countries mainly in the Pacific region. But even though it is a Pacific country, China's application for membership has been ruthlessly turned down. An ominous omen.

Then, came the real acid test in 2019 with the Covid pandemic. The virus stalled the global growth engine in China, which happened to be the epicentre of the Covid outbreak at the end of 2019. In the following three years until 2022, China implemented a draconian 'zero tolerance lockdown'. Assembly lines in China were stopped, cargo planes grounded; container ocean liners heading for China berthed; and global supply chains broken. Suddenly, there was a trading world without China for three long years in a 'perfect storm'.

The immediate impact of China's unilateral lockdown on the rest of the world was man-made scarcity of simple manufactured items such as facial masks and personal protection outfits on an industrial scale. Worldwide, trade tied to 'global value chains' (GVC) declined by 30 per cent, compared with a 20 per cent fall in trade linked to non-GVC industries.[71] The G7, which traded heavily with China, saw their goods trade in free fall.[72] Table 5.8 shows that on average the G7 suffered a 17.9 per cent and 24.2 per cent decline in exports and imports, respectively. The total decline in foreign trade was 42.1 per

Table 5.8. Impact of Covid on G7 Trade, in Value, 2019–2022

Country	Change in exports, peak-to-trough %	Change in imports, peak-to-trough %	Change in total trade, peak-to-trough %
Canada	−19.0	−21.0	−40.0
France	−31.3	−23.0	−54.3
Germany	−23.0	−14.4	−37.4
Italy	−28.2	−21.5	−49.7
Japan	−20.8	−4.1	−24.9
UK	−22.7	−24.2	−46.9
USA	−24.4	−17.3	−41.7
Average	−24.2	−17.9	−42.1

Note: For pre-Covid patterns, see figures 5.9–5.12.
Source: 'Recent trends in the international trade flows of G7 economies', 10 October 2022, https://www.ons.gov.uk/businessindustryandtrade/internationaltrade/articles/recenttrendsintheinternationaltradeflowsofg7economies/2022-10-10.

cent. The worst hit economies were France (−54.4 per cent in total trade) and Italy (−49.7 per cent in total trade), followed by the UK, USA, and Canada (−46.9 per cent, −41.7 per cent and −40 per cent, respectively).

However, by 2023, the GDP of the G7 economies had all recovered.[73] Apart from innate recovery mechanisms from economic injury, much can be attributed to a combination of supply diversification away from China, known as 'global decoupling', on the one hand, and reindustrialisation in G7 economies under tariff protection on the other.[74]

In comparison, China's recovery from the Covid shock has been far from ideal. Regardless of what official GDP figures show, China's domestic production has shrunk,[75] deflation has taken over the economy,[76] and the unemployment rate has risen even among the best educated. Data in table 5.9 show that post-Covid (2023 and 2024), the unemployment rate among postgraduates rose from 43.3 per cent to 55.5 per cent, an increase of 12.2 per cent. This was six times higher than the increase faced by undergraduates (a 2 per cent increase in the unemployment rate from 52.5 per cent to 54.5 per cent). In cold comfort, youngsters with polytechnic qualifications reversed slightly their double-digit unemployment rate by 2.2 per cent. But the high-end labour market is a long way from fully recovering from the Covid shock now that the once celebrated 'China Model' has been marginalized by the international community.

China is making every effort to maintain the pre-Covid low-tariff world order after the unprecedented experiment of global trade

Table 5.9. Unemployment Rates, High-end Labour Market, 2023–2024

Level	2023	2024	Mean
Postgraduate schools	43.3%	55.5%	49.4%
Universities	52.5%	54.5%	53.5%
Polytechnic institutes	45.6%	43.4%	44.5%
Average	47.1%	51.1%	49.1%

Source: https://www.mbachina.com/html/xw/202407/593182.html.

without China in 2020–2. So, China's Foreign Minister Wang Yi told his BRICS counterparts in 2020 that China wanted to return to the pre-Covid order:[77]

> A few countries have now constructed 'walled backyards' and built a 'parallel universe' with their irresponsible macro-economic and monetary policies. This has increased uncertainties and disequilibrium in the global [Chinese] economic recovery. . . . We must resist against such an approach that divides the world.

The response to Wang's nostalgic plea was a global ban on sales of advanced computer chips to China, first announced in October 2022.[78] It was followed by two more bans on chips for China in 2023 and 2024, respectively.[79] It was then escalated to an unprecedented 145 per cent tariff on China's exports to the United States in 2025 to tax China out of the American market.[80] The signal is clear. The G7 are no longer as open to China's high-tech shopping or to China's dumping of cheap exports as they were before. This change fundamentally undermines China's import-export combo and thus makes the China Model unsustainable. There is very little China can do about it.

7. The Fallacy of the 'Global Value Chain' and What China May Look Like by 2030

What is common to both Adam Smith and David Ricardo is an international trading system made up of countries with fixed national boundaries. 'Nation-to-nation' trade was a workable and mainstream model until 1995 when GATT passed its baton on to the WTO. One may call it a 'block-to-block' system, each block representing a nation. The interface between nations is trade. If lucky, a nation/block gains twice from international trade in terms of accounting cost efficiency (Adam Smith) and opportunity cost efficiency (David Ricardo).

The novel concept of a 'global value chain' was invented only in the 2000s, not so long ago.[81] What the new system does is transcend a block-based (i.e. nation-based) international order by allowing factors of production, typically capital and technology, to flow freely across multiple nations whose traditional national boundaries are dissolved, and then links these boundaryless nations up into a chain.

It is called a 'global value chain economy' (GVCE) because it follows a strictly Smithian system of absolute advantage for the formation of a chain where each nation produces a semi-finished product for a multinational group, be it Nike shoes, Apple phones, or Tesla cars. Intellectual property rights and business profit belong to the 'chain owner'. This is also known as the 'smile curve',[82] in which R&D (the 'technology stakeholder') and marketing (the 'marketing stakeholder') at the top of the smile curve control the chain. Chain workers – factories that physically make the products – receive orders from chain owners. But only the chain owner designs the product and handles finished goods. In other words, it is an unequal relationship between chain owners and chain workers in a closed circuit. This is an effective way to ringfence the chain from competitors.

The global low tariff regime under the WTO provides the GVCE with near-perfect conditions to operate. In other words, the WTO helps create the GVCE. It was only a matter of time for fully fledged GVCE to go rampant. Now it is worthwhile revisiting the WTO rules that facilitate the GVCE. Going by the preamble of the 1994 Marrakesh Agreement, low tariffs are central:

> [The party has agreed on] raising standards of living, ensuring full employment and a large and steadily growing volume of real income and effective demand, . . . seeking both to protect and preserve the environment. . . . There is a need for positive efforts designed to ensure that developing countries, and especially the least developed among them, secure a share in the growth of international trade commensurate with the needs of their economic development, *being desirous* of contributing to these objectives by entering reciprocal and mutually advantageous arrangements directed to the substantial reduction of tariffs and other barriers to trade.[83]

But here low tariffs have been romanticised to deliver too many good things, ranging from (1) full employment, (2) more real income, (3) higher living standards, (4) better environmental conditions, and (5) more growth in developing countries. In reality, abuse of and free riding on low tariffs are on the cards, not only for China but also for all the other WTO signatories.

From China's own track record, apart from more growth, impact on full employment, higher real incomes, higher living standards, and a protected environment is questionable (chapters 3, 4, and 5), not to mention accusations of dumping and export subsidies by China which violate the WTO's 'reciprocal and mutual' principle to the core (table 5.6).

Like China, the owner of GVCE takes full advantage of low tariffs and operates freely across national boundaries. Undoubtedly, when a value chain reaches a low-income and labour-abundant nation, it creates employment for the local population. It may even support modern infrastructure (such as roads and electricity) and education, which produce certain 'positive externalities' to help local development. However, inside a value chain, production participants (chain workers) are paid wages much lower than in chain owners' home countries. This is just a new version of an old game of international arbitrage. But when wages are no longer low enough to provide an accounting cost advantage, the chain will shift elsewhere. There are plenty of low-income countries on the waiting list. This is just the nature of the Smithian game.

Thus, at some point, the GVCE will turn its back on China, either because China's workforce is no longer the cheapest, or because chain owners are called back by their home-country governments. Or both. These are the forces behind 'decoupling' and 'de-globalisation'. The episode of a world without China during the Covid pandemic has served as a highly visible dry run on a global scale. In other words, China is by definition replicable and will be replaced by countries like Mexico, India, Vietnam, and so forth. This is already happening, as chain owners constantly hunt for the next cheap-labour victim in an 'absolute advantage' hunting ground. This will lead to unemployment and low growth (which contradicts WTO rules), but it is acceptable in the Smithian playbook.

China may decide to become a chain owner. But it will face stiff resistance, as demonstrated by the crippling of Huawei 5G as well as by the *de facto* demise of 'Made in China 2025'.

Moreover, the general public of the home nations of chain owners may rebel against the mobility of chain capital and chain technology once unemployment rates in these advanced economies become too high. This seems inevitable because the precondition for forming a value chain is for chain owners to leave their home countries where labour and environmental costs are too high. So, the GVCE necessarily creates unemployment in advanced economies (which contradicts WTO full employment). At some point, the general public in rich countries will vote in a nationalist government that passes laws to discourage off-shore value chains. Indeed, the MAGA Movement and the consequent Trump Administration have ticked these boxes. More specifically, the American government has now moved towards imposing a 25 per cent tariff on Apple products if they are produced through an international value chain outside the United States.[84] In this context, it is highly likely that China may lose its American market, on which half of China's import-export combo depends. The European Union and Japan are likely to be next. That will dismantle China's import-export combo.

What will China's response be? Its exports may find their way to non-G7 countries to compensate for the loss of G7 markets. But China's prime mover of import dependency may stop working without the G7. Meanwhile, modelled after China, too many low-income countries have begun to join the supply side of the world market and to export, often more cheaply than China. In Western shopping centres, increasingly more garments are made in India and Bangladesh, and more electronics are made in Vietnam and Malaysia. These suppliers are persistently elbowing China out.

Under such a crossfire and together with its own four inescapable growth limits, China needs a miracle to bounce back to its pre-Covid growth trajectory.

8. Final Remarks

It has become clear that the well-publicised China Model depends heavily on imports from the outside world, manly from the advanced capitalist West to operate. Such dependency is often hidden behind the camouflage of China's swaggering outflow of exports and its astronomical foreign trade earnings. The ultimate goal of the China Model is, however, to catch up and surpass the capitalist West. These seemingly contradictory approaches – depending on and then prevailing over the West – can only be understood from the Marxian assertion that communism is the final destiny of humanity on this planet which has been taken as *the* axiom by Marx's devoted followers.

The real challenge that China now faces is how to continue operating the model if the capitalist West is prepared to kick away the ladder, as famously argued by Ha-Joon Chang,[85] to prevent China, or any other communist power, from rising to global ascendance. China cannot produce an answer.

CONCLUSION

China has gone a long and bumpy way since the Ming era of openness characterised by vigorous exports of manufactures in exchange for foreign silver, wide diplomatic connections and undisputed sea power. Sophisticated technology and a complex division of labour were also present then. China seems to have been on top of the world *c.*1600. The Ming episode is very important for understanding China's experiences 400 years down the line.

But history is unpredictable. China did not continue along the Ming trajectory. The Qing state promoted a mono-agrarian or physiocratic economy controlled by a small state. The imbalance and mismatch between an enlarged peasantry and a tiny state ushered in an era of large-scale social unrest in the nineteenth century, which effectively ended China's bureaucratic empire system when the Qing state could no longer control the masses. Fundamental changes began at the provincial level with a new breed of local power-holders – militocrats – who needed guns rather than books to rule China's provinces. This planted the seed of Maoism. When the militocrats rebelled in 1911, China's growth trajectory was once again altered.

Despite his Eurocentric wrapping, Mao was a direct successor of the late-Qing militocrats. Mao's political alliance with Stalin enhanced his legitimacy. But genuine believers of European communism, both inside and outside of China, questioned Mao's ideological credentials. Mao answered them with ruthless purges. Meanwhile, astonishingly, Mao's China failed to match the low standards of economic performance achieved by the later Qing despite Stalin's aid. Rather, economic Maoism led China down a cul-de-sac of low-level education, peace-time famine, mass poverty, ruralisation of the economy, and so forth. These were symptoms of the anti-growth and anti-development stance that Mao adopted as China's ultimate agrarian-autarkical dictator.

Deng Xiaoping emerged after Mao died in 1976. Deng's mission was to reverse the damage inflicted by Mao's rule. Deng's roadmap for the country was to learn from China's past as well as from the West (which can be traced back to the period when Deng was a teenager in France). His income-multiplying plan and modernisation schemes all worked for China, partly because the economy could not decline any further, and partly because a synergy between recovery and growth came from China's own past in a renaissance of the market and school education, both of which were still within living memory for many.

However, what China has achieved in the past half a century has been accompanied by the busy and visible hand of the state that manipulates China's imports, exports, prices and quantities in order to catch up with the West (as every authentic Leninist-Stalinist has believed since the 1917 Revolution). In that regard, China's ongoing 'import-export combo' began with Mao and remained on Deng's priority list in the post-Mao era. The game was simple: to achieve modernity by buying foreign imports with China's exports. However, one key element has not been factored in so far: the West keeps progressing and China has to shoot at a fast-moving target. If so, the 'import-export combo' will have to continue indefinitely in the future if 'catching up' remains at the top of the CCP's agenda.

A consequence of the well-oiled 'import-export combo' has been production overcapacity well in excess of the size of China's domestic market. Indeed, the dogma of transnationalism associated with the WTO has created the illusion that overseas markets will always be there for China's exports. In other words, the WTO implies *unlimited* global demand for China's *limited* supply of manufactures. So, the stage was set in China's favour. China has not disappointed the WTO by now becoming the second largest economy in the world. With hindsight, China may keep going for another 50 or 100 years, depending on how soon it catches up with the West in a holistic fashion.

But what has been overlooked by international observers and trade practitioners is that China's 'import-export combo' is not 'value-free' for China's trading partners. Typically, in a zero-sum game, cheap Chinese manufactures capture foreign markets and force local factories to close down, local unemployment then goes up, and local aggregate demand for Chinese manufactures declines. This in turn drives Chinese firms to sell their products even more cheaply until their profit margin disappears completely. Unfriendly countries simply resort to tariff protection to block the flow of cheap goods from China. Either way, as international demand now changes, China's 'import-export combo' becomes vulnerable.

Then, came a 'natural experiment' in the form of the Covid-19 pandemic, an evil omen for the China Model. Unlike other worldwide crises, such as the 1997–9 Asian Financial Crisis and the 2008 Bank Meltdown when international economic connections continued, the virus created a world without China, as China unilaterally stalled its own 'import-export combo'. To the horror of the CCP leadership, life without China has continued in the outside world, and the West has progressed further away from the PRC.

At home, as the combo has created overcapacity where output cannot possibly be absorbed by China's domestic consumers, the retreat of China's export sector is inevitable. This time China is having a taste of its own medicine.

Is there any way out of China's current crisis of overproduction? The answer is affirmative. If we go back to figure 5.5, China's GDP grew 141-fold versus 13-fold for industrial wages. When the RMB–US$ exchange rate is factored in, manufacturing wages grew only five-fold (see figure 5.6). Finally, the notorious 996 Regime lowered manufacturing wage growth further to merely two-fold (see figure 5.7). So, the solution is to increase China's industrial wages in line with China's GDP in the region of 141-fold to 'serve the people', to quote Mao himself. But to allow ordinary Chinese to get that much (a 141-fold wage increase) requires two fundamental changes.

Internally, China needs a democracy which enshrines ordinary people's rights in general, and empowers ordinary waged workers in particular, to share proportionately in the fruits of China's remarkable national economic growth. This is a simple concept that has been practised in many parts of the world reasonably successfully. But this is easier said than done in the current political environment in Mainland China simply because it has been a taboo there for public grievances to be openly displayed, including going on strike for better pay. A precedent was set in June 1989 when troops were sent in with live ammunition to Beijing's Tiananmen Square to crack down on a mass gathering. Nowadays, to prevent similar 'social unrest', China's spending on internal security and surveillance has exceeded its national defence budget against external threats,[1] meaning that the PRC authorities are constantly on guard against their own citizens. In this context, any bottom-up demands for an increase in workers' wages will be nipped in the bud by the authorities. This phenomenon only proves the historical fact that although all democratic societies have a market, not all market economies tolerate a democracy. Thus, it is naïve to believe that a market economy automatically leads to a democracy.

Externally, economic dependency on the West is China's Achilles' heel. As the G7 group is keen on 'kicking away the ladder' available until recently for China with import tariffs (from the US) and import restrictions (from Japan and the EU), China's 'import-export combo' is in serious jeopardy. As a result, despite being a Pacific country, China has been ringfenced out of trans-Pacific trade partnerships since 2016, another evil omen for the China Model.[2] Although China has tried extremely hard to open a 'second front' in Russia, India, and 'Belt and Road' countries to compensate for its export losses in the G7 market, this second front by default downgrades the ability of China's 'import-export combo' to catch up with the West. Even if such a second front works, China will at best become a supplier of manufactures to the non-G7 world at lower prices than to the G7. To maintain such a supply-driven position, China's wages would have to stay low indefinitely.

Additionally, many other developing countries have their fingers on the same pie of the international market in which China operates. Wages in those countries are even lower than in China as we speak, yet another evil omen for the China Model. If so, capital flight from China – to countries such as, in Asia alone, Vietnam, Thailand, Indonesia, Cambodia, and Laos – is inevitable. China's capital flight will create domestic unemployment which will in turn force Chinese wages down.

Therefore, the chances are that China's domestic wages will be capped and its domestic demand will remain weak for the foreseeable future. If so, similar to other Asian export economies like Japan in the 1980s and South Korea in the 1990s, China is now facing a long and painful economic recession for decades to come.

APPENDIX 1: CHANGES IN CHINA'S REGIONAL POPULATION DENSITIES

This appendix contains detailed demographic patterns in China's main regions. Overall, China population growth stagnated during the Ming period (1368–1644). Figures A–1.1–A–1.3 capture population changes in core economic regions situated in the Yellow and

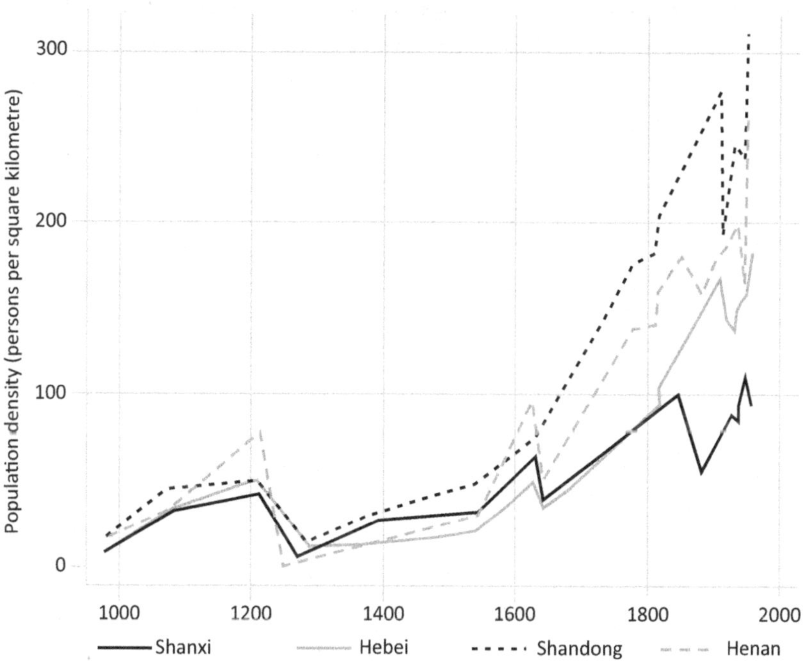

Figure A–1.1. Population Density, Yellow River Region, 1000–1910

Sources are available in the separate section of 'Figure Sources'.

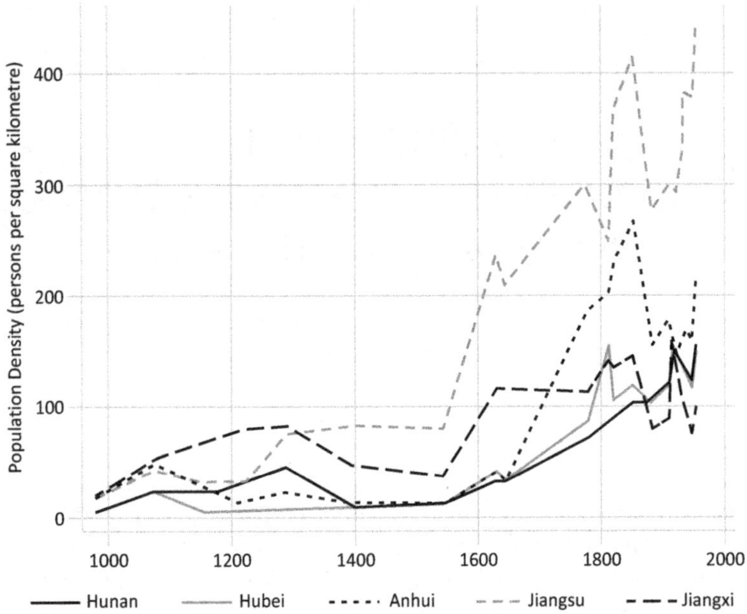

Figure A–1.2. Population Density, Yangzi River Region, 1000–1910

Sources are available in the separate section of 'Figure Sources'.

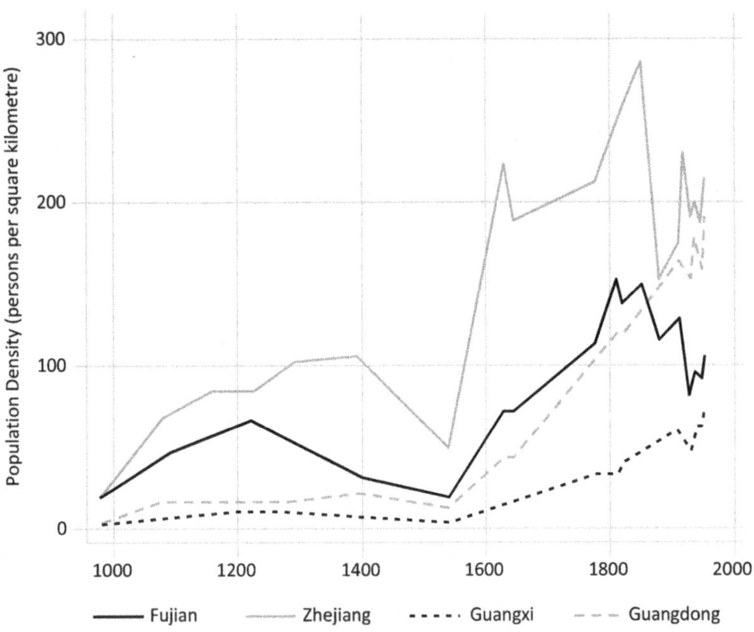

Figure A–1.3. Population Density, South-east Coast, 1000–1910

Sources are available in the separate section of 'Figure Sources'.

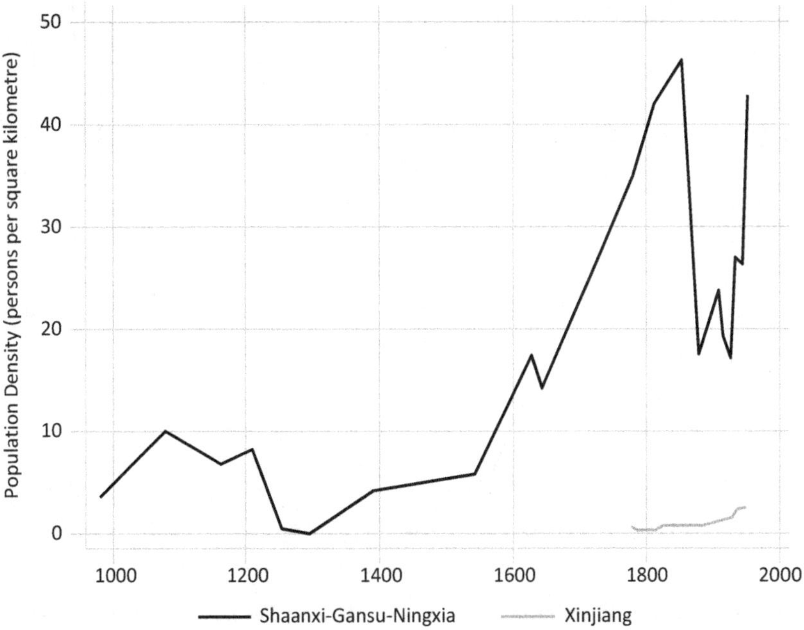

Figure A–1.4. Population Density, North-west Hinterland, 1000–1910

Sources are available in the separate section of 'Figure Sources'.

Yangzi river valleys and along China's east and south-east coasts. These regions benefitted from China's openness. Even so, there was a demographic trough between around 1300 and 1600, measured by population density.

Figures A–1.4 and A–1.5 capture the demographic pattern in the hinterlands. The Shaanxi-Gansu-Ningxia belt, which was characterised by a mixed economy of farming (Shaanxi) and farming-pasteurism (Gansu and Ningxia), shared a demographic pattern with the core regions (figure A–1.4). Population growth in the north-east and south-west hinterlands was also modest, including rice-farming Sichuan (figure A–1.5).

The region known as Manchuria, whose population density is shown in figure A–1.6, had not been part of the Empire of China until 1644. But, like all other regions, population growth occurred only during the Qing (1644–1911).

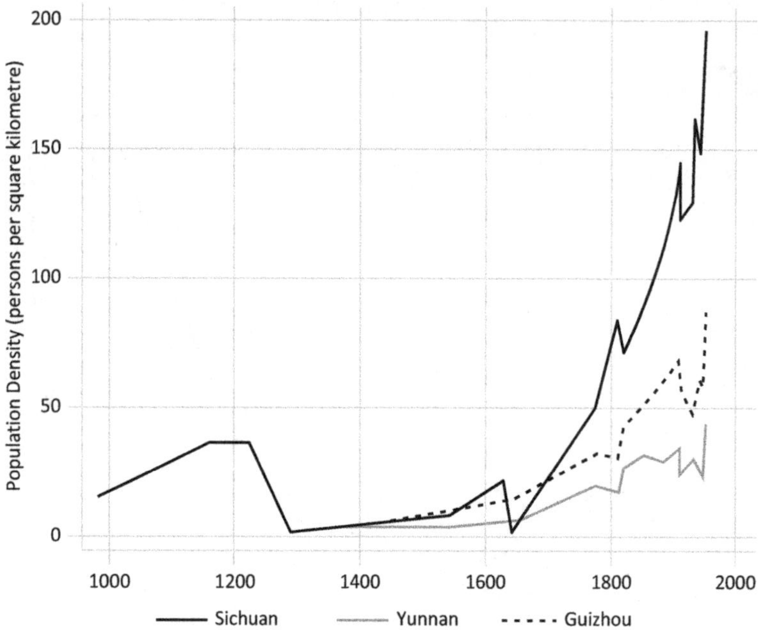

Figure A–1.5. Population Density, South-west Hinterland, 1000–1910

Sources are available in the separate section of 'Figure Sources'.

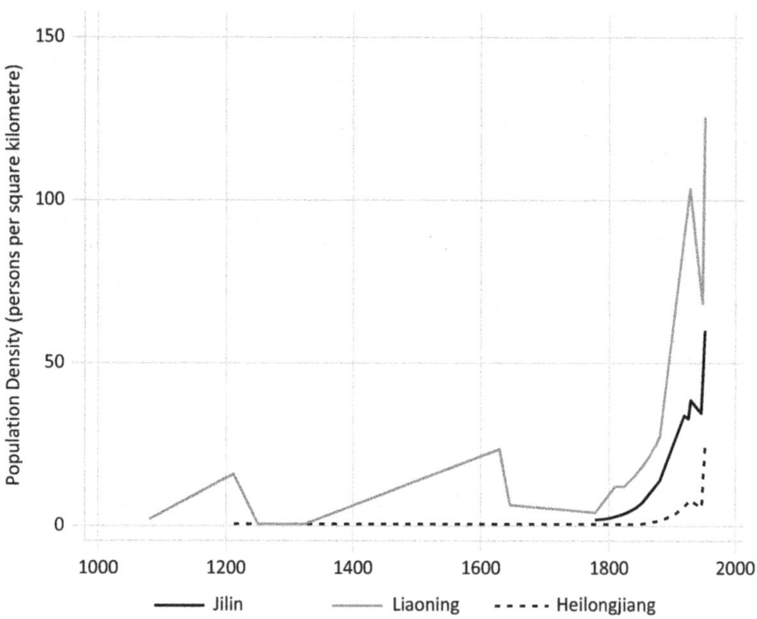

Figure A–1.6. Population Density, North-east Hinterland, 1000–1910

Sources are available in the separate section of 'Figure Sources'.

APPENDIX 2: DOMESTIC FLOWS OF COTTON GOODS DURING QING TIMES

Cotton manufacturing and trade dominated China's domestic manufacturing during the Qing period. Figure A–2.1 shows its scale and scope.

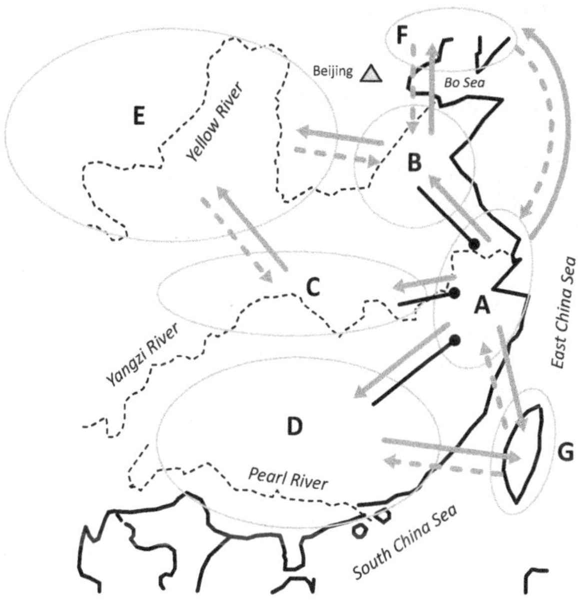

Figure A–2.1. Cotton Trade Patterns, *c.*1750–1800

Note: Solid arrows: directions for hand-woven cotton cloth to move in. Solid round-heads: directions for loose cotton wool to move in. Broken arrows: directions for non-cotton goods to move in. Region A, Lower Yangzi, a main cotton-weaving region. B, North China Plain, an auxiliary cotton-weaving region, and a region where the cotton plant was farmed.[1] C and D, the middle reaches of the Yangzi and the Pearl River valleys that supplied cotton wool and re-sold cloth further. E, F, and G, net cotton recipient regions. Actual quantities of cotton goods produced in the economy have been debated without a clear conclusion.

Sources are available in the separate section of 'Figure Sources'.

APPENDIX 3: TECHNICAL ILLUSTRATIONS OF ECONOMIC MECHANISMS

This appendix contains illustrations of economic mechanisms for technically minded readers.

A–3.1. The Ming Silver Trade as a Burden on the Economy

To highlight the Ming plight, in figure A–3.1, the X axis represents China's exportable goods (be they porcelain wares or silk textiles), part of which was indeed exported to buy silver to implement the silver tax payment law. The Y axis is China's non-exportable goods (mainly food). Ming China did not import food from other economies. So, as long as the same amount of food was domestically produced, the size of the population was maintained.[1] Point α is the Ming self-sufficient output required to sustain the population size without foreign trade. At point α, the tax burden was twice the Qing level. So, Ming demographic growth momentum was halved, *ceteris paribus*. After the One Whip Method was implemented, demand for silver was artificially created to support the increase in 'state capacity'.[2] Point β is China's new output combination after the silver tax payment law was implemented, which warranted an increase in the manufacturing output of the economy.[3] All the time, the food availability remained unchanged.

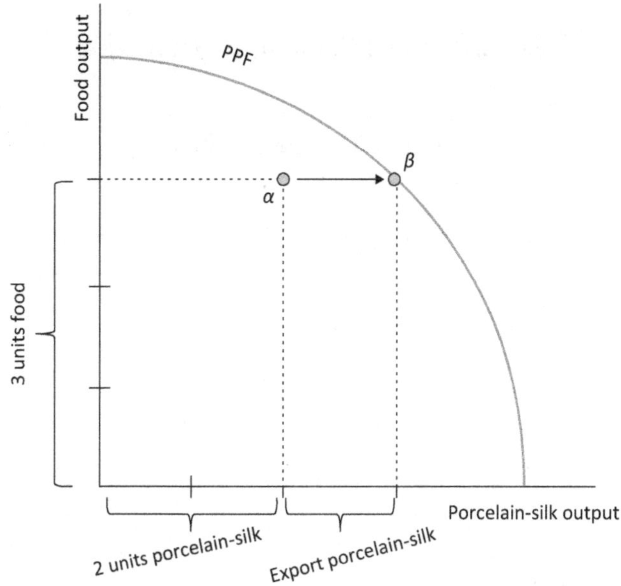

Figure A–3.1. Ming Silver Trade as a Burden on the Economy

Note: X-axis: Exportable manufactures (porcelain and silk textiles); Y-axis: Non-exportable outputs (food). Point *α*: Original output combination to sustain domestic population size. Point *ß*: New outputs with extra output of porcelain and silk textiles to facilitate silver imports. Meanwhile, China's total output reaches an envelope of efficiency, commonly called 'production possibility frontier' ('PPF'), which is immobile unless new resources become available.[4]

Sources are available in the separate section of 'Figure Sources'.

A–3.2. Ending Population Stagnation

In figure A–3.2, China's output ceiling shifts outwards (to PPF_2), whereby more food is produced to sustain higher population density.

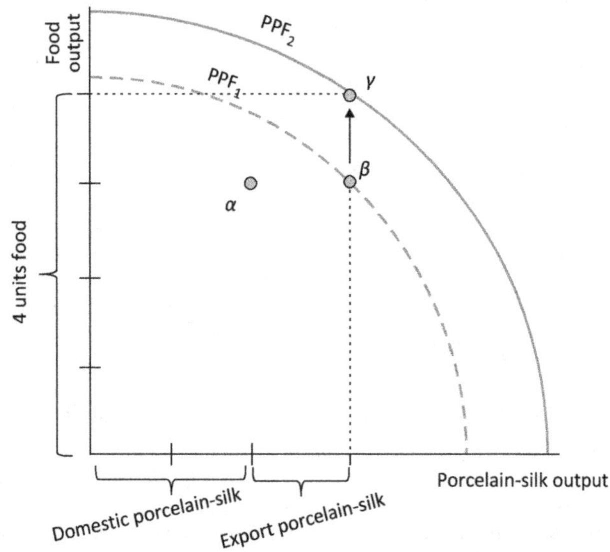

Figure A–3.2. Ending Population Stagnation

Note: X-axis: Manufactures (porcelain and silk textiles); Y-axis: Non-exportable foods. Points *α* and *ß*: Obsolete output combinations as the economy moves on. Point *γ*: New output combination to sustain the same level of annual silver imports with an increase in food for population growth. PPF_1 is the obsolete output envelope. PPF_2 is the new output envelope.

Sources are available in the separate section of 'Figure Sources'.

A–3.3. Maoist Rural Growth Trap

Figure A–3.3 simplifies the Maoist rural economy by representing the efficient production of food along the output envelope (PPF) at point α in the beginning.[5] With Mao's artificial push for rural iron and steel production from 0 to ß, there is a reduction in food output from α to α'. Now, the original output equilibrium at point α slides to point γ due to a lack of technological progress (seen from a million backyard furnaces). Consequently, 'rural furnaces ate people', as the economy ended up with a loss in food output which led to large-scale famine. This was inevitable as in his stratocratic thinking, Mao viewed the rural sector as his political power base.

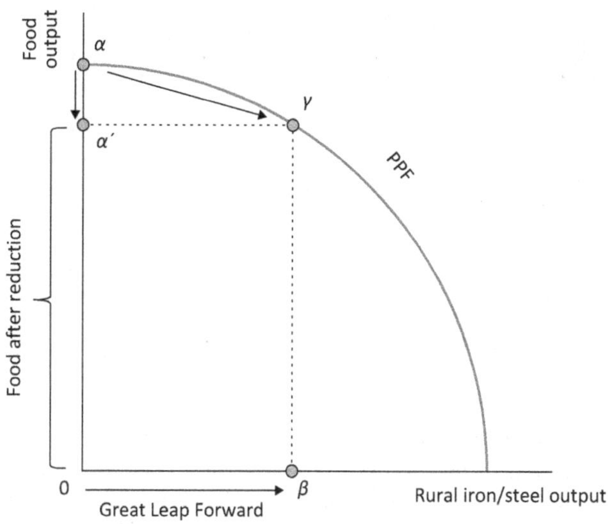

Figure A–3.3. Maoist Rural Growth Trap

Note: This model produces two outputs: food and iron/steel. Point α is the aggregate food output to feed the population. At this point, there is no room for extra iron and steel in the economy. When the political centre asks for iron and steel, resources have to come from point α, thus the reduction of α to α', and a food shortage is inevitable.

Sources are available in the separate section of 'Figure Sources'.

A–3.4. Mao's Rurally Based Iron/Steel Growth Model

Mao's rural iron/steel fiasco shrank China's output envelope (from PPF_0 to PPF_1) with new food output at point *α'* in figure A–3.4. One cannot help thinking that with such a wasteful track record, the 30–40 million famine victims all died in vain.

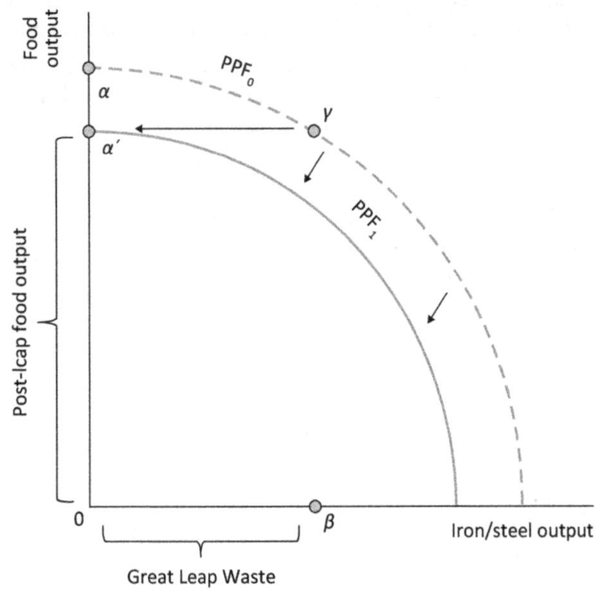

Figure A–3.4. Economic Decline under Mao's Rule

Note: After the wasteful Great Leap Forward in rural iron/steel, point *β* became obsolete because two-thirds of the iron/steel output were useless. On the farming front, a sharp decline of 30–40 million in the rural population caused the output envelope to remain at point *α'* as the new equilibrium point. The corresponding output envelope now shifted inwards from PPF_0 to PPF_1. China's total GDP became smaller, which is testified by China's food deficits.

Sources are available in the separate section of 'Figure Sources'.

A–3.5. Post-Mao Production Possibility Frontier (Superior Output Envelope)

The process is highlighted in figure A–3.5 where point α' is the Maoist 'corner solution' along the inefficient or obsolete output envelope PPF_1, which is associated with mass poverty with subsistence living, minimal urbanisation, and low industrial progress. The reforms pushed China to PPF_2 with a new output combination at point γ' where food output increases to point α'' and industrial output reaches point β' hand in hand with a new army of non-farming workers.

There are data to support this shift in China's production frontier: Total GDP grew 222-fold from 1978 to 2020 at an annual average of 13.7 per cent; the primary sector (mainly farming) increased 64-fold at 10.4 per cent per year; manufacturing enlarged 177 times, or 13.1 per cent a year; and services exploded 477 times or 15.8 per cent a year.

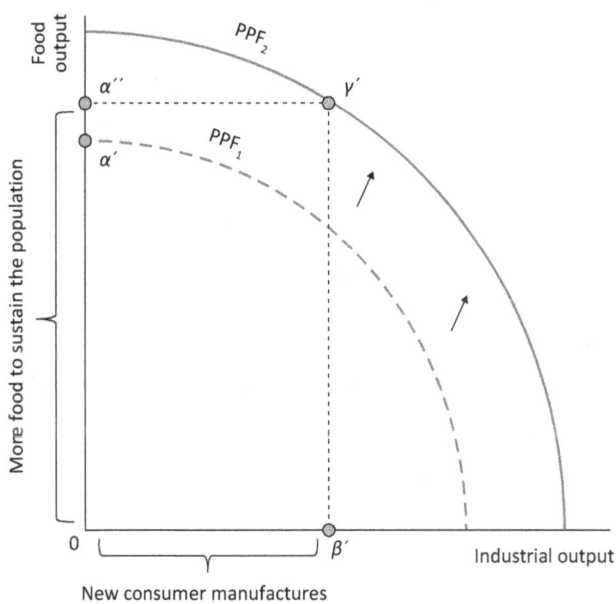

Figure A–3.5. Post-Mao Production Possibility Frontier

Sources are available in the separate section of 'Figure Sources'.

A–3.6. RMB Depreciation and Rise in External Demand

Figure A–3.6 demonstrates how China's goods exports benefitted from getting RMB exchange rates wrong thanks to a 'price elastic market' in the West,[6] typically for garments and consumer electronics. RMB depreciation facilitates China's external market expansion only (marked by G7 dd_2) as currency depreciation has no impact on China's domestic price structure and resource allocation.

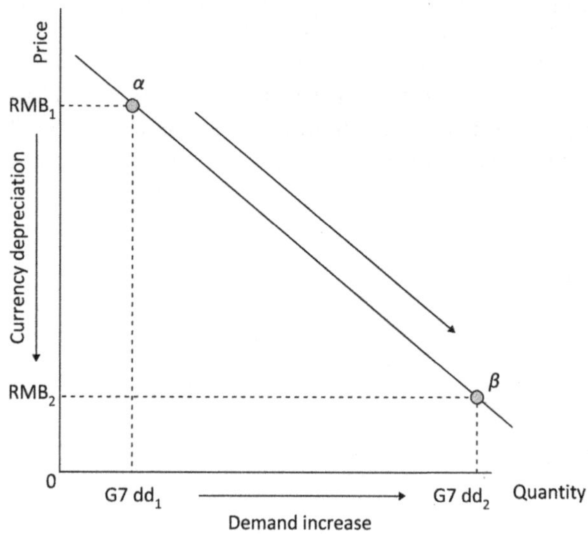

Figure A–3.6. RMB Depreciation and Rise in External Demand

Note: Points *α* and *β* are two marketable points with two prices and their corresponding quantities. This is a 'highly elastic market' in which an *n*% decrease in price causes more than an *n*% increase in demand. The amount of goods traded increases in response to cheaper RMB.

Sources are available in the separate section of 'Figure Sources'.

A–3.7. Negative Externalities

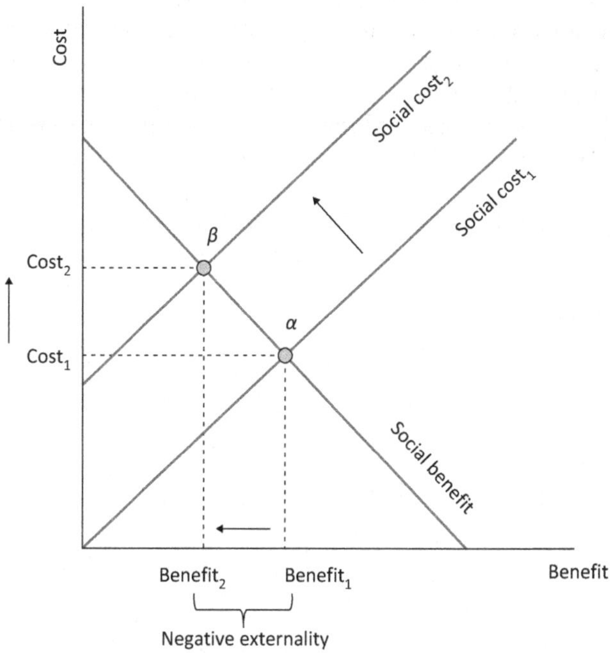

Figure A–3.7. Negative Externalities

Note: Neo-classically, one can lump government rent-seeking and industrial waste together as necessary evils, as they are unavoidable burdens and reduce social benefit (marked by Social $Cost_1$). The equilibrium starts at point α. As time goes by, corruption and pollution set in and shift the cost curve to Social $Cost_2$. Consequently, a new equilibrium appears at point β with which social benefit declines from $Benefit_1$ to $Benefit_2$; and ordinary citizens become worse off. Extra-economic means such as laws and regulations may help society move back to Social $Cost_1$ and restore $Benefit_1$.

Sources are available in the separate section of 'Figure Sources'.

A–3.8. Supply-Driven Model in the World Market

Conceptually, as shown in figure A–3.8, the international consumer market begins with equilibrium at point α together with a price level at P_1 and quantity of goods sold at Q_1. When a new supplier joins in the supply side and hence pushes the supply level from $Supply_1$ to $Supply_2$, a new equilibrium along the same demand curve rests at point β where quantity of goods sold increases to Q_2. China is more capable of shifting from Q_1 to Q_2 than any economy on earth. However, the market price level has to drop to P_2 to absorb the extra goods (such as 800 million shirts). After such reshuffling, total revenue shrinks from $(P_1 \times Q_1)$ to $(P_2 \times Q_2)$. This is a common problem with a supply-drive model: growth can only be achieved by more price-cutting which is self-defeating in the long run.

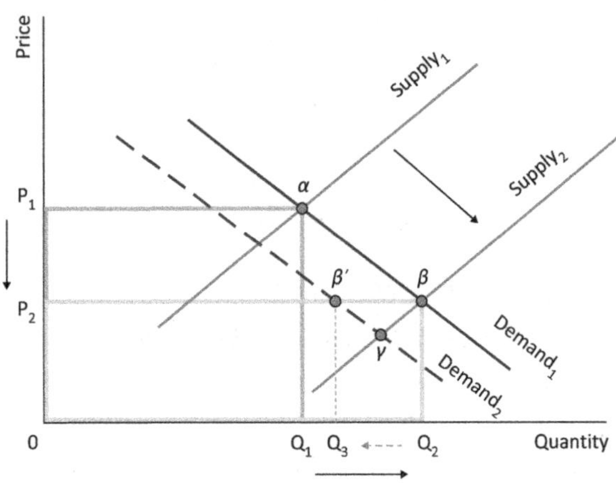

Figure A–3.8. Supply-Driven Model and the World Market

Note: P_1: the original price level. Q_1: the original quantity of goods. Point α: the original demand and supply equilibrium where the market clears itself. P_2: the new price level after new supply joining in. Q_2: the new quantity of goods after new supply joining in. Point β: the new demand and supply equilibrium where the market clears itself. Now, in comparison, the original total revenue $(P_1 \times Q_1)$ is greater than the new total revenue $(P_2 \times Q_2)$. Over time, the demand side may collapse and retreat to $Demand_2$ due to high unemployment rates. When this happens, the best scenario will be point β' along the broken line demand curve if the price level P_2 is considered as the floor price that cannot drop any lower. So, point γ is bypassed. Then, the corresponding quantity of goods sold reduces to Q_3. Eventually, the price level may have to drop below P_2 which is dictated by point γ. But such an ultra-low price may cause the supply side to go bust in the end.

Sources are available in the separate section of 'Figure Sources'.

A–3.9. China's Stifled Domestic Consumer Manufactures Market

Figure A–3.9 represents China's domestic consumer manufactures market, be it for toys, clothes, white goods, or consumer electronics. The need for household savings distorts the demand curve and makes it less elastic. Afterwards, any sizeable drop in the price level (from P_1 to P_2) only leads to a small increase in goods purchases (from Q_3 to Q_4). Therefore, all government consumption stimulation schemes since 2007 have yielded very limited results.[7] The shaded area represents loss in market size due to the distortion on the demand side.

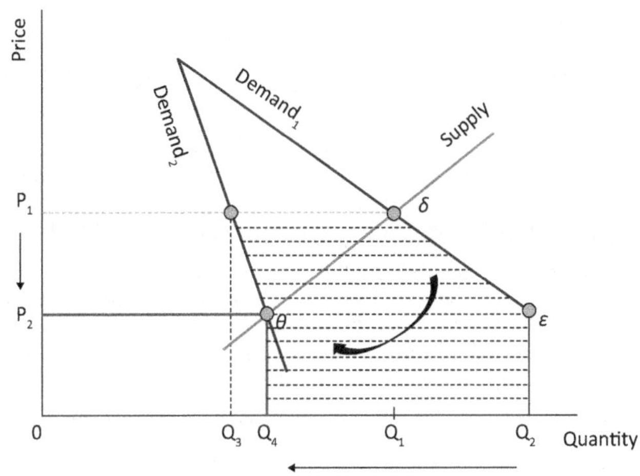

Figure A–3.9. China's Stifled Domestic Consumer Manufactures Market

Note: The model has a fixed supply curve. $Demand_1$ is a 'normal demand curve'. Point δ is the original equilibrium with a price level at P_1 and quantity of manufactures sold at Q_1. When the price drops to P_2, the quantity of manufactures sold increases to Q_2 in a price elastic manner. Now, under the pressure from household budgeting, the demand curve slants inwards and becomes steeper ($Demand_2$). The shaded area represents the amount now devoted to household savings. After that, market capacity shrinks from Q_1 to Q_3 even if the price level stays at P_1. Moreover, when the price drops to P_2, it only generates a marginal increase in manufactures sold (from Q_3 to Q_4). Point θ is the new equilibrium if the supply curve remains unchanged. The combination of the price change (P_1 to P_2) and quantity change (Q_2 to Q_4) is commonly associated with market deflation.

Sources are available in the separate section of 'Figure Sources'.

A–3.10. Tariffs and Their Impact on the Supply Side of the Market

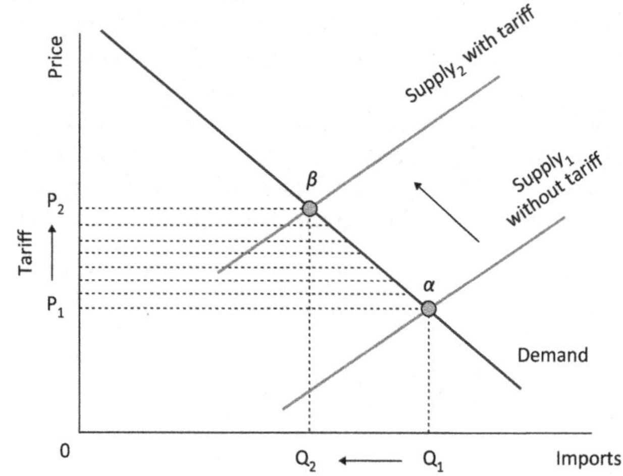

Figure A–3.10. Tariffs and Their Impact on the Market

Note: Point *α* is the original market equilibrium point; point *β*, a new equilibrium after tariffs. Tariffs push the price level up (from P_1 to P_2) in an income and price elastic consumer market. They cause the quantity of consumer goods sold to reduce (from Q_1 to Q_2), enough to drive the unwanted supply out of the market (from $Supply_1$ to $Supply_2$). The shaded area is the loss that the supply side faces.

Sources are available in the separate section of 'Figure Sources'.

APPENDIX 4: QING SALARY BONUSES AND THEIR ABOLITION

Table A–4.1 shows the pay scheme of honesty and uprightness bonuses when they began. The earmarked salary bonuses were routinely preyed upon by Beijing in the name of good-deed donations and eventually boomeranged back to the state coffers.[1]

Table A–4.2 shows the scale of the problem. After donations, hardly anything was left for the bonus beneficiaries. Also, arrears were common.[2]

As such, a reserve army of 'sub-official functionaries' was a red herring. So, the judgement of the Qing super-slim state stands.

Table A–4.1. Annual Honesty and Uprightness Bonuses, *c.*1720–1740

Rank	Name	Annual bonuses in silver *taels*
1st Grade, Proper	*Tidu* (Admiral)	2000
1st Grade, Proper	*Dachen* (Minister)*	900
2nd Grade, Proper	*Zongbing* (Field Marshal)	1500
2nd Grade, Proper	*Tongling* (Army Chief)*	600
2nd Grade, Minor	*Fujiang* (Deputy Chief)	800
3rd Grade, Proper	*Canjiang* (Regional Chief)	500
4th Grade, Proper	*Zongwei* (Regional Chief)*	400
5th Grade, Proper	*Shoubei* (Station Commander)	200
8th Grade	*Yizhang* (Local Commander)*	200

Note: * Reserved for members of the Manchu Banners (*ba qi*). It is puzzling that the Manchus were rewarded less than their Han Chinese counterparts. Perhaps the latter were more inclined to corruption.

Source: Pu Zhengwei and Feng Zongchen, 'Qingdai Yanglianyin Zhidu Yanjiu' (Archival Study of the Qing Honesty and Uprightness Bonuses), *Yunnan Dang-an* (*Yunnan Archives*), 5 (2023): 28–9.

Table A–4.2. Donation of Honesty and Uprightness Bonuses, 1820

North	% Bonuses donated	South	% Bonuses donated
Shanxi	79.7	Anhui	48.6
Shaanxi	80.0	Hubei	65.1
Henan	50.0	Hunan	59.1
		Jiangsu	113.0
		Zhejiang	162.0
		Guangdong	143.1
Average %	70.0		98.5

Source: Zhou Jiang, 'Qingdai Caizhengzhong De Tanjuan' (Forced Donation as a Qing Fiscal Policy), *Zhongguo Jingjishi Yanjiu* (*Study of China's Economic History*), 3 (2012): 148.

Therefore, the Qing state did not have the manpower to distribute famine relief handouts among the masses, not to mention the information costs to govern a large empire. Delays and failures in famine relief food handouts were expected, given that to disperse centrally held food stock to masses in villages was a labour-intensive undertaking.

APPENDIX 5: CRUDE INFORMATION FROM THE GDP ACCOUNTING APPROACH

Fundamentally, GDP accounting is suited only for crude indications of economic magnitudes largely due to the component of 'average prices', which is often inaccurate and/or biased. GDP figures should be treated as such accordingly. In this appendix, GDP figures are considered less accurate for our purpose. They thus serve as rough indicators only.

A–5.1. GDP as Second-Order Evidence: Agriculture

Once physical output volumes are established, one can then consider GDP as the second-order evidence (figure A–5.1). However, as mentioned, China's GDP data have been notoriously unreliable.[1] As recently as 2004, China's best sectoral GDP data were only 67 per cent reliable;[2] and from the 1990s to 2010s, China's provincial GDP figures did not add up to the national total.[3]

Now with this health warning in mind, China's growth rates are as follows: sectoral GDP at 7.2 per cent a year, per capita GDP at 7.7 per cent a year, state agricultural expenditure at 8.2 per cent a year, and food imports (to ease the pressure from the domestic demand) at 6.6 per cent a year. Of these rates, the government's role in terms of state expenditure and food imports is obvious.

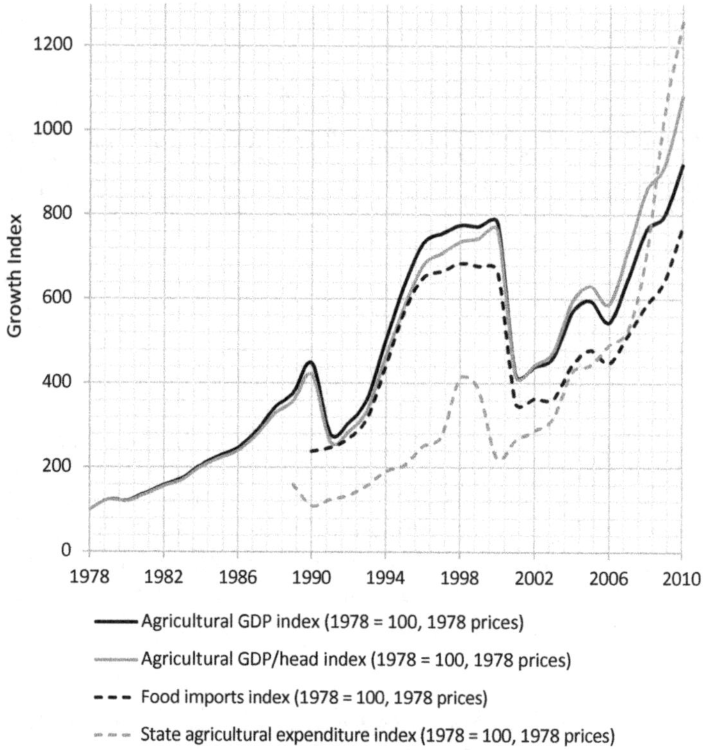

Figure A–5.1. Agricultural GDP*, State Expenditure and Food Imports, Indexes, 1980–2010

Note: * The GDP figures should be treated with caution as they are not reliable. The constant price is based on National Bureau of Statistics, *Statistical Year Book, 2023*, ch. 3.

Sources are available in the separate section of 'Figure Sources'.

A–5.2. GDP as Second-Order Evidence: National Economy

Figure A–5.2 takes on all sectors of the economy.

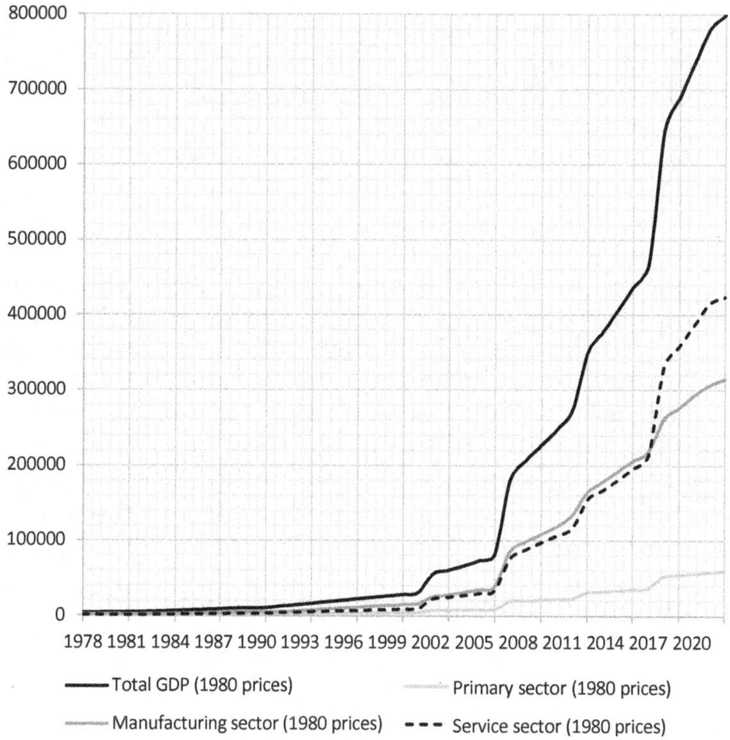

Figure A–5.2. China's GDP Leap*, 1980–2020 (RMB 100 Million, 1980 Prices)

Note: * Any GDP number should be treated with caution. Not much was going on under Mao's rule. Pro-Mao propaganda finds no supporting evidence.

Sources are available in the separate section of 'Figure Sources'.

A–5.3. Sectoral GDP Shares and GDP Returns per Worker, 1980–2020

From 1980 to 2020, the agricultural share in China's total GDP shrank from over a third to 7.5 per cent with an annual decline of 3.5 per cent. The manufacturing share experienced a mild decline (–0.5 per cent growth per year) from half to 40 per cent of the total GDP.[4] The growth champion was the services sector that doubled its share from a quarter to over half of China's total GDP with an annual growth of 1.8 per cent (table A–5.1). China's economy finally looked modern.

In terms of inputs, economic structural changes are also embodied in GDP returns per worker (labour efficiency), calculated by 'sectoral share of China's total GDP' ÷ 'sectoral share of China's total workforce' (hence % GDP ÷ % workers), as shown in table A–5.2. The most efficient sector (with the highest GDP returns per worker) is that of services (one unit of workforce producing 0.5–0.9 units of GDP); and the least efficient sector is farming (one unit of workforce producing 0.2–0.3 units of GDP). Manufacturing is in the middle (one unit of workforce producing 0.3–0.7 units of GDP). One senses that China's macro-level structural change was driven mainly by the market, as services were not on Deng's priority list at all.

Table A–5.1. Sectoral GDP Shares*, % Total, 1980–2020

Year	Primary	Manufacturing†	Services
1980	23.3	52.3	24.4
1985	26.6	46.6	26.8
1990	22.2	48.7	29.0
1995	18.2	51.1	30.7
2000	12.8	54.8	32.4
2005	11.1	47.8	41.2
2010	8.4	49.0	42.5
2015	7.8	46.7	45.5
2020	7.5	39.4	53.1
Average	15.3	48.5	36.2

Note: * The GDP figures should be treated with caution, as they are not reliable.
† It is almost certain that the total GDP for this sector was inflated in the 1980s and 1990s.
Source: National Bureau of Statistics, *Statistical Year Book, 2021*, ch. 3.

Table A–5.2. Sectoral Labour-GDP Efficiency Indexes*, 1980–2020

Year	Lower bound (primary sector)	Middle (manufacturing)	Upper bound services)
1980	33.9	34.8†	53.7
1985	42.6	44.6†	62.7
1990	36.9	43.9	63.8
1995	34.9	45.0	80.8
2000	25.6	41.1	84.9
2005	24.8	49.8	76.2
2010	22.9	58.6	81.4
2015	27.9	63.6	93.0
2020	31.8	72.8	89.8
Average	31.3	50.5	76.3

Note: * Indexes are based on 'Sectoral share of China's total GDP' ÷ 'Sectoral share of China's total workforce'. † Manufacturing did not have a clear labour-output advantage over farming at this stage.

Source: National Bureau of Statistics, *Statistical Year Book, 2021*, chs 3 and 4.

A–5.4. China's Tax-to-GDP Ratio

Figure A-5.3 displays a general trend. More GDP estimates are available in tables A–5.3, A–5.4, and A–5.5. They serve only as rough indicators.

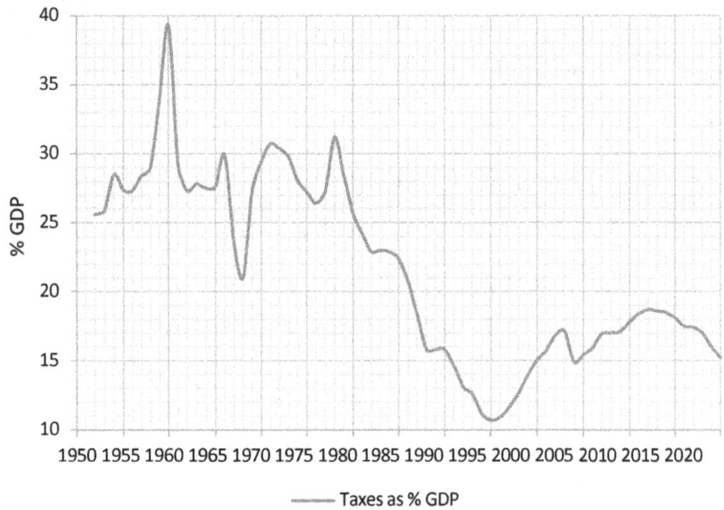

Figure A–5.3. China's Tax-to-GDP Ratio*, 1950–2020

Note: * GDP figures should be treated with caution. China's GNP and GDP overlapped from 1950 to 1980. Data exclude the tax hidden in housing prices.

Sources are available in the separate section of 'Figure Sources'.

Table A–5.3. China's Tax Revenue-to-GDP Ratio, 1880s

Estimates	Chang	Feuerwerker	Liu et al.	Average
Total GDP* (I)	104,300	125,200	131,600	120,370
State total revenue (II)				5,801
II/I (%)				4.8

Note: * In tonnes of pure silver, converted from silver *taels*. Numbers in this table are all estimates.

Sources: Chung-li Chang, *The Income of the Chinese Gentry* (Seattle: University of Washington Press, 1962), p. 296; Albert Feuerwerker, *The Chinese Economy, 1870–1949* (Ann Arbor: Center for Chinese Studies of the University of Michigan, 1995), p. 16; Liu et al., *Early Modern China*, p. 66.

Table A–5.4. Tax Revenue-to-GDP Ratios in Advanced Economies, 1760–1860

Period	Country	Taxes as % GDP*	1880 China = 100
*c.*1760	Prussia	35	729
*c.*1790	Austria	27	563
*c.*1810	Britain	43	896
*c.*1840	France	19	396
*c.*1860	Japan	20	416
Average		28.8	600

Note: GDP figures should be treated with caution.
Sources: Michael Mann, *The Sources of Social Power, The Rise of Classes and Nation States, 1760–1914*) (Cambridge: Cambridge University Press, 1993), vol. 2, p. 366. The British data are the maximum including its national debt payments. For Japan, see E.H. Norman, *Japan's Emergence as a Modern State* (Westport, CT: Greenwood Press, 1973), p. 23; Penelope Francks, *Japanese Economic Development, Theory and Practice* (London: Routledge, 1992), pp. 30, 103; Mikiso Hane, *Modern Japan: A Historical Survey* (New York: Westview Press, 2001), p. 50.

Table A–5.5. Taxes as % GDP, China vis-à-vis other Economies, 2013–2020

Year	G7 average	OECD average	Asia-Pacific average (36 countries)	Taiwan*	China
2013	34.8	32.6	18.8	12.1	18.6
2014	35.0	32.9	18.2	12.3	18.5
2015	35.4	32.9	18.4	12.4	18.1
2016	35.4	33.6	17.8	12.6	17.5
2017	35.7	33.3	18.6	12.8	17.4
2018	35.6	33.5	19.1	13.0	17.0
2019	35.5	33.4	19.3	13.2	22.1
2020	36.0	33.6	18.3	13.5	20.1
2021	36.7	34.2	18.8	14.0	21.0
2022	37.1	34.0	19.3	14.5	20.1
Average	35.7	33.4	18.7	13.0	19.0
China's average = 100	188	176	98	68	100

Note: * GDP figures should be treated with caution. In Taiwan, the Confucian ideology has remained strong since 1949.
Sources: OECD: 'Global Revenue Statistics Database', https://www.oecd.org/en/publications/revenue-statistics-2024_c87a3da5-en.html; Ministry of Finance, *Year Books of Public Finance Statistics, 2013–2022*, https://www.mof.gov.tw/eng/singlehtml/260?cntId=290009d7327a40b9a67572a21d6ffc52.

A–5.5. Import Dependency Seen from China's GDP

Figure A–5.4 shows the weight of foreign imports as an input factor in China's national economy. The long-term average of imports is equivalent to one-sixth (17.2 per cent) of China's total GDP, which can be seen as China's 'import dependency rate'. Not surprisingly, acceleration occurred after China's 2001 WTO membership.

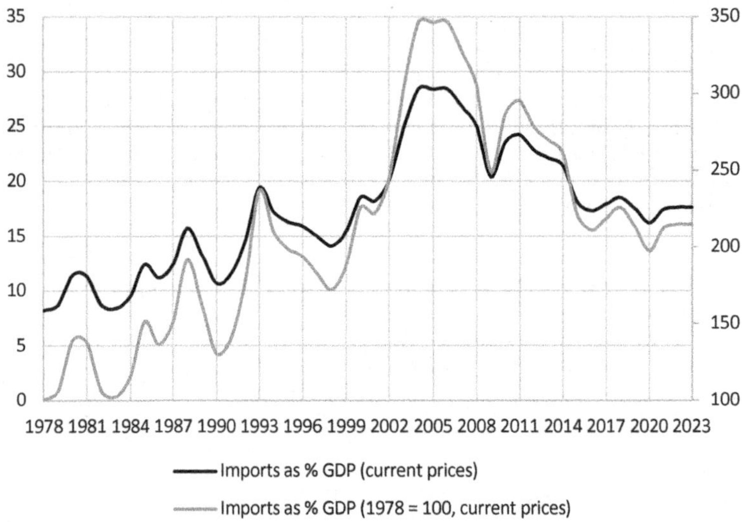

Figure A–5.4. Import Dependency Seen from China's GDP, %, 1978–2023

Note: Left Y-axis: Imports as % of China's annual GDP.
Right Y-axis: Growth index of foreign imports as % of China's annual GDP.

Sources are available in the separate section of 'Figure Sources'.

A–5.6. CO_2 Emissions per Unit of GDP

Information for 1978–2022 shows that CO_2 emissions for each unit of Chinese GDP have plunged by a factor of 33 (or 8.3 per cent per year), meaning that technology has played a role in improving energy efficiency (figure A–5.5).[5]

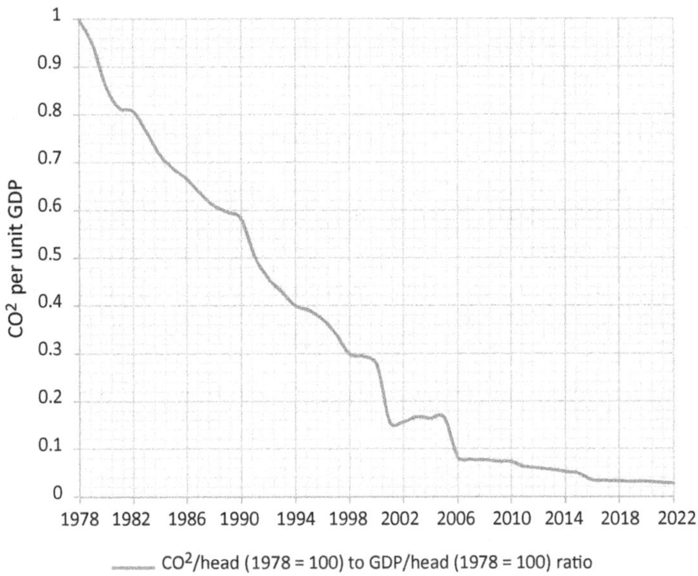

Figure A–5.5. CO_2 Emissions per Unit of GDP*, 1978–2022

Note: * GDP figures should be treated with caution due to their innate inaccuracy. Numbers are indexed in per capita terms. China's official GDP constant price conversions, see National Bureau of Statistics, *Statistical Year Book, 2023*, ch. 3.

Sources are available in the separate section of 'Figure Sources'.

A–5.7. GDP Recovery of the G7 from the Covid Shock

According to information in table A–5.6, the G7 economies were fully recovered by 2023.

Table A–5.6. Economic Recovery of the G7, 2023 versus 2019

Country	Benchmark GDP, 2019	Post-Covid GDP, 2023
Canada	100	104
France	100	101
Germany	100	99
Italy	100	103
Japan	100	101
UK	100	99
USA	100	105
Average	100	102

Source: https://www.statista.com/statistics/1392678/g7-gdp-growth-since-covid-19-pandemic/.

APPENDIX 6: CHINA'S IMPORT DEPENDENCY

China's import dependency has been G7-specific. Figure A–6.1 shows that non-industry-related items (food) account for about 20 per cent of all imports from the United States. In figure A–6.2, non-industry-related items account for about 10 per cent of all imports from the European Union.

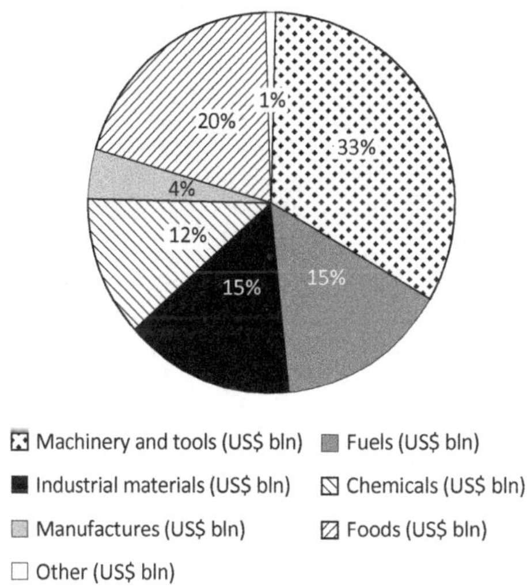

Figure A–6.1. Pattern of China's Imports from the United States, % Shares, 2023

Note: % shares are based on value in US$ billion.

Sources are available in the separate section of 'Figure Sources'.

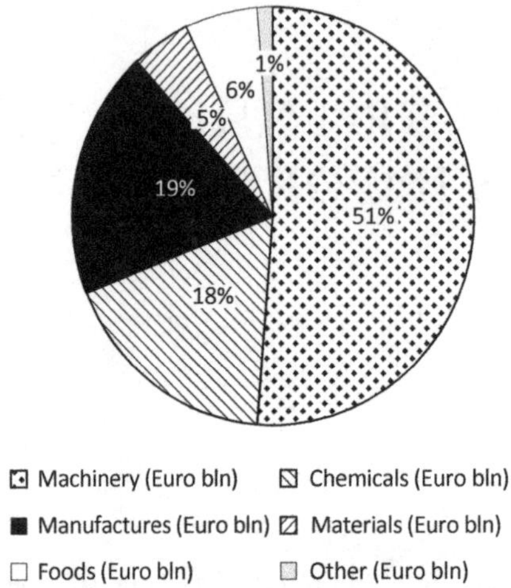

Figure A–6.2. Pattern of China's Imports from the European Union, % Shares, 2023

Note: % shares are based on value in Euro billion.

Sources are available in the separate section of 'Figure Sources'.

APPENDIX 7: DISTRIBUTION OF ISSUES IN CHINA'S STATE FIVE-YEAR PLANS

The following tables are based on seven consecutive five-year plans covering 35 years from 1986 to 2020 (including 1986 itself). The observations are based on (1) the ordinal ranking of the issues according to their importance for the state planners, and (2) the percentage weight (in word count) of each of these issues in official documents. The information reveals how the state handles the economy and its growth and development.

Table A–7.1. Ranks and Weights of Issues on Government To Do List, 1986–1990

Official ranking of importance	Text (word count)	Textual weight (% Total)
1. Tasks and targets	2,146	11.3
2. Economic performance*	10,628	55.9
3. Technology and education	2,045	10.7
4. Foreign trade	1,452	7.6
5. Investment	1,021	5.4
6. Social welfare	1,729	9.1
Total	19,021	100.0

Note: * Including 'sectorial balances', 'regional growth', and 'urbanisation'.
Source: 'People's Republic of China's National Economic and Social Development and the Seventh Five-Year Plan Outline (1986–1990)', April 1986, https://www.ndrc.gov.cn/fggz/fzzlgh/gjfzgh/200709/P020191029595676468654.pdf.

Table A–7.2. Ranks and Weights of Issues on Government To Do List, 1991–1995

Official ranking of importance	Text (word count)	Textual weight (% Total)
1. Economic performance*	2,214	45.8
2. Technology and education	1,123	23.2
3. Social welfare	544	11.3
4. Institutions	551	11.4
5. Foreign trade	402	8.3
Total	4,834	100.0

Note: * Including 'sectorial balances', 'regional growth', and 'urbanisation'.
Source: 'People's Republic of China's Ten-Year National Economic and Social Development Programme and the Eighth Five-Year Plan Outline (1991–1995)', April 1991, https://www.ndrc.gov.cn/fggz/fzzlgh/gjfzgh/200709/P020191029595681819982.pdf.

Table A–7.3. Ranks and Weights of Issues on Government To Do List, 1996–2000

Official ranking of importance	Text (word count)	Textual weight (% Total)
1. Economic performance*	18,990	63.7
2. Technology and education	2,435	8.2
3. Institutions	4,685	15.7
4. Foreign trade	1,666	5.6
5. Social welfare	2,020	6.8
Total	29,796	100.0

Note: * Including 'sectorial balances', 'regional growth', and 'urbanisation'.
Source: People's Republic of China's National Economic and Social Development and the Nineth Five-Year Plan (1996–2000)', 17 March 1996, https://www.ndrc.gov.cn/fggz/fzzlgh/gjfzgh/200709/P020191029595686994247.pdf.

Table A–7.4. Ranks and Weights of Issues on Government To Do List, 2001–2005

Official ranking of importance	Text (word count)	Textual weight (% Total)
1. Economic performance*	8,939	43.3
2. Technology and education	2,680	13.0
3. Resources	2,155	10.4
4. Foreign trade	4,323	21.0
5. Social welfare	2,536	12.3
Total	20,633	100.0

Note: * Including 'sectorial balances', 'regional growth', and 'urbanisation'.
Source: People's Republic of China's National Economic and Social Development and the Tenth Five-Year Plan (2001–2005)', 15 March 2001, https://www.gov.cn/gongbao/content/2001/content_60699.htm.

Table A–7.5. Ranks and Weights of Issues on Government To Do List, 2006–2010

Official ranking of importance	Text (word count)	Textual weight (% Total)
1. Tasks and targets	1,449	13.9
2. Economic performance*	3,916	37.4
3. Environment	930	8.9
4. Foreign trade	2,209	21.1
5. Technology and education	907	8.7
6. Social welfare	1,044	10.0
Total	10,457	100.0

Note: * Including 'sectorial balances', 'regional growth', and 'urbanisation'.
Source: People's Republic of China's National Economic and Social Development and the Eleventh Five-Year Plan Outline (2006–2010)', 24 March 2006, https://www.gov.cn/ztzl/2005-10/19/content_79386.htm.

Table A–7.6. Ranks and Weights of Issues on Government To Do List, 2011–2015

Official ranking of importance	Text (word count)	Textual weight (% Total)
1. Tasks and targets	2,331	5.6
2. Economic performance*	18,888	45.4
3. Regional balance	4,251	10.2
4. Environment	4,751	11.4
5. Technology and education	2,977	7.2
6. Urbanisation	4,141	10.0
7. Social welfare	4,852	11.6
8. Foreign trade	2,416	5.8
9. Defence industry	1,139	2.7
Total	41,495	100.0

Note: * Including 'sectorial balances', 'regional growth', and 'urbanisation'.
Source: People's Republic of China's National Economic and Social Development and the Twelfth Five-Year Plan Outline (2011–2015), 16 March 2011, https://www.gov.cn/2011lh/content_1825838_17.htm.

Table A–7.7. Ranks and Weights of Issues on Government To Do List, 2016–2020

Official ranking of importance	Text (word count)	Textual weight (% Total)
1. Tasks and targets	5,787	12.1
2. Institutions	5,145	10.7
3. Economic performance*	10,087	39.1
4. Ecology	5,893	12.3
5. Foreign trade	3,958	8.3
6. Education	1,633	3.4
7. Social welfare	6,791	14.2
Total	47,897	100.0

Note: * Including 'sectorial balances', 'regional growth', and 'urbanisation'.
Source: People's Republic of China's National Economic and Social Development and the Thirteenth Five-Year Plan Outline (2016–2020)', 17 March 2016, https://www.gov.cn/xinwen/2016-03/17/content_5054992.htm.

NOTES

Introduction

1 See 'General Comparative Chronological Chart, 300 BC to 2000 AD', in Joseph Needham, *Science and Civilisation in China* (Cambridge: Cambridge University Press, 1954), vol. 1, p. 80.
2 For example, Wen Chen, Xilu Chen, Chang-tai Hsieh, and Zheng (Michael) Song, 'A Forensic Examination of China's National Accounts', *Brookings Papers on Economic Activity*, 7 March 2019, https://www.brookings.edu/articles/a-forensic-examination-of-chinas-national-accounts/.
3 Iacob N. Koch-Weser, 'The Reliability of China's Economic Data: An Analysis of National Output', *U.S.-China Economic and Security Review Commission Staff Research Project*, 28 January 2013, p. 16, https://www.uscc.gov/sites/default/files/Research/TheReliabilityofChina'sEconomicData.pdf.
4 Ibid., p. 36.

Chapter 1

1 For example, John K. Fairbank and Denis Twitchett (eds), *The Cambridge History of China, Volume 10: Late Ch'ing, 1800–1911, Part 1* (Cambridge: Cambridge University Press, 1978); Jonathan D. Spence, *The Search for Modern China* (New York: W.W. Norton, 1999); John K. Fairbank and Merle Goldman. *China: A New History* (Cambridge, MA: Harvard University Press, 2006).
2 Gang Deng, *Chinese Maritime Activities and Socioeconomic Development, c. 2100 B.C.–1900 A.D* (Westport, CT: Greenwood Press), ch. 5.
3 Alain le Pichon, *China Trade and Empire* (Oxford: Oxford University Press, 2006), p. 3.
4 Paul van Dyke, *The Canton Trade: Life and Enterprise on the China Coast, 1700–1845* (Hong Kong: Hong Kong University Press, 2005), pp. 33, 113.
5 Pichon, *China Trade and Empire*, p. 16.
6 Ibid., p. 9.

7 Ibid., p. 19.
8 Ibid., pp. 365, 524, 527, 528.
9 Ibid., pp. 36–51.
10 Zhang Tingyu, *Ming Shi* (*The History of the Ming Dynasty*), vols 320–328 'Waiguo Zhuan' (Foreign Nations) and vols 329–332 'Xiyu Zhuan' (Central Asian Nations), in *Er-shi-wu Shi* (*Twenty-Five Official Histories*) (Shanghai: Shanghai Classics Press, 1986), vol. 10, pp 8682–763.
11 They all adopted Chinese names: Giulio Aleni (艾儒略, 1582–1649), Diego de Pantoja (庞迪我, 1571–1618), Sabbatino de Ursis (熊三拔, 1575–1620), Johannes Schreck (邓玉函, 1576–1630), Johann Adam Schall von Bell (汤若望, 1592–1666), Nicolas Longobardi (龙华民, 1565–1655), Jacques Rho (罗雅各, 1593–1638), Ferdinand Verbiest (南怀仁, 1623–88), Thoma Pereira (徐日升, 1645–1708), Philippus Maria Grimaldi (闵明我, 1639–1712), Joachim Bouvet (白晋, 1656–1730), Jean Francois Gerbillon (张诚, 1654–1707), Bernard-Kiliam Stumpf (纪理安, 1655–1720), Joseph Giuseppe Castiglione (郎世宁, 1688–1766), Ignatius Koegler (戴进贤, 1680–1747), Andre Pereira (徐懋德, 1690–1743), Augustin de Hallerstein (刘松龄, 1721–74), William A. Martin (丁韪良, 1827–1916), and John Fryer (傅兰雅, 1839–1928).
12 Andre Gunder Frank, *ReOrient: Global Economy in the Asian Age* (Berkeley: University of California Press, 1998), ch. 3; Jerry Bentley, Sanjay Subrahmanyam, and Merry Wiesner-Hanks (eds), *The Cambridge World History, Vol. 4* (Cambridge: Cambridge University Press, 2015), ch. 7.
13 Deng Gang, *Maritime Sector, Institutions and Sea Power of Premodern China* (Westport, CT: Greenwood Press, 1999), pp. 131–2.
14 For Ming 'market openness' allowing foreign silver to flow in, see Frank, *ReOrient*, chs 2–3; Dennis O. Flynn and Arturo Giráldez, 'Born with a "Silver Spoon": The Origin of World Trade in 1571', *Journal of World History*, 6/2 (1995): 201–21; Kent Deng, 'Miracle or Mirage? Foreign Silver, China's Economy and Globalisation of the Sixteenth to Nineteenth Centuries', *Pacific Economic Review*, 13/3 (2008): 320–57. For the impact of this market openness, see, e.g., Richard von Glahn, *Fountain of Fortune: Money and Monetary Policy in China, 1000–1700* (Berkeley: University of California Press, 1996), ch. 4; Timothy Brook, *The Confusions of Pleasure: Commerce and Culture in Ming China* (Berkeley: University of California Press, 1999), pp. 238–40; William Atwell, 'Ming China and the Emerging World Economy, *c.*1470–1650', in Denis Twitchett and Frederick Mote (eds), *Cambridge History of China, Vol. 8* (Cambridge: Cambridge University Press, 2008), ch. 8.
15 As recorded in the official history of the Ming Dynasty; see Zhang Tingyu, *Ming Shi* (*The History of the Ming Dynasty*), vol. 30 'Li Zhi', vol. 31 'Li Zhi', and vol. 326 'Waiguo Zhuan', in *Er-shi-wu Shi* (*Twenty-Five Official Histories*) (Shanghai: Shanghai Classics Press, 1986), vol. 10, pp. 7841, 7843, 8703–4.
16 Tan Qixiang, *Jianming Zhongguo Lishi Dituji* (*Concise Maps of China's Past*) (Beijing: China's Map Press, 1991), pp. 65–70. The measures responsible for the Russian colonisation and semi-colonisation of China from 1689 to 1924, over 235 years, can be specified as the Treaty of Nerchinsk (1689), Treaty of Kyakhta (1727), Treaty of Aigun (1858), Convention of Peking (1860), Treaty of Tarbagatai (1864), Treaty of Saint Petersburg (1881).

In addition, after the 1900 Boxer Rebellion, Russia occupied Manchuria with the pretext of protecting its railway interests in the region (known as the 'Chinese Eastern Railway' and the 'South Manchuria Railway'). The Russian ambition was checked by the 1904 Russo-Japanese War. The most recent case was the creation of the Mongolian People's Republic in 1924.

17 Gang Deng, *The Chinese Premodern Economy – Structural Equilibrium and Capitalist Sterility* (London: Routledge), p. 4.

18 For example, Dennis O. Flynn and Arturo Giraldez, 'Silk for Silver: Manila-Macao Trade in the 17th Century', *Philippine Studies*, 44/1 (1996): 52–68; Peter Gordon and Juan José Morales, *The Silver Way: China, Spanish America, and the Birth of Globalisation, 1565–1815* (London: Penguin Press, 2017); Richard von Glahn, 'The Changing Significance of Latin American Silver in the Chinese Economy, 16th–19th Centuries', *Revista de Historia Economica*, 38/S3 (2020): 553–85; Xu Jin, *Empire of Silver: A New Monetary History of China* (New Haven, CT: Yale University Press, 2021).

19 Zhao Erxun, *Qingshi Gao* (*Drafted History of the Qing Dynasty*), vol. 124, 'Economy', in *Twenty-Five Official Histories*, vol. 11, p. 9275; and vol. 25, 'Biography of Xuantong', in *Twenty-Five Official Histories*, vol. 11, p. 8933.

20 China's registered population was 377.6 million (1887) and 368.1 million (1911); see Liang Fangzhong, *Zhongguo Lidai Hukou Tiandi Tianfu Tongji* (*Dynastic Data for China's Households, Cultivated Land and Land Taxation*) (Shanghai: Shanghai People's Press, 1980), p. 10.

21 One may intuitively extrapolate backwards the amount of silver received by China for the 1565–1644 period with the assumption that silver went to China in a linear manner. If true, roughly another 4000 tonnes of silver ended up in China modelled after the pattern from 1644 to 1730, or about 45 tonnes per year. This amount is within the range of Hang-Seng Chuan's 2–3 million *pesos* (50–75 tonnes) a year from 1600 to 1680 and William Atwell's 94 tonnes a year during the seventeenth century. See Hang-Seng Chuan, 'The Inflow of American Silver into China from the Late Ming to the Mid-Qing Period', *Journal of the Institute of Chinese Studies of the Chinese University of Hong-Kong*, 2/1 (1969): 62; William Atwell, 'Notes on Silver, Foreign Trade, and the Late Ming Economy, *Ch'ing-Shih Wen-T'i*, 3/8 (1977): 1–33. Chin-Keong Ng cites 2–4 million *pesos* (50–100 tonnes) a year for Fujian during the whole Manilla Galleon period; see Chin-Keong Ng, *Trade and Society: The Amoy Network on the China Coast, 1683–1735* (Singapore: Singapore University Press, 1983), p. 85. Meanwhile, the total Manilla annual silver shipment has been estimated at between 120 and 300 tonnes; see John TePaske, 'New World Silver, Castile, and the Philippines, 1590–1800', in John F. Richards (ed.), *Precious Metals in the Later Medieval and Early Modern Worlds* (Durham, NC: Carolina Academic Press), pp. 425–46. About half of the silver delivered to Manilla ended up in China; see Chuan, 'The Inflow of American Silver', p. 72.

22 Gang Deng, 'An Evaluation of the Role of Admiral Zheng He's Voyages in Chinese Maritime History', *International Journal of Maritime History* 7/2 (1995): 1–19.

23 Zhu Di was 'Duke of Yan' (*yan wang*) before his emperorship.

24 Kent Deng, *China's Political Economy in Modern Times* (London: Routledge, 2012), p. 17.

25 Liang, *Dynastic Data*, p. 8.
26 See Han Rulin, *Yuanchao Shi* (*A History of the Yuan Dynasty*) (Beijing: People's Press, 1986), vol. 1, pp. 391, 429; vol. 2, p. 48; Guo Zhengzhong, *Zhongguo Yanye Shi* (*A History of the Salt Sector in China*) (Beijing: People's Press, 1997), vol. 1, pp. 302, 493.
27 Han, *Yuan Dynasty*, vol. 1, pp. 391, 429; vol. 2, p. 48.
28 See Danial Coughlin, 'History's Most Expansive Megaprojects, from China's Great Wall to the US Interstate', 28 September 2021, https://www.lovemoney.com/gallerylist/83144/historys-most-expensive-megaprojects-from-chinas-great-wall-to-the-us-in?utm_source=chatgpt.com.
29 The number of Ming-registered households for taxation purposes was between 10 and 11 million; see Liang Fangzhong, *Zhongguo Lidai Hukou Tiandi Tianfu Tongji* (*Dynastic Data for China's Households, Cultivated Land and Land Taxation*) (Shanghai: Shanghai People's Press, 1980), pp. 8–10.
30 Anon. 'Beijing', *Britannica*, https://kids.britannica.com/students/article/Beijing/273153?utm_source=chatgpt.com.
31 Deng, 'Admiral Zheng He's Voyages'; Deng, *Chinese Maritime Activities*, ch. 3; Deng, *Maritime Sector*, ch. 4.
32 Commonly, one cites the experiment and full implication of the 'One Whip Method' (*yi tiao bian fa*) of 1522–1581, which combined land and poll taxes and made all direct taxes payable in silver; see Zhang, *Ming Dynasty*, vol. 78, 'Shihou Zhi', in *Twenty-Five Official Histories*, vol. 10, p. 7983.
33 Deng, 'Miracle or Mirage?', p. 326.
34 Transaction costs represent any obstacles to commodities and market information moving freely. Market information or power asymmetricity is a typical form of such a cost.
35 Austin Dean, *China and the End of Global Silver, 1873–1937* (Ithaca, NY: Cornell University Press, 2020), ch. 2.
36 Flynn and Giráldez, 'Born with a "Silver Spoon"', p. 205. Also see Frank, *ReOrient*, ch. 3; William Atwell, 'Another Look at Silver Imports into China, ca. 1635–1644', *Journal of World History*, 16/4 (2005): 467–89.
37 Juan Rivas-Moreno, *The Capital Market of Manila and the Pacific Trade, 1668–1838* (Cham: Palgrave Macmillan, 2024), p. 38.
38 A technical illustration can be found in Appendix 3, figure A–3.1.
39 Liang, *Dynastic Data*, pp. 8–10.
40 Typically, the Ming 'demography trough' was replaced by a linear growth which was back extrapolated from the Qing; see Angus Maddison, *Chinese Economic Performance in the Long Run* (Paris: OECD, 1998), pp. 26, 169.
41 A technical illustration can be found in Appendix 3, figure A–3.2.
42 Fairbank and Goldman, *China*, p. 203; Eric L. Jones, *Growth Recurring, Economic Change in World History* (Ann Arbor: University of Michigan Press, 2000), ch. 8.
43 The Qing territorial expansion was associated with Kangxi (r.1662–1722) and Qianlong (r.1736–95).
44 By the 1820s, the new farmland in the Balikun and Yili regions of Xinjiang (also known as 'Chinese Turkistan') alone totalled 908,500 *mu* or 121,735 hectares; see Chen Hua, *Qingdai Quyu Shehui Jingji Yanjiu* (*Regional Socio-Economic Conditions during the Qing Period*) (Beijing: People's University Press, 1996), p. 265; see also Jane K. Leonard and John R. Watt

(eds), *To Achieve Security and Wealth: The Qing Imperial State and the Economy, 1644–1911* (Ithaca, NY: Cornell University East Asia Program, 1992), pp. 21–46.

45 The common speculation around China's adoption of New World Crops – maize and sweet potatoes – is not well supported by China's records.

46 Kenneth Pomeranz, *The Great Divergence: Europe, China and the Making of the Modern World Economy* (Princeton, NJ: Princeton University Press, 2000), pp. 20, 241.

47 For a spatial survey, see Yeh-chien Wang, *Late Taxation in Imperial China, 1750–1911* (Cambridge, MA: Harvard University Press, 1973), p. 85.

48 For the eighteenth century, see Pierre-Etienne Will, *Bureaucracy and Famine in Eighteenth-Century China* (Stanford: Stanford University Press, 1990), pt. 2. See also W.J. Peterson (ed.), *The Cambridge History of China* (Cambridge: Cambridge University Press, 2002), vol. 9, p. 567.

49 Anon., *Qing Gaozong Shilu* (*Veritable Records of Emperor Gaozong of the Qing Dynasty*) (1799, reprint 1964, Taipei: Hualian Press), vol. 311, Entry 'Shisannian Sanyue' (The Third Month of the Thirteenth Year under the Gaozong Reign); Zhang Limin, 'Chuang Guandong Yiminchao Jianxi' (Advancing to Manchuria), *Zhongguo Shehui Jingjishi Yanjiu* (*Study of Chinese Socio-Economic History*) 2 (1998): 57–64.

50 Tian Fang and Chen Yijun, *Zhongguo Yimin Shilue* (*Brief History of Migration in China*) (Beijing: Knowledge Press, 1986), pp. 110–12.

51 The Qing state imposed a ban on permanent immigration to Manchuria (1668–1860) and Mongolia (1740–1897). There was little control over seasonal migrants to both regions. Moreover, by the time the restriction was introduced, a large number of immigrants had already settled; see Zhao, *Drafted History*, vol. 120, 'Economy', in *Twenty-Five Official Histories*, vol. 11, p. 9253.

52 James Lee, 'Population Growth in Southwest China, 1250–1850', *Journal of Asian Studies*, 41/4 (1982): 711–46.

53 Yuan Yida and Zhang Cheng, *Zhongguo Xingshi: Qunti Yichuan He Renko Fenbu* (*Chinese Surnames: Group Genetics and Demographic Distribution*) (Shanghai: East China Normal University Press, 2002), pp. 6–57.

54 An economic measurement for 'factor's input–output efficiency'. Conceptually, excessive labour input yields less or no additional output. If such labour input harms crops, the responding output becomes negative (e.g., after excessive digging, weeding, and irrigation).

55 See Wu Chengming, *Zhongguode Xiandaihua, Shichang Yu Shehui* (*China's Modernization: Market and Society*) (Beijing: Sanlian Books, 2001), pp. 154–6; see also Mark Elvin, *The Pattern of the Chinese Past* (Stanford: Stanford University Press, 1973), p. 214; Pomeranz, *Great Divergence*, p. 226; *cf.* Dwight H. Perkins, *Agricultural Development in China, 1368–1968* (Edinburgh: Edinburgh University Press, 1969), p. 210, fn 1.

56 See Zhang Haiying, *Mingqing Jiangnan Shangpin Liutong Yu Shichang Tixi* (*Commodity Flows and Market Structure in the Jiangnan Region during the Ming-Qing Period*) (Shanghai: East China Normal University Press, 2001), pp. 198–206. See also Myers and Wang, 'Economic Developments', vol. 9, p. 613.

57 Zhang Jiayan, 'Mingqing Jianghan Pingyuande Nongye Kaifa Dui Shangren Huodong He Shizhen Fazhande Yingxiang' (Impact of Agricultural

Development in the Yangtze-Han Plain on Commercial Activities and Urbanization during the Ming-Qing Period), *Zhongguo Nongshi* (*Agricultural History of China*) 4 (1995): 42.

58 Chen, *Regional Socio-Economic Conditions*, ch. 4.

59 Wang, *Late Taxation*, p. 90.

60 See James Lee and Wang Feng, *One Quarter of Humanity: Malthusian Mythology and Chinese Realities, 1700–2000* (Cambridge, MA: Harvard University Press, 1999), pp. 34–5, 38.

61 Kent G. Deng, 'Unveiling China's True Population Statistics for the Pre-Modern Era with Official Census Data', *Population Review* 43/2 (2004): Appendix 2.

62 Liang, *Dynastic Data*, pp. 387, 390–6.

63 Yan Zhongping, *Zhongguo Jindai Jingjishi Ziliao Xuanji* (*Selected Data for Early Modern Economic History of China*) (Beijing: Science Press, 1955), pp. 31–2.

64 For example, Ping-ti Ho, 'The Introduction of American Food Plants into China', *American Anthropologist*, 57/2, Part 1 (1955): 191–201; Walter H. Mallory, *China: Land of Famine* (New York: American Geographical Society, 1926); Lee, 'Population Growth'; Jack Goldston, 'Feeding the People, Starving the State: China's Agricultural Revolution of the 17th and 18th Centuries', Hong Kong University of Science and Technology Conference Papers, 2003, https://repository.hkust.edu.hk/ir/Record/1783.1-75412; Shuo Chen and James K. Kung, 'Of Maize and Men: The Effect of a New World Crop on Population and Economic Growth in China', *Journal of Economic Development*, 21/1 (2016): 71–99.

65 They are called 'inferior goods' or 'Giffen Goods' whose consumption is positively correlated to economic hardships and poverty and negatively correlated to incomes and prices. This notion clearly goes against what economists call 'price and income inelasticity of food', meaning that consumers will put up with a price increase in food and/or an income decrease for food and keep their diet unchanged.

66 Seee www.nutri-facts.com.

67 Ibid.

68 Hallett Abend, *My Years in China, 1926–1941* (London: John Lane, 1944), p. 63.

69 Chen Xiaoqing, Li Jifeng, and Zhu Lexian, *Kangzhan Shiwu Nian* (*Fifteen Years of Counter-Japanese Invasion*) (Nanning: Guangxi Normal University Press, 2008), p. 118.

70 Ibid., pp. 341, 349, 365.

71 Ibid., p. 314.

72 Maize first landed in China in the 1570s; and sweet potatoes in the 1590s.

73 John L. Buck, *Land Utilization in China: Atlas* (London: Oxford University Press, 1937), p. 82.

74 Ibid., pp. 62, 106.

75 This assessment is supported by a regional study of rural diet in the Lower Yangzi in the 1820s: maize and sweet potatoes were both absent on people's dinner table; see Li Bozhong, 'Xiangminmen Chide Bucuo – Shijiu Shiji Chuqi Songjiang Shiwu Xiaofei Shuiping Yanjiu' ('Rural Folks Eating Well' – A Study of Food Consumption Level in Songjiang in the Early 19th Century), in Ancient History Centre of Peking University (ed.), *Deng*

Guanming Jiaoshou Bainian Shouchen Jinian Wenji (*Collected Essays to Mark the 100th Birthday of Professor Deng Guanming*) (Beijing: Zhonghua Books, 2008), pp. 715–35. See also Li Bozhong, *Duoshijiao Kan Jiangnan Jingjishi* (*A Multifaceted Economic History of the Lower Yangzi Region*) (Shanghai: Sanlian, 2003), ch. 9.

76 John L. Buck, *Land Utilization in China: Statistics* (London: Oxford University Press, 1937), pp. 311, 314, 316.

77 Gilbert Rozman, *Urban Networks in Ch'ing China and Tokugawa Japan* (Princeton, NJ: Princeton University Press, 1973), pp. 279–82; Cao Shuji, *Zhongguo Renkou Shi* (*A Demographic History of China*) (Shanghai: Fudan University Press, 2000), vol. 5, pp. 828–9.

78 William W. Skinner, *The City in Late Imperial China* (Stanford: Stanford University Press, 1977), pp. 228–9.

79 William W. Skinner, 'Marketing and Social Structure in Rural China', *Journal of Asian Studies*, 24/1 (1964): 3–44; 24/2 (1965): 195–228; 24/3 (1965): 363–400; Robert B. Marks, 'Rice Prices, Food Supply, and Market Structure in Eighteenth-Century South China', *Late Imperial China*, 12/2 (1991): 64–116; Li Wenzhi, 'Lun Mingqing Shidai Nongmin Jingji Shangpinlü' (Marketing Rates of the Peasant Products in Ming-Qing Times), *Zhongguo Jingjishi Yanjiu* (*Study of Chinese Economic History*), 1 (1993): 21–42.

80 For 30 per cent marketable surpluses, see Victor Lippit, 'The Development of Underdevelopment in China', *Modern China*, 4/3 (1978): 293; Li, 'Marketing Rates', pp. 21–42. For the 20–40 per cent commercial output, see Ramon H. Myers, *The Chinese Peasant Economy: Agricultural Development in Hopei and Shangtung, 1890–1949* (Cambridge, MA: Harvard University Press, 1970), pp. 12–13; Perkins, *Agricultural Development*, p. 115; Albert Feuerwerker, *State and Society in Eighteenth-Century China: the Ch'ing Empire in Its Glory* (Ann Arbor: Center for Chinese Studies of the University of Michigan), p. 86. For higher percentages, see Buck, *Statistics*, p. 343.

81 See Yutong Wang, Jingyuan Guo and Kent Deng, 'Inputs, Outputs and Living Standards in Rural China during the 1920s and 30s – A Quantitative Analysis', *Working Papers of Department of Economic History, LSE*, No. 359, September 2023.

82 This project avoids the use of estimates in general and GDP estimates in particular, with a general principle that one cannot possibly settle disputes over estimates with yet more estimates. Thus, it is more constructive to stick to real data.

83 For example, Chung-li Chang, *The Income of the Chinese Gentry* (Seattle: University of Washington Press, 1962), p. 296; Albert Feuerwerker, *The Chinese Economy, 1870–1949* (Ann Arbor: Center for Chinese Studies of the University of Michigan, 1995), p. 16; Liu Foding, Wang Yuru and Zhao Jin, *Zhongguo Jindai Jingji Fazhanshi* (*A History of Economic Development in Early Modern China*) (Beijing: Tertiary Education Press, 1999), p. 66.

84 Including Land-Poll of 90 million *taels* per year (3,375 tonnes); see Zhou Yumin, *Wanqing Caizheng Yu Shehui Bianqian* (*Late Qing Public Finance and Social Changes*) (Shanghai: Shanghai People's Press, 2000), p. 237. Or, 102.4 million *taels* for 1908 (3,840 tonnes); see Wang, *Late Taxation*, p. 75.

85 This is more optimistic than the estimates of 30–40 million *piculs* of unhusked rice for the same period; see Hou Chi-ming (ed.), *Modern Chinese Economic History* (Taipei: The Institute of Economics, *Academia Sinica*, 1979), p. 434. The period price was 2.0–2.4 *taels* of silver per *picul* for unhusked rice, the total value of the grain would be a maximum of 80 million *piculs* of unhusked rice. One Qing *picul* makes 103 litres; see Ts'ui-Jung Liu and J.C.H. Fei, 'An Analysis of the Land Tax Burden in China, 1650–1865', *Journal of Economic History*, 43/3 (1977): 375. One Qing *picul* of unhusked rice weights 72.5 kg; see Liang *Dynastic Data*, p. 545; Kang Chao, *Man and Land in Chinese History: An Economic Analysis* (Stanford: Stanford University, 1986), p. 209. These 80 million *piculs* are enough to feed 21.9 million adult males for a year at the subsistence level. These 21.9 million people occupied 5.5 per cent (based on China's 398.9 million of 1833) of China's total population; see Deng, 'True Population Statistics', Appendix 2. According to William Skinner, China's urbanisation rate was 5.1 per cent for 1843 and 6.0 per cent for 1893. Even in the most affluent Jiangnan region, the rate was merely 7.4 per cent for 1843 and 10.6 per cent for 1893; see Skinner, *City in Late Imperial China*, pp. 228–9. So, the grain trade was about enough to maintain China's urban population.

86 As far as one can tell, among China's rural population, 90 per cent of work clothes and 70 of social clothes were made of domestically made cotton goods; silk clothes accounted for only 12 per cent; see Buck, *Statistics*, pp. 349–51, 355.

87 A more detailed pattern of cotton flows is available in Appendix 2, figure A–2.1.

88 Buck, *Statistics*, p. 311.

89 Jan de Vries, 'The Industrial Revolution and the Industrious Revolution', *Journal of Economic History*, 54/2 (1994): 249–70; Robert Allen and Jacob Weisdorf, 'Was There an "Industrious Revolution" before the Industrial Revolution?' *Journal of Economic History*, 64/3 (2011): 715–29.

90 For example, Akira Hayami, *Japan's Industrious Revolution: Economic and Social Transformations in the Early Modern Period* (London: Springer, 2015).

91 Yu Tongyuan, 'Mingqing Jiangnan Zaoqi Gongyehua Shehuide Xingcheng Yu Fanzhan' (Formation and Development of Early Industrial Society in the Lower Yangzi during the Ming-Qing Period), *Shixue Yuekan* (*Historical Study Monthly*), 11 (2007): 53–61. The debate has not yet been settled.

92 A bolt = 2.2 Qing *chi* by 40 Qing *chi*, or 0.7 m by 12.8 m. For the *chi* to metre conversion standard, see Liang, *Dynastic Data*, p. 543.

93 For the common rule, see https://www.google.com/search?q=estimate+of+how+much+cloth+is+needed+for+a+pair+of+trousers+for+an+adult+in+square+metres&client=safari&sca_esv=706a3250d026367c&channel=mac_bm&sxsrf=ADLYWIKVrpEdESf-hSQwWHGAI1e9aV2GOA%3A1734979725639&source=hp&ei=jbBpZ6WuJOrXhbIPytTmoAI&iflsig=AL9hbdgAAAAAZ2m-nRmvEqEpWQlf3sjA5s1LP6x2CNvc&oq=es&gs_lp=Egdnd3Mtd2l6IgJlcyoCCAAyBBAjGCcyCxAAGIAEGJECGIoFMgsQABiABBiRAhiKBTIKEAAYgAQYQxiKBTIKEAAYgAQYQxiKBTIKEAAYgAQYQxiKBTIKEAAYgAQYQxiKBTIWEC4YgAQYsQMY0QMYQxiDARjHARiKBTIKEAAYgAQYQxiKBTIKEAAYgAQYQxiKBUjuE1AAWL0BcAB4AJABAJgBeqABzwGqAQMxLjG4AQHIAQD4A

QGYAgKgAvcBwgIKECMYgAQYJxiKBcICERAuGIAEGLEDGNEDGIMBGMcBwgIEEAAYA8ICDhAuGIAEGLEDGNEDGMcBmAMAkgcDMS4xoAeqGQ&sclient=gws-wiz; https://www.google.com/search?q=estimate+of+how+much+cloth+is+needed+for+a+shirt+for+an+adult+in+square+metres&client=safari&sca_esv=706a3250d026367c&channel=mac_bm&sxsrf=ADLYWILN96n7fX9lvl3ZguQbFl-gLfXbog%3A1734979733935&ei=lbBpZ5nAOLTXhbIPkNjo6A4&ved=0ahUKEwjZ3u6Vx76KAxW0a0EAHRAsGu0Q4dUDCBA&uact=5&oq=estimate+of+how+much+cloth+is+needed+for+a+shirt+for+an+adult+in+square+metres&gs_lp=Egxnd3Mtd2l6LXNlcnAiTmVzdGltYXRlIG9mIGhvdyBtdWNoIGNsb3RoIGlzIG5lZWRlZCBmb3IgYSBzaGlydCBmb3IgYW4gYWR1bHQgaW4gc3F1YXJlIG1ldHJlc0gAUABYAHAAeAGQAQCYAQCgAQCqAQC4AQPIAQD4AQGYAgCgAgCYAwCSBwCgBwA&sclient=gws-wiz-serp.

94 Export of the *nankeen* cotton cloth increased 10-fold in 1865 to 1875; see Xu Xinwu, *Jiangnan Tubu Shi* (*A History of Traditional Cotton Textiles in the Yangzi Region*) (Shanghai: Shanghai Social Sciences Press, 1989), pp. 105–6; see Yan Zhongping, *Zhongguo Mianyezhi Fazhan* (*Development of Cotton Textile Industry in China*) (Shanghai: Commercial Press, 1944), p. 70.

95 For example, Hosea B. Morse, *The Chronicles of the East India Company Trading to China, 1635–1834* (Oxford: Clarendon Press, 1926–1929); Tan Chung, 'The Britain–China–India Trade Triangle (1771–1840)', *Proceedings of the Indian History Congress*, 34/2 (1973): 77–91; Michael J. Twomey, 'Employment in Nineteenth Century Indian Textiles', *Explorations in Economic History*, 20/1 (1983): 40, 42 and 46; Hue Bowen, 'The Integration of the Asian Cotton Textile Industry: Trade, Empire, and British Exports of Raw Cotton from India to China during the Late Eighteenth and Early Nineteenth Centuries', *LSE Global Economic History Network Working Paper Series*, November 2005.

96 Le Pichon, *China Trade*, pp. 9, 12.

97 So, from 1840 to 1900, China signed twenty-six treaties with twelve foreign powers with seventy-three concessions; see Zhang Dongqing, *Zhongguo Jingjishi Cidan* (*Encyclopaedia of Chinese Economic History*) (Wuhan: Hubei Books, 1990), pp. 874–80.

98 John S. Mill, *Principles of Political Economy with Some of their Applications to Social Philosophy* (London: John W. Parke, 1848); Arthur C. Pigou, *The Economics of Stationary State* (London: Macmillan, 1935); Elvin, *Chinese Past*, p. 313.

99 Albert Feuerwerker, 'The State and the Economy in Late Imperial China', *Theory and Society* 13/3 (1984): 300.

100 Angus Maddison, *Chinese Performance in the Long Run 960–2030*, 2nd edn (Paris: OECD, 2007); Peng Kaixiang, 'Lishi GDP Gusuanzhongde Jijia Wenti Chuyi' (Critique of Price-based Historical GDP Estimates), *Zhongguo Jingjishi Yanjiu* (*Research into Chinese Economic History*), 4 (2011): 53–60; Liu Ti, *Qian Jindai Zhongguo Zongliang Jingji Yanjiu, 1600–1840* (*Estimations of China's Total GDP, 1600–1840*) (Shanghai: Shanghai People's Press, 2010); R.C. Feenstra, H. Ma and J.P. Neary, 'Who Shrunk China? Puzzles in the Measurement of Real GDP', *Economic Journal*, 123/573 (2013): 1100–29; Ni Yuping, 'Ping Qianjidai Zhongguo Zongliang Jingji Yanjiu, 1600–1840' (Review of China's Total GDP of

Early Modern Times, 1600–1840), *Zhongguoshi Yanjiu* (*Study of Chinese History*), 1 (2013): 186–93; Zhong Weimin and Qiu Yongzhi 'Shuju Gusuan Yu Lishi Zhenshi, Zhongguoshi Zhong GDP Gusuan Yanjiu Pingshu' (Quantitative Estimates and Historical Reality), *Shixue Yuekan* (*Historical Study Monthly*), 2 (2014): 105–14; Kent Deng and Patrick O'Brien, 'China's GDP per Capita from the Han Dynasty to Communist Times', *World Economics Journal*, 17/2 (2016): 79–123; S. Broadberry, H. Guan, and D. Li, 'China, Europe and the Great Divergence: A Study in Historical National Accounting, 980–1850', *Journal of Economic History*, 78/4 (2018): 955–1000; Peter M. Solar, 'China's GDP: Some Corrections and the Way Forward', *Journal of Economic History*, 81/3 (2021): 943–57. The list may go on.

101 Estimated GDP for the 1830s is 3,603 million *taels*; see Liu Ti, '1600–1840 Nian Zhongguo Guonei Shengchan Zongzhide Gusuan' (Estimation of China's GDP between 1600 and 1840), *Jingji Yanjiu* (*Economic Study*), 10 (2009): 144–55. GDP estimate for 1750, around 1,713 million *taels* is based on Feuerwerker, 'The State and the Economy', pp. 297–326.

102 Cao, *Demographic History*, vol. 6, pp. 236, 257, 266, 274, 281, 298.

103 See Chris Ogden, *Oxford Dictionary of Politics and International Relations in India* (Oxford: Oxford University Press, 2019).

Chapter 2

1 For example, Lee and Wang, *One Quarter of Humanity*; Angus Maddison, *The World Economy Historical Statistics* (OECD Publishing; 2003), p. 275.

2 Rodney Gilbert, *The Unequal Treaties, China and the Foreigner* (London: John Murray, 1929).

3 Frank Dikötter, *The Age of Openness: China before Mao* (Berkeley: University of California Press, 2008).

4 For example, Theodore Hamberg, *The Visions of Hung-Siu-tshuen, and Origin of the Kwang-si Insurrection* (Hong Kong: China Mail Office, 1854); Rudolf G. Wagner, *Reenacting the Heavenly Vision: The Role of Religion in the Taiping Rebellion* (Berkeley: University of California, Institute of East Asian Studies, 1982); John K. Fairbank and E.O. Reischaver, *China: Tradition and Transformation* (London: Allen and Unwin, 1979); John K. Fairbank, *The United States and China*, 4th edn (Cambridge, MA: Harvard University Press, 1983); John K. Fairbank and Kwang-ching Liu (eds), *Cambridge History of China, Late Ch'ing, 1800–1911* (Cambridge: Cambridge University Press, 1980); Robert A. Scalapina and George T. Yu, *Modern China and Its Revolutionary Process* (Berkeley: University of California Press, 1985); Jonathan D. Spence, *God's Chinese Son* (New York: W.W. Norton, 1996); Spence, *Modern China*.

5 Jack Brad, *How Mao Conquered China* (Berkeley: Independent Socialist Press, 1970); Otto Braun, *A Comintern Agent in China* (London: C. Hurst, 1982); Jiang Zhongzheng (Chiang Kai-shek), *Su-e Zai Zhongguo* (*Soviet Russia Operating in China*) (Taipei: Central Cultural Relics Bureau, 1983).

6 Sun was in Denver in the United States and became aware of the Wuhan Mutiny through the American media. Sun continued to behave as an

outsider until December 1911 by which time the game was largely over. In 1911, Sun was but an armchair revolutionary.

7 Deng, *China's Political Economy*, p. 33.

8 Ibid., p. 25.

9 Zhu Kezhen, 'Woguo Jinwuqiannianlai Qihou' (Climate Changes in China in the Past 5000 Years), *Kaogu Xuebao* (*Acta Archaeologica Sinica*), 1/1 (1972): 15–38; Kam-biu Liu, Caiming Shen, and Kin-Sheun Louie, 'A 1,000-Year History of Typhoon Landfalls in Guangdong, Southern China, Reconstructed from Chinese Historical Documentary Records', *Annals of the Association of American Geographers*, 91/3 (2001): 453–64; Lingbo Xiao, Xiuqi Fang, Jingyun Zheng, and Wanyi Zhao, 'Famine, Migration and War: Comparison of Climate Change Impacts and Social Responses in North China between the Late Ming and Late Qing Dynasties', *The Holocene*, 25/6 (2015): 900–10.

10 Bret Hinsch, 'Climatic Change and History in China', *Journal of Asian History*, 22/2 (1988): 155.

11 The difference was that the Song state was large and actively interfered with farming, manufacturing, and commerce. See Kent Deng and Lucy Zheng, 'Economic Restructuring and Demographic Growth, Demystifying Growth and Development in Northern Song China, 960–1127', *Economic History Review*, 68/4 (2015): 1107–31.

12 Zhao, *Drafted History*, vol. 260, 'Biographies 47', in *Twenty-Five Official Histories*, vol. 12, p. 9889; vol. 263, 'Biographies 50', in *Twenty-Five Official Histories*, vol. 12, p. 9808; vol. 285, 'Biographies 72', in *Twenty-Five Official Histories*, vol. 12, p. 9932; vol. 344, 'Biographies 131', in *Twenty-Five Official Histories*, vol. 12, p. 10048; vol. 345, 'Biographies 132', in *Twenty-Five Official Histories*, vol. 12, p. 10053; vol. 404, 'Biographies 191', in *Twenty-Five Official Histories*, vol. 12, p. 10142. Also see Institute of History of the Chinese Academy of Social Sciences, *Qing Zhongqi Wusheng Bailianjiao Qiyi Ziliao* (*Materials of the White Lotus Uprising in Five Provinces in the Mid-Qing Period*) (Nanjing: Jiangsu People's Press, 1981), vols 1–5.

13 Mallory, *China: Land of Famine*; Lillian M. Li, 'Introduction: Food, Famine and the Chinese State', *Journal of Asian Studies*, 41/4 (1982): 687–707; Lillian M. Li, *Fighting Famine in North China* (Stanford: Stanford University Press, 2007); James K-S. Kung and Justin Y. Lin, 'The Causes of China's Great Leap Famine, 1959–1961', *Economic Development and Cultural Change*, 51/2 (2003): 51–73.

14 The work by Pierre Étienne Will concentrates on the Province of Zhili; see his *Bureaucracy and Famine*. The follow-up study by Will and Wong covered seven provinces and only in the form of rice aid; see Pierre-Etienne Will and R.B. Wong, *Nourish the People: the State Civilian Granary System in China, 1650–1850* (Ann Arbor: University of Michigan Center for Chinese Studies, 1991).

15 Zhao, *Drafted History*, vol. 121 'Economy', in *Twenty-Five Official Histories*, vol. 11, p. 9236. It takes 0.5 kg of husked grain per day to sustain an adult (about 1,850 kcal per head per day). A husking or milling process loses 30 per cent of the original weight of the grain. So, the required amount of unhusked grain is 0.65 kg per day, or 237 kg per year, to sustain an adult.

16 Will and Wong, *Nourish the People*, pp. 21, 482–3; Peterson, *Cambridge History of China*, vol. 9, p. 602; Carol H. Shiue, 'The Political Economy of Famine Relief in China, 1740–1820', *Journal of Interdisciplinary History*, 1/36 (2005): 33–55; also see Li, 'Food, Famine and the Chinese State'.
17 Zhao, *Drafted History*, vol. 121 'Economy', *Twenty-Five Official Histories*, vol. 11, p. 9262.
18 Ibid., p. 9263.
19 Ibid.
20 Pomeranz, *Great Divergence*, p. 34.
21 Zhao, *Drafted History*, vol. 121 'Economy', in *Twenty-Five Official Histories*, vol. 11, pp. 9262–3.
22 Ibid., p. 9262.
23 Ibid., p. 9263.
24 Ibid.
25 Deng, 'True Population Statistics', Appendix 2; Cao, *Demographic History*, vol. 5, p. 704.
26 This impression was valid inside the government bureaucracy: Officials were tightly controlled by their superior; punishments were often severe. Such rules did not apply to the general population. See Deng, *Chinese Premodern Economy*, ch. 3.
27 Yang Zhimei, *Zhongguo Gudai Guanzhi Jiangzuo* (*Bureaucracy of Premodern China*) (Beijing: Zhonghua Books, 1992), pp. 420–1; and Zhang Deze, *Qingdai Guojia Jiguan Kaolue* (*The State Apparatus of the Qing Period*) (Beijing: Xueyuan Press, 2001), pp. 6, 39, 43, 57, 79, 106, 127. Officials in the Qing central government worked very long hours to keep the vital departments running 24 hours a day; see Wanyan Shaoyuan, *Dao Yanmen Shangbanqu* (*Go to Work in Government Offices*) (Taipei: Yuanliu Press, 2005), pp. 172–81.
28 This should be the maximum, including 120,000 Eight Banners (*baqi*) and 660,000 Green Standards (*lüying*, literarily 'green corps'); see Zhao, *Drafted History*, vol. 131, 'Military', in *Twenty-Five Official Histories*, vol. 11, pp. 9305, 9307.
29 See Zhao, *Drafted History*, vols 54–81, 'Administrative Geography', in *Twenty-Five Official Histories*, pp. 9071–131; Yang, *Bureaucracy*, pp. 420–1. Note that after 1882, Fengtian, Jilin, Heilongjiang, Xinjiang, and Taiwan became full provinces.
30 Sun Haiquan, 'Qingdai Zhongye Zhili Diqu Xiangcun Guanli Tizhi' (Rural Management Institutions in Zhili during the Mid-Qing Period), *Zhongguo Shehui Kexue* (*Social Sciences in China*), 3 (2003): 189–204. For the relevant principle–agent problem, see Madeleine Zelin, *The Magistrate's Tael: Rationalizing Fiscal Reform in Eighteenth-Century Ch'ing China* (Berkeley: University of California Press, 1984), pp. 257–8.
31 Cheng Qi and Ying Jie (eds), *Qinding Hubu Zeli* (*Regulations of Ministry of Revenue, Made by Imperial Order*) (N.d. Reprint, Taipei: Chengwen Press, 1968), vol. 73, 'Honesty and Uprightness Bonus'; see also Zuo Bofu, *Qingdai Yongzhengchaode Yanglianyin Yanjiu* (*A Study of 'Honesty and Uprightness Bonuses' under the Yongzheng Reign, 1723–35*) (Taipei: Taiwan Commercial Press, 1976); Zelin, *Magistrate's Tael.*

32 He Changling and Wei Yuan (eds), *Huangchao Jingshi Wenbian* (*Collection of Documents of the Qing Administration*) (N.d. Reprint, Beijing: Zhonghua Books, 1992), p. 868.
33 Chen Feng, 'Lun Haoxian Guigong' (Silver Wear and Tear as a New Tax), *Qinghua Daxue Xuebao* (*Bulletin of Tsinghua University*), 3/24 (2009): 17–38.
34 See Zuo Bofu and Zheng Liangsheng, *Qing Yongzhengchaode Yanglianyin Yanjiu* (*A Study of the 1723–35 Honesty and Uprightness Bonuses*) (Taipei: Taiwan Commercial Press, 1976). See also Feng Yuankui, 'Lun Qingchao Yanglianyin Zhidu' (The Qing Honesty and Uprightness Bonuses), *Fudan Xuebao* (*Bulletin of Fudan University*), 2 (1991): 62–70.
35 Cheng and Ying, *Regulations of Ministry of Revenue*, vol. 73, 'Honesty and Uprightness Bonuses'; see also Zuo, *Honesty and Uprightness*; Zelin, *Magistrate's Tael.*
36 In 1853, the Taipings captured the Nanjing granary loaded with 2 million *piculs* of grain (145,000 tonnes); see Guo Yisheng, *Taiping Tianguo Jingjishi* (*An Economic History of the Taiping Regime*) (Nanning: Guanxi People's Press, 1991), p. 112.
37 For the whole picture of mass rebellions in China, see Deng, *Premodern Chinese Economy*, pp. 364–76.
38 Chinese Historical Society (ed.), *Taiping Tianguo* (*Heavenly Kingdom of Great Peace*) (Shanghai: Shenzhou Guoguang Press, 1952), vol. 4, p. 465.
39 The notion of a 'moral economy' emphasises traditional rights and entitlements; see E.P. Thompson, 'The Moral Economy of the English Crowd in the Eighteenth Century', *Past & Present*, 50/1 (1971): 76–136; James Scott, *The Moral Economy of the Peasant Rebellion and Subsistence in Southeast Asia* (New Haven, CT: Yale University Press, 1976).
40 Zhao, *Drafted History*, vol. 8, 'Biography of Shengzu', in *Twenty-Five Official Histories*, vol. 11, p. 8850; vol. 9, 'Biograph of Shizong', in *Twenty-Five Official Histories*, vol. 11, p. 8853; and vol. 121, 'Economy', in *Twenty-Five Official Histories*, vol. 11, p. 9261.
41 Zhou Qirong, 'Mingqing Yinshua Shuji Chengben, Jiage Jiqi Shangpin Jiazhide Yanjiu' (Costs, Prices and Market Value of Books in the Ming-Qing Period), *Zhejiang Daxue Xuebao* (*Bulletin of Zhejiang University*), 1 (2010): 5–17.
42 Fairbank, *United States and China*, p. 77.
43 Song Yuanqiang, *Qingchaode Zhuangyuan* (*Champions of the Qing Imperial Examinations*) (Changchun: Jilin Culture and History Press, 1992), pp. 52, 451–5.
44 E Ertai (Ortai), *Shoushi Tongkao* (*Compendium of Works and Days*) (1742. Reprinted, Beijing: Zhonghua Books,1956), pp. 1073, 1077–8, 1083–4.
45 Wang Yuhu, *Zhongguo Nongxue Shulu* (*Bibliography of Chinese Classical Agronomy*) (Beijing: Agriculture Press, 1964), Appendix III.
46 Wei Zaitian, Xu Xuechu, and Li Yawei (eds), *Kangxi Zhiguo Shengxun* (*Emperor Kangxi's Instructions on State Management*) (Beijing: Expatriates' Press, 1995), p. 193.
47 Liu and Fei, 'Land Tax Burden', pp. 373, 375–6.
48 Deng, 'True Population Statistics'.
49 Susan Mann, *Local Merchants and the Chinese Bureaucracy, 1750–1950* (Stanford: Stanford University Press, 1987), p. 16.

50 Deng, *China's Political Economy*, ch. 3.
51 Li Yi, *The Structure and Evolution of Chinese Social Stratification* (Lanham, MD: University Press of America, 2005), p. 83.
52 See http://blog.sina.com.cn/s/blog_4b8bd1450102edb0.html.
53 John K. Fairbank and Edwin O. Reischauer, *East Asia: The Great Tradition* (Boston: Houghton Mifflin, 1960), p. 115.
54 Numerous works on state capacity, e.g. Douglass North, and Barry R. Weingast, 'Constitutions and Commitment: The Evolution of Institutions Governing Public Choice in Seventeenth-Century England', *Journal of Economic History*, 49/4 (1989): 803–32; Douglass North, *Institutions, Institutional Change and Economic Performance* (Cambridge: Cambridge University Press, 1990); Hillel Soifer and Matthias Vom Hau, 'Unpacking the Strength of the State: The Utility of State Infrastructural Power', *Studies in Comparative International Development*, 43 (2008): 219–30; Cullen S. Hendrix, 'Measuring State Capacity: Theoretical and Empirical Implications for the Study of Civil Conflict', *Journal of Peace Research*, 47/3 (2010): 273–85; Francis Fukuyama, 'What Is Governance?', *Governance*, 26/3 (2013): 347–68; Jonathan K. Hanson, 'Forging then Taming Leviathan: State Capacity, Constraints on Rulers, and Development', *International Studies Quarterly*, 58/2 (2014): 380–92; Daron Acemoglu, Camilo García-Jimeno, and James A. Robinson, 'State Capacity and Economic Development: A Network Approach', *American Economic Review*, 105/8 (2015): 2364–409; Daron Acemoglu, Jacob Moscona, and James A. Robinson, 'State Capacity and American Technology: Evidence from the Nineteenth Century', *American Economic Review*, 106/5 (2016): 61–7; Matt Andrews, Lant Pritchett, and Michael Woolcock, *Building State Capability: Evidence, Analysis, Action* (Oxford: Oxford University Press, 2017); Elissa Berwick and Fotini Christia, 'State Capacity Redux: Integrating Classical and Experimental Contributions to an Enduring Debate', *Annual Review of Political Science*, 21/1 (2018): 71–9; Luciana Cingolani, 'The Role of State Capacity in Development Studies', *Journal of Development Perspectives*, 2.1/2 (2018): 88–114; Stuti Khemani, 'What Is State Capacity?', *World Bank Policy Research Working Paper*, No. 8734 (2019).
55 Deng, *China's Political Economy*, chs 5 and 6.
56 Franz Michael, 'Military Organization and Power Structure of China during the Taiping Rebellion', *Pacific Historical Review*, 18/4 (1949): 469–83.
57 These militocrats imposed military rule on each province they controlled, gave the priority to security, gained autonomy from Beijing in personnel hiring, tax collection, and foreign diplomacy. See Deng, *China's Political Economy*, ch. 5.
58 Li Jie, *Wenwu Beiyang* (*Achievements of the 'Northern Modern' Elite*) (Nanning: Guangxi Normal University Press, 2004), p. 109.
59 Augustus F. Lindley, *Ti-Ping Tien-Kwoh: the History of the Ti-ping Revolution* (London: Day and Son, 1866), vol. 2, pp. 671–3.
60 As observed in 1853 by Sir George Bonham, see Cao Shuju, 'Yingguo Zhengfu Lanpishuzhong Zhi Taiping Tianguo Shiliao' (Historical Materials on the *Heavenly Kingdom of Great Peace* from the British Government Documents), in Chinese Historical Society, *Heavenly Kingdom of Great*

Peace, vol. 6, pp. 892, 896; see also Ssu-yü Teng, *The Taiping Rebellion and the Western Powers: A Comprehensive Survey* (Oxford: Oxford University Press, 1971), p. 331.

61 Zhang Shujun and Qi Sheng, *Zhongguo Gongchandang Zhongda Huiyi Shilu* (*Veritable Records of Important Meetings of the Chinese Communist Party*) (Changsha: Hunan People's Press, 2006), p. 57.

62 Zhao, *History of the Qing Dynasty*, vol. 132, 'Military', in *Twenty-Five Official Histories*, vol. 11, p. 9311.

63 Zhao, *Drafted History*, vol. 422, 'Biographies of Wang Maoyi *et al.*', in *Twenty-Five Official Histories*, vol. 12, p. 10178; see also Edwin G. Beal, *The Origin of Likin, 1853–1864* (Cambridge, MA: Harvard University Press, 1958).

64 Later, the Meiji reformers in Japan called such an approach 'departing from Asia and joining Europe', announced in 1885 (*datsu-a nyu-o*).

65 Mao Zedong, '1917 Nian 8 Yue 23 Ri Zhi Li Jinxi Xin' (Letter to Li Jinxi in 23 August 1917), in Institute of Documents of Chinese Communist Party Central Committee and Hunan Provincial Committee of the Chinese Communist Party, eds, *Mao Zedong Zaoqi Wengao* (*Early Writings of Mao Zedong*) (Changsha: Hunan Press, 1990), p. 85.

66 Li Ying (ed.), *Cong Yida Dao Shiliuda* (*Memoirs of Participants in the First to Sixteenth Congress of the Chinese Communist Party*) (Beijing: Central Documents Press, 2003), vol. 1, p. 316.

67 Mao Zedong, *Mao Zedong Xuanji* (*Selected Works of Mao Zedong*) (Beijing: People's Press, 1961), vol. 2, p. 535.

68 Anon., 'Hengsao Yiqie Niugui Sheshen' (Sweeping Clear All Devils), *Renmin Ribao* (*People's Daily*), 1 June 1966, p. 1.

69 Li Rui, *Li Rui Tan Mao Zedong* (*Li Rui's Memoir on Mao Zedong*) (Hong Kong: Time International Publishing, 2005), p. 176.

70 Up until this moment, Mao's life trajectory was very similar to (if not identical with) Hong Xiuquan (1814–1864), the leader of the Taiping Movement, who repeatedly failed to obtain the lowest qualification in the Qing Imperial Examinations. So, Hong rebelled.

71 Li, *Li Rui's Memoir*, pp. 13–14, 323, 324, 327.

72 Liu Zhichao and Hu Yuhai, *Minguo Junfa Shilue* (*A History of Warlords during the Republic Period*) (Shenyang: Liaoning University Press, 1998), p. i. Note that this period has also been viewed as the state of 'anarchy' and the impact of 'anarchism' from the viewpoint of normativism; see, e.g., https://en.wikipedia.org/wiki/Anarchism_in_China.

73 Yu Keli and Zhu Xianlong, *Zhongguo Guomindang Quanshu* (*Encyclopedia of the Citizens' Party of China*) (Xi-an: Shaanxi People's Press, 2001), pp. 5–8.

74 John K. Fairbank (ed.), *The Cambridge History of China, Republican China 1912–1949, Part I* (Cambridge: Cambridge University Press, 1983), vol. 12, p. 36; Li, *Memoirs of Participants*, vol. 1, pp. 26–7.

75 This is generously derived from 3 million industrial workers for 10 per cent of China's total GDP; based on Mao Zedong, 'Lun Renmin Minzhu Zhuanzheng' (On People's Democratic Dictatorship), in Mao, *Selected Works*, vol. 4, p. 148.

76 Li, *Memoirs of Participants*, vol. 1, p. 187.

77 Yang Kuisong, *Zhuoxiang Polie, Mao Zedong Yu Mosikede Enen Yuanyuan* (*Communist Break-up, Personal Scores of Mao Zedong with Moscow*) (Hong Kong: Sanlian Books, 1999), p. 188.
78 Li, *Li Rui's Memoir*, pp. 36, 199; Jung Chang and Jon Halliday, *Mao: The Unknown Story* (London: Vintage Books, 2005), ch. 3.
79 Deng, *China's Political Economy*, ch. 5.
80 Peter Vladimirov, *The Vladimirov Diaries, Yenan, China: 1942–1945* (New York: Doubleday, 1975), pp. 355, 421, 425.
81 Zhou, 'Sixth National Congress', vol. 1, p. 316.
82 Zhou, 'Assessment of the Sixth National Congress', vol. 1, p. 298. Note: the other two Comintern agents were the Indian-born Comintern operator Manabendra Nath Roy and the Russian Mikhail Markovich (Михаúл Бородúн) commonly known by his code name 'Borodin'.
83 Mao Zedong, 'Gongzou Fangfa Liushi Tiao' (Sixty Methods of the Party Work), in Institute of Documents of the Chinese Communist Party Central Committee (ed.), *Mao Zedong Wenji* (*Selected Works of Mao Zedong*) (Beijing: People's Press, 1999), vol. 8, p. 352.
84 It has been commonly held that Mao created this phrase in 1963. It was first published in 1970 in *People's Daily*'s Editorial, 'Jieji Douzheng Yizhua Jiuling' (Class Struggle Works Perfectly Every Single Time), *Renmin Ribao* (*People's Daily*), 11 April 1970, p. 1.
85 In Mao's own phrase in 1958, 'the philosophy of the Communist Party is indeed one for struggles'; see his 'Origins of Machineguns, Mortar Guns and So On', in Mao, *Selected Works*, vol. 5, p. 344.
86 Statistically, the nuclear weapon is at best an 'outlier' and thus cannot be taken as a mean value for the whole economy. In other words, the nuclear weapon has little to do with the general degree of modernisation and industrialisation of a country, and thus should be ignored. See Chang and Halliday, *Mao*, ch. 45.
87 Central Liaison Department of the Chinese Communist Party (ed.), *Dangnei Shici Luxian Douzheng Ziliao* (*Materials of Ten Two-Line Struggles within the Chinese Communist Party*) (Beijing: The Central Liaison Ministry of the Chinese Communist Party, 1972).
88 See Central Committee of the Chinese Communist Party, *Wu Yao Liu Tongzhi* (*Circular of the Central Committee of the Chinese Communist Party on 16th May 1966*) (Beijing: People's Press, 1967); Zhang Hua and Su Caiqing (eds), *Huishou Wenge, Zhongguo Shinian Wenge Fenxi Yu Fansi* (*Recollection of the Decade of Cultural Revolution, Analyses and Soul-Researching*) (Beijing: Chinese Communist Party History Press, 2000), vol. 1, pp. 325, 327; vol. 2, p. 914.
89 Zhang and Su, *Decade of Cultural Revolution*, vol. 1, p. 359.
90 In real terms, it was the 'party-peasant alliance under the leadership of the Communist Party' simply because the number of full-time waged workers in China was negligible until the 1980s.
91 Mao Zedong, 'Lun Renmin Minzhu Zhuanzheng' (On People's Democratic Dictatorship), in Mao, *Selected Works*, vol. 4, pp. 147–66.
92 In 1955, an internal passport system called residential identification (*hukou*) was designed and reinforced to keep the urban population small and social mobility minimal.

93 Urbanisation has been commonly recognised as an index of industrialisation and modernity; see, e.g., Arthur Lewis, 'Economic Development with Unlimited Supplies of Labour', in Mark Gersovitz (ed.), *Selected Economic Writings of W. Arthur Lewis* (New York: New York University Press), pp. 139–76; Raymond Williams, *The Country and the City* (London: Chatto & Windus, 1973); David Barnett, *London: Hub of the Industrial Revolution* (London: I.B. Tauris, 1998); Jeffrey G. Williamson, *Coping with City Growth during the British Industrial Revolution* (Cambridge: Cambridge University Press, 2002); Miriam R. Levin, Sophie Forgan, Martina Hessler, Robert H. Kargon, and Morris Low, *Urban Modernity* (Cambridge, MA: MIT Press, 2010); John R. Short, *Globalization, Modernity and the City* (London: Routledge, 2011); Louise Young, *Beyond the Metropolis* (Berkeley: University of California Press, 2013).

94 Mao Zedong, 'Zuzhi Qilai' (To Get Organised), in Mao, *Selected Works*, p. 932.

95 Zhang Xianwen (ed.), *Zhonghua Minguo Shi* (*A History of the Republic of China*) (Nanjing: University of Nanjing Press, 2005), vol. 2, p. 236.

96 International Politics Department, Peking University (ed.), *Zhongguo Xiandaishi Tongji Ziliao Xuanbian* (*Selected Statistics for Early Modern History of China*) (Zhengzhou: Henan People's Press, 1985), p. 396.

97 See Larry I. Bland (ed.) *George C. Marshall's Mediation Mission to China* (Lexington: George C. Marshall Foundation, 1998), p. 287.

98 Ibid., pp. 432, 442.

99 Zhang, *Republic of China*, vol. 4, pp. 227–35.

100 Cui Zhiqing, *Guomindang Zhengzhi Yu Shehui Jiegou Zhi Yanbian* (*Changes in Political and Social Structures of the Citizens' Party*) (Beijing: Social Science Literature Press, 2007), vol. 3, p. 1512.

101 Shen Zhihua, *Mao Zedong, Sidalin Yu Chaoxian Zhanzheng* (*Mao Zedong, Stalin and the Korean War*) (Guangzhou: Guangdong People's Press, 2003); Chang and Halliday, *Mao*, ch. 34.

102 The 156 projects were not gifts from Stalin but Soviet exports to China. China paid full prices for them, hence the beginning of 'import-oriented industrialisation' in China's modern history.

103 Anon., 'International Trade of Communist China, 1950–65', CIA, 21 October 1966, Approved For Release 2001/04/30: CIA-RDP79T01049 A003300110001-2, pp. 10–11, 13; https://www.cia.gov/readingroom/docs/CIA-RDP79T01049A003300110001-2.pdf?utm_source=chatgpt.com.

104 For example, Dong Zhikai and Wu Jiang, *Xin Zhongguo Gongyede Dianjishi: 156 Xiang Jianshe Yanjiu, 1950–2000* (*New China's Industrial Foundation: 156 Projects, 1950–2000*) (Guangzhou: Guangdong Economic Press, 2004), p. 158.

105 Zhihua Shen and Guy Alitto, 'A Historical Examination of the Issue of Soviet Experts in China: Basic Situation and Policy Changes', *Russian History*, 29/2.4 (2002): 380; Sen Zhihua, *Sulian Zhuanjia Zai Zhongguo, 1948–1960* (*Soviet Advisors in China, 1948–1960*) (Beijing: China's International Broadcasting Press, 2003).

106 Based on the total of 1,280,000 communist cadres at the time, of whom 27.2 per cent were illiterate and were thus unlikely to be qualified as officials in post-war China. See Shen and Alitto, 'Soviet Experts in China', p. 383.

107 See https://en.wikipedia.org/wiki/Population_history_of_China.
108 Li, *Chinese Social Stratification*, p. 83.
109 See http://blog.sina.com.cn/s/blog_4b8bd1450102edb0.html.
110 Robert A. Lewis and Richard H. Rowland, 'Urbanization in Russia and the USSR: 1897–1966', *Annals of the Association of American Geographers*, 59/4 (1969): 782.
111 'Russia Urban Population – Historical Data', https://www.macrotrends.net/global-metrics/countries/RUS/russia/urban-population.
112 Lewis and Rowland, 'Urbanization in Russia', p. 793.
113 $R^2 = 0.79$; see Lewis and Rowland, 'Urbanization in Russia', p. 791.
114 Sheila Fitzpatrick, *Stalin's Peasants: Resistance and Survival in the Russian Village after Collectivization* (New York: Oxford University Press, 1994), pp. 225–6, 363; Volodar V. Kraevskii, 'The Soviet Union's Experience in the Elimination of Adult Illiteracy', *Convergence: An International Journal of Adult Education*, 20/2 (1987): 20–5.
115 Mark Harrison, 'Soviet Economic Growth since 1928: The Alternative Statistics of G.I. Khanin', *Europe-Asia Studies*, 45/1 (1993): 146.
116 For the Soviet 1927 census (147.0 million), see Soviet Union Information Bureau, 'Area and Population, https://www.marxists.org/history/ussr/government/1928/sufds/ch01.htm?utm_source=chatgpt.com. For the Soviet 1989 census (286.7 million), see Anon., '1989 Soviet census', https://en.wikipedia.org/wiki/1989_Soviet_census?utm_source=chatgpt.com.
117 Archival Institute, Central Committee of the Chinese Communist Party, *Jianguo Yilai Zhongyao Wenxuan Xuanbian* (*Selected Important Archival Materials since 1949*) (Beijing: Central Archival Press, 1995), vol. 13 p. 475.
118 Justin Y. Lin, 'Rural Reforms and Agricultural Growth in China', *American Economic Review*, 82/1 (1992): 38.
119 Zhang and Su, *Decade of Cultural Revolution*, vol. 1, p. 169.
120 Ibid., vol. 1, p. 186.
121 Wei Li and Dennis Tao Yang, 'The Great Leap Forward: Anatomy of a Central Planning Disaster', *Journal of Political Economy*, 113/4 (2005): 846.
122 The estimation is based on (1) China's population of 647 million – of whom 517 million were rural, and (2) there were on average five people per household, so 647 million and 517 million can be converted to 127 and 103 million households. Thus, 81 per cent of households were affected China-wide.
123 Xue Muqiao, *Xue Muqiao Huiyilu* (*Memoir of Xue Muqiao*) (Tianjin: Tianjin People's Press, 1996), p. 269.
124 Chang and Halliday, *Mao*, ch. 40.
125 Li Rui, *Lushan Huiyi Shilu* (*Records of the 1959 Lushan Conference*) (Beijing: Spring-Autumn Press, 1989), p. 182; Xue, *Memoir*, p. 255.
126 National Bureau of Statistics, *Jianguo Sanshinian Quanguo Nongye Tongji Ziliao* (*National Agricultural Statistics of 30 Years since 1949*) (Beijing: China's Statistics Press, 1979), p. 5.
127 Ibid., pp. 45–9.
128 National Committee for Agriculture (ed.), *Nongye Jitihua Zhongyao Wenjian Huibian* (*Collection of Key Documents on Agricultural Collectivisation*) (Beijing: Central Party Academy Press, 1981), vol. 2, p. 136; Li, *1959 Lushan Conference*, p. 107.

129 This is the generally agreed range; see Jasper Becker, *Hungry Ghost, China's Secret Famine* (London: John Murray, 1996), ch. 18; Jin Hui, 'Sannian Ziyanzaihai Beiwanglu' (Memorandum on the Alleged Three Years of Natural Disasters, 1959–62), *Shehui* (*Society*), 4–5 (1993): 13–22; Cao Shuji, *Da Jihuang, 1959–1961 Niande Zhongguo Renkou* (*Great Famine and China's Population in 1959–1961*) (Hong Kong: Times International Publishing, 2005); see also He Shu, 'Lun Zaofanpai' (A Study of the 'Cultural Revolutionaries'), in Song Yongyi (ed.), *Wenhua Dageming: Lishide Zhenxiang He Jiti Jiyi* (*The Cultural Revolution: Historical Truth and Collective Memories*) (Hong Kong: Tianyuan Books, 2007), vol. 1, pp. 516–17; Li Jingyan, 'Qiqianren Dahuide Gongji Jiqi Juxianxing' (Merit and Limit of the "'7,000 Party Officials" Conference'), *Yanhuang Chunqiu* (*History of Chinese*), 8 (2007): 4–5; Yang Jisheng's *Mubei – Zhongguo Liushi Niandai Dajihuang Jishi* (*Gravestone for the Great Leap Famine Victims, Evidence from History*) (Hong Kong: Tiandi Books, 2008). The weather conditions in 1958–59 were favourable for farming; see Wang Hong, 'Yueru Gongchan Zhuyide Beizhuan Shijian' (Sad Practice of Communism), *Yanhuang Chunqiu* (*History of Chinese*), 1 (2006): 26.

130 These rates were 16.0% (1959), 14.4% (1960), 18.2% (1961), 13.8% (1962), 11.6% (1963), 12.1% (1964), 11.3% (1965), and 10.8% (1966); see Zheng Weidong, 'Jitihua Shidaide Fenpei Zhidu Yu Renko Shengyu' (Distribution System and Baby Births during the Collective Era), *Kaifang Shidai* (*Age of Openness*), 5 (2010): 112.

131 Anon., 'Wei Quanmiandi Tizao Wancheng He Chao-e Wancheng Wunian Jihua Er Fendou' (Our Campaign for Comprehensively Over-fulfilling Our Five-year Plan Ahead of the Schedule), *Renmin Ribao* (*People's Daily*), 1 January 1965, p. 1.

132 Modern industrial workers totalled 1.13 million across sixteen cities; see Tuoni Lichade (Tony Richard), *Zhongguode Tudi He Laodong* (*Land and Labour in China*) (1966. Chinese edition, Beijing: Commercial Press, 2014), p. 216.

133 Kent Deng, Jim Shen, and Jingyuan Guo, 'Mechanisms and Performance of the Maoist Economy – A Holistic Approach, 1950–1980', *Journal of Social and Economic History of the Orient*, 4/67 (2024): 646–701.

134 Note that GDP or PPP figures are manipulation far more easily manipulated than workers' head-count.

135 Various social surveys in the 1910s and 1920s reveal urban food consumption, which was on average 3,000+ kilocalories per person per day, about 30% higher than Mao's food availability. See Ta-chung Liu and Kung-chia Yeh, *The Economy of the Chinese Mainland: National Income and Economic Development, 1933–1959* (Princeton, NJ: Princeton University Press, 1965), p. 31; Li Wenhai, Xia Mingfang, and Huang Xingtao (eds), *Minguo Shiqi Shehui Diaocha Congbian, Chengshi Laogong Shenghuojuan* (*Selected Social Surveys of the Republican Period, Volume on Urban Workers*) (Fuzhou: Fujian Education Press, 2005), vol. 1, pp. 35, 47, 276, 386; vol. 2, p. 829; William H. Adolph, 'Diet Studies in Shantung', *Chinese Medical Journal*, 37/12 (1923): 1016; Simon Yang, *An Index of the Cost of Living in Peiping* (Peiping: China Foundation, 1928); Shao-Kang Yang and Kung-Lee Tao, *A Study of the Standard of Living of Working Families in Shanghai* (Peiping: Institute of Social Research, 1930); Makino Fumio

(牧野文夫), '中国関内地域の農業生産, 1931–1947年' (Agricultural Production in Interior China, 1931–47),中国経済研究 (*Studies of China's Economy*), 2/1 (2004): 44.

136 Zhang and Su, *Decade of Cultural Revolution*, vol. 2, p. 890.

137 Yu Guangyuan (ed.), *China's Socialist Modernization* (Beijing: Foreign Language Press, 1984), p. 584.

138 Xue, *Memoir*, p. 348.

139 Ibid., p. 478.

140 Based on the situation in the mid-1990s as a proxy; see Gu Xin, 'Danwei Fuli Shehui Zhuyi Yu Zhongguode Zhiduxing Shiye' (Enterprise-based Welfare Socialism and China's Structural Unemployment), *Xinhua Wenzhai* (*Xinhua Compilation*), 11 (1998): 61; Niu Renliang, 'Lun Zai Jiuye' (Re-Employment), *Xinhua Wenzhai* (*Xinhua Compilation*), 2 (1998): 56.

141 It was an official policy known as 'three jobs to be shared by five workers', Xue, *Memoir*, p. 479.

142 A technical illustration is available in Appendix 3, figure A–3.3.

143 Zhang and Su, *Decade of Cultural Revolution*, vol. 1, p. 11.

144 Ibid., vol. 1, p. 442.

145 Amartya K. Sen, *Resources, Values and Development* (Oxford: Blackwell, 1984), p. 497.

146 Amartya K. Sen, *Poverty and Famines: An Essay on Entitlement and Deprivation* (Oxford: Clarendon Press, 1981), p. 49.

147 Ibid., p. 45.

148 Jean Dreze and Amartya K. Sen, *Hunger and Public Action* (New Delhi: Oxford University Press, 1989), pp. 210–14, 222.

149 Li, '"7,000 Party Officials" Conference', pp. 4–5.

150 Wang, 'Sad Practice of Communism', p. 24. After he reported it to his superior, Wang was labelled a 'rightist opportunist', which ended his career.

151 Xue, *Memoir*, p. 280.

152 National Bureau of Statistics, *Labour Statistical Year Book, 1999*, ch. 3

153 Xue, *Memoir*, p. 269.

154 Ibid., p. 275.

155 A technical illustration is available in Appendix 3, Appendix A–3.4.

156 The values for the coefficient of variation (CV) are (1) rural north 0.45, (2) rural south 0.58, (3) Beijing (urban north) 0.53, and (4) Shanghai (urban south) 0.55. So, food rationing in rural China was less egalitarian than in cities.

157 Note that Deng Xiaoping's criterion for 'modest comfortable life' (*xiaokang*) includes 2,600 kilocalories and 80 grams of protein per day for all; see Ma Hong and Sun Shangqing (eds), *1992–1993 Zhongguo Jingji Xingshi Yu Zhanwang* (*China's Economic Situation and Prospect, 1992–1993*) (Beijing: China's Development Press, 1993), p. 263. Meanwhile, the national target for 2010 was 2,300 kilocalories and 77 grams of protein per day per head; see National Committee for Development and Reforms, 'Quanguo Nongye He Nongcun Jingji Fazhan Dishige Wunian Jihua (2001–2005)' (The Tenth National Five-Year Plan for Agriculture and Rural Economic Development, 2001–2005), https://www.ndrc.gov.cn/fggz/fzzlgh/gjjzxgh/200506/W020191104623910180258.pdf.

158 Stephen L. Morgan, 'Richer and Taller, Stature and the Standard of Living in China, 1979–1995', *China Journal*, 44 (2000): 1–39, especially tables 6 and

7; Stephen L. Morgan, 'Economic Growth and the Biological Standard of Living in China, 1880–1930', *Economics and Human Biology*, 2/2 (2004): 197–218; Stephen L. Morgan, 'Stature and Famine in China: the Welfare of the Survivors of the Great Leap Forward Famine, 1959–61', Paper for Asia-Pacific Economic and Business History Conference, University of Sydney, 2007, figures 8, 9, and 10.

159 Gao Wangling, *Zhongguo Nongmin Fanxingwei Diaocha* (*Investigation into a Quiet Rebellion of the Chinese Peasantry against Maoism*) (Beijing: Central Party History Press, 2006), p. 51.

160 Mao's rural egalitarianism made family income positively correlated with its size; Zheng, 'Baby Births', p. 109; see also Li Shangyong, 'Jianguo Qian 20-nian Renkou Duodu Pengzhangde Zhidu Yuanyin' (Institutional Cause for China's Population Overdrive in the First 20 Years of the PRC), 27 April 2017, http://lishangyong.blog.caixin.com/archives/162301.

161 See Zheng, 'Baby Births', p. 106.

162 Ibid., pp. 103–16; Li, 'Population Overdrive'.

163 See, e.g., World Bank, 'GDP per Capita (Current US$) – China', https://data.worldbank.org/indicator/NY.GDP.PCAP.CD?locations=CN; Anon., 'Historical GDP of China', https://en.wikipedia.org/wiki/Historical_GDP_of_China.

164 National Committee for Agriculture, *Agricultural Collectivisation*, vol. 2, pp. 16, 74.

165 Gao, *Quiet Rebellion*, p. 73.

166 The 1978 official exchange rate between Renminbi *yuan* and US Dollar was RMB 1.55 for 1 US$.

167 Ling Zhijun, *Lishi Buzi Paihuai* (*History, No More Hesitation*) (Beijing: People's Press, 1997), pp. 102–3.

168 Lu Xueyi, *Dangdai Zhongguo Shehui Jieceng Yanjiu Baogao* (*Survey of Social Strata in Contemporary China*) (Beijing: Social Science Literature Press, 2002), p. 165.

169 Even Deng Xiaoping openly admitted it by saying that '[Mao's] rural communes were in fact backwards together and impoverished together'; see Deng Xiaoping, *Deng Xiaoping Wenxuan* (*Selected Essays of Deng Xiaoping*) (Beijing: People's Press, 1993), vol. 3, p. 155.

170 This applied to the wealthy Yangzi Valley where social mobility stopped under Mao's rule; see Ying Dai, 'Lineage Genealogies as a New Source for Researching the Occupational Structure of Twentieth-Century China: Tradition (Partially) Transformed', *Historical Methods*, 58/1 (2025): 71.

171 National Bureau of Statistics, *Zhongguo Nongcun Zhuhu Diancha Nianjian, 2002* (*China's Rural Households Survey Year Books, 2002*) (Beijing: China's Statistics Press, 2002), p. 11; National Bureau of Statistics, *Zhongguo Tongji Nianjian, 2003* (*China's Statistical Year Book, 2003*), p. 99.

172 Hu Qili, 'Zhonggong Zhongyang Guanyu Jiaoyu Tizhi Gaigede Jueding Chutai Qianhou' (How was Educational Reform Decided by the Chinese Communist Party Central Committee), December 2008, https://www.aisixiang.com/data/101596.html.

173 Zhang and Su, *Decade of Cultural Revolution*, vol. 1, p. 441.

174 Total GDP has been recognised as a crude and inaccurate parameter for measuring a country's growth and development; see, e.g., Herman Daly, *Beyond Growth: The Economics of Sustainable Development* (Boston,

MA: Beacon Press, 1996); Amartya Sen, *Development as Freedom* (New York: Alfred A. Knopf, 1999); Tim Jackson, *Prosperity Without Growth: Foundations for the Economy of Tomorrow* (London: Routledge, 2009); Joseph Stiglitz, *Mismeasuring Our Lives: Why GDP Doesn't Add Up* (New York: New Press, 2010); Diane Coyle, *GDP: A Brief but Affectionate History* (Princeton, NJ: Princeton University Press, 2014); Kate Raworth, *Doughnut Economics: Seven Ways to Think Like a 21st-Century Economist* (London: Random House, 2017).

175 Ministry of Finance, *Financial Year Book, 1997*, p. 479; National Bureau of Statistics, *Statistical Year Book, 2002*, p. 51.

176 Robert M. Solow, 'A Contribution to the Theory of Economic Growth', *Quarterly Journal of Economics*, 70/1 (1956): 65–94; Trevor W. Swan, 'Economic Growth and Capital Accumulation', *Economic Record*, 32/2 (1956): 334–61.

177 See https://zh.wikipedia.org/zh-hans/.

178 Yu, *Socialist Modernization*, p. 458.

179 Ibid., pp. 471–2.

180 Loren Brandt and Xiaodong Zhu, 'Accounting for China's Growth', Institute for the Study of Labor, *Discussing Paper, No. 4764* (2010): figure 7a.

181 Measured using 'total factor productivity' (a reliable parameter for efficiency), the performance of the agricultural sector was poor from 1954 to 1984; see Guanzhong James Wen, 'Total Factor Productivity Change in China's Farming Sector: 1952–1989', *Economic Development and Cultural Change*, 42/1 (1993): 27, 37. The performance of the industrial sector was equally poor from 1952 to 1992; see Selin Ozyurt, 'Total Factor Productivity Growth in Chinese Industry: 1952–2005', *Oxford Developmental Studies*, 37/1 (2009): 11, 14. Also, the state sector remained the most inefficient during the post-Mao Era; see Brandt and Zhu, 'Accounting for China's Growth', figure 3.

182 National Bureau of Statistics, *Zhongguo Keji Tongji Nianjian, 1991* (*China's Statistical Year Book of Science and Technology, 1991*) (Beijing: China's Statistics Press, 1992), p. 24; Ma Hong (ed.), *2000 Niande Zhongguo Kexue Jishu* (*China's Science and Technology in 2000*) (Beijing: Social Science Press, 1988), p. 5.

183 Zong Fengming, *Zhao Ziyang Ruanjinzhongde Tanhua* (*Conversations with Zhao Ziyang under House Arrest*) (Hong Kong: Open Press, 2007), p. 243.

184 Zhang and Su, *Decade of Cultural Revolution*, vol. 1, p. 446.

185 He Qinglian, *Women Rengzai Yangwang Xingkong* (*We Are Still Praying*) (Guilin: Lijiang Press, 2001), pp. 84–5.

186 Rostow rightly defined the final goal as 'mass high consumption'; see Walt W. Rostow, *The Stages of Economic Growth, a Non-Communist Manifesto* (Cambridge: Cambridge University Press, 1966), ch. 2.

187 He, *Still Praying*, p. 8.

188 Liu Xin and Liu Gang, *Zhongguo Jingjixue Sanshinian* (*Economics in China in the Past Thirty Years*) (Beijing: China's Finance and Economy Press, 2008), p. 115.

189 Li Qiang, *Shehui Fenceng Yu Pinfu Chabie* (*Social Stratification and Income Inequality*) (Xiamen: Lujiang Press, 2000), p. 69.

Chapter 3

1 Zhou, 'Sixth National Congress', vol. 1, p. 316.
2 Known as the 'underground literature' by liberal thinkers; see, e.g., Gu Zhun, *Cong Lixiang Zhuyi Dao Jingyan Zhuyi* (*From Idealism to Empiricism*) (Beijing: Zhonghua Books, 1980), his *Gu Zhun Kuaiji Biji* (*Gu Zhun's Accounting Notes*) (Beijing: China's Finance and Economy Press, 1981), and *Gu Zhun Wenji* (*Collected Essays*) (Shanghai: Sanlian Books, 1994). What Gu demonstrated in his works is that there cannot be genuine 'communist economic planning', rather the most reliable methods all come from capitalism; see Gu Zhun, *Gu Zhun Kuaiji Wenji* (*Collected Essays on Accounting*) (Shanghai: Lixin Accounting Press, 2010).
3 The total number of waged workers in China's modern industry in the 1920s was estimated as about one million (or 0.2 per cent of China's total population of 440 million). If one adds 10 million traditional urban handicraftsmen and service workers, the total waged labourers made up 2.5 per cent of China's population; see Fairbank, *Cambridge History of China*, vol. 12, p. 36; Li, 'Formation of the Chinese Communist Party', pp. 26–7.
4 Lü Xiaoji, 'Liu Shaoqi Hezuoshe Sixiang Yanjiu' (Liu Shaoqi's View on Cooperatives), Party History Institute of Chinese Communist Party Central Committee, 24 March, 2014, https://www.dswxyjy.org.cn/n1/2019/0228/c423964-30918426.html.
5 Alexander V. Chayanov, *The Theory of Peasant Economy* (Madison: University of Wisconsin Press, 1925, reprinted in 1986).
6 For a case called the 'Narrow Valley' (*Jiabian Gou*) in the Gobi Desert in remote Gansu, see survivors' accounts: He Fengming, *Jingli – Wode 1957 Nian* (*The Year 1957 When A Disaster Struck on Me*) (Lanzhou: Dunhuang Literature and Art Press, 2001); Yang Xianhui, *Jiabian Gou Jishi* (*Diary in the Narrow Valley*) (Shanghai: Shanghai Literature and Art Press, 2003).
7 Chinese Communist Party Central Committee, *Tudifa Dagang* (*General Guideline of Land Law*) (N.p.: Taiyue New China Books, 1947), p. 2.
8 Lu, *Survey of Social Strata*, p. 163; Chen, *Revolution and Rural China*, p. 188; Yao Liwen and Liu Jianping, 'Xinminzhuzhuyide Mingyun He Liu Shaoqide Shibai' (Fate of New Democracy and Liu Shaoqi's Defeat), *Yanhuang Chunqiu* (*History of Chinese*) 2 (2009): 4.
9 Luo Pinghan, 'Jianlun 1957 Nian Nongcun Liangtiao Daolude Dabianlun' (The 1957 Debate on the Two Developmental Paths in Rural China), *Shixue Yuekan* (*History Review Monthly*), 11 (2002): 58–65.
10 Ibid.
11 Gao, *Quiet Rebellion*, pp. 71, 91.
12 Ibid., p. 110.
13 Fieldwork indicates that 85 per cent of founding members of agricultural cooperatives were poor peasants (*pinnong*) and thus self-selected to a great extent; see Chen Yiyuan, *Geming Yu Xiangcun* (*Revolution and Rural China*) (Shanghai: Shanghai Social Sciences Press, 2006), pp. 201, 255.
14 Gao, *Quiet Rebellion*, p. 71.
15 National Committee for Agriculture, *Agricultural Collectivisation*, vol. 1, p. 648.
16 Li Rui, *Dayuejin Qinli Ji* (*Personal Experience of the Great Leap Forward*) (Shanghai: Far East Press, 1996), p. 341.

17 Chang and Halliday, *Mao*, ch. 37.
18 Luo, '1957 Debate', p. 42.
19 Gao, *Quiet Rebellion*, p. 112.
20 Ibid., p. 85.
21 Ibid., p. 90.
22 Ibid., p. 68; Chen Bing-an, *Da Tao Gang* (*Exodus to Hong Kong*) (Guangzhou: Guangdong People's Press, 2011). For estimates (10,000 to 120,000 people a year under Mao's rule), see Ronald Skeldon, 'Migration from China', *Journal of International Affairs*, 49/2 (1996): 439. For a personal case, see Kent Wong, *Swimming to Freedom: My Untold Story of Escaping the Cultural Revolution* (New York: Harry N. Abrams, 2021). Some provincial leaders decided to let hungry farmers leave; see Chen Zuohan, 'Xi Zhongxun, Toudu Shi Renmin Neibu Maodun' (Xi Zhongxun's Attitude towards Exodus to Hong Kong: It was People's Internal Conflict), *Yangcheng Wanbao* (*Guangzhou Evening*), 29 November 2014, https://news.ifeng.com/a/20141129/42603142_0.shtml.
23 Song, *Cultural Revolution*, vol. 1, p. 208.
24 Li, *1959 Lushan Conference*, p. 156.
25 Liu Kai, Nie Gege, and Zhang Sen, 'Zhongguo 1951–2018 nian Qiwen He Jiangshuide Shikong Yanbian Tezheng Yanjiu' (Spatio-temporal Evolution of Temperature and Precipitation in China from 1951 to 2018), *Diqiu Kexue Jinzhan* (*Progress in Earth Science*), 35/11 (2020): 1113–26.
26 Luo Pinghan, *Nongcun Renmin Gongshe Shi* (*A History of Rural People's Communes*) (Fuzhou: Fujian People's Press, 2006), p. 72.
27 Song Haiqing, *Renmin Gongshe Xingwang Lu* (*Rise and Fall of the People's Commune*) (Urumqi: Xinjiang Youth Press, 2000), vol. 2, pp. 362, 366–9.
28 Luo, *People's Communes*, p. 188.
29 Song, *Rise and Fall*, vol. 2, p. 427.
30 Zong, *Conversations with Zhao Ziyang*, p. 38.
31 Xue, *Memoir*, p. 280.
32 Gao, *Quiet Rebellion*, pp. 39, 131, 134; Elisabeth Croll, *The Family Rice Bowl, Food and the Domestic Economy in China* (Geneva: UNRISD, 1983), pp. 158, 163. Croll's estimate is 200 kilograms of grain for each family member per year which is about 50 per cent of the official annual ration, which is roughly another 1,300 calories per day. This is not a generous food intake by any standard.
33 Ling, *No More Hesitation*, pp. 323–4. This was very similar to Russia where 4 per cent of 'private plots' produced 24–38 per cent of all rural output in the 1990s; see Gavin Kitching, 'The Revenge of the Peasant? The Collapse of Large-Scale Russian Agriculture and the Role of the Peasant "Private Plot" in that Collapse, 1991–97', *Journal of Peasant Studies*, 26/1 (1998): 53.
34 Ling, *No More Hesitation*, p. 324.
35 Li Honglin, 'Wode Lilun Gongzuozhe Jingli' (My Experience as a Party Theorist), *Yanhuang Chunqiu* (*History of Chinese*), November, 2008, https://www.aisixiang.com/data/101597.html.
36 Yu, *Socialist Modernization*, pp. 264–5.
37 Ling, *No More Hesitation*, p. 324.

38 Xing Tongyi, 'Gansu Nongcunde Fanyoupai Yundong' (Anti-Rightist Movement in Rural Gansu), *Yanhuang Chunqiu* (*History of Chinese*), 2 (2009): 65.
39 Gao, *Quiet Rebellion*, p. 96.
40 Anon., *Mao Zedong Sixiang Wansui* (*Long Live Mao Zedong's Thought*) (Beijing: Peking University, August 1969, SOAS Library Copy), p. 284.
41 Gao Wangling, *Zudian Guanxi Xinlun: Dizhu, Nongmin He Dizu* (*New Theory of Tenancy: Landlords, Tenants and Rents*) (Shanghai: Shanghai Book Press, 2005), pp. 39, 44.
42 Mancur Olson was right, the Soviet collective farms were organised for 'collections of food for the state', not for 'collective governance' by the peasantry itself; Mancur Olson, *Power and Prosperity, Outgrowing Communist and Capitalist Dictatorships* (New York: Basic Books, 2000), p. 128.
43 Yu, *Socialist Modernization*, pp. 471–2.
44 It was documented in 1963 that a Soviet-aided truck factory had to balance 20 different costs which was beyond Mao's cadres' ability. See Gu, *Accounting Essays*, p. 460.
45 Mao Zedong, 'Speech in Supreme State Council', in Institute of Documents of the Chinese Communist Party Central Committee, *Collected Essays*, pp. 38–71.
46 Zong, *Conversations with Zhao Ziyang*, p. 243.
47 See Ministry of Finance, *Zhongguo Caizheng Nianjian, 1997* (*China's Financial Year Book, 1997*) (Beijing: China's Finance Magazine Press, 1997), pp. 479, 482.
48 Huan Guoying and Huan Guorui, *Huan Xiang Wangshi* (*Memoirs of Huan Xiang*) (Beijing: Contemporary China Press, 2020), pp. 205–15.
49 Lin and his *entourage* were killed in an aeroplane crash in Outer Mongolia on their way to the Soviet territory. So, the travellers' intention was beyond reasonable doubt: they were leaving China for the Soviet Union, the enemy territory of the time. See Chang and Halliday, *Mao*, ch. 52.
50 Mao was deeply shaken by Lin's betrayal, as described vividly by Li Zhisui who was Mao's personal physician. See Li Zhisui, *The Private Life of Chairman Mao* (London: Random House, 1994): ch. 76.
51 The Gang of Four were four dodgy characters: (1) Jiang Qing (1914–91), Mao's fourth wife who had no role in the party until the Cultural Revolution, (2) Zhang Chunqiao (1917–2005), a party propogandist with no military experience, (3) Yao Wenyuan (1931–2005), a party propogandist with no military experience, and (4) Wang Hongwen (1935–92), a demobilised army foot soldier who made his career during the Cultural Revolution as a thuggish 'rebel leader' in Shanghai. See Chang and Halliday, *Mao*, ch. 56.
52 For example, A. Cheng, 'Ting Ditai' (Listening to Enemy Radios), in Li Tuo and Bei Dao (eds), *Qishi Niandai* (*Life in the Seventies*) (Hong Kong: Oxford University Press, 2019), ch. 8; Donald Santacaterina, 'Transnational Environments and "Mixed Signals" in Radio Propaganda: The Voice of America, the BBC, and the People's Republic of China, 1949–1976', *TMG Journal for Media History*, 24/1–2 (2021): 10, 15; Huang Aihe, 'Touting Ditaide Rizi: Dangshi Jihu Quanshijie Doushi Diduiguo' (Days of Underground Listening to Enemy Radios: At the Time When Almost the Entire World Was Our Enemy), 16 November 2021, https://mp.weixin.qq.com/s/urkkX7bj1ZPozVrVNwqoow.

53 Anon., 'Listening to the Voice of America in Communist China', Record Group 306, U.S. National Archives and Records Administration (NARA); Anon., 'Jiemi Shike: Touting Ditai Meiguo Zhiyin' (Time to Declassify: Underground Listening to the Voice of America), VOA, 3 October 2014, https://www.voachinese.com/a/history-mystery-listen-to-voa-in-the-dark-20141020/2470752.html; Anon., 'Xiaoshihou Ni Toudingguo Ditai Ma?' (Did You Listen to Enemy Radios When You Were Little?), 18 July 2014, https://baijiahao.baidu.com/s?id=1804893830646347465; Lonán Ó Briain and Min Yen Ong, *Sound Communities in the Asia Pacific* (London: Bloomsbury, 2021), ch. 9; Yu Wang, 'Listening to the Enemy: Radio Consumption and Technological Culture in Maoist China, 1949–1965', *Twentieth-Century China*, 47/2 (2022): 154–70.

54 Hugh Howse, 'The Use of Radio in China', *China Quarterly*, 1/2 (1960): 59–68; Thomas W. Hoffer and James D. Rayburn II, 'The Broadcast Blitz against Revisionism: Radio and the Chinese Cultural Revolution', *Journalism and Mass Communication Quarterly*, 54/4 (1977): 730–9; Jie Li, 'Revolutionary Echoes: Radios and Loudspeakers in the Mao Era', *Twentieth-Century China*, 45/1 (2020), pp. 25–45.

55 George P. Jan, 'Radio Propaganda in Chinese Villages', *Asian Survey*, 7/5 (1967): 313.

56 Howse, 'Radio in China', p. 63.

57 See https://en.wikipedia.org/wiki/Deng_Xiaoping.

58 Ibid.

59 Feng was deeply involved in the Republican Movement and served as Deputy Director of the Executive Board (*xingzheng yuan*) in 1928–30 and Minister of Army of the Republic of China in 1928–9.

60 Liu received Soviet training at Far East University in Moscow during 1921–2.

61 Deng, *Selected Essays*, vol. 3, p. 228.

62 Ibid., vol. 3, p. 225.

63 Deng Xiaoping, 'Zai Wuchang, Shenzhen, Zhuhai, Shanghai Dengdide Tanhua Yaodian' (Outline of Talks in Wuchang, Shenzhen, Zhuhai, and Shanghai), in Deng, *Selected Essays*, vol. 3, p. 370. Here, 'June Fourth Juncture in 1989' is slang for the Tiananmen Massacres on 4 June 1989.

64 Ma Licheng, *Jiaofeng Sanshi Nian* (*Thirty Years of Confrontation*) (Nanjing: Jiangsu People's Press, 2008), p. 293.

65 According to authentic Marxism, once the proletariat class takes over the state power and socialises (not nationalises) all capital, all classes, including the proletariat, cease to exist. So, Marx's class struggle is a one-off weapon to terminate class division among citizens. To declare a perpetual class struggle only betrays one's ignorance of Karl Marx.

66 Chinese Communist Party Central Committee (ed.), *Guanyu Jianguo Yilai Dangde Ruogan Lishi Wentide Jueyi* (*The Resolution on Various Historical Issues since 1949*) (Beijing: People's Press, 1981), pt. 5; Cong Jin, *Quzhe Fazhande Suiyue* (*Period of Tortuous Development*) (Zhengzhou: Henan People's Press, 1989), p. 61; Mi Hedu, *Jujiao Hongweibing* (*Re-Examining Red Guards*) (Hong Kong: Sanlian Books, 2005), p. 131; Song, *Cultural Revolution*, vol. 1, p. 487.

67 See zh.wikipedia.org.

68 Deng, *Selected Essays*, vol. 3, p. 228.

69 Ibid., vol. 3, p. 226.
70 Li Li-an and Zheng Keyang (eds), *Deng Xiaoping Yu Gaige Kaifang Shisi Nian* (*Deng Xiaoping and Fourteen Years of Reforms and Opening Up*) (Beijing: Beijing Normal University Press, 1993), pp. 13, 19, 25, 28, 30, 34, 41, 45, 46–7, 51, 55.
71 'State Council Communiqué of the People's Republic of China, 10 October 1985', https://www.gov.cn/gongbao/shuju/1985/gwyb198527.pdf.
72 See https://www.163.com/dy/article/GHI77DRO0536NZ17.html.
73 The data for state educational expenditures are only published by China's National Bureau of Statistics.
74 See National Bureau of Statistics, *Statistical Year Books, 2004–2013*, chs 20 and 21.
75 Jingyuan Guo and Kent Deng, 'Laying Off Old Guards to Rebuild State Capacity: Deng Xiaoping's Bloodless *Coup D'état* in post-Mao China, 1980–2000', *Working Papers of Department of Economic History, LSE*, No. 372, November 2024.
76 Shan S. Huang, *The Political Economy of Reforms and the Remaking of the Proletarian Class in China, 1980s–2010s* (Cham: Palgrave Macmillan, 2023).
77 Ma, *Confrontation*, p. 38.
78 Li and Zheng, *Fourteen Years of Reforms and Opening Up*, p. 21.
79 Ling, *No More Hesitation*, p. 335.
80 Ibid., pp. 297, 303, 305.
81 Ibid., pp. 305, 306.
82 Chris Bramall and M.E. Jones, 'Rural Income Inequality in China since 1978', *Journal of Peasant Studies*, 21/1 (1993): 53.
83 Wu Fangwei, Meng Lingjie, and Xiong Shiping, *Zhongguo Nongyede Zengzhang Yu Xiaolü* (*Growth and Efficiency of China's Agriculture*) (Shanghai: Shanghai Finance and Economics University, 2000), pp. 106–10.
84 He, *Still Praying*, pp. 84–5; Chen, *Losses of State Assets*, p. 82; also Ministry of Finance, *Zhongguo Caizheng Nianjian, 1997* (*China's Financial Year Book, 1997*) (Beijing: China's Finance Magazine Press, 1997), p. 482.
85 Chen Zhengyun, Yang Wenshu, and Sun Ming, *Zhongguo Guozi Liushi Zhuangkuang Diaocha* (*Investigation of Losses of State Assets in China*) (Beijing: Law Press, 2000), p. 25.
86 He, *Still Praying*, p. 21.
87 National Bureau of Statistics, *Statistical Year Book, 2003*, pp. 186, 461.
88 Ma, *Confrontation*, p. 250.
89 See http://www.weforum.org/pdf/summitreports/eastasia2006/security.htm.
90 Clyde Prestowitz, *Three Billion New Capitalists: the Great Shift of Wealth and Power to the East* (New York: Basic Books, 2003), p. 76. In 2005, the wage level in China was about 5 per cent of that of the United States and Japan, 6 per cent of South Korea and 42 per cent of Mexico; see International Labour Office, *Year Book of Labour Statistics* (Geneva: International Labour Organisation, 2006), pp. 763–838.
91 Ministry of Finance, *Financial Year Book, 1997*, pp. 499–501, 505–7; Ministry of Finance, *Financial Year Book, 1998*, pp. 498–501.
92 Chen et al., *Losses of State Assets*, pp. 5–6, 88, 91.

93 He Qinglian, *Xiandaihuade Xianjing* (*Trap of Modernisation*) (Beijing: Today's China Press, 1998), pp. 96–7.
94 Ma Ling and Li Ming, *Wen Jiabao Xinzhuan* (*New Biography of Wen Jiabao*), 8th edn (Hong Kong: Mingpao Press, 2003), p. 222.
95 He, *Trap of Modernisation*, pp. 98–9.
96 It is called 'income and price elastic' versus food which is 'income and price inelastic'. It means that one cannot have too many gadgets but one can only have one stomach for a fixed amount of food. This income and price elasticity is the force that drives growth in the manufacturing sector.
97 Xue, *Memoir*, p. 280.
98 Li and Zheng, *Fourteen Years of Reforms and Opening Up*, p. 22.
99 Andrew Walder, 'Local Government as Industrial Firm: An Organizational Analysis of China's Transitional Economy', *American Journal of Sociology*, 101/2 (1995): 266; Jean C. Oi, *Rural China Takes Off: Institutional Foundations of Economic Reform* (Berkeley: University of California Press, 1999), pp. 193–6.
100 Chun Chang and Yijing Wang, 'The Nature of the Township-Village Enterprise', *Journal of Comparative Economic Studies*, 19/3 (1994): 434–52; David D. Li, 'A Theory of Ambiguous Property Rights in Transition Economies: The Case of the Chinese Non-state Sector', *Journal of Comparative Economic Studies,* 23/1 (1996): 1–19; Jiahua Che and Yingyi Qian, 'Institutional Environment, Community Government, and Corporate Governance: Understanding China's Township-Village Enterprises', *Journal of Law, Economics & Organization,* 14/1 (1998): 1–23.
101 For the role of clans, see Xin Wang, *Sunan Moshede Zhongjie* (*The Ending of the South Jiangsu Model*) (Beijing: Sanlian Books, 2005), pp. 116–25, 150–2. For shareholding, see Zhang Zuoyuan, Hu Jiayong, and Liu Xuemin, *Lun Zhongguo Suoyouzhi Gaige* (*Ownership Reforms in China*) (Nanjing: Jiangsu People's Press, 2001), pp. 161–3; T. Sonobe, D. Hu, and K. Otsuka, 'From Inferior to Superior Products: an Inquiry into the Wenzhou Model of Industrial Development in China', *Journal of Comparative Economics*, 32/3 (2004): 542–63; Xin, *South Jiangsu Model*, pp. 65, 86–7; Z.H. Huang, X.B. Zhang, and Y.W. Zhu, 'The Role of Clustering in Rural Industrialization', *China Economic Review*, 19/1 (2008): 409–20.
102 Rural industry is rather common in many parts of the world. See, e.g., Yujiro Hayami, Masao Kikuchi, and Esher B. Marciano, 'Structure of Rural-based Industrialization: Metal Craft Manufacturing on the Outskirts of Greater Manila, the Philippines', *Development Economies*, 35/2 (1998): 132–54.
103 Yu Dechang, *Nonghu Jingji Xingwei Ji Laodong Shijian Liyong Tiaocha Ziliaoji* (*Survey Data for Rural Households' Economic Behaviour and Labour Input Patterns*) (Beijing: China's Statistical Press, 1992), p. 354.
104 Ibid., p. 352.
105 National Bureau of Statistics, *Statistical Year Book, 2003*, pp. 447, 448, 450, 451.
106 Li and Zheng, *Fourteen Years of Reforms and Opening Up*, p. 53; National Bureau of Statistics, *Statistical Year Book, 2003*, p. 448.
107 National Bureau of Statistics, *Statistical Year Book, 2003*, chs 4 and 5.
108 National Bureau of Statistics, 'Xin Zhongguo 50 Nian Xilie Fenxi Baogao Zhi Liu' (Report on China's 50 Years' Growth, No. 6), 18 September 1999,

https://www.stats.gov.cn/zt_18555/ztfx/xzg50nxlfxbg/202303/t20230301_1920444.html.

109 National Bureau of Statistics, *Statistical Year Book, 2001*, ch. 5; Vudayagi N. Balasubramanyan and Xiaolan Fu, 'Township and Village Enterprises in China', *Journal of Development Studies*, 39/4 (2003): 28.

110 Deng, *Selected Essays*, vol. 3, p. 238.

111 Fei Xiaotong, *Fei Xiaotong Quanji* (*Collected Essays of Fei Xiaotong*) (Huhehot: Inner Mongolia People's Press, 2009), vol. 13, p. 451.

112 National Bureau of Statistics, 'China's 50 Years' Growth'; National Bureau of Statistics, *Statistical Year Book, 2003*, p. 452.

113 Balasubramanyan and Fu, 'Township and Village Enterprises', p. 28.

114 Chen Xiao, 'The Evolution of China's Township and Village Enterprises', Center for International Knowledge on Development, 27 October 2020, https://en.cikd.org/knowledge-detail?id=1650668295360262145.

115 National Bureau of Statistics, 'China's 50 Years' Growth'.

116 Balasubramanyan and Fu, 'Township and Village Enterprises', p. 28.

117 The LSE-trained Chinese sociologist Professor Fei Xiaotong spent 15 years of his life on this topic. See his *Collected Essays*, vol. 10, pp. 85–7, 192–233, 349–68, 396–428, 504–32; vol. 11, pp. 336–42; vol. 12, pp. 89–106; vol. 13, pp. 407–13, 436–40, 441–56; vol. 14, pp. 200–5, 206–10; vol. 15, 162–70; vol. 16, pp. 374–87.

118 Note: if so, marginal returns (also called 'marginal product of labour') in farming should be close to zero.

119 Fei, *Collected Essays*, vol. 11, pp. 364–5.

120 See, e.g., James Kai-sing Kung and Yi-min Lin, 'The Decline of Township-and-Village Enterprises in China's Economic Transition', *World Development*, 35/4 (2007): 569–84.

121 Lu, *Survey of Social Strata*, p. 237.

122 Ibid., p. 238.

123 National Bureau of Statistics, *Statistical Year Book, 2003*, p. 72.

124 Lu, *Survey of Social Strata*, p. 225; Li Peilin, Li Qiang, and Sun Liping, *Zhongguo Shehui Fenceng* (*Social Stratification in Contemporary China*) (Beijing: Social Science Literature Press, 2004), p. 318.

125 Lu, *Survey of Social Strata*, p. 214.

126 Li, *Chinese Social Stratification*, pp. 201, 203. The official figure was 6.2 million.

127 Ma, *Confrontation*, p. 229.

128 Communist bureaucrats have unrivalled advantage to benefit from market-based reform and are the most desirable candidates to become the new bourgeoisies. For the Hungarian case, see Akos Rona-Tas, 'The First Shall Be Last? Entrepreneurship and Communist Cadres in the Transition from Socialism', *American Journal of Sociology*, 100/1 (1994): 40–69.

129 Li, *Chinese Social Stratification*, p. 202.

130 Will Hutton, *The Writing on the Wall, China and the West in the 21st Century* (Boston, MA: Little, Brown, 2007), p. 139.

131 According to a survey in 1994, 75 per cent of the respondents believed that the wealthy class obtained their riches from the state-owned assets; see He Zengke, *Fan Fu Xin Lu* (*New Path to Combat Corruption*) (Beijing: Central Compilation and Translation Press, 2002), pp. 207–8.

132 He, *To Combat Corruption*, pp. 109–12, 229–35; Li et al., *Social Stratification*, p. 342.
133 He, *To Combat Corruption*, p. 109.
134 Lu, *Survey of Social Strata*, pp. 36–7.
135 Hutton, *Writing on the Wall*, p. 140.
136 Li, *Chinese Social Stratification*, p. 197.
137 Ibid., p. 236.
138 Ministry of Finance, *Financial Year Book, 2004*, p. 411.
139 There have been numerous surveys, the highest profile one being Personnel Department of the Party Central Committee, *2000–2001 Zhongguo Diaocha Baogao: Xinxingshixiade Renmin Neibu Maodun Yanjiu* (*2000–2001 Report of Survey of China's Internal Conflicts in the New Era*) (Beijing: Central Translation Services Press, 2001). Others include Li, *Social Stratification*; Sun Liping, *Shiheng: Duanlieshehuide Yunzuo Luoji* (*Disequilibrium: Mechanisms of Broken Society*) (Beijing: Social Science Literature Press, 2004); Zhong Zeqi, *Dangdai Zhongguo Shehui Fenceng Zhuangkuangde Bianqian* (*Changes in Contemporary Social Stratification in China*) (Shijiazhuang: University of Hebei Press, 2004); Zheng Hangsheng and Li Lulu (eds), *Dangdai Zhongguo Chengshi Shehui Jiegou: Xianzhuang Yu Qushi* (*Social Structure in Contemporary Urban China, Current Situation and Future Trends*) (Beijing: People's University of China Press, 2004); Li Peilin, *Shehui Chongtu Yu Jieji Yishi* (*Social Conflicts and Class Consciousness*) (Beijing: Social Science Literature Press, 2005).
140 Ju Li, 'From "Master" to "Loser": Changing Working-Class Cultural Identity in Contemporary China', *International Labor and Working-Class History*, 88 (2015): 190–208; Marc Blecher, *The Making of China's Working Class A World to Lose* (London: Routledge, 2025).
141 Xian Taijiong, *Zhongguo Zhengdang Zhengfu Yu Shichang* (*The Party-State Government and the Market in China*) (Beijing: Economic Daily Press, 2002), p. 100.
142 See Jiang Zemin, 'Gaoju Deng Xiaoping Lilun Weida Qizhi, Ba Jianshe You Zhongguo Tece Shehuizhuyi Shiye Quanmian Tuixiang 21 Shiji' (Holding High Deng Xiaoping's Theoretical Banner and Pushing Socialism with Chinese Characteristics towards the 21st Century), *Renmin Ribao* (*People's Daily*), 12 September 1997, p. 1; and his 'Quanmian Jianshe Xiaokang Shehui, Kaichuang Zhongguo Tece Shehuizhuyi Shiye Xinjumian' (Building an Economy of 'Reasonably Comfortable Life' and Opening up a New Page of Socialism with Chinese Characteristics), *Renmin Ribao* (*People's Daily*), 14 November 2002, p. 1.
143 Data show that about half of China's post-1978 entrepreneurs wore 'red hats'; see Li et al., *Social Stratification*, pp. 323–4.
144 Hutton, *Writing on the Wall*, p. 139.
145 Ma and Li, *Wen Jiabao*, p. 232.
146 Fei, *Selected Works*, vol. 11, p. 500; see also Koji Hirata, *Industrial Manchuria and the Transnational Origins of Chinese Socialism* (Cambridge: Cambridge University Press, 2024), pp. 265–93.
147 Walder, 'Local Government', p. 266; Oi, *Rural China*, pp. 193–6.
148 Deng, *Selected Essays*, vol. 3, p. 138.
149 Xian, *Party-State Government*, pp. 106–7.
150 He, *To Combat Corruption*, p. 197.

151 In 2011, the state-controlled capital investment by shareholding was first published as RMB 30 trillion, 3.7 times the genuine state capital investment of RMB 8.2 trillion in the same year; see National Bureau of Statistics, *Statistical Year Book, 2012*, ch. 5–14. It means that the state invested from its own pocket at least RMB 15 trillion to qualify as the legal 'controlling shareholder'; see Li Youxing and Pan Zhifeng, 'Shangshi Gongsi Konggu Gudong, Shiji Kongzhiren' (Controlling Shareholders and *De Facto* Company Controllers), Shanghai Jintiancheng Law Firm, 12 April 2017, https://www.investor.org.cn/about_us/introduction_to_investor_service_center/research_planning/investor/investor_s1_2842/202109/P020210908525084387619.pdf.
152 National Bureau of Statistics, *Statistical Year Book, 2018*, ch. 10. Data for 2013 are RMB 43.6 trillion versus 11.0 trillion; 2014, RMB 50.1 trillion versus 12.5 trillion; 2015, RMB 55.2 trillion versus 14.0 trillion; 2016, RMB 59.7 trillion versus 12.9 trillion; see National Bureau of Statistics, *Statistical Year Book, 2014–2017*, ch. 10.
153 Yu Sheng, Xiaohui Tian, Weiqing Qiao, and Chao Peng, 'Measuring Agricultural Total Factor Productivity in China: Pattern and Drivers over the Period of 1978–2016', *Australian Journal of Agricultural and Resource Economics*, 64 (2019): 95.
154 For the crude GDP figures, see Appendix 5, table A–5.1.
155 National Bureau of Statistics, *Statistical Year Book, 2012*, ch. 3. Finally, after 62 years, China passed this threshold compared with the aforementioned thirty-four years of the Soviet Union's track record.
156 See Special Commentator, '*Shijian Shi Jianyan Zhenlide Weiyi Biaozhun*' (Practice as the Sole Testing Criterion for Truth or Fallacy), *Guangming Ribao* (*Bright Daily*), 11 May 1978, p. 1.
157 The term 'price and income inelasticity' here means that one can only eat so much each day when his or her income increases. So, when a household's income increases, say, 10-fold, its food bill does not enlarge *pro rata* and *pari passu*.
158 See Wang Zijian, 'Zhongguo Laogong Shenghuo Chengdu' (Living Standards of the Working Class in China), *Shehui Kexue* (*Social Sciences*), 2/2 (1931): 234–43.
159 Liu and Liu, *Economics in China*, p. 251.
160 Anon., *Summary of the 571 Project* (*571 Gongcheng Jiyao*), http://www.epochtimes.com/gb/8/1/10/n1971918p.htm.
161 Chen et al., *Losses of State Assets*, p. 92.
162 Huang Weiting, *Zhongguode Yinxing Jingji* (*China's Invisible Economy*) (Beijing: China's Commerce Press, 1996), p. 64.
163 Lu, *Survey of Social Strata*, p. 180; National Bureau of Statistics, *Statistical Year Book, 2003*, pp. 99, 123.
164 Li, *Chinese Social Stratification*, p. 219.
165 A technical illustration is available in Appendix 3, figure A–3.5.
166 For crude GDP information, see Appendix 5, figure A–5.2.
167 Ministry of Finance, *Financial Year Book, 2004*, pp. 331, 415.
168 Ministry of Commerce, *Zhongguo Duiwai Jingji Maoyi Nianjian, 2001* (*China's Foreign Trade Year Book, 2001*) (Beijing: *China's Foreign Trade Press*, 2001), p. 487.
169 Ministry of Commerce, *Foreign Trade Year Book, 2001*, p. 486.

170 In the same year, Party General Secretary Xi Jinping announced the 'China's Dream' blueprint.
171 In terms of the 'Cobb–Douglas Production Function', China's capital investment sources can be defined as $Y\ (L,\ K_{DOM}+K_{FDI}) = A\ L^{\alpha}\ (K_{DOM}+K_{FDI})^{1-\alpha}$, where Y stands for total output, A for technological input (called 'total factor productivity'), L for labour input, which is domestically supplied, and K for capital input with two separate sources, one domestic K_{DOM} and another foreign K_{FDI}. But, $K_{DOM} > K_{FDI}$, by a factor of nine, which is not trivial.
172 Deng was disappointed by the slowness in SEZs' switching to export; see Deng, *Selected Essays*, vol. 3, pp. 133, 239.
173 Ibid., vol. 3, p. 133.
174 Ibid., vol. 3, p. 239.
175 For example, Joseph Persky, 'Retrospectives: The Ethology of Homo Economicus', *Journal of Economic Perspectives*, 9/2 (1995): 221–31.
176 Liu and Liu, *Economics in China*, p. 109.
177 Li and Zheng, *Fourteen Years of Reforms and Opening Up*, p. 31; Ling, *No More Hesitation*, p. 131.

Chapter 4

1 For example, Alexander Gerschenkron, *Economic Backwardness in Historical Perspective* (Cambridge, MA: Harvard University Press, 1962); Lars Magnusson, *Nation, State and the Industrial Revolution: The Visible Hand* (London: Routledge, 2009). Numerous works on state capacity include North, *Institutions, Institutional Change*; Acemoglu et al., 'State Capacity and Economic Development'; Mark Dincecco and Gabriel Katz, 'State Capacity and Long-Run Economic Performance', *Economic Journal*, 126/590 (2016): 189–218; Mark Dincecco and Yuhua Wang, 'State Capacity in Historical Political Economy', *Oxford Handbook of Historical Political Economy*, C13-P1 (2022).
2 José Antonio Cheibub, 'Political Regimes and the Extractive Capacity of Governments: Taxation in Democracies and Dictatorships', *World Politics*, 50/3 (1998): 349–76; Timothy Besley and Torsten Persson, 'The Origins of State Capacity: Property Rights, Taxation, and Politics', *American Economic Review*, 99/4 (2009): 1218–44; Luz M. Arias, 'Building Fiscal Capacity in Colonial Mexico: From Fragmentation to Centralization', *Journal of Economic History*, 73/3 (2013): 662–93; Tuan-Hwee Sng and Chiaki Moriguchi, 'Asia's Little Divergence: State Capacity in China and Japan before 1850', *Journal of Economic Growth*, 19 (2014): 439–70.
3 Neil A. Englehart, 'State Capacity, State Failure, and Human Rights', *Journal of Peace Research*, 46/2 (2009): 163–80; Robert I. Rotberg (ed.), *When States Fail: Causes and Consequences* (Princeton, NJ: Princeton University Press, 2010); Daron Acemoglu and James A. Robinson, *Why Nations Fail: The Origins of Power, Prosperity, and Poverty* (New York: Crown Business Press, 2013).
4 Zong, *Conversations with Zhao Ziyang*, pp. 158, 171, 286.
5 Ibid., p. 254.
6 Ibid., p. 285.

7 We can list the following books: Li Buyun and Liu Han (eds), *Jianshe Gaodu Minzhude Shehuizhuyi Zhengzhi Zhidu* (*Establishing a High Democracy under a Socialist Political System*) (Beijing: Red Flag Press, 1984); Chen Hefu, *Lun Zhongguo Minzhu Zhengzhi* (*On China's Political Democracy*) (Beijing: Social Science Literature Press, 1995); Rui Mingjie (ed.), *Minzhu Guanli* (*Democratic Management*) (Hangzhou: Zhejiang People's Press, 1997); Gu Zhun, *Minzhu Yu 'Zhongjide Mudi'* (*Democracy and the 'Ultimate Goal'*) (Beijing: Chinese Youth Press, 1999); Cong Riyun, *Dangdai Shijiede Minzhuhua Langchao* (*The Current Tide of Democratisation in the World*) (Tianjin: Tianjin People's Press, 1999); Li Liangdong, *Dangdai Zhongguo Minzhu Wenti Yanjiu* (*The Issue of Democracy in Contemporary China*) (Beijing: Contemporary World Press, 2001); Lin Shangli, *Dangnei Minzhu: Zhongguo Gongchandangde Lilun Yu Shijian* (*Internal Democracy of a Party: Theory and Practice of the Chinese Communist Party*) (Shanghai: Shanghai Social Sciences Press, 2002); Tang Wei, *Difang Lifade Minzhuhua Yu Kexuehua Ganxiang* (*Conception of Democratisation and Scientification of Regional Legislation*) (Beijing: Peking University Press, 2002); Yuan Dayi and Guo Zhiping, *Nongcun Minzhu Jianshe Yanjiu* (*Study of Rural Grassroots Democracy*) (Beijing: China's Social Press, 2003); Ma Jun, *Zhongguo Gonggong Yusuan Gaige – Lixinghua Yu Minzhuhua* (*Reform in China's Public Budget – Rationality and Democratisation*) (Beijing: Central Compilation and Translation Press, 2005); News Bureau of the State Council, *Zhongguode Minzhu Zhengzhi Jianshe* (*Formation of China's Political Democracy*) (Beijing: New Star Press, 2005); Li Jingde and Wen Xiaoling, *Beijing Minzhu Zhengzhi Jianshe Chuangxin Anli Yanjiu* (*Case Studies of Political Democracy in Beijing*) (Beijing: China's Personnel Press, 2005); Guo Daojiu, *'Yi Shehui Zhiyue Quanli': Minzhude Yizhong Jiexi Shijiao* (*'To Use Society to Restrict the State Power': An Angle to Explain Democracy*) (Tianjin: Tianjin People's Press, 2005); Xiao Lihui, *Zhongguo Gongchandang Dangnei Minzhu Jianshe Yanjiu* (*Building an Internal Democracy in the Chinese Communist Party*) (Chongqing: Chongqing Press, 2006); Xu Yaotong and Liu Changxiong, *Zhengzhi Wenming Jianshe Yu Minzhu Zhengzhi Fazhan* (*Political Civilisation and Development of Political Democracy*) (Beijing: China's Economy Press, 2006); Liu Cheng, *1989–2002 Zhongguo Minzhu Fazhi Jianshe* (*China's Democracy and Rule of Law, 1989–2002*) (Beijing: Social Science Literature Press, 2007); Wang Changjiang, Zhou Hongyun, and Wang Yongbing (eds), *Dangnei Minzhu Zhidu Chuangxin* (*Institutional Innovation of Internal Democracy of the Chinese Communist Party*) (Beijing: Central Translation Press, 2007); and Fang Ning, *Caogen Jingji Yu Minzhu Zhengzhi* (*Grassroots Economy and Political Democracy*) (Beijing: Social Science Literature Press, 2008).

8 Yan Jian (ed.), *Minzhu Shige Haodongxi: Yu Keping Fangtan Lu* (*Democracy Is Desirable: Interview with Yu Keping*) (Beijing: Social Science Literature Press, 2006).

9 Ma Licheng and Ling Zhijun, *Jiaofeng, Dangdai Zhongguo Sanci Sixiang Jiefang Shilu* (*Confrontations, A History of Three Ideological Emancipations in Modern China*) (Beijing: China Today Press, 1998), p. 301.

10 Ibid., p. 302.

11 Wang et al., *Institutional Innovation*, p. 159.

12 Ma and Ling, *Confrontations*, p. 296.

13 Ibid., p. 341.

14 Melanie Manion, 'The Electoral Connection in the Chinese Countryside', *American Political Science Review*, 90/4 (1996): 736–48; Bai Yihua, *Lun Zhongguodalu Nongcunde Cunmin Zizhi Zhidu* (*Village Autonomy in Rural China*) (Taipei: Guiguan Press, 1998); Robert Pastor and Qingshan Tan, 'The Meaning of China's Village Elections', *China Quarterly*, 162 (2000): 490–512; He Baogang and Lang Youxing, 'Dalu Cunmin Xuanju Yu Zizhi Zhiduzhong Minzhuxingde Shengzhang Yu Fazhan' (Growth and Development of Democracy in Village Elections and Autonomy in Mainland China), *Zhonggong Yanjiu* (*Research into Chinese Communist Party*), 35/12 (2001): 85–96; Jamie Horsley, 'Village Elections: Training Ground for Democratization', *Chinese Business Review*, 28/2 (2001): 44–52; Chen Chubin, 'Dalu Nongcun Cuminweiyuanhui Xuanjude Shijian, Xiaoguo Yu Pinggu' (Practice, Impact and Assessment of Village Committee Elections in Mainland China), *Zhongguo Dalu Yanjiu* (*Research into Mainland China*), 45/1 (2002): 39–62; Lianjiang Li, 'The Politics of Introducing Direct Township Election in China', *China Quarterly*, 171 (2002): 704–23; Fubing Su and Dali Yang, 'Elections, Governance and Accountability in Rural China', *Asian Perspective*, 29/4 (2005): 125–57; Melanie Manion, 'Democracy, Community, Trust, the Impact of Elections in Rural China', *Comparative Political Studies*, 39/3 (2006): 301–24; Wang *et al.*, *Internal Democracy*.

15 Wang et al., *Institutional Innovation*, pp. 296–8.

16 Hutton, *Writing on the Wall*, p. 139.

17 They were officially announced in 1979: (1) communism (as a social system), (2) people's dictatorship (as the method to rule), (3) party's leadership (as the decision-making centre), and (4) Marx-Leninism and Maoism (as the decision-making guidance).

18 For example, North and Weingast, 'Constitutions and Commitment'; John Brewer, *The Sinews of Power: War, Money and the English State 1688–1783* (Cambridge, MA: Harvard University Press, 1990). Other aspects of state capacity include national security and social justice which are not the concerns of the present project. For national security, see, e.g., Noel Johnson and Mark Koyama, 'Legal Centralization and the Birth of the Secular State', *Journal of Comparative Economics*, 41/4 (2013): 959–78; and for social justice, see Acemoglu and Robinson, *Why Nations Fail*, and Francis Fukuyama, *The Origins of Political Order from Prehuman Times to the French Revolution* (London: Profile Books, 2011).

19 At this stage, the current study does not see the point of re-working China's GDP. It is good enough to take the average amongst the available estimates to see some general trends.

20 Rough GDP estimates are available in Appendix 5, tables A–5.3 and A–5.4.

21 Before 1990, China's gross national product (GNP) and GDP were identical due to small quantities of exports. So, GDP is used to avoid confusion.

22 For crude GDP information, see Appendix 5, figure A–5.4.

23 The common leasehold term is 70 years.

24 The six purses are two from the bride's parents, two from the bridegroom's parents, and two from the new couple. Six purses are all the savings of the three families, enough for the 20 per cent downpayment. The remaining 80 per cent depends on a bank mortgage loan over 30 years as a standard.

25 Jing Xiaolei, 'House Slaves', *Beijing Review*, 14 April 2007, https://www.bjreview.com/nation/txt/2007-04/02/content_248755.htm; Anon., 'Confessions of a Mortgage "Slave"', *China Daily*, 21 December 2009, https://www.chinadaily.com.cn/cndy/2009-12/21/content_9205018.htm; Liu Juan, 'Fangnu Jietao Sanbuqu' (Trilogy of Mortgage-debt Slaves), 7 May 2008, http://www.pingan.com/cms-tmplt/finance/knowledge/investknowledge/74504.html; Sun Lijian, *Shui Chuangzaole Fangnu, Chenu He Kanu* (*The Making of Mortgage-debt Slaves, Car Loan Slaves and Credit Card Slaves*) (Beijing: Zhongxin Press, 2011); Anon., 'Bacheng Gaoxiao Qingnian Jiaoshi Cheng Fangnu' (80% of Young Academics in Universities Have Become Mortgage-debt Slaves), 14 September 2012, http://www.shuobozhaopin.com/News/732012914155935.html.

26 Anon., 'Rise in Mortgage Defaults in China Raises Risks for Banks and Developers', 18 July 2022, https://www.fitchratings.com/research/corporate-finance/rise-in-mortgage-defaults-in-china-raises-risks-for-banks-developers-18-07-2022; Anon., 'Household Sector Risks in China', October 2019, https://www.rba.gov.au/publications/fsr/2019/oct/box-a-household-sector-risks-in-china.html.

27 Buck, *Land Utilization in China: Atlas*; Buck, *Statistics*, ch. 3.

28 'Constitution of the People's Republic of China (1954)', https://news.12371.cn/2015/03/18/ARTI1426665514681575.shtml.

29 Luo, '1957 Debate', p. 42.

30 Li Changping, 'Zhongguo Tudi Zhidu Bianqian Yu Sannong Xingshuai' (Changes in Land Systems and Ups and Downs of the Rural Economy), *Yanhuang Chunqiu* (*History of Chinese*), 6 (2007): 41–7.

31 Liang, *Dynastic Data*, p. 290; Qi Xia, *Songdai Jingjishi* (*An Economic History of the Song*) (Beijing: Zhonghua Books, 2009), vol. 1, p. 299.

32 'Constitution of the People's Republic of China (1982)', https://news.12371.cn/2015/03/18/ARTI1426664689523381.shtml.

33 The legal meaning of 'all-people's ownership' can only be 1.4 billion multiple owners in society, everyone holding an equal share.

34 See https://news.12371.cn/2015/03/18/ARTI1426664689523381.shtml. All urban land is owned by the state, and state ownership is for all citizens, all rural land is owned by local communities. Either way, land should be free for citizens. See Constitution of the PRC, https://www.elegislation.gov.hk/hk/A7%21zh-Hant-HK.assist.pdf.

35 Based on Chen Jian, *Liushide Zhongguo* (*Losses of State Assets*) (Beijing: China's Urban Press, 1998), p. 1; Chen et al., *Losses of State Assets*, pp. 8, 21.

36 Anon., *Mao Zedong's Thought*, pp. 69, 70, 131.

37 Xue, *Memoir*, p. 167.

38 Anon., *Mao Zedong's Thought*, pp. 69, 71.

39 Anon., 'Budongchan Zhengshou' (*Real Estate Taxation*), https://zh.wikipedia.org/wiki/%E4%B8%8D%E5%8A%A8%E4%BA%A7%E5%BE%81%E6%94%B6?utm.

40 For example, Hongyan Du, Yongkai Ma, and Yunbi An, 'The Impact of Land Policy on the Relation between Housing and Land Prices: Evidence from China', *Quarterly Review of Economics and Finance*, 51/1 (2011): 19–27; Jinfeng Du and Richard B. Peiser, 'Land Supply, Pricing and Local Governments' Land Hoarding in China', *Regional Science and Urban*

Economics, 48 (2014): 180–9; Fox Z.Y. Hu and Jiwei Qian, 'Land-based Finance, Fiscal Autonomy and Land Supply for Affordable Housing in Urban China: A Prefecture-Level Analysis', *Land Use Policy*, 69 (2017): 454–60; Jiawei Mo, 'Land Financing and Economic Growth: Evidence from Chinese Counties', *China Economic Review*, 50 (2018): 218–39; Xiaoyan Shen, Xianjin Huang, Huan Li, Yi Li, and Xiaofeng Zhao, 'Exploring the Relationship between Urban Land Supply and Housing Stock: Evidence from 35 Cities in China', *Habitat International*, 77 (2018): 80–9; Joseph Gyourko, Yang Shen, Jing Wu, and Rongjie Zhang, 'Land Finance in China: Analysis and Review', *China Economic Review*, 76 (2022): Article 101868.

41 Mortgage loans are to be paid continuously. The loan interest is yet another form of taxation because capital in state banks ultimately comes from public savings. As a result, a large proportion of China's population has been indebted since 1998 thanks to the artificially created 'housing market' together with 'housing prices'.

42 Alice H. Amsden, *Asia's Next Giant: South Korea and Late Industrialization* (New York: Oxford University Press, 1989), ch. 6; Robert Wade, *Governing the Market: Economic Theory and the Role of Government in East Asian Industrialisation* (Princeton, NJ: Princeton University Press, 1990), ch. 10.

43 Gerschenkron, *Economic Backwardness*, ch. 2.

44 Party Central Committee Document No. 4 (1979) on 'Increase in Procurement Prices'; State Council Document No. 55 (1990) on 'Grain Procurement Monopsony'; State Council Document No. 12 (1995) on 'Tightening Grain Purchase Control'.

45 State Council Document No. 35 (1998) on 'Deregulating Food Price Protection': State Council Document No. 1 (2004) on 'Marketizing Food Prices'; Party Central Committee Document No. 1 (2007) on 'Subsidising Food Producers'.

46 See footnote 90 in chapter 3.

47 A technical illustration is available in Appendix 3, figure A–3.6.

48 See https://www.safe.gov.cn/safe/2012/0416/4533.html.

49 See https://ielaw.uibe.edu.cn/fgal/wgfl/qt/18384.htm.

50 See https://ielaw.uibe.edu.cn/fgal/wgfl/qt/18384.htm?utm.

51 See https://jsnews.jschina.com.cn/zt2024/fzsxxxpt/hdxf/xzfg/202404/t20240417_3392225.shtml.

52 The origin of this tactic comes from China's ancient 'Thirty-six Stratagems' (*sanshiliu ji*) of *Master Sun's Art of War* (*Sunzi Bingfa*). It is Stratagem Number 25: 'Substituting a superior pillar with an inferior one' (*touliang huanzhu*).

53 The percentage increases were as follows: 26.3% (1979), 29.3% (1980), 14.5% (1981), 10.8% (1982), 20.6% (1983), 49.5% (1984), 24.7% (1985), 20.2% (1986), 19.4% (1987), and 46.7% (1988), averaging 26.2% a year which was 6.6 times China's GDP growth during the same period. With such an annual rate, China's monetary supply would increase over 10-fold each decade. See Huang, *China's Invisible Economy*, pp. 244–5.

54 For China's official GDP constant price conversions, see National Bureau of Statistics, *Statistical Year Book, 2023*, ch. 3.

55 See, e.g., https://chineseposters.net/themes/chinese-dream; and https://en.wikipedia.org/wiki/Chinese_Dream; https://www.bbc.co.uk/news/world-asia-china-22726375.

56 See, e.g., Ronald H. Coase, 'The Problem of Social Cost', *Journal of Law and Economics*, 3/1 (1960): 1–44; James Buchanan and Wm. Craig Stubblebine, 'Externality', *Economica*, 29/116 (1962): 371–84; William J. Baumol, 'On Taxation and the Control of Externalities', *American Economic Review*, 62/3 (1972): 307–22; Frances Stewart and Ejaz Ghani, 'How Significant Are Externalities for Development?' *World Development*, 19/6 (1991): 569–94; Donald J. Boudreaux and Roger Meiners, 'Externalities: Origins and Classifications', *Natural Resources Journal*, 59/1 (2019): 1–34.

57 A technical illustration is available in Appendix 3, figure A–3.7.

58 Garrett Hardin, 'The Tragedy of the Commons', *Science*, 162 (1968): 1243–48; Fikret Berkes, *Common Property Resources* (London: Belhaven Press, 1989); Elinor Ostrom, *Governing the Commons* (New York: Cambridge University Press, 1990); Brett M. Frischmann, Alain Marciano, and Giovanni Battista Ramello, 'Retrospectives: Tragedy of the Commons after 50 Years', *Journal of Economic Perspectives*, 33/4 (2019): 211–28.

59 Chenggang Xu and Juzhong Zhuang, 'Why China Grew: the Role of Decentralisation', in Peter Boone, Stanislaw Gomulka, and Richard Layard (eds), *Emerging from Communism: Lessons from Russia, China, and Eastern Europe* (Cambridge, MA: MIT Press, 1998), pp. 183–212; Chenggang Xu, 'China's Political-Economic Institution: Regionally Decentralized Authoritarianism (RDA)', in Sheggen Fan, Ravi Kanbur, Shang-Jin Wei, and Xiaobo Zheng (eds), *Oxford Companion to the Economics of China* (Oxford: Oxford University Press, 2014), pp. 515–19.

60 Zhong Dajun, *Guomin Daiyu Bupingdeng Shenshi* (*Assessment of Unequal Entitlement amongst Citizens*) (Beijing: China's Workers' Press, 2002), p. 186.

61 China's Investment Year Book Committee, *Zhongguo Touzi Nianjian, 2006* (*China's Investment Year Book, 2006*) (Beijing: China's Water Control and Hydro-electricity Press, 2006), p. 918.

62 Elizabeth C. Economy, *The River Runs Black: The Environmental Challenge to China's Future* (Ithaca, NY: Cornell University Press, 2010); Congbo Song, Lin Wu, Yaochen Xie, et al., 'Air Pollution in China: Status and Spatiotemporal Variations', *Environmental Pollution*, 227 (2017): 334–47; Jun Liu, Yixuan Zheng, Guannan Geng, et al., 'Decadal Changes in Anthropogenic Source Contribution of $PM_{2.5}$ Pollution and Related Health Impacts in China, 1990–2015', *Atmospheric Chemistry and Physics*, 20/13 (2020): 7783–99; Qingyang Xiao, Guannan Geng, Tao Xue, Shigan Liu, Cilan Cai, Kebin He, and Qiang Zhang, 'Tracking $PM_{2.5}$ and O_3 Pollution and the Related Health Burden in China 2013–2020', *Environmental Science & Technology*, 56/11 (2021): 9622–32.

63 Typically, CO_2, CH_4, and N_2O.

64 For crude information, see Appendix 5, figure A–5.5.

65 Lu et al., 'Air Pollution Control'; Chen Xuan, Xiaoran Shan, Zhaoji Shi, Jia-en Zhang, and Qin Zhong, 'Analysis of Spatio-Temporal Changes in Acid Rain and Their Causes in China (1998–2018)', *Journal of Resources and Ecology*, 12/5 (2021): 593–9.

66 For example, World Bank, *Cost of Pollution in China* (Washington, DC: World Bank, 2007).

67 Hu Angang and Guo Yong, 'Woguo Shuyu Shijieshang Fubai Bijiao Yanzhongde Guojia Zhiyi' (China Now Belongs to One of Most Corrupt

Countries in the World), *Zhongguo Guoqing Fenxi Yanjiu Baogao* (*Report on China's National Conditions*), Paper No. 344, Tsinghua University Centre for National Conditions, 15 August 2001.

68 Kathleen Eisenhardt, 'Agency Theory: An Assessment and Review', *Academy of Management Review*, 14/1 (1989): 57–74; Jean-Jacques Laffont and David Martimort, *The Theory of Incentives: The Principal–Agent Model* (Princeton, NJ: Princeton University Press, 2002); Rose M. Baker, 'The Agency of the Principal–Agent Relationship: An Opportunity for HRD', *Advances in Developing Human Resources*, 21/3 (2019): 303–18. For the PRC case, see, e.g., Hutton, *Writing on the Wall*; Dexter Roberts, *The Myth of Chinese Capitalism* (New York: St. Martin's Press, 2020); Desmond Shum, *Red Roulette: An Insider's Story of Wealth, Power, Corruption, and Vengeance in Today's China* (London: Simon & Schuster, 2021); Peter Schweizer, *Red-Handed – How American Elites Get Rich Helping China Win* (New York: HarperCollins, 2022). For small sample-based studies, see Yong Guo, 'Corruption in Transitional China: An Empirical Analysis', *China Quarterly*, 194 (2008): 349–64; Yuhua Wang, 'China's Corruption Investigations Dataset', https://search.dataone.org/view/sha256:cb64891d4cc38c5f06b1f1c099b86f0752cb9ef59dbc702b259bb7d3c9e0af98.

69 Yang Yu, *Shehui Zhuanxingqi Fan Fubai Yanjiu* (*Combating Corruption in a Social Transition Period*) (Tianjin: Tianjin People's Press, 2001), p. 66.

70 Ibid., p. 211.

71 See https://www.dni.gov/files/ODNI/documents/assessments/ODNI-Unclassified-CDA-CCP-Leadership-202503.pdf.

72 For the joint communiqué of the Communist Party Central Committee and the State Council, see Chen Bo, *Zhongguo Fan Fubai Ershi Nian* (*Twenty Years of Fighting against Corruption in China*) (Beijing: People's Press, 2000), p. 8.

73 He, *To Combat Corruption*, pp. 37, 109–10, 161, 232.

74 Ma and Li, *Wen Jiabao*, p. 198.

75 Hutton, *Writing on the Wall*, p. 129. See also Zong, *Conversations with Zhao Ziyang*, p. 244. A higher estimate is 17 per cent of GDP; see Ma and Li, *Wen Jiabao*, p. 192.

76 Zong, *Conversations with Zhao Ziyang*, p. 225; National Bureau of Statistics, *Statistical Year Book, 2002*, p. 51.

77 Yang, *Combating Corruption*, p. 40.

78 Huang, *China's Invisible Economy*, p. 137; Ministry of Finance, *Financial Year Book, 1997*, pp. 499–501, 505–7; Ministry of Finance, *Financial Year Book, 1998*, pp. 498–501.

79 Ma and Li, *Wen Jiabao*, p. 222.

80 He Qinglian, 'Zhongguo Yinhang Huaizhang Zai Re Guanzhu' (Bad Debts in China's Banks Causing Concerns Again), 27 May 2006, http://archives.cnd.org/HXWK/author/HE-Qinglian/kd060527-7.gb.html. China's 2005 GDP was RMB 18.4 trillion; see National Bureau of Statistics, *Statistical Year Book, 2006*, ch. 3.

81 Fred, 'Bank Non-performing Loans to Gross Loans for China', 7 May 2024, https://fred.stlouisfed.org/series/DDSI02CNA156NWDB; Anon., 'Zhongguode Yinhang Huaizhang Wenti Zheng Gungun Erlai' (Arising Bad Debts in China's Banks), 29 March 2024, https://caus.com/all-articles/news/402832/.

82 Yang, *Combating Corruption*, p. 168.

83 Anon., 'Jinrong Fanfu Jiali!' (Anti-Banking-Corruption Intensified!), *Shanghai Observer*, 18 November 2012, https://www.jfdaily.com/wx/detail.do?id=425135.

84 Jin Zhong, 'Yinhang Xidai Lingyude Fubai Yicheng Jinrong Fubaide Zuida Bingyin' (Bank Loan Corruption as the Root Cause of Financial Corruption), *China's Finance News*, 18 February 2025, http://www.financeun.com/newsDetail/60022.shtml.

85 Yang, *Combating Corruption*, p. 7; Ai Sha and Cao Li, 'Huaizhang Yinhang Huarong Jiang Huo Guozi Jiuzhu' (The 'Bad-Debt Bank' Huarong to Be Rescued by Government Capital), *New York Times (Chinese)*, 20 August 2021, https://cn.nytimes.com/business/20210820/huarong-bailout-china/.

86 James Stent, *China's Banking Transformation: The Untold Story* (New York: Oxford University Press, 2017); Hu Bin, Cheng Lian, and Zheng Liansheng, *Zhongguo Jinrong Fengxian 2022* (*Report on Financial Risks in China, 2022*) (Beijing: China's Social Sciences Press, 2023); Han Qing, 'Xijuan Quanguode Jinrong Fanfu Fengbao' (National Sweeping Anti-Corruption in the Financial Sector), *China's Finance Web*, 2 March 2025, http://www.financeun.com/newsDetail/60138.shtml.

87 Chen, *Fighting against Corruption*, p. 260; He, *To Combat Corruption*, pp. 225–6.

88 Yang, *Combating Corruption*, pp. 47–8; Han Jie, 'Si Bumen: Quanguo Faxian Xiao Jinku Yu 4 Wan-ge Jin-e Chao 200 Yi Yuan' (Four Agencies' Joint Report: Over 40,000 Secret Coffers Discovered Nation-wide with over RMB 20 Billion), *Central Government of PRC*, 28 January 2011, https://www.gov.cn/jrzg/2011-01/28/content_1794835.htm.

89 Yang, *Combating Corruption*, p. 3.

90 Wu Jiejun, 'Gaoxiao Jiceng Danwei Xiao Jinku Wenti Guankui' (Secret Coffers in University Departments), *Caikuai Yuekan* (*Accounting Monthly*), 10 (2005): 26–7; Ma Haitao and Xiao Fei Danqing, 'Xiao Jinku Zhili Nande Yuanyin Ji Duice' (Challenges from Control over Secret Coffers and Solutions), *Caizheng Jiandu* (*Financial Control*), 19 (2009): 9–10; Lu Fei, 'Jiyu Xiao Jinku Shijiaode Guoyou Qiye Guoyou Zichan Liushi Wenti Yanjiu' (Secret Coffers and Losses of State Assets in State-owned Enterprises), *Zhongyang Caijing Daxue Xuebao* (*Bulletin of Central Finance and Economics University*), 7 (2012): 20–5; Dong Yuting, 'Xiao Jinku Wentide Fanzuixue Fenxi' (A Criminological Analysis of Secret Coffers), *Xueshu Jiaoliu* (*Academic Exchanges*), 2 (2013): 47–50; Wang Haimin, 'Tielu Qiye Jingji Huodongzhong "Xiao Jinku" Xianzhuang Ji Chengyin' (Status and Causes of Secret Coffers in Economic Activities of the Railway Sector)', *Shenji Yu Licai* (*Auditing and Financial Management*), 1 (2024): 22–4.

91 Yang, *Combating Corruption*, pp. 65–7. See also, Chen, *Fighting against Corruption*, pp. 259–63.

92 Ma and Li, *Wen Jiabao*, p. 200.

93 See He, *To Combat Corruption*, pp. 1–2, 113; Li Youjun and Liu Xiaolin, 'Zhongguo Zuzhi Tanguan Waitao' (China Stops Corrupt Officials from Escaping), *Renmin Ribao* (*People's Daily*), 10 September 2004, p. 7.

94 For the sensational cases of Lai Xiaomin (who was found guilty and sentenced to death), Sun Deshun (guilty and also sentenced to death), Fan

Yifei (guilty and also sentenced to death), and Liu Lianke; see Li Ting, 'Lai Xiaominde Huarong Diguo Shimo' (The Ups and Downs of Lai Xiaomin's Banking Empire), *Hong Kong O1*, 1 May 2021, https://www.hk01.com/即時中國/570515/賴小民建華融帝國始末-被銀監會4度邀請才接手－9年打造萬億金控; Qi Ning, 'Sun Deshun Shouhui Jin 10 Yi Beipan Sihuan' (Sun Deshun Received BRM 1 Billion, Sentenced to Death), *First Financial News*, 11 November 2023, https://www.yicai.com/news/101901638.html; Fan Fu, 'Fan Yifei Jin 30 Nian Tanfu 3.8 Yi!' (Fan Yifei: Near 30 Years' Embezzlement for RMB 380 Million), *Shanghai Observer*, 10 October 2024, https://www.jfdaily.com/staticsg/res/html/web/newsDetail.html?id=805593; and Voice of Germany, 'Jinrong Tanfuan Lianlian, Zhongguo Yinhang Yuanhangzhang Renzui' (Banking Corruption Continuing, the Former Director of Bank in China Pleaded Guilty', *Voice of Germany*, 24 April 2024, https://www.dw.com/zh/金融贪腐案连连-中国银行原行长认罪/a-68911013.

95 Da He, '2025 Nian 1 Yuan Jinrong Fanfu Zhanbao: 12 Wei Jinrong Gaoguan Luoma' (Anti-Corruption Report of January 2025: 12 High Ranking Officials in the Banking Sector Deposed), *China's Financial News*, 25 January 2025, http://www.financeun.com/newsDetail/59915.shtml.

96 For similar information, see Chen, *Fighting against Corruption*, p. 255; Yang, *Combating Corruption*, p. 168; He, *To Combat Corruption*, pp. 2–3.

97 Carsten A. Holz, 'Have China Scholars All Been Bought?' *Far Eastern Economic Review*, 170/3 (April 2007): 38.

98 According to a survey in 1994, 75 per cent of the respondents believed that the wealthy class obtained their riches from state-owned assets; see He, *To Combat Corruption*, pp. 207–8.

99 Ibid., pp. 2, 50.

100 Xuezhi Guo, 'Controlling Corruption in the Party: China's Central Discipline Inspection Commission', *China Quarterly*, 219 (2014): 602.

101 Anon., 'Xi Jinping Has Been Good for China's Communist Party; Less so for China', *Economist*, 14 October 2017, https://www.economist.com/news/briefing/21730138-contradicting-deng-xiaoping-mr-xi-has-concentrated-vast-power-his-own-hands-xi-jinping-has.

102 See Zhang Hui, 'China Punished 4.7 Million People in Decade-long Anti-graft Campaign', *Global Time*, 30 June 2022, https://www.globaltimes.cn/page/202206/1269498.shtml. Note that the report by the Director of National Intelligence of the United States in March 2025 cites this number, see https://www.dni.gov/files/ODNI/documents/assessments/ODNI-Unclassified-CDA-CCP-Leadership-202503.pdf.

103 Guodong Du, 'China Party Says Nearly 5 Million Members Probed for Graft', 17 October 2022, https://apnews.com/article/health-china-business-covid-economy-6618e65ef6148e0c75fce4dc2a28011f?

104 Anon., 'Crime Rate in China', https://www.chinajusticeobserver.com/a/crime-rate-in-china-2021?

105 Timothy Besley and James A. Robinson, 'Quis Custodiet Ipsos Custodes? Civilian Control over the Military', *Journal of the European Economic Association*, 8/2–3 (2010): 655–63; Peter Corning, *The Fair Society: The Science of Human Nature and the Pursuit of Social Justice* (Chicago: University of Chicago Press, 2011), p. 146.

106 https://www.transparency.org/en/cpi/2024.
107 Hutton, *Writing on the Wall*, p. 123.
108 Yang, *Combating Corruption*, ch. 4.

Chapter 5

1 For example, Joshua Cooper Ramo, *The Beijing Consensus* (London: The Foreign Policy Centre, 2004); Minxin Pei, *China's Trapped Transition: The Limits of Developmental Autocracy* (Cambridge, MA: Harvard University Press, 2006); Dani Rodrik, 'Goodbye Washington Consensus, Hello Washington Confusion?' *Journal of Economic Literature* 44 (2006): 937–87; Azar Gat, 'The Return of Authoritarian Great Powers', *Foreign Affairs*, 86/4 (2007): 59–69; Stefan Halper, *The Beijing Consensus: How China's Authoritarian Model Will Dominate the Twenty-First Century* (New York: Basic Books, 2010); Suisheng Zhao, 'The China Model: Can it Replace the Western Model of Modernization?' *Journal of Contemporary China*, 19/65 (2010): 419–36; Arif Dirlik, 'The Idea of a "Chinese Model": A Critical Discussion', *China Information*, 26/3 (2012): 277–302; Thomas Ambrosio, 'The Rise of the "China Model" and "Beijing Consensus": Evidence of Authoritarian Diffusion?' *Contemporary Politics*, 18/4 (2012): 381–99; Daniel A. Bell, *The China Model: Political Meritocracy and the Limits of Democracy* (Princeton, NJ: Princeton University Press, 2015); Weitseng Chen (ed.), *The Beijing Consensus: How China Has Changed Western Ideas of Law and Economic Development* (Cambridge: Cambridge University Press, 2017).

2 Jean-Marc Blanchard and Colin Flint, 'The Geopolitics of China's Maritime Silk Road Initiative', *Geopolitics*, 22/2 (2017): 223–45; David Brewster, 'Silk Roads and Strings of Pearls: The Strategic Geography of China's New Pathways in the Indian Ocean', *Geopolitics*, 22/2 (2017): 269–91; Maria A. Carrai, 'China's Malleable Sovereignty along the Belt and Road Initiative: The Case of the 99-Year Chinese Lease of The Hambantota Port', *Journal of International Law & Politics*, 51/4 (2019): 1062–98; Mohamed Ibrahim Mohamed Irfan and Mohamed Anifa Mohamed Fowsar, 'Learning from the Chinese Model of Development and Moulding China–Sri Lanka Relations', *Journal of Politics and Law*, 3/13 (2020): 57–63; Theodor Tudoroiu, *The Geopolitics of China's Belt and Road Initiative* (London: Routledge, 2024); Ganeshan Wignaraja, Dinusha Panditaratne, Pabasara Kannangara, and Divya Hundlani, 'Chinese Investment and the BRI in Sri Lanka', *Chatham House Research Paper*, 24 March 2024, https://www.chathamhouse.org/2020/03/chinese-investment-and-bri-sri-lanka.

3 For example, Anon., 'Nobel Prize Winner Sees Transformation in China's Growth Model', 24 March 2019, https://news.cgtn.com/news/3d3d674d7967544e33457a6333566d54/index.html; Anon., 'Interview with James Heckman: Nobel Prize Winner on US–China Trade War and AI Race', 14 July 2019, https://news.cgtn.com/news/79636a4d784d4464776c6d636a4e6e62684a4856/index.html; Anon., 'China's Commitment to Innovation Shines Bright on Quality Development: Nobel Laureate Edmund Phelps', 28 March 2024, https://www.globaltimes.cn/page/202403/1309731.shtml.

4 Anon., 'GT Voice: What Does China's $96b AI Industry Mean for the World?', 27 April 2025, https://www.globaltimes.cn/page/202504/1332992.shtml.

5 In economic jargon, this is called the 'corner solution' along the production possibility frontier (PPF), which is efficient.

6 David Ricardo, 'On Foreign Trade', in *On The Principles of Political Economy and Taxation* (1817. Reprint. Cambridge: Cambridge University Press, 2015), ch. 7.

7 For the debate, see, e.g., Gary Gereffi and Miguel Korzeniewicz, *Commodity Chains and Global Capitalism* (London: Bloomsbury Academic, 1994); Folker Frobel, Jürgen Heinrichs, and Otto Kreye, *The New International Division of Labour: Structural Unemployment in Industrialised Countries and Industrialisation in Developing Countries* (Cambridge: Cambridge University Press, 1980).

8 See Nigar Hashimzade, Gareth Myles, and John D. Black (eds.) *Dictionary of Economics*, 5th edn (Oxford: Oxford University Press, 2017), p. 459.

9 For example, Daniel M. Bernhofen and John C. Brown, 'A Direct Test of the Theory of Comparative Advantage: The Case of Japan', *Journal of Political Economy*, 112/1 (2004): 48–67.

10 Adam Smith, *An Inquiry into the Nature and Causes of the Wealth of Nations* (1776. Reprint. Chicago: University of Chicago Press, 1977), Book IV, Ch. 2.

11 Data for 2022, see World Bank, 'Population 2022', https://databankfiles.worldbank.org/public/ddpext_download/POP.pdf.

12 Here, a conventional economic judgement and explanation come from the Cobb–Douglas production function $Y = AL^{\alpha}K^{1-\alpha}$, where Y (total output) is the function of the product of L (labour input) times K (capital input). A represents 'technology' that is embodied in labour and capital, which is taken for granted. The power of labour α and the power of capital $1-\alpha$ mean that labour and capital are substitutable or exchangeable in producing the same output Y. Thus, if China uses 44.3 units of labour to produce more than 44.3 units of output and exports, the extra output and exports are likely to be a result of capital inputs. Extra capital inputs in turn qualify 'capital intensive production'.

13 Note: if so, marginal returns (also called 'marginal product of labour') in farming should be close to zero.

14 In terms of the Cobb–Douglas production function, $Y (L, K) = A\ L^{\alpha}\ K^{1-\alpha}$ where Y stands for total output, A for technological input (called 'total factor productivity'), L for labour input, and K for capital input. L and K are interchangeable, hence $\alpha + (1 - \alpha) = 1$. What TVEs in China have created is a 'free labour' production function. If so, the owners of technology and capital gain all the returns. That will be the nirvana for capitalism.

15 Even Deng Xiaoping noticed SEZs' problem of being unable to perform export-led growth; see Deng, *Selected Essays*, vol. 3, pp. 133, 239.

16 Kaoru Sugihara, *Labour-Intensive Industrialization in Global History* (Farnham: Ashgate, 2013).

17 See Anthony Clothier, Ferenc Schmél, Song Wen Xian, and Su Chaoying, 'The Chinese Footwear Industry and Its Influence on the World Trade', Conference Paper for 15th Meeting of the UNIDO Leather Panel, León, Mexico, 10–14 September 2005, https://leatherpanel.org/sites/default/files

/publications-attachments/chineese_footwear_industry.pdf; for the Wenzhou footwear production centre, see Huang et al., 'Rural Industrialization', pp. 409–20; Y.H. Dennis Wei, 'China's Shoe Manufacturing and the Wenzhou Model: Perspectives on the World's Leading Producer and Exporter of Footwear', *Eurasian Geography and Economics*, 50/6 (2009): 720–39.

18 Robert E. Scott, 'The China Trade Toll, Widespread Wage Suppression, 2 Million Jobs Lost in the U.S.' *Briefing Paper No. 219*, 30 July, 2008, Economic Policy Institution (Washington, DC), https://www.epi.org/publication/bp219/.

19 For the construction industry, see Anon., 'Tuoqian Gongzi, 2023–2025' (Wage Arrears, 2023–2025), *China Labour Bulletin*, https://maps.clb.org.hk/?i18n_language=zh_CN&map=1&startDate=2023-01&endDate=2025-01&eventId=&keyword=拖欠工资&addressId=&parentAddressId=&address=&parentAddress=&industry=10400,10401,10402,10403,10404,10405&parentIndustry=4&industryName=建筑业&pageEmbed=. For a general picture, see Anthony Blair, 'Protests Erupt in China after Furious Workers Demand Back Pay as Trump's Tariffs on Imports Jolt Economy', 6 May 2025, https://nypost.com/2025/05/06/world-news/protests-erupt-in-china-as-trumps-steep-tariffs-bite-extremely-anxious/.

20 Ministry of Human Resources and Social Security, 'Tuoqian Laodong Baochu Dianxing Anjian, 2021–2022' (Case Studies of Wage Arrears, 2021–2022), https://www.mohrss.gov.cn/ldjcj/LDJCJgongzuodongtai/202201/t20220129_433905.html.

21 Anon., '1,866 individuals prosecuted for crimes related to wage arrears in China in 2024', *China Daily*, 21 January 2025, https://www.chinadaily.com.cn/a/202501/21/WS678f3f88a310a2ab06ea84bd.html.

22 Anon., 'Chinese Courts Initiate Special Winter Action to Tackle Wage Arrears', The Supreme People's Court, 26 December 2024, https://english.court.gov.cn/2024-12/26/c_1059728.htm.

23 Anon., 'China's 996 Work Culture is Driving Young People Out of Megacities', *Bloomberg*, 11 June 2024, https://www.bloomberg.com/news/newsletters/2024-06-11/china-s-996-work-culture-is-driving-young-people-out-of-megacities; Ryan McMorrow and Nian Liu, 'We're Like Gears Grinding Until They Break: Chinese Tech Companies Push Staff to the Limit', *Financial Times*, 24 June 2024, https://www.ft.com/content/c94d046c-570a-4222-bfc5-463fdcfc66c2; Luna Sun, 'Are China's biggest firms turning the page on 996-style work culture?', *South China Morning Post*, 10 March 2025, https://www.scmp.com/economy/china-economy/article/3301815/are-chinas-biggest-firms-turning-page-996-style-work-culture.

24 'Labour Law of the People's Republic of China', https://www.gov.cn/banshi/2005-05/25/content_905.htm.

25 Or, workers should be paid 2.3 times what they get; see https://996.icu/#/zh_CN.

26 US Representative Benjamin L. Cardin, and US Representative Christopher H. Smith, 'Section 301 Petition [on China's Repression of Workers' Rights], 2006', see Scott, 'China Trade Toll'.

27 Anita Chan, *China's Workers Under Assault Exploitation and Abuse in a Globalizing Economy* (London: Routledge, 2001); Pun Ngai, *Made in China: Women Factory Workers in a Global Workplace* (Durham, NC: Duke University Press, 2005); David Dorn and Peter Levell, 'Labour Market

Impacts of the China Shock: Why the Tide of Globalisation Did Not Lift All Boats', *Labour Economics*, 91 (2024): 1–14.

28 'Trade Union Law of the People's Republic of China', https://www.mohrss.gov.cn/xxgk2020/fdzdgknr/zcfg/fl/202011/t20201102_394624.html.

29 For example, Andong Zhu and David M. Kotz, 'The Dependence of China's Economic Growth on Exports and Investment', *Review of Radical Political Economics*, 43/1 (2010): 9–32; Yilmaz Akyuz, 'Export Dependence and Sustainability of Growth in China', *China and World Economy*, 1/19 (2011): 1–23; Vivek B. Arora and Roberto Cardarell, *Rebalancing Growth in Asia – Economic Dimensions for China* (Washington, DC: IMF, 2011), ch. 4.

30 Deng, *Selected Essays*, vol. 3, p. 88.

31 Ibid., vol. 3, p. 279.

32 Ibid., vol. 3, p. 112. Note: In the CCP jargon, 'socialism' here means 'an early stage of communism', and 'communism' means 'fully fledged communism'.

33 Ibid., vol. 3, pp. 363–4.

34 At the age of 25, the young tsar dirtied his hands in shipyards in Amsterdam and Deptford (near London) to learn shipbuilding for the sake of building a navy for Russia.

35 Deng, *Selected Essays*, vol. 3, p. 356.

36 Ibid., vol. 3, p. 376.

37 This was first established by the Harvard Economist Alexander Gerschenkron in his *Economic Backwardness in Historical Perspective* (Cambridge, MA: Harvard University Press, 1962). It has continued in China; see Lin Yifu and Zhang Pengfei, 'Houfa Youshi, Jishu Yinjin He Luohou Guojiade Jingji Zengzhang' (The Advantage of Late Economic Developer, Technology Importation and Economic Growth in Less Developed Countries), *China Economic Quarterly*, 5/1 (2005): 55–74.

38 He Zhixing, 'Lun Wandao Chaoche Yu Houfa Youshi' (Overtaking the West by a Cut on a Bend with the Advantage of a Later Developer), *Jingjixue Jia* (*Economists*), 11/7 (2010): 22–7; Wang Yi, 'Zhuazhu Wandao Chaochede Lishi Jiyu' (Seize the Historical Opportunity to Overtake the West by a Cut on a Bend), 22 February 2016, *People's Daily*, http://www.casisd.cn/zkcg/zjsd/201706/t20170621_4816120.html; Yu Zujun, 'Wandao Chaoche Shixian Zhongguo Meng' (Overtaking the West by a Cut on a Bend to Realise the China Dream), *China's Urban Newspaper*, 4 July 2016, p. 4, http://paper.people.com.cn/zgcsb/html/2016-07/04/content_1693512.htm.

39 Lin and Zhang, 'Advantage of Late Economic Developer', p. 69.

40 Deng, *Selected Essays*, vol. 2, p. 133.

41 For crude GDP information, see Appendix 5, figure A–5.4.

42 More detail is available in Appendix 6, figures A–6.1 and A–6.2.

43 According to one snapshot of 1995–8, manufactures counted for 58.4–66.5 per cent of South Korea's total imports; minerals including fuels, 20.3–26.2 per cent; and food, 10–10.9 per cent. This is similar to Deng's China. See Oliver Morrissey and Dirk Willem te Velde, 'Trade, FDI and Equity in the Republic of Korea in the 1990s', p. 16, https://assets.publishing.service.gov.uk/media/57a08d3eed915d3cfd0018e6/R8003b.pdf&ved=2ahUKEwiRm_nU44ePAxWOaEEAHYHKCewQFnoECC0QAQ&usg=AOvVaw2A5yHDJkl42EZm6ksiEpUB.

44 Deng, *Selected Essays*, vol. 3, p. 119.

45 Ibid., vol. 3, p. 106.

46 Zhao Ziyang, 'Guanyu Zhiding Qiwu Jihua Jianyide Shuoming' (Elaboration on the Seventh Five-Year Plan Initiatives), 18 September 1985, https://www.gov.cn/gongbao/shuju/1985/gwyb198527.pdf.
47 See Deng, *Selected Essays*, vol. 3, pp. 133, 239.
48 For example, Zhu and Kotz, 'Dependence of China's Economic Growth'; Akyuz, 'Export Dependence'; Arora and Cardarell, *Rebalancing Growth*, ch. 4.
49 Dong He and Wenlang Zhang, 'How Dependent is the Chinese Economy on Exports and in What Sense Has Its Growth Been "Export-Led"?', *Journal of Asian Economics*, 21/1 (2010): 87–104.
50 Anon., 'Bayijian Chenshan Huan Yijia Kongke A380' (China's 800 Million Shirts Exchange for One A380 Passenger Jet), *Sina Net*, 9 May 2005, https://finance.sina.cn/sa/2005-05-09/detail-ikknscsi2145430.d.html.
51 In terms of research paper index, China overtook Italy in 2002, France in 2004, Germany and Japan in 2006, and Britain in 2007; see Jonathan Adams and Martin Szomszor, 'A Converging Global Research System', *Quantitative Science Studies*, 3/3 (2022): 726.
52 Hui-Zhen Fu and Yuh-Shan Ho, 'Independent Research of China in Science Citation Index Expanded during 1980–2011', *Journal of Informetrics*, 7/1 (2013): 213.
53 A technical illustration is available in Appendix 3, figure A–3.8.
54 For example, Robert E. Scott, 'Rising China Trade Deficit Will Cost One-Half Million U.S. Jobs in 2010', *Economic Policy Institute Briefing Paper No. 283*, 20 September 2010 (Washington, DC: Economic Policy Institute), https://www.epi.org/publication/ib283/; Thieß Petersen and Cora Jungbluth, 'Globalization among G7 Nations Has Faltered since 2000', *New Perspectives on Global & European Dynamics Paper*, 15 September 2016, https://globaleurope.eu/globalization/globalization-among-g7-nations-has-faltered-since-2000/; Jim O'Neill and Alessio Terzi, 'The G7 is Dead, Long Live the G7', *Bruegel*, 13 June 2018, https://www.bruegel.org/blog-post/g7-dead-long-live-g7; Kristina Morkunaite, 'A Secular Decline in Capital Productivity in G7 Countries', *Intereconomics*, 54/6 (2019): 385–90; Khuong Vu, Nobuya Haraguchi, and Juergen Amann, 'Deindustrialization in Developed Countries amid Accelerated Globalization: Patterns, Influencers, and Policy Insights', *Structural Change and Economic Dynamics*, 59/3 (2021): 454–69.
55 Scott, 'The China Trade Toll', pp. 1 and 6.
56 A technical illustration is available in Appendix 3, figure A–3.9.
57 Sutirthos Patranobis, 'First Survey on Natural Disaster Risks Shows China Has 600 Million Buildings', *Hindustan Times*, 25 February 2023, https://www.hindustantimes.com/world-news/first-survey-on-natural-disaster-risks-shows-china-has-600-million-buildings-101677239693131.html.
58 All economics textbooks view domestic savings as the main source of domestic investment.
59 Seehttps://www.bnpparibas-am.com/en-gb/esg-thematic-etfs/?utm_campaign=etf-010125-uk&utm_source=google&utm_medium=cpc&utm_content=text&gclsrc=aw.ds&gad_source=1&gad_campaignid=21357143753&gbraid=0AAAAA9kz2cAzOWZXEflvhR6XXktotiF-i&gclid=Cj0KCQjw_8rBBhCFARIsAJrc9yAxXveiSktzn6nBUTCkjy9Cjrl1xt0DE2I2e3uzQPbPZBevV5X39oEaAuDeEALw_wcB.

60 Andrew Cainey and Christiane Prange, *Xiconomics: What China's Dual Circulation Strategy Means for Global Business* (Rickmansworth: Agenda Publishing, 2023); Mandy Zuo, 'How China's "Dual Circulation" Drive Is Shaping Up – and What's Next', *South China Morning Post*, 26 June 2024, https://www.scmp.com/economy/china-economy/article/3267963/how-chinas-dual-circulation-drive-shaping-and-whats-next-agenda.

61 In G7, methods to reverse government financial burden are (1) privatisation of state-owned assets such as coal mines, railways, and residential buildings (as in the case of British Thatcherism), and (2) cutting back government overspending (as with 'DOGE' under the Trump Administration). Neither is available for the PRC.

62 Note here that household debts (such as mortgages and car loans) are excluded because they are based on private decisions and are no more than over-drafted family future incomes.

63 Stewart Paterson, *China, Trade and Power: Why the West's Economic Engagement Has Failed* (London: London Publishing Partnership, 2018); Lawrence J. Lau, *The China–U.S. Trade War and Their Future Economic Relations* (Hong Kong: Chinese University of Hong Kong Press, 2019); Guoyong Liang and Haoyuan Ding, *The China–US Trade War* (London: Routledge, 2011); Raj Bhala, *Trade War – Causes, Conduct, and Consequences of Sino–American Confrontation* (Durham, NC: Carolina Academic Press, 2024).

64 Walter F. Hatch, *Asia's Flying Geese, How Regionalization Shapes Japan* (Ithaca, NY: Cornell University Press, 2011).

65 For a comprehensive review, see Jost Wübbek, Mirjam Meissner, Max J. Zenglein, Jaquelline Ives, and Björn Conrad, 'Made in China 2025 – The Making of a High-Tech Superpower and Consequences for Industrial Countries', *MERICS Paper on China No. 2*, Mercator Institute for China Studies, 2016.

66 See, e.g., 'The East Rising and the West Declining', https://zh.wikipedia.org/wiki/%E6%9D%B1%E5%8D%87%E8%A5%BF%E9%99%8D; 'Warrior Wolf Diplomacy', https://zh.wikipedia.org/wiki/%E6%88%B0%E7%8B%BC%E5%A4%96%E4%BA%A4.

67 Bonnie S. Glaser, *Made in China 2025 and the Future of American Industry* (Washington, DC: Center for Strategic and International Studies (CSIS), 2022); Ali Iravanipour, *'Made in China 2025' Exploring Economic Impacts for German Original Equipment Manufacturers* (Munich: GRIN, 2025).

68 Shiping Hua, *The Political Logic of the US–China Trade War* (Lanham, MD: Lexington Books, 2022).

69 Barry Naughton, 'Understanding the Chinese Stimulus Package', unpublished paper, 2009, https://www.researchgate.net/publication/265565305_Understanding_the_Chinese_Stimulus_Package; Wenjun Xue, Hakan Yilmazkuday, and Jason E. Taylor, 'The Impact of China's Fiscal and Monetary Policy Responses to the Great Recession: An Analysis of Firm-Level Chinese Data', *Journal of International Money and Finance*, 101 (2020): 102113; Maho Shiraishi and Go Yano, 'The Financial Crisis in 2008, the Stimulus Package, and Distortion of Financial Intermediation in China: A Survival Analysis Approach', *Comparative Economic Studies*, 64/4 (2021): 280–323.

70 Short for 'Silk Road Economic Belt' over land and 'Maritime Silk Road' across sea. It boasts 149 member countries with 3,000 projects backed by a total investment of RMB 1 trillion; see 'Numerous Key Infrastructure Projects

Launched as Part of Belt and Road Initiative', *TV BRICS*, 24 October 2022, https://tvbrics.com/en/news/numerous-key-infrastructure-projects-launched-as-part-of-belt-and-road-initiative/.

71 IMF, 'World Economic Outlook' (Washington, DC: IMF, 2022), https://www.elibrary.imf.org/display/book/9781616359423/CH004.xml.

72 Anon., 'Recent trends in the international trade flows of G7 economies', 10 October 2022, https://www.ons.gov.uk/businessindustryandtrade/internationaltrade/articles/recenttrendsintheinternationaltradeflowsofg7economies/2022-10-10.

73 Crude data for G7 recovery are available in Appendix 5, table A–5.6.

74 For the United States' 'One Big Beautiful Bill Act', see Kevin Freking and Lisa Mascaro, 'Trump's "Beautiful" Bill Spans More Than 1,000 Pages, 21 May 2025, https://apnews.com/article/00ce1ff8a7b7fea7a894d38398748c6b; For the EU, see Eric Albert, 'Europe's Reindustrialization: A Challenging Work in Progress', 9 May 2024, https://www.lemonde.fr/en/economy/article/2024/05/09/europe-s-reindustrialization-a-challenging-work-in-progress_6670854_19.html.

75 China's producers' price indexes – 'Producers' Price Index' (30 items), 'Producers' Purchasing Price Index for Industrial Products' (15 items), 'Producers' Purchasing Price Index for Means of Production', and 'Producers' Price Index for Consumer Goods' – are all negative monthly in 2024; see National Bureau of Statistics, 'Producer Price Index in the Industrial Sector for December 2024', 10 January 2025, https://www.stats.gov.cn/english/PressRelease/202501/t20250114_1958198.html.

76 Junhua Zhang, 'China Trapped in a Cycle of Deflation', *GIS Reports*, 27 January 2025, https://www.gisreportsonline.com/r/china-deflation/; Fan Chen and Jane Cai, 'China's Consumer Prices Fall in April, Fuelling Fears of Deflation', *South China Morning Post*, 10 May 2025, https://www.scmp.com/economy/economic-indicators/article/3309834/chinas-consumer-prices-fall-april-fuelling-fears-deflation.

77 Zhao Jia, *China Daily*, 20 May 2022, https:/cn.chinadaily.com.cn/a/202205/20/WS6286fd61a3101c3ee7ad644c.html.

78 Department of Commerce, 'Commerce Implements New Export Controls on Advanced Computing and Semiconductor Manufacturing Items to the People's Republic of China (PRC)', 24 October 2022, https://www.bis.doc.gov/index.php/documents/about-bis/newsroom/press-releases/3158-2022-10-07-bis-press-release-advanced-computing-and-semiconductor-manufacturing-controls-final/file.

79 Anon., 'U.S. AI Chip Export Restrictions', https://www.cimphony.ai/insights/us-ai-chip-export-restrictions-impact-on-nvidia-amd; Chase D. Kaniecki, Ryan Brown, and Catherine Johnson, 'BIS Further Restricts Exports of Artificial Intelligence and Advanced Chips to China', 4 April 2025, https://www.clearytradewatch.com/2025/04/bis-further-restricts-exports-of-artificial-intelligence-and-advanced-chips-to-china/.

80 White House, 'Amendment to Reciprocal Tariffs and Updated Duties as Applied to Low-Value Imports from the People's Republic of China', 'Executive Order 14257', 8 April 2025, https://www.whitehouse.gov/presidential-actions/2025/04/amendment-to-recipricol-tariffs-and-updated-duties-as-applied-to-low-value-imports-from-the-peoples-republic-of-china/. A technical illustration is presented in Appendix 3, figure A–3.10.

81 Gary Gereffi, John Humphrey, and Timothy Sturgeon, 'The Governance of Global Value Chains', *Review of International Political Economy*, 12/1 (2005): 78–104. This new concept sounds very similar to 'supply chain', which is by definition a factory-level logistic management concept. See, e.g., Macharia Brown, 'SC 2020: Toyota Production System and Supply Chain', Dissertation of Master of Engineering, United States Military Academy, West Point, 2005, https://ctl.mit.edu/sites/default/files/Mac_TPS_thesis.pdf; Sitong Yang, 'Analysis for Supply Chain Management: Evidence from Toyota', *BCP Business and Management*, 34 (2022): 1204–9.
82 Jim H. Shen, Kent Deng, and Sarah Tang, 'Re-evaluating the "Smile Curve" in Relation to Outsourcing Industrialization', *Emerging Markets Finance and Trade*, 57/5 (2021): 1247–70.
83 World Trade Organisation, *Marrakesh Agreement Establishing the World Trade Organization (WTO Agreement)* (Cambridge: Cambridge University Press, 2017), vol. 1.
84 Dan Milmo, 'Trump Threatens 25% Tariff on Apple and Samsung Phones Not Made in US', *The Guardian*, 23 May 2025, https://www.theguardian.com/us-news/2025/may/23/donald-trump-threatens-25-percent-tariff-iphones-not-made-in-us.
85 Ha-Joon Chang, *Kicking Away the Ladder: Development Strategy in Historical Perspective* (London: Anthem Press, 2002).

Conclusion

1 Sheena C. Greitens, 'Rethinking China's Coercive Capacity: An Examination of PRC Domestic Security Spending, 1992–2012', *China Quarterly*, 232 (2017): 1002–25; Diana Fu and Greg Distelhorst, 'Grassroots Participation and Repression under Hu Jintao and Xi Jinping', *The China Journal*, 79 (2018): 100–22.
2 They have been 'Trans-Pacific Partnership' (TPP) of 12 member countries (2016) and its successor 'Comprehensive and Progressive Agreement for Trans-Pacific Partnership' (CPTPP) of also 12 member countries (as of 2023). In the case of CPTPP, China does not meet any of the membership prerequisites, regarding data freedom, labour rights, environmental standards, and deregulation of SOEs.

Appendix 2

1 Mainly Shandong, Hebei and Henan; see Buck, *Statistics*, p. 176.

Appendix 3

1 This is no doubt a Malthusian approach. It suits the current minimalistic, subsistence argument.
2 Numerous works on state capacity, e.g. North and Weingast, 'Constitutions and Commitment'; North, *Institutions, Institutional Change*; Soifer and Hau, 'Unpacking the Strength of the State'; Hendrix, 'Measuring State Capacity';

Fukuyama, 'What Is Governance?'; Hanson, 'Forging then Taming Leviathan'; Acemoglu, et al., 'State Capacity and Economic Development'; Acemoglu, et al., 'State Capacity and American Technology'; Andrews, et al., *Building State Capability*; Berwick and Christia, 'State Capacity Redux'; Cingolani, 'Role of State Capacity'; Khemani, 'What Is State Capacity?'.

3 It has been estimated that China exported 800 tonnes of silk textiles in the early seventeenth century in exchange for silver. See George Souza, *The Survival of the Empire: Portuguese Trade and Society in China and the South China Sea, 1630–1754* (Cambridge: Cambridge University Press, 1986), p. 46.

4 The concave shape of the curve is determined by 'Pareto efficiency'; see https://www.investopedia.com/terms/p/pareto-efficiency.asp.

5 In economics jargon, it is called 'a corner solution'.

6 Price elasticity of demand (PED) shows how sensitive market demand is to a price change. The formula: (% change in quantity of goods demanded) ÷ (% change in price of the same goods).

7 They include (1) 'home electronics for the countryside' (*jiadia xiaxiang*) from 2007 to 2013, https://zh.wikipedia.org/zh-hans/家電下鄉; (2) 'cars for the countryside' (*qiche xiaxiang*) in 2009, https://www.gov.cn/gongbao/content/2009/content_1456080.htm; (3) 'trading in old white goods' (*yijiu huanxin*) in 2024, https://cn.chinadaily.com.cn/a/202403/04/WS65e53632a3109f7860dd3c92.html; (4) 'buying urban houses to get urban residence' (*maifang song hukou*) in 2024, https://finance.sina.com.cn/roll/2024-06-30/doc-incanfxu4448128.shtml.

Appendix 4

1 Liu Fengyun, 'Yanglianyin Wuyi Yanglian' (How Honesty and Uprightness Bonuses Did Not Support Honesty and Uprightness), *Shixue Yuekan* (*Historic Study Monthly*), 11 (2020): 28–43; Liu Fengyun, 'You Qiangliang Kuikong Kan Kang-Yong-Qian Shiqi Canzheng Zhidu Chuangli de Yinguo Guanxi' (Causal Factors in the Qing Financial Institution Seen from Revenue Deficits in 1662–1795), *Mingqing Yanjiu* (*Study of Ming-Qing History*), 1 (2022): 41–58.

2 He Yongzhi, 'Qingdai Hubu Fanyin Yu Jingguan Yanglianyin Zhidu Shanbian' (Per Diem Subsidies from the Ministry of Revenue and the Evolution of Honesty and Uprightness Bonuses for Officials Working for the Central Administration), *Zhongguoshi Yanjiu* (*Study of China's History*), 2 (2023): 185–203.

Appendix 5

1 For example, Chen et al., 'Forensic Examination'.

2 Koch-Weser, 'Reliability of China's Economic Data', p. 16.

3 Ibid., p. 36.

4 Caution is required here. It is almost certain that the total GDP for this sector was inflated, which was easy to do. Also, the authorities had strong incentives to inflate GDP. Besides, there has been no independent auditing in China so far. In comparison, workers' numbers are less likely to be fabricated.

5 For recent studies, see Xi Lu, Shaojun Zhang, Jia Xing, et al., 'Progress on Air Pollution Control in China and Its Challenge in the Ecological Civilization Era', *Engineering*, 6/12 (2020): 1423–31; Chi Li, Melanie S. Hammer, Bo Zheng, and Ronald C. Cohen, 'Accelerated Reduction of Air Pollutants in China, 2017–2020', *Science of the Total Environment*, 803 (2022): 150011.

FIGURE SOURCES

Figure 1.1: Zhang Tingyu, *Ming Shi* (*The History of the Ming Dynasty*), vol. 32 'Li Zhi', in *Er-shi-wu Shi* (*Twenty-Five Official Histories*) (Shanghai: Shanghai Classics Press, 1986), vol. 10, p. 7849.

Figure 1.2: Based on Li Longsheng, 'Qingdai (1645–1911) Meinian Liuru Zhongguo Baiyin Shuliangde Chubu Guji' (Estimation of the Annual Inflow of Silver to China during the Qing Period, 1645–1911), *Renwen Ji Shehui Kexue Qikan* (*Journal of Humanities and Social Sciences*), 5/2 (2009): 45–56. To take China's silver intake from Japan prior to the Manilla Galleon Trade, see Kishimoto Mio, 'The Edo Period as China's Silver Sink: The Silver Trade and China's Economy', *International Journal of Asian Studies*, 4/1 (2007): 85–112; Kent Deng, 'Miracle or Mirage? Foreign Silver, China's Economy and Globalisation of the Sixteenth to Nineteenth Centuries', *Pacific Economic Review*, 13/3 (2008): 320–57.

Figure 1.3: Qian Jiang, 'Shiliu – Shiba Shiji Guojijian Baiyin Liudong Jiqi Shuru Zhongguozhi Kaocha' (International Silver Flux and Silver Imports by China), *Nanyang Wenti Yanjiu* (*Study of Southeast Asia*), 2 (1988): 81–91.

Figure 1.4: Cao Shuji, *Zhongguo Renkou Shi* (*A Demographic History of China*) (Shanghai: Fudan University Press, 2000), vol. 5, p. 704. Farmland, based on Liang, *Dynastic Data*, pp. 10, 380, 384, 396, 400, 401.

Figure 1.5: (1) Silver imports; Li, 'Annual Inflow of Silver', 31–58; see Alejandra Irigoin, 'The End of a Silver Era: The Consequences of the Breakdown of the Spanish Peso Standard in China and the United States, 1780s–1850s', *Journal of World History*, 20/2 (2009): 211. (2) Treasury's silver stock; see Lu Jian, 'Kang Yong Qian Hubu Yiku Linian Cunyin Shu' (Annual Silver Stock Held by Ministry of Revenue during 1667 to 1774), *Lishi Dang-an* (*Historical Archives*), no. 4 (1984): 19–21.

Figure 1.6: John L. Buck, *Land Utilization in China, Atlas* (London: Oxford University Press, 1937), p. 9.

Figure 1.7: Buck, *Statistics*, pp. 289–91.

Figure 1.8: (1) Bronze coins/silver tael, silver imports; see Li, 'Annual Inflow of Silver'; Yu Yaohua, *Zhongguo Jiage Shi* (*A History of Prices in China*) (Beijing: China's Price Press, 2000), pp. 857–62. (2) Silver imports; Li, 'Annual Inflow of Silver'.

Figure 1.9: The benchmark is based on Albert Feuerwerker, 'The State and the Economy in Late Imperial China', *Theory and Society*, 13/3 (1984): 297–326; Liu Ti, '1600–1840 Nian Zhongguo Guonei Shengchan Zongzhide Gusuan' (Estimation of China's GDP between 1600 and 1840), *Jingji Yanjiu* (*Economic Study*), 10 (2009): 144–55. The actual growth is based on Liu Foding and Wang Yuru, *Zhongguo Jindaide Shichang Fayu Yu Jingji Zengzhang* (*Market Development and Economic Growth in Early Modern China*) (Beijing: Tertiary Education Press, 1996), p. 44; Liu Foding, Wang Yuru and Zhao Jin, *Zhongguo Jindai Jingji Fazhan Shi* (*A History of Economic Development in Early Modern China*) (Beijing: Tertiary Education Press, 1999), p. 66; National Bureau of Statistics, *Zhongguo Laodong Tongji Nianjian, 2002* (*China's Statistical Year Book, 2002*) (Beijing: China's Statistics Press, 2002), p. 51.

Figure 2.1: Yi Xin and Zhu Xueqin, *Qinding Pingding Guizhou Miaofei Fanglue* (*Strategies and Tactics to Suppress Miao Bandits in Guizhou, Made by Imperial Order*) (1896. Reprint, Taipei: Chengwen Press, 1968), vols 1–40; Yi Xin and Zhu Xueqin, *Qinding Pingding Shaangan Xinjiang Huifei Fanglue* (*Strategies and Tactics to Suppress the Muslim Bandits in Shaanxi, Gansu and Xinjiang, Made by Imperial Order*) (1896, reprint, Lanzhou: Lanzhou Classics Replica Press, 1990), vols 1–320; Yi Xin and Zhu Xueqin, *Qinding Pingding Yunnan Huifei Fanglue* (*Strategies and Tactics to Suppress the Muslim Bandits in Yunnan, Made by Imperial Order*) (1896. Reprint, Taipei: Chengwen Press, 1968), vols 1–50; Yi Xin and Zhu Xueqin, *Qinding Pingding Yuefei Fanglue* (*Strategies and Tactics to Suppress Guangdong Taiping Bandits, Made by Imperial Order*) (1896. Reprint, Taipei: Wenyuan Press, 1965), vols 1–420. See also F.H. Michael (ed.), *The Taiping Rebellion, History and Documents* (Seattle: University of Washington Press, 1966–71), vol. 1, p. 216; John K. Fairbank and Kwang-ching Liu (eds), *The Cambridge History of China, Late Ch'ing, 1800–1911* (Cambridge: Cambridge University Press, 1980), vol. 11, pt. 2, p. 216; Jonathan D. Spence, *The Search for Modern China* (New York: W.W. Norton, 1999), p. 187. Additionally, see Li Guangbi, Qian Junye, and Lai Xinxia, *Zhongguo Nongmin Qiyi Lunji* (*On Chinese Peasant Rebellions*) (Beijing: Sanlian Books, 1958); Zhang Shaoliang and Zheng Xianjin, *Zhongguo Nongmin Geming Douzhengshi* (*A History of Revolutionary Struggle of the Chinese Peasantry*) (Beijing: Qiushi Press, 1983); D.G. Atwill, *The Chinese Sultanate: Islam, Ethnicity and the Panthay Rebellion in Southwest China, 1856–1873* (Stanford: Stanford University Press, 2006).

Figure 2.2: (1) Disasters: Chen Gaoyong, *Zhongguo Lidai Tianzai Renhuo Bian* (*Chronological Tables of Natural and Man-made Disasters in China*) (Shanghai: Jinan University Press, 1937); (2) Disaster relief: Data for Qing disaster relief are from Zhao, *Drafted History*, vols 4–25, 'Biographies of the Qing Emperors', and vols 54–81, 'Administrative Geography', in *Twenty-Five Official Histories*, vol. 11, pp. 8827–8937, 9071–9131.

Figure 2.3: National Bureau of Statistics, *Statistical Year Book, 2021*, ch. 4.

Figure 2.4: See table 2.15.

Figure 2.5: Ansley J. Coale, *Rapid Population Change in China, 1952–1982* (Washington, DC: National Academy Press, 1984), p. 47; Yuan Yongxi, *Zhongguo Renko (Zonglun)* (*China's Demography [Overview]*) (Beijing: China's Finance and Economy Press, 1991), p. 126.

Figure 2.6: (1) Population data, based on National Bureau of Statistics, *Statistical Year Book*, ch. 2. (2) Private household savings, based on National Bureau of Statistics, *Statistical Year Book, 2008*, ch. 9; *Statistical Year Book, 2013*, ch. 11; *Statistical Year Book, 2014*, ch. 19; *Statistical Year Book, 2018*, ch. 18; *Statistical Year Book, 2024*, ch. 18.

Figure 3.1: National Bureau of Statistics, *Statistical Year Books, 2004–2013*, chs 20 and 21.

Figure 3.2: National Bureau of Statistics, *Statistical Year Books, 2001–21*, chs 5, 6, and 10.

Figure 3.3: National Bureau of Statistics, *Statistical Year Book, 2001*, ch. 12; *Statistical Year Book, 2008*, ch. 12; *Statistical Year Book, 2024*, ch. 2.

Figure 3.4: National Bureau of Statistics, *Statistical Year Books, 2000, 2003, 2015, and 2024*, ch. 13.

Figure 3.5: Data for GDP for 1980 to 2000, see National Bureau of Statistics, *Statistical Year Book, 2021*, chs 2 and 3.

Figure 3.6: National Bureau of Statistics, *Statistical Year Book, 2012*, ch. 10.

Figure 3.7: National Bureau of Statistics, *Statistical Year Book, 2003*, ch. 3.

Figure 3.8: National Bureau of Statistics, *Statistical Year Book, 2011*, ch. 3.

Figure 3.9: National Bureau of Statistics, *Statistical Year Book, 2024*, ch. 11.

Figure 3.10: National Bureau of Statistics, *Statistical Year Books, 2001–21*, chs 5, 6, and 10.

Figure 4.1: National Bureau of Statistics, *Statistical Year Book, 1999*, ch. 8; *Statistical Year Book, 2001*, chs 3 and 8; *Statistical Year Book, 2021*, chs 3 and 7; *Statistical Year Book, 2021*, ch. 7.

Figure 4.2: National Bureau of Statistics, *Statistical Year Book, 2023*, ch. 19.

Figure 4.3: National Bureau of Statistics, *Statistical Year Books, 1999–2001*, ch. 14; *Statistical Year Book, 2005*, ch. 15; *Statistical Year Books, 2008–9*, ch. 14; *Statistical Year Books, 2010–11*, ch. 15; *Statistical Year Book, 2014*, ch. 15; *Statistical Year Book, 2020*, ch. 19; *Statistical Year Book, 2023*, ch. 14.

Figure 4.4: National Bureau of Statistics, *Statistical Year Book, 2001*, ch. 4; *Statistical Year Book, 2006*, ch. 8; *Statistical Year Book, 2007*, chs 4 and 8.

Figure 4.5: National Bureau of Statistics, *Statistical Year Book, 2024*, ch. 11; Anon., 'Dollar Yuan Exchange Rate – 35 Year Historical Chart', https://www.macrotrends.net/2575/us-dollar-yuan-exchange-rate-historical-chart.

Figure 4.6: National Bureau of Statistics, *Statistical Year Book, 2024*, ch. 11.

Figure 4.7: National Bureau of Statistics, *Statistical Year Book, 2012*, ch. 6; *Statistical Year Book, 2024*, chs 11, 18.

Figure 4.8: National Bureau of Statistics, *Statistical Year Book, 2012*, ch. 6; *Statistical Year Book, 2024*, chs 11 and 18.

Figure 4.10: Qin et al., 'Analysis of Changes in Water Quality'.

Figure 4.11: Hannah Ritchie, Max Roser, and Pablo Rosado, 'CO_2 and Greenhouse Gas Emissions', *OurWorldinData.org* (2020), https://ourworldindata.org/co2-and-greenhouse-gas-emissions; National Bureau of Statistics, *Statistical Year Book, 2023*, ch. 2.

Figure 4.12: (1) 1980–2000: He Zengke, *Fan Fu Xin Lu* (*New Path to Combat Corruption*) (Beijing: Central Compilation and Translation Press, 2002), p. 229. (2) After 2000: 'Annual Bulletins of the Supreme People's Court of PRC', https://www.spp.gov.cn/spp/gzbg/200602/t20060222_16381.shtml; https://www.spp.gov.cn/spp/gzbg/200602/t20060222_16397.shtml; http://gongbao.court.gov.cn/Details/2a5153c1cd3d120fe8b64b8f86cf49.html; http://gongbao.court.gov.cn/Details/d89cbf4c890f108b76eb94fd3d024c.html; http://gongbao.court.gov.cn/Details/9f473f0c3f798273294b8877ad5c6e.html; http://gongbao.court.gov.cn/Details/09d347f9fc0792c975dca381f23396.html; http://gongbao.court.gov.cn/Details/418cef91a5d2eadae75be8b42a274b.html; http://gongbao.court.gov.cn/Details/1fdb8e0f028681071deb95e408248b.html; http://gongbao.court.gov.cn/Details/1387a39eb10a886fc87cafaa8ab26f.html; http://gongbao.court.gov.cn/Details/ff04437c0ee2798097031c34314d07.html; http://gongbao.court.gov.cn/Details/3a82b22d6c8acbf96732d4e61e2a3c.html; http://gongbao.court.gov.cn/Details/a870810bf0c5835ba4f08b1ae3dfef.html; http://gongbao.court.gov.cn/Details/845e61faec8aaf0fa47ac8247ab80a.html; http://gongbao.court.gov.cn/Details/7ba6d177431a690096341e4fd5e527.html; http://gongbao.court.gov.cn/Details/0991c1055c4811d3c927d1ce0dfe57.html; http://gongbao.court.gov.cn/Details/27e1cd92304feeeffd132e8244441a.html; http://gongbao.court.gov.cn/Details/faccf2e3c1216069f9c87cd2dc535d.html; http://gongbao.court.gov.cn/Details/c15ac3fd6bd534567eec8e047941eb.html; http://gongbao.court.gov.cn/Details/c70030ba6761ec165c3c2f0bd2a12b.html; http://gongbao.court.gov.cn/Details/fcadfe71e8d5a54acd8f840f768e65.html; http://gongbao.court.gov.cn/Details/0bce90201fd48b967ac863bd29059b.html; http://gongbao.court.gov.cn/Details/a6c42e26948d3545aea5419fa2beaa.html; http://gongbao.court.gov.cn/Details/20587eaef248beb61ed6596018865c.html; http://gongbao.court.gov.cn/Details/a3e86176b272dc94a05d9cb012c2d5.html.

Figure 4.13: He, *To Combat Corruption*, p. 52.

Figure 4.14: 'Transparency International', https://www.transparency.org/en/cpi/2024.

Figure 5.1: (1) Top ten producers of silicon: https://en.wikipedia.org/wiki/List_of_countries_by_silicon_production; (2) top ten cement producers, https://worldpopulationreview.com/country-rankings/cement-production-by-country; (3) top ten producers of rare earths, https://www.nasdaq.com/articles/top-11-countries-rare-earth-metal-production-updated-2024; (4) top ten producers of steel, https://www.worldsteel.org/; (5) top ten builders of high-speed railway tracks, https://uic.org/IMG/pdf/20231001_high_speed_lines_in_the_world.pdf; (6) top ten producers of coal, https://www.iea.org/reports/coal-market-update-july-2023/supply; (7) top ten exporters of toys, games, and sports accessories, https://www.worldstopexports.com/top-toys-exporters-for-traditional-toys-versus-video-games/; (8) top ten exporters of solar panels, https://

www.worldstopexports.com/best-solar-wind-exporters-powering-international-energy-sales/; (9) top ten exporters of textiles, https://worldpopulationreview.com/country-rankings/textile-exports-by-country; (10) top ten mineral importers (excluding mineral fertilisers), https://wits.worldbank.org/trade/comtrade/en/country/ALL/year/2023/tradeflow/Imports/partner/WLD/product/253090; (11) top ten most populous countries, World Bank, 'Population 2022', https://databankfiles.worldbank.org/public/ddpext_download/POP.pdf.

Figure 5.2: National Bureau of Statistics, *Statistical Year Books, 1999–2007, 2010–12*, ch. 11; *Statistical Year Books, 2008–2009*, ch. 10; *Statistical Year Book, 2012*, ch. 4.

Figure 5.3: National Bureau of Statistics, *Statistical Year Books, 2004–2008, 2010–12*, ch. 14; *Statistical Year Books, 2001–2003, 2009*, ch. 13.

Figure 5.4: https://www.statista.com/statistics/1025570/china-footwear-export-volume/.

Figure 5.5: (1) Total GDP, National Bureau of Statistics, *Statistical Year Book, 2024*, chs 2 and 3; (2) Urban wages of the private sector, National Bureau of Statistics, *Statistical Year Book, 2003*, ch. 5; *Statistical Year Book, 2009*, ch. 4; *Statistical Year Book, 2024*, ch. 4.

Figure 5.6: (1) Total GDP and urban wages of the private sector are the same as in figure 5.5. (2) RMB–US$ exchange rates, see National Bureau of Statistics, *Statistical Year Book, 2024*, ch. 11; Anon., 'Dollar Yuan Exchange Rate'.

Figure 5.7: (1) Total GDP and urban wages of the private sector are the same as in figure 5.5. (2) RMB–US$ exchange rates, see National Bureau of Statistics, *Statistical Year Book, 2024*, ch. 11; Anon., 'Dollar Yuan Exchange Rate'. (3) 996 Regime, https://996.icu/#/zh_CN.

Figure 5.8: 'China Labour Bulletin Strike Map Data Analysis', 29 January, 2025, https://clb.org.hk/en/content/china-labour-bulletin-strike-map-data-analysis-2024-year-review-workers%E2%80%99-rights.

Figure 5.9: Anon., 'International Trade of Communist China, 1950–65', CIA, 21 October, 1966, Approved For Release 2001/04/30: CIA-RDP79T01049A003300110001-2, p. 58, https://www.cia.gov/readingroom/docs/CIA-RDP79T01049A003300110001-2.pdf.

Figure 5.10: https://www.statista.com/statistics/873128/china-integrated-circuit-import-value/.

Figure 5.11: United States Census, 'Trade in Goods with China', https://www.census.gov/foreign-trade/balance/c5700.html.

Figure 5.12: See Appendix 7.

Figure 5.15: (1) Annual completed construction floor area, see National Bureau of Statistics, *Statistical Year Books, 1998–2002*, ch. 14; *Statistical Year Books, 2003–2006*, ch. 15; *Statistical Year Books, 2007–2009*, ch. 14; *Statistical Year Books, 2010–2012*, ch. 15; *Statistical Year Books, 2013–2024*, ch. 14. (2) Fast rail rack length, based on 'High-speed rail in China', https://en.wikipedia.org/wiki/High-speed_rail_in_China.

Figure 5.16: FRED, 'General government gross debt for China', https://fred.stlouisfed.org/series/GGGDTACNA188N; National Bureau of Statistics, *China's Statistical Year Book, 2024*, ch. 3.

Figure A–1.1: Population figures are based on Cao, *Demographic History*, vols 3–6. Land areas are based on Tan Qixiang, *Zhongguo Lishi Ditu Ji* (*Collected Maps of China's Past*) (Beijing: China's Map Press, 1982), vols 6–8.

Figure A–1.2: See figure A–1.1.

Figure A–1.3: See figure A–1.1.

Figure A–1.4: See figure A–1.1.

Figure A–1.5: See figure A–1.1.

Figure A–1.6: See figure A–1.1.

Figure A–2.1: Buck, *Statistics*, pp. 349–50; Yan Zhongping, *Zhongguo Mianfangzhi Shigao* (*Drafted History of Cotton Textiles in China*) (Beijing: Science Press, 1963), ch. 8 (Appendix); Fan Shuzhi, 'Suzhou Songjiang Mianbuye Shizhende Xingshuai' (Ups and Downs of Local Cotton Towns in Suzhou), *Zhongguo Jingjishi Yanjiu* (*Study of China's Economic History*), 4 (1984): 57–72; Wu Chengming, *Zhongguo Zibenzhuyi Yu Guonei Shichang* (*Capitalism and Domestic Market in China*) (Beijing: Social Science Press, 1985), pp. 25, 253–64; Xu Dixin and Wu Chengming, *Zhongguo Zibenzhuyide Mengya* (*Budding Capitalism in China*) (Beijing: People's Press, 1985), vol. 1, pp. 282–4, 318–29; Zhang Zhongmin, 'Yapian Zhanzhengqian Shanghai Diqu Mian Bu Chanliang Guji' (Estimation of Cotton Wool and Cotton Cloth Outputs in Shanghai prior to the Opium War), *Shanghai Jingji Yanjiu* (*Shanghai Economic Review*), 4 (1987): 66–8. Li Bozhong, *Jiangnande Zaoqi Gongyehua* (*Early Industrialisation in the Lower Yangzi*) (Beijing: Economic Literature Press, 2000), chs 3 and 8.

Figure A–5.1: National Bureau of Statistics, *Statistical Year Book, 2012*, chs 2 and 3.

Figure A–5.2: National Bureau of Statistics, *Statistical Year Book, 2021*, chs 3 and 4.

Figure A–5.3: National Bureau of Statistics, *Statistical Year Book, 1999*, ch. 8; *China's Statistical Year Book, 2001*, ch. 8; *China's Statistical Year Book, 2021*, chs 3 and 7.

Figure A–5.4: 'World Bank National Accounts Data', https://data.worldbank.org/indicator/NE.EXP.GNFS.ZS?locations=CN.

Figure A–5.5: National Bureau of Statistics, *Statistical Year Book, 2023*, chs 2 and 3; Hannah Ritchie, Max Roser, and Pablo Rosado, 'CO_2 and Greenhouse Gas Emissions', *OurWorldinData.org* (2020), https://ourworldindata.org/co2-and-greenhouse-gas-emissions.

Figure A–6.1: https://tradingeconomics.com/china/imports/united-states.

Figure A–6.2: https://www.statista.com/statistics/873128/china-integrated-circuit-import-value/.

INDEX

5G technology, 168, 173
996 Regime, 148–9, 177
1911 Revolution, 32–3

absolute advantage, 128, 142, 144–6, 151, 159–60, 168, 172–3
AI technology, 139
anti-corruption, 134–6
anti-rightists, 51, 74, 81
arbitrage, 14, 94, 118–19, 131, 173
armies, 2, 20, 33, 38, 41, 43, 45, 47, 50–2, 56, 65, 80, 145, 189, 195
Asian Tigers, 136, 152
autarky, 59, 70, 105, 139, 142, 169, 176

Bacon, Frances, 81
barrel-of-a-gun doctrine, 44, 46, 50, 79
Beijing, 11–13, 23, 32, 34–5, 38–9, 42, 65, 71, 111, 134, 183, 196
  Consensus, 138
Belt and Road scheme, 138, 169, 178
birth control policies, 2, 66
  rates, 66, 68
block-to-block trade, 171–2
bonuses, 38–9, 195–6
bourgeoisie, 50, 72, 93, 111, 117
BRICS, 171
Britain (including UK), 27, 45, 54, 170, 203, 206
budgeting and budgets, 83, 96, 104, 151, 164, 177, 193
bureaucracy, 2, 37–8, 42
bureaucrats, 38–40, 42, 147
capital accumulation, 67, 92, 94
  deadweight, 70
  formation, 68, 70, 119
  intensiveness, 142, 162, 164
  investment, 68, 70, 96–8, 102, 106, 142, 164
  productivity, 71
capitalism, 69, 72, 80, 111, 138, 151
cash crops, 74–5
catching-up growth, 155, 159, 176
Catholic Church, 9–10
CCP, 9, 72, 79–80, 94, 107, 111, 135, 150–1, 176–7
Chayanov, theory of, 72, 145
Chiang Kai-shek, 45, 47–8, 53–4
choices, 46–7, 49, 74–5, 86, 110, 150
civil wars, 30, 71, 80
civilians, 41–2, 71, 80
class struggle, 49, 52, 72, 81–2
collectivisation, 56, 73–4, 134
colonies, 9–10
Comintern, 48–9, 52–3
communism, 32–3, 47–9, 53, 55, 57, 74–6, 78, 80–1, 87, 117, 150–2, 174–5
communists, 45, 48, 52–5, 80, 111
comparative advantage, 138
compulsory currency conversion, 15, 122
Confucianism, 40, 42, 113, 137–8
constitutions, 79, 82, 117–18
constructions, 11–13, 70, 85, 90, 100, 113–16, 118, 142, 146–50, 165–6

consumer goods, 55, 83, 88–90, 95, 100, 115, 153, 155–6, 160–2, 164–5, 167, 189, 193–4
consumers, 21, 113–14, 159, 177
corner solution, 189
corruption, 127, 129–37, 191, 195
Covid-19, 166, 169–71, 173–4, 177, 206
CPTPP, 169
crises, 19, 33, 96, 107, 151, 163, 169, 177
cropping systems, 21–2, 26
crops, 20–2, 58, 74–5
  see also New World crops
Cultural Revolution, 49–51, 59, 69, 78–81

de-ruralisation, 103–4
debts, 88, 117, 124, 131, 167, 203
decoupling, 170, 173
defence, 1, 3, 12, 63, 151, 177, 211
deflation, 170, 193
demand-driven growth, 85
democracy, 6, 47–8, 80, 110–11, 134, 137, 177–8
  see also elections, and May Fourth Movement
demography, 1, 18, 23, 29, 37, 100, 179, 181, 184
Deng Xiaoping, 2–3, 51, 72, 74, 79–83, 88, 92, 96–7, 100, 102, 104, 109, 112–13, 129, 142, 151, 155, 157, 159, 176, 200
dictatorship, 3, 48, 50, 52, 73, 109, 149, 176
diplomacy, 1, 8, 13, 32, 78, 168, 175
disaster relief, 33–4
  see also famine relief
distortion, 119, 193
division of labour, 27, 139, 175

East India Company, 7, 19
economic development, 172
  performance, 11, 30–1, 38, 57, 68, 70, 97–8, 100, 147, 151, 158, 162, 175, 209–12
  planning, 55–6, 63–4, 77, 91, 162–3
    see also five-year plans
  reforms, 3, 5, 42, 61–2, 79, 81–2, 87–8, 95–7, 100, 102, 104–5, 109–13, 118, 125, 127–9, 146, 151, 157, 162, 189
  returns, 78, 132, 164, 200
economics, 5, 7, 20, 91, 93, 150
efficiency, 63–4, 68, 78, 112, 128, 139, 150, 171, 185, 200–1, 205
elasticity, 88, 98, 159, 190, 193–4
elections, 42, 111–12
emperors, 2, 11–12, 40–2, 47
employment, 16, 23, 52, 58–9, 61, 63, 68, 90–2, 103, 156, 164, 172–3
encircling cities, tactic of, 46, 49, 88
energy, 20, 65, 75, 83, 88, 99, 128, 205
Engel coefficients, 89, 101–2
entrepreneurship, 93–4
environment, 127–8, 136, 138, 172–3, 177, 211
EOI, 92, 107, 143–5, 157
ethnicity, 33, 39–40, 107
EU, 105, 174, 178, 207–8
Europe, 1, 3, 8–10, 15, 48, 55, 62, 72, 78, 80, 88, 119–20, 175
exchange rates, 14, 28, 67, 121, 130, 134, 146–8, 158, 177, 190
exports, 3–4, 13, 23–7, 90, 92, 104–8, 120–2, 124, 126, 140–3, 145, 151–4, 156–8, 160–4, 167, 169–71, 173–8, 185–6, 190
externalities, 126–7, 129, 136, 173, 191

famine relief, 35–6
famines, 5, 20, 36, 39, 41, 58, 63–4, 66, 76, 81, 91, 95, 142, 151, 175, 187–8, 196
farmers, 16, 22, 64, 67, 74, 76, 86, 89, 92, 94
farming sector, 29, 59
farmland, 15–20, 22, 24, 52, 56–8, 76, 117–18
FDI, 104, 106–8, 122–7, 144–6, 163
feudalism, 2, 7, 41
five-year plans, 56, 159, 162, 209
food shortages, 58, 61, 75
foreign collaborators, 9, 45, 80, 140
  invasions, 53
  radios, 79
  reserves, 75, 99, 121–6
  sponsors, 45
  trade, 62, 83, 104–6, 121–2, 125, 146,

151, 154, 156, 162–3, 169, 174, 184, 209–12
France, 3, 54, 79–80, 170, 176, 203, 206
free-riding, 75, 172
frontiers, 17, 53, 74
furnaces, traditional, 58, 64, 76, 187

G7, 138, 156, 159, 162, 167–71, 174, 178
GDP, 4, 24, 29, 32, 48, 57, 64, 66, 68–70, 82, 87–8, 90–2, 94, 98–102, 105, 107–8, 112–13, 127, 131, 134, 138–9, 141, 146–7, 149–52, 159, 167, 170, 177, 188–9, 197–206
  fallacy of, 5, 59
Germany, 45, 55, 106, 170, 206
globalisation, 3, 168–9
granaries, 35–8, 77
Great Leap Forward, 58, 63–4, 66, 76, 81, 187–8
Great Wall, 11–12, 15, 23, 71
growth limits, 5–6, 61, 158, 165, 168, 174
  rates, 8, 30, 37, 57, 102, 113, 150
  trajectories, 1, 4, 11, 27, 29–30, 33, 39, 47, 59, 61–2, 125, 174–5

heavy industry, 55, 70, 77–8, 88–9, 95, 164–5
higher education (including tertiary education), 82, 84–5, 100, 104, 127, 162
Hong Kong, 9, 51, 74, 106, 136
housing market, 113–16, 118, 120, 126, 162, 164–6, 202
  prices, 114–16, 120, 126, 162, 164, 166, 202
human capital, 82, 85, 100

ideology, 32, 48, 81–2, 112, 138, 175, 203
Imperial Examinations, 2, 40, 42, 84
import dependency, 153–7, 160, 162–3, 167, 174, 204, 207–8
import-export combo, 3, 6, 13, 151–3, 159, 162–3, 168, 171, 174, 176–8
import goods, 55, 62, 70, 87, 141, 152–5, 157–8, 160, 168, 174, 176, 197–8, 204, 207–8
  silver, 11, 13–16, 19, 28, 185–6
incentives, 11, 64, 68, 75, 78, 86, 90, 109, 126, 132, 134, 164
India, 8, 14, 27, 173–4, 178
industrial workforce, 52, 58–9, 63–4, 71, 91–2, 94–5
industrialisation, 3–4, 23, 56–9, 61, 63–4, 87, 90, 92, 107, 143, 145, 152, 160, 170
inefficiency, 70, 87–8, 168, 189
inelasticity, 101, 161
inflation, 28, 60, 96, 124–5
internal security, 41, 77, 168, 177
investment bias, 77, 91
IOI, 3–4, 56, 107, 145, 152

Japan, 7, 13–14, 23, 25–6, 45, 47, 52, 105–6, 136, 155, 170, 174, 178, 203, 206
Jesuits, 8–10, 13
Jiang Zemin, 95, 112, 132

knowledge transfer, 8–10, 110
Korean War, 55, 58

labour inputs, 58, 99
  intensiveness, 21, 99, 164, 196
  market, 59, 63, 90, 146, 170–1
  productivity, 29, 59, 76, 86, 91
land input, *see* farmland
  ownership, 86, 113, 117
  productivity, 29
landholding, 24, 53, 86, 100, 109, 117
landlords, 50, 93
leadership, 50, 52, 78, 81, 93, 100, 107, 130, 132, 149, 156, 177
Lenin, 46, 79, 109, 152, 176
Leninism (including Bolshevism), 9, 46–8, 80, 149
Lin Biao, 78
literati, 8, 42
Little Ice Age, 2, 33, 35, 42, 45
Liu Shaoqi, 72, 80
living standards, 23, 78, 83, 97–8, 109, 152, 168, 172–3
losses, 37, 129, 131, 148, 161, 174, 178, 187, 193–4

Macao, 8–10, 32, 106
majority, 24, 67, 73, 93, 95, 112, 137, 143

Manchuria, 16–18, 54, 181
Manchus, 12, 39–41, 195
Manilla Galleon Trade, 10, 13–14
manufacturing, 1, 3, 5–6, 8, 24, 26, 56, 60, 82–3, 85, 88–92, 95, 105–6, 115, 119, 137, 139, 142, 146–50, 161–2, 164–5, 167–9, 175–8, 183–6, 189, 193, 207–8
Mao Zedong, 2–3, 5, 44–59, 63–8, 70–2, 75–84, 86–7, 93, 95, 100, 109, 112, 117, 142, 152, 154, 175–7, 187
  legacy, 63, 68–9, 71
  victims, 50–1, 58, 82, 86, 188
  victim reinstatements, 82, 86
Maoism, 5, 11, 23, 31, 42, 57, 64, 73, 78, 81, 83, 86, 88, 96, 100, 102, 110, 112, 175
maritime bans, 7–8, 39, 56
  legacy, 63, 68–9, 71
market economy, 3, 18, 29, 112, 126, 129, 150, 178
  equilibrium, 124, 194
  expansion, 146, 190
Marx, Karl, 48, 72, 95
Marxism, 46–7, 72, 75, 95, 109, 149, 174
May Fourth Movement, 32, 48, 112
media, 93, 147, 167
meritocracy, 3, 42, 82, 112
migrants, 17, 61
migration, 16–18, 57, 68, 102
military (including troops), 2, 33, 38–40, 42–4, 46–8, 50, 52–5, 63, 70–1, 78, 80, 151, 177
militocrats, 2, 42, 44–5, 47–8, 50, 52, 175
Ming armada, 12, 23, 71
  emperors, 11–12
modernisations, 80–1, 92, 99, 138, 153–4, 168, 176
  see also Westernisation Movement
modernity, 31, 64, 80, 161, 168, 176
monopoly, 70, 88–9, 114, 119
moral economy, 39, 50, 52
mortgages, 113, 117–18, 124, 133, 150
Moscow, 48–9, 52, 72, 79–80
  Moscovians, 80
  see also Comintern
national economy, 95, 100, 117, 119, 199, 204
National People's Congress, 80–1, 94–5
nationalisation, 56, 118, 134
nationalists, 52, 55
New Cultural Movement, 32–3
  see also May Fourth Movement
New World crops, 20, 22

obsoleteness, 12, 110, 186, 188–9
OECD, 112, 115–16, 203
opening-up, 27, 82, 92, 104, 107, 110, 124, 152, 157
opium trade, 11, 39, 137, 152
Opium War, 7–9, 22–4, 26–8, 32–3
opportunity cost, 139–40, 142
overproduction, 163, 177
overseas incomes, 124
  markets, 3, 90, 92, 107, 122, 159–60, 162, 167, 176
ownership, 52, 56, 64, 100, 117–18, 124, 127, 134

Pareto optimal, 140, 150
Party Central Committee, 81, 111
Party General Secretary, 80, 95, 111, 136
party members, 93–4, 134–5
  members convicted, 81, 131–2, 135
  officials (including cadres), 41, 56, 75–8, 86, 94, 110, 112, 130–5, 137, 147
party-state, 52, 56, 72, 79, 86, 93, 100, 103, 125–6, 129–30
  policy priorities, 57, 85, 135, 151, 159, 162–4, 176, 200
path dependence, 1, 55, 109, 162, 169
peasantry, 53, 64, 72–3, 75–7, 86, 109, 175
Peer Group of Top 10, 140–1, 168
people's communes, 57–8, 75–6, 86, 117
physical inputs and outputs, 5, 141, 152, 197
physiocracy, 23, 31, 175
political alliance, 50, 52, 77, 175
  campaigns, 77, 130–2, 134–6
  economy, 50, 52, 56
  leaders, 3, 33, 42, 45, 47–9, 79–80, 129
  power, 31, 44, 46, 112, 187

power bases, 12, 52, 56, 187
purges, 2, 50–2, 73, 81–2, 86, 95, 175
resistance, 2, 72–3, 77–9, 109
pollution, 127–9, 137, 168, 191
population density, 15–16, 179–82, 186
growth, 12–13, 15–16, 19, 22–3, 32, 59, 61–2, 66, 179, 181, 186
Portuguese, 8–10
poverty, 2, 5, 68, 81, 89, 151, 175, 189
PRC, 32, 68, 94, 106–7, 118, 122, 124, 138, 151, 177
price controls, 90, 119
manipulations, 110, 119–21, 126, 146
primary sector, 5, 25, 59–60, 105, 189, 199–201
see also farming sector
principle-agent problem, 76, 134
production possibility frontiers, 64, 185, 189
productivity, 29, 59, 63, 71, 76, 86–7, 91, 113, 158
proletariat, 20, 48–9, 63, 72, 74, 95
property rights, 17, 29, 91, 93, 137, 172
provincial independence, 42–3, 45–6
public goods, 2, 12, 37–8, 67, 71, 103, 110

Qing emperors, 2, 39–42, 47
officials, 36, 38–9, 71
salaries, 38–9, 195
Quesnay's model, 59

R&D, 157, 159, 172
rationing, 52, 64–6, 75–7, 89–90, 101, 142
rebellions, 2, 33–5, 37, 39, 41–2, 47
recessions, 6, 64, 119, 165, 178
red bases, 53, 80
capitalists, 100
rent-seeking, 37, 116, 118, 191
rents, 73, 114, 119, 133
Republicans, 33, 42, 45, 48, 51, 53–5
resources, 15–16, 18, 56, 70, 127, 168, 185, 187, 210
revenues, 1, 13, 23–5, 39, 41, 44, 83, 91–2, 113–14, 118–19, 126, 130, 133, 137, 192, 202–3
revolutions, 2, 24, 26–7, 32–3, 46, 48–51, 56, 59, 69, 73, 78–81, 109, 176
Ricardo, David, 29, 139–40, 142, 171
Ricci, Matteo, 9–10, 32
RMB exchange rates, 121, 146–9, 158, 166, 177, 190
depreciation, 190
ruralisation, 2, 57, 61, 79, 175
Russia, 9–10, 33, 48, 57, 109, 178

savings, 67–8, 89–90, 100–2, 119, 126, 140, 149, 162–4, 166–7, 193
schooling, 3, 47, 52, 68, 70, 84–6, 171, 176
sea power, 13, 175
Second World War, 31, 48, 54, 60, 155
self-defeating patterns, 3, 5, 165, 192
separatism, 41, 46
services sector, 56, 91, 189, 199–201
SEZ-EOI combo, 107
SEZs, 4, 83, 107–8, 143, 145, 157
silver deadweight, 11, 15
imports, *see* imports, silver
Smith, Adam, 64, 140, 142, 145, 168, 171–3
social mobility, 63, 68, 83–4, 109, 173
security, 63, 147
unrest, 2, 33, 36–9, 42, 45, 175, 177
welfare, 2, 16, 20, 78, 139, 150, 162, 164, 209–12
SOEs, 77, 87–8, 90–1, 95–6, 113, 129, 131, 134
Soviet Union (including USSR), 3, 45, 47–50, 52–3, 55–6, 59, 62, 73, 78–9, 152–4
specialisation, 20, 23, 91, 139
stagnation, 1–2, 15, 30, 186
Stalin, 53–5, 79, 152, 175
Stalinism, 46, 109, 176
state capacity, 1, 11–12, 15, 31, 35, 39, 45, 110, 112–13, 126, 137, 184
failures, 2, 16, 31–3, 39, 42, 110
ownership, 52, 56, 77, 87–8, 94, 117–19, 131–2, 162
State Council, 83, 122, 124
studying abroad, 123, 159
subsidies, 120, 134, 161, 173
subsistence, 2, 52, 61, 64, 67, 101, 189

Sun Yat-sen, 33, 42, 45, 80
supply-driven growth, 3, 165–6, 168, 178, 192
surpluses, 15, 19, 23, 27, 61, 66, 83, 86, 113, 119, 121–3, 125, 139, 142, 146
sustainability, 81, 111, 150, 167

Taiping Rebellion, 32–5, 37, 39, 43, 46, 71
Taiwan, 10, 48, 54, 79, 82, 106, 110, 113, 136, 155–6, 203
take-off, 30, 70, 95, 99, 127–8
tariffs, 114, 168, 170–4, 177–8, 194
tax burden, 2, 12–13, 15, 23, 37, 41, 113, 118, 184
taxation, 12, 32, 41–2, 112, 118
technocrats, 51, 57, 80
technology, 3, 8, 36, 42, 44, 52, 55, 70, 80, 85, 95, 104, 107, 128, 143–4, 154–8, 168, 172–3, 175, 205, 209–11
  intensiveness, 157–8
textiles (including weaving), 8, 13, 24–7, 55, 79, 141–2, 145, 183–6
TFP, 71, 87, 158
Tiananmen Movement, 111, 134, 177
trade balance, 121, 146
trade unions, 48, 149
tragedy of the commons, 66, 127
treaties, 7, 9, 27
Trotskyism, 49–50, 52, 72–3, 109
truth debate, 81, 86, 100
TVEs, 90–6, 100, 103, 144–5
two systems in one country, 83

unemployment, 3, 63, 83, 94–6, 162, 170–1, 173, 176, 178, 192
unilateral changes, 39, 120–1, 158, 168–9
unintended consequences, 11, 23, 126–8
United States (including America, US and USA), 45, 54, 79, 88, 105–6, 120, 130, 138, 160–1, 167–8, 170–1, 174, 178, 206–7
universities, 47, 64, 80, 83–5, 131, 133, 171
  see also higher education
urbanisation, 23, 52, 57, 59, 61–3, 68, 71, 102, 127, 189, 209–12
  see also de-ruralisation
USI, 90–2, 95, 100, 104, 107, 127, 144
USI-EOI combo, 92

value chains, 169, 171–4
VAT, 113–14

wage goods, 89–90
waged labourers, 48, 72, 95, 143, 148–9, 171
wages, 59–60, 66–7, 83, 119, 126, 128, 142, 144–50, 157, 160–1, 164, 173, 177–8
warlords, 45, 53, 71
wars, 2, 7–9, 12, 22–4, 26–8, 30–3, 42, 44, 46, 49, 54–5, 58, 72, 80, 155
wastes, 64, 76, 78, 87, 188, 191
West, 3, 32–3, 42, 54, 58, 82, 111–12, 128, 151, 153–5, 157–60, 167–9, 174, 176–8, 190
Westernisation Movement, 42, 45, 58, 152
world market, 14, 140, 174, 192
world order, 156, 168, 170
WTO, 3, 93, 106, 112, 119, 143, 157, 160, 168–9, 171–3, 176, 204

xenophobia, 32, 45
Xi Jinping, 130, 136

Yangzi River, 34, 180–1, 183
Yellow River, 16, 26, 34, 127, 179, 183
Yuan Shikai, 42, 45, 47, 71

Zeng Guofan, 42, 46–8, 52, 54
zero-sum game, 96, 159, 168, 176
Zhao Ziyang, 111

Praise for Kiss Me Like You Mean It

'This book was just PERFECT, the ideal balance of sweet and sexy. 10/10 for plot, characterisation, sexual tension, community and jeopardy'
Marian Keyes

'Packed with all the best tropes, this book will sweep you away into a world of small-town charm and irresistible romance'
Liz Tomforde

'This is cosy, small-town romance at its best. Swoony, sweeping and cinematic. I loved every minute with Lee and Nico!'
Elle McNicoll

'Nobody does yearning quite like her and the yearning in *Kiss Me Like You Mean It* was one for the record books'
Sarra Manning

'Featuring some of the hottest kiss scenes I've ever read and filled with the kind of yearning that will send hopeless romantics swooning'
Catherine Walsh

'I AM STILL SWOONING SO HARD. I don't feel like I will ever get over this book – and I don't want to'
Lucy Vine

'It's so romantic, sexy, with all of Laura's trademark charm'
Louise O'Neill

'Hijinks and hilarity, schemes and swooning: this is Laura Wood at her best. A big-hearted, classic of a romcom'
Lizzie Huxley-Jones

'The most delicious, indulgent, funny and emotionally charged romcom I have read in a long time – it ranks up there with my favourite ever romances'
Cressida McLaughlin

'*Kiss Me Like You Mean It* had me from the dedication. Lee and Nico together are absolute tropey perfection'
Rebecca Ryan

'A joyful tribute to chosen family, to community, and to finding the lasting love we've always hoped for in the most unexpected place'
Sarah Chamberlain

'A complete master of deeply fanciable characters, towns you'll want to move to, and the perfect degree of aching yearn'
Kate Young

'Everything I look for in a love story . . . This book will delight Wood's fans and win over plenty more'
Laura Marie Meyers

'The kind of yearning that'll have readers squealing with excitement'
Sophie Jo